CHÉTICAMP
HISTORY AND ACADIAN TRADITIONS

Anselme Chiasson

Chéticamp

History and
Acadian Traditions

Preface by Luc Lacourcière

Translation by Jean Doris LeBlanc

Breton Books
Wreck Cove, Nova Scotia
1998

ORIGINALLY PUBLISHED in French in 1962, *Chéticamp* was awarded the PRIX CHAMPLAIN 1962 du Conseil de la Vie Française en Amérique and the PRIX DES CONCOURS LITTERAIRES ET SCIENTIFIQUES des Affaires Culturelles de la Province de Québec. The first English edition was translated by Jean Doris Le-Blanc in 1986. Our thanks to Clyde Rose, Breakwater Books, for permission to publish this new edition. With the exception of the *Cape Breton's Magazine* photographs of Marie Deveau and Alexandre Boudreau, all photographs are courtesy of Anselme Chiasson.

Editor: Ronald Caplan
Production: Bonnie Thompson
Typesetting: Carlotta Weatherbee
Cover Photos of Chéticamp and Les Trois Pignons: Warren Gordon

THIS BOOK IS A CAPE BRETON CLASSIC, and we have not changed the original edition. We thank Anselme Chiasson for updating the final chapter, bringing it to 1998.

Handpumps are no longer the miracle they were in the 1960s. And it'll be a long time before the fishermen are bringing home 40 or 50 thousand pounds of cod to Chéticamp harbour. But what refuses to change is the vitality and ingenuity of the remarkable people of Chéticamp.

**We acknowledge the support of
the Canada Council for the Arts for our publishing program.**

**We also acknowledge support from Cultural Affairs,
Nova Scotia Department of Education and Culture.**

Canadian Cataloguing in Publication Data

Chiasson, Anselme, 1911-

   Chéticamp

   Translation of: Chéticamp : histoire et traditions acadiennes.
   Includes bibliographical references and index.
   ISBN 1-895415-29-2

1. Acadians — Nova Scotia — Chéticamp — Social life and customs.
2. Chéticamp (N.S.) — History. I. Title.

FC2349.C43C4413 1998   971.6'91   C98-950165-5
F1039.5.C5C513 1998

Table of Contents

Preface
by Luc Lacourcière

WITH THE PUBLICATION OF THIS BOOK, Father Anselme Chiasson realizes a dream which has been in the making for more than thirty years: that of writing for the people of Chéticamp the account of what they have been since the beginning, and of what they became in the somewhat isolated countryside where they live between the sea and the mountains of the Cabot Trail.

About 1927, young Chiasson, who was studying with the Capuchin Fathers, began compiling historical notes on the village of his birth, as well as recording memories and observations made more vivid through long absences, each time he returned to Cape Breton.

Finally, in the course of these last years, increasing his contacts among the older people of the area, he was able to penetrate most deeply the study of the oral traditional history of this small transplanted fragment of Acadia. Father Chiasson's personal collection of more than six hundred recordings of songs, tales, legends and various accounts is proof of this.

The way seems long because he has often been thwarted or delayed by the demands of his ministry and by teaching in other productive areas. But the goal that Father Anselme aimed for in his youth never changed, nor was there any lessening in his passion, love and curiosity to know his people. The feelings which had inspired him at the beginning of his career, remained his best support in this noble enterprise.

It is truly remarkable that this son of Chéticamp, who could have lived as a fisherman, simply tending his nets, became, in spite of the absences imposed on him by the rule of St. Francis, the greatest fisherman of oral and written traditions of Chéticamp.

Stirred by the desire to know his corner of the world and its beginnings, evolution, progress, as well as the present state of the people who dwell there, he never departed from his wonderful optimism nor his unshakeable confidence in this, his first project.

Like the ancient chroniclers, he lays open to us perspectives on all elements which form the basis of life in the village of his birth—social, economic, religious, traditional, and even political, but without, however, becoming a slave to any of those present disciplines which force one to divide the study of human groups into infinite compartments.

Curious concerning the total life of the populace but especially all those things most familiar to him and about which he felt most deeply, his spontaneous folklorist character would not permit him to follow the absolute theories and abusive techniques that one meets more and more in the science of man. His ingenuity, if I may say so, permitted him to write a very human book, a book of great faith in which, happily, humour is not absent.

A mirror of concrete and picturesque realities, this learned treatise is all the more important because we know so few of the facts of each of our Acadian communities.

With all the numerous general stories on the ups and downs of the Acadian people, there are few local treatises which give us, as agreeably as this one, the descriptions of their daily customs, the oral tradition of events, and small historical facts of their people. It is, however, that human substance which gives to this story its true dimensions and ensures it an audience that surpasses the boundaries of regional interest, not only in Cape Breton, but in all of Acadia.

Father Anselme did more than add a remarkable title to the too-short list of stories of Acadian parishes; he inscribed Chéticamp on the international list of comparative studies which specifically have for their objective the popular French traditions. This is, in our opinion, worthy of very high merit; it is also our reward for having encouraged the author in this magnificent work.

Luc Lacourcière
Director of the Archives of Folklore
Université Laval
Easter 1961

Introduction

THE ACADIAN PEOPLE RESEMBLE A TREE whose growth was vigorous in the beginning (1632-1755), after which a squall (1755-1763) sprang up and defoliated its branches, still laden with promising fruit. Uprooted from the soil, buffeted in its roots, the tree itself was carried by the tempest. After having been torn up and scattered in fragments all along the coast of the Atlantic and the Gulf, it was replanted. And its numerous shoots, little by little, have reclaimed the lost land.

Thus it is that today some French groups from several corners of old Acadia have come into view, full of life and rich in traditions and all manner of folklore. By their heroic and legendary past, by their old way of speaking with its own characteristics and pungency, by their customs and traditions imported from the Motherland, these pockets of survival of a dispersed people constitute ethnic groups worthy of interest, and their story continually arouses our admiration.

Of all the regions where prolonged isolation has faithfully preserved the charm of olden times, Chéticamp on the west coast of Cape Breton, without fear of contradiction, takes first place.

"If the question were put to us," writes Brother Antoine Bernard, "'Where can one find, today, the type of people which has most faithfully preserved the Acadian character of former days?'—we would answer without hesitation: 'Go to the coast of Chéticamp.' There, on the shores which will perhaps never see a railroad, among that population, half farming and half fishing, you will discover treasures of faith, considerate charity and delicate hospitality."[1]

In the past, the Acadian communities of New Brunswick, St. Mary's Bay and Prince Edward Island were better known by the general public. Chéticamp had been there a long time and, enveloped by morning fogs, was white and beautiful, but impenetrable, not only because of its geography, but its history as well. Its history was nonexistent under the French regime, and the people, who for a long time were under English domination, wished to remain hidden, with good reason! However, the chronicle of events which bind us to the past of Chéticamp, the stronghold of Acadian life in Cape Breton, writes a beautiful page in our history—Acadian and French.

Unfortunately, our people know too little of their own Acadian history. In general, they possess no more than a vague idea of the Expulsion itself. This is regrettable, for the heroic example of our ancestors would serve well to instill within us a genuine pride in our forefathers. We also forget too often that these are the same deportees of 1756 and 1758 and their children, born in exile, who founded most of our beautiful Acadian parishes of today. The tenacity of their desire to return, their courage and endurance in the hardships of building these new establishments, their resourcefulness in absolute destitution, their unshakable loyalty to their language, and their enduring faith in God, furnish admirable pages of inner history.

Our ancestors were poor in material things. The conditions they had to face in the beginning, and the ostracism that they too often would meet later on because of their lack of education, were hard to take. However, they left us a culturally-rich patrimony that we haven't known how to appreciate until now, an inheritance we must hurry to rescue from oblivion.

Their French language was very colourful, though it has become archaic today. Their vocabulary was of an astonishing richness. We recall with emotion the polished language of some illiterate old people who knew the correct word for everything. The songs they would sing and the role these songs would play in the primitive Acadian communities would merit a study in itself. Their songs, tales and traditions are of incomparable value. This is what we wished to bring out in this parish monograph of Chéticamp: the epic of the pioneers, their life and troubles in the beginning, the subsequent developments—economic, religious and cultural, but also, and just as important, the richness of their traditions both as French people and as human beings.

With some very irregular intervals we have worked on this book for thirty years. We have used the rare leisure hours that we were permitted between our other observing tasks elsewhere, imposed by our profession. The principal archives consulted were the parish registers and the old papers of the families of Chéticamp, the registers of the missionary period of Carleton and Caraquet, The Public Archives of Canada, The Public Archives of Nova Scotia, those of the Archbishop of Québec and the Bishop of Antigonish. Finally, we spent several vacations in Chéticamp to consult the living traditions.

More than anyone, we are aware of the shortcomings of this book. In the first place, with regard to the Archives, there were some documents we couldn't find, others that we couldn't attain. Then, as to the style of the book, it is certainly not that of an academician.

Introduction

Being a native of Chéticamp, we are a victim of a school system claimed to be bilingual where all our life we suffered from a deficient French teaching, received in grammar school. Just the same, we have the temerity to hope that the reader will show an interest in this modest work.

We want to express here our gratitude to our Superiors for their continued encouragement; to the population of Chéticamp for their zealous collaboration; to Mr. Éphrem Boudreau of Ottawa for his technical aid; to Mr. Luc Lacourcière for his counsel and encouragement; and, finally, to all those who, from near or far, enabled us to bring our work to a successful conclusion.

CHAPTER ONE

Dawning of Acadia
and the English Conquest

ACADIA, FOUNDED THE FIRST TIME IN 1604 by Pierre du Gast (Sieur de Monts), Jean de Biencourt (Sieur de Poutrincourt), Louis Hébert, Samuel de Champlain and Marc Lescarbot, experienced very little success and was destroyed in 1613 by the English pirate Samuel Argall.

The real work of establishing the colony began in 1632 with Isaac de Razilly who brought over "three hundred picked men recruited in Touraine and Poitou," all "French, Catholic, and of irreproachable conduct" as Richelieu had required.[1] Six Capuchin missionary priests were part of the expedition. After the death of Razilly in 1635, Charles de Menou (Sieur d'Aulnay) continued the work already begun and brought over other French families who united with the first group to give birth to the Acadian people.

"Judging the fertile valley of Port Royal better for colonization than the rocky coast of La Hève" where Razilly had established the young colony, d'Aulnay "carried there the seat of government and most of the colonists who came...in 1632."[2] Little by little the mother cell grew and some entire families went off to found Beaubassin, Grand Pré, Piziguit and Chipoudy, which would later become flourishing parishes.

The lands were fertile. Trade grew. Also, in spite of the fratricidal battles waged between d'Aulnay and Charles de la Tour, an original settler of 1610, and in spite of the sometimes disastrous attacks of the Bostonians, the young colony prospered. At the time of the Expulsion the Acadians enjoyed a life of remarkable ease. "Each inhabitant of the district of Minas Basin," for example, "in 1755 owned about fifteen cattle, thirty sheep and fourteen hogs." "Lawrence especially mentioned his desire to lay his hands on some 120,000 head of cattle belonging to the Acadians."[3]

Acadia was even too prosperous in the eyes of the neighboring English colony, Boston, which feared its growth. Although trade was regular between the two colonies, though often clandestine, the English authorities looked with a jaundiced eye at the French colony growing so close to them. They used every occasion to attack it. Unfortunately, these occasions were not lacking. The European wars between France and England gave hardly any respite.

In 1654 a Boston fleet commanded by Sedgewick took control of the fortified towns in Acadia, the forts of St. John, Port Royal and La Hève, and drove the governor and the missionaries from Acadian territory. It was only in 1667 that Acadia became French again by the Treaty of Bréda and the French flag once again flew over Acadian land.

Not for long, though. Port Royal fell again in 1690 under the blows of William Phipps and remained under English rule until the Treaty of Ryswick in 1697. Finally, during the war of the Spanish succession the Bostonians renewed the attack on the French colony which fell, definitely, in 1710.

The Treaty of Utrecht in 1713 sealed the fate of the peninsula of Nova Scotia which became, decisively, the possession of the English, whereas Cape Breton, Prince Edward Island, New Brunswick and the rest of Canada were still under the crown of France.

By the Treaty of Utrecht (Article 14) it is expressly stated that the Acadians of the peninsula "shall have the liberty, for one year, to withdraw to another place, at their convenience, and carry away with them all their personal belongings." Three months later Queen Anne herself intervened and fixed conditions much more favourable for the Acadian people: "It is our wish and our good pleasure that all those who hold any lands under our government in Acadia and Newfoundland, who became our subjects under the last treaty of peace and who wished to stay under our authority, have the right to preserve their said lands and holdings and of enjoying them without any trouble, as fully and as freely as our other subjects may possess their lands and inheritances, and also, that they may sell the same, if they prefer to establish themselves elsewhere."[4]

Soon after this treaty France made plans to fortify Louisbourg in Cape Breton, to colonize Prince Edward Island and to attract to these places Acadians of the peninsular region. But these Acadians were attached to their lands, "the best in the world,"[5] and their English rulers, for their part, tried everything possible to prevent their leaving the area. The English were quite conciliatory as long as they themselves were few in numbers and militarily ineffective. But with the founding of Halifax in 1749 and the arrival of considerable reinforcements, they showed their true colours and the situation changed.

Farsighted Acadians saw hanging over their heads a storm-filled sky. Consequently, emigration to Prince Edward Island, begun about 1740, intensified to such a point by the end of 1749 that the English were alarmed. Cornwallis built forts on the exit route (Fort Edward at Piziguid and Fort Lawrence at Beaubassin) and placed warships in Northumberland Strait to prevent this exodus. In spite of all that "a great number of Acadians succeeded in avoiding the patrols and arrived at Prince Edward Island. From 1749 to 1755 more than 3,000 arrived there."[6] Others, in smaller numbers, emigrated to the Canso region in Cape Breton.

The founders of Chéticamp or their ancestors were part of these groups of emigrants, some from Prince Edward Island and others from the Canso area.

Deportation of 1755

With the coming of Charles Lawrence to the post of governor of Nova Scotia in 1753, the threats and exactions increased. But the cruelty with which the blow of 1755 was executed surpassed the most odious the imagination could invent.

On September 3, 1755, the Acadians, from whom the English had taken away their guns and boats, were lured into their churches by a wily stratagem and made prisoners of the King. All their goods, so long coveted by the English, were confiscated. This was the Expulsion: they forced everyone at bayonet point to embark on boats in the midst of confusion, without any concern as to whether they put on the same boat members of the same family. On October 8 the boats left, filled with dismembered families, death and despair in the soul, carrying away an entire people that they had sworn to get rid of forever. These human cargoes were dispersed, some here and some there, along the Atlantic coast from Boston to Georgia[7] with the hope that they would be lost forever in the Anglo-Saxon colonies to the south.

Exile without end and a shame without equal in history. Thrown on distant shores, separated from each other, we saw them wander from town to town, without friends, without homes, without human hope, resigned, and only asking of the land, a tomb. [Longfellow]

At Beaubassin and Port Royal the Acadians got wind of Lawrence's trap. Instead of answering his call they took to the woods. The governor then ordered a merciless manhunt, where the fate of Acadians who fell under the bullets of the English soldiers was, perhaps, preferable to that of those who were taken captive.

With the taking of Louisbourg on July 27, 1758, this manhunt extended to all the coasts and forests of the three provinces of the Gulf. It lasted ten long years—interminable years, bloody, indescribable, where the inoffensive Acadians, tracked like wild animals, slaughtered like dogs or deported without mercy to areas where the people were fanatically hostile, wandered like ghosts in a nightmare of tears and blood.

Deportation of 1758 and the End of the French Régime in Acadia

With Louisbourg still standing the Acadians from the Canso area, from Fort Dauphin (St. Anne), from Prince Edward Island and from the coast of New Brunswick, with their brothers who escaped from Grand Pré and joined them, were enjoying a certain security. But Louisbourg fell and the manhunt began again in all those regions where all the horrors of 1755 were renewed.[8]

The English sowed ruin, desolation and death. "We have done a great deal of harm and spread the terror of the armies of His Majesty all along the Gulf, without adding anything to His glory," wrote Wolfe the day after his victory, December 30, 1758.[9]

In effect, the Expulsion was as cruel as that of Grand Pré. The brutality was the same and the separations equally heart-rending. The only difference was that the heartbreaking scenes of departure were succeeded by the tragic scenes of the crossing of the Atlantic. These people were deported to Europe.

Embarked on miserable boats, a good number of the passengers never made it to their destinations;[10] the ocean swallowed up their bodies and their sufferings. "The greater part of the...boats were damaged before leaving Canso," says H. Blanchard,[11] and two of them were lost. Of nine boats mentioned, "one stayed three months outside Plymouth with its 170 passengers with hardly any food and dying of thirst; another, storm-ridden, landed at Boulogne with 179 survivors; two others sank, taking 700 victims to their deaths beneath the waves. The Honorable Brook Watson spoke in a letter to Dr. Andrew Brown of 1,300 Acadians who were lost in the crossing from America to Europe."[12] Of five beautiful parishes established on Prince Edward Island—with their churches, their priest, their population of about 6,000 souls—nothing remained.

But here and there some had succeeded in escaping. Entire families had fled to the woods. When the storm was over these people, with great timidity, returned in small groups. Other exiles

plucked up courage to follow them, and soon we saw them...those unfortunates wandering over devastated fields, where a short time ago stood their homes, their villages and their churches. It is useless to try to tell with what pangs they travelled through these mournful places, that they had previously seen so full of life. What had become of the majority of those they had known? Alas! disappeared forever: some dead from extreme poverty, others victim of unknown disasters; the survivors relegated to such faraway shores that life would run out before we could learn anything of them.[13]

Holland's report of 1768 shows us that the numbers of Acadians is very sparse in all these regions. On Prince Edward Island:

There are about thirty families, he says; they are treated as prisoners, on the same footing as those of Halifax. Their poverty is extreme, they live in small cabins in the woods, which also give them their firewood. They live on fish that they catch in the summer and on game which they kill: hare, partridge, lynx, otter, marten, and muskrat, their pressing hunger forcing them to refuse nothing.[14]

At this time the Acadian people are certainly a tree pulled up by its roots, fragmented by the hurricane, the débris of which is scattered all around.

Is this the end? Is the tree going to die? We know it is not. All the fragments have taken root and today are in a magnificent state of bloom.

This brings us to the branch that has produced Chéticamp.

CHAPTER TWO

Geographical and Political Position of Chéticamp

Cape Breton Island: The "Old and New" Counties

The importance of Cape Breton Island, known as Isle Royale during the long battles waged between the French and the English while they were disputing the sovereignty of Canada, is well known. Can we not apply to Cape Breton, due mostly to its stronghold Louisbourg, what the Intendant Jacques de Meules said in 1685 of the whole of Acadia: "The position of this country...is so well disposed that it seems to have been set here to gain control of the whole of America."[1]

On July 27, 1758, three years after the Expulsion of the Acadians from La Baie Française (Bay of Fundy), and five years before the fall of Canada (1763), the great fortress of Louisbourg fell into the hands of the English admiral Boscawen and the whole island came under the domination of the English for good.

Ruled for five years by a military régime, Cape Breton Island was annexed politically to Nova Scotia in 1763.[2] In 1784 it became a distinct province, then in 1820[3] it was again annexed to Nova Scotia. This annexation has lasted to the present day.

During the fourteen years that followed 1820, the whole island formed one county, the County of Cape Breton. In 1834-35 this county was divided into three electoral districts: Cape Breton, Richmond and Juste-au-Corps. Finally, in 1851, the County of Cape Breton was broken up into the two present counties of Cape Breton and Victoria.

And what about the County of Inverness?

It was in 1837 that, on the suggestion of Sir William Young, its first representative in Halifax, the name of Juste-au-Corps was changed to Inverness.[4] Himself a native of the county with this name in old Scotland, he wanted to satisfy his feeling of filial devotion by erasing from the map an old French name. The county had taken its name from the principal village, Juste-au-Corps, which also received a new name. Nevertheless, the Acadians continued to call it Juste-au-Corps, the principal French settlement on this coast of Cape Breton[5] until the end of the nineteenth century, but for the English and on modern geographical maps it became Port Hood.

The Site of Chéticamp

The county of Inverness extends along the Gulf, from Point Tupper in the south to Cape St. Lawrence in the north, for a coastal distance of about 130 miles. Its average width is about thirty miles.[6]

Running along its precipitous coastline, surmounted by capes, the coast transforms itself here and there into wide gaps which open onto gracious valleys where magnificent rivers run towards the sea in wide expanses of water. Some villages, "isolated from the rest of the world between the Atlantic and a barrier of rocks,"[7] are spread out all along the coast. These are, from south to north: Port Hood, Mabou, Inverness, Margaree, Saint-Joseph-du-Moine; then, at the entrance to the famed National Park on the Cabot Trail, we greet Chéticamp.

The Name of Chéticamp

The name of Chéticamp, like so many others in Canada, is derived from the language of the Mi'kmaq Indians, a tribe which is still numerous in Cape Breton. "The origin is certain," wrote Father Pacifique, "I got it from the Indians themselves, who write Aotjatotj (pronounce: Aoutchadoutch). This word means 'rarely full.'"[8] This must be referring to the exit of the harbour which, before the digging out of the channel, presented dry, vast sandbanks called "The Bar" that low tide widened still more.

The name and spelling of Chéticamp has changed over the years. In 1660, a map in Latin made by Father P. Ducreux, Jesuit, refers to Chéticamp as "I. Ochatisia"; and Coronelli, in 1689, writes "Ochatis" on his map.[9] For their part, the French and Acadians pronounced it "Le Chady,"[10] "Le Grand Chady,"[11] "Le Chady Grand," "I. de Chedagan,"[12] and "Chatican," as the Acadians still say. "Chétican," wrote the missionaries, such as Lejamtel and others, as well as Bishop J.-O. Plessis, himself; "Chéticamps" was already written in 1752 by Sieur de la Roque,[13] "Chétifcamp" is the name we find in the Cahier des Visites Pastorales of Bishop Denault in 1803.[14] Finally, "Chéticamp" was written by the missionary, Father Antoine Manseau, in the parish registers on May 3, 1815.[15] This last spelling has prevailed.[16]

Topography

The distinctive characteristic of Chéticamp is its harbour. This is an immense basin, one-half mile wide and three miles long, formed by a peninsula called "the Island"—"which runs to the north parallel to the mainland.... The isthmus which joins it" to the south "is only a sandbank beaten by the sea on both sides without ever covering it."[17]

The principal inhabited area along the harbour on the mainland constitutes, along with the church, hospital, consolidated school, convent, and stores, the centre of the parish, and is called Chéticamp. The other less populated areas are two or three miles apart: Petit-Étang to the northeast, La Prairie, Belle-Marche and Le Platin to the east, Le Plateau, Point Cross and Le Lac to the south, and, finally, to the northwest: the Island.[18] Two main highways cross the parish from one end to the other. One, more modest, runs through the back settlements of the parish, while the other follows the coast to arrive at the harbour, and from there, through the capes and Petit-Etang, rushes headlong to meet the high mountains of the Cabot Trail.

Numerous streams, two rivers—of which one, the river of La Prairie, is of incomparable splendour—valleys, hills, headlands, bays, immense beaches, mountains in the background which attain, in certain cases, one thousand feet in altitude, and in front, the sea, always the sea, as far as the eye can reach—this is the majestic décor in which the Chéticantins live.

The Toponymy or Given Names of Areas

Apart from the names of the localities we have already listed, the population has bedecked every angle and every undulation of the terrain in the parish with often picturesque names. Some are a description of the land itself, as La Terre Rouge (Red Earth), others grew out of an historic fact, as La Cave-à-Loup (Wolf Cave), and, finally, others are simply the assignment of a corner of earth to its owner, as Le Buttereau-à-John (John's Hill).

Following is a list of these popular names that we have collected, following a northeasterly direction:

Le Buttereau à John; la Terre rouge; la Pointe; le Collet à Orignal; le Chêne; la Prairie. In the meadow we have: les Bouleaux; les Grandes Parts; les Prés rondes. Les Caves; la Cave à loup; l'Etang à Eusèbe; le Plé (wild berries here); la Frênière; le Chemin du portage; la Petite Prairie (along the coast); l'Anse du bois marié; les Caveaux; le Gabion; les Caps; le Quai à Braquette; le Ruisseau creux; la Digue; le Petit Havre; la Pointe à cochons; le Pont de ciment; la Butte à l'ours; le Redman; la Pointe aux pois; le P'tit Plé or Belle-Marche; la Butte à Hubert à Henri; le Brûlé; la Petite Source; la Source bouillante; le Platin; la Petite Allée; le Chemin des vieux; la Butte de la commune; le Plé des boeufs; le Grand Plé; la Butte des Constant; la Butte à Élie; la Butte du cimetière; le Plateau; la Butte à John à Raymond; les Buttes; la Ferme; le Ruisseau de la ferme; le Lac; le Ruisseau du Lac.

In the neighbouring mountains: L'Abîme; la Montain des Écureaux; le Trou à Pochard; le Buttereau à Pierrot; la Coulèche; la Rigwash; le Ruisseau du mât; Panwax à Piquet; la Sucrerie.

On the Island: La Digue; le Gros Cap or le Nique-du-Corbeau; la Pointe Enragée; le Havre à Marcel; le Ruisseau de l'Île; l'Anse du bois marié; la Source des Bostonnais; l'Anse au brick; le Ruisseau du mitan de l'Île; la Grosse Tête; l'Étang à Phirin; le Four à Pierre Bois; la Pointe; le Havre de la Pointe; le Banc; and on leaving le Banc: l'Anse aux huileux and les Bras.

Climate

Chéticamp enjoys a temperate climate. The thermometer seldom dips below zero degrees Fahrenheit in the winter and rarely passes seventy-five degrees in the summer. Thanks to the sea, the heat is never excessive during the summer months nor the cold unbearable during the winter months.

September and October are often pleasant months, but November brings on the cold rains from the northeast which make the horses shiver in the fields and cause the children to run between shelter stations on their way home from school.

Winter rarely shows its bad temper before well into January, when the ice arrives from the north, reaching our coasts and pounding our headlands and cliffs. "We no longer have winter today," say the old ones, "there is no longer any snow." Whereas, about thirty years ago, the snow blocked the roads, it was piled so high—right to the top of the telegraph poles. It was necessary to transport the mail by dogsled from Cap Rouge to Chéticamp. Today, the situation is so different! The roads are always kept open, not only in Chéticamp, but from one end of Cape Breton Island to the other.

Spring arrives late in this area, because the ice remains so long along the coasts and is sometimes still there at the end of April.

Summer is incomparably mild. Breezes from the sea temper the heat of the day, and evenings are always cool. We never experience the overpowering heat of Montréal and Ottawa. It is good to live in Chéticamp, and the future of the tourist industry there looks very promising.

The terrible "suêtes" (southeast winds). This calm earthly paradise that the seabreezes caress so softly, can change its whole aspect in the space of a few hours and become the scene of violent hurricanes which sweep away everything in their path; these hurricanes are caused by extreme southeast winds, the suêtes, as the people call them.

Familiarized through hard experience, transmitted from one generation to another, the people are well able to recognize the signs of these storms hours in advance. Immediately, if anyone is *au large* (out at sea), he gets under way and heads for shore as quickly as possible. At home, the horse-wagon is readied and on its way to the school to fetch the children. Everything is secured. Enough wood is brought in for the night, along with several buckets of water. Shutters and storm doors are closed. Everyone stays home.

Then the storm begins. Rumbling can be heard in the distant mountains. From time to time a strong gust of wind sweeps the fields, followed by another, then another. Stray pieces of board are thrown against the fences; stray buckets crazily bounce from one obstacle to another in search of shelter; everything flies around. All hell breaks loose. The wind pounds the sea into foam, trees bend and wail and houses crack enough to terrify one. Everyone is worried. If it is nighttime, no one goes to bed for the duration of the storm.

In these regions, some people, perhaps, are afraid of thunder and fire. But they are especially afraid of the suête, and with good reason.

It does occur that the roofs of barns and houses are carried away by the wind, that buildings too old are flattened, that enclosures are smashed and trees uprooted. This is why, in the past, we would see homes attached by steel cables to stakes anchored in the ground.

Are these suêtes frequent? No, there are only a few each summer and winter; this is more than enough, however, to cause damage which, often costly, sometimes has dramatic consequences.

Previously, in 1812, Bishop Plessis had written in his travel journal:

The prevalent southerly and southwesterly winds in this place, are powerful to a point difficult for one to imagine.... A hurricane which has passed along this coast has turned a section of the woods topsy-turvy, such that one can see as many trees lying down as standing up.[19]

One and one-half centuries have passed, but the suête has lost none of its power. One can only imagine the damage it can cause when it is preceded by a heavy sleet which weighs down the electric wires, the branches, and finally, everything else. In 1947, a suête knocked down 280 electric poles from Belle-Côte to Chéticamp. Hardly was the damage repaired when, the following week, a second squall downed another 200 in the same place, some old and some new.

Rarely does a summer pass without one noticing some serious damage, such as this reported in a newspaper:

On August 14th, a terrible hurricane beat against Cape Breton and caused considerable damage...several fishing boats dragged their anchors and were damaged. Baptiste LeFort's boat was smashed against Johnnie (à Charles) Deveau's wharf, and Henri (à Jean) Roach's boat was hurled against the Cooperative wharf. The two boats were completely broken up. Two other large fishing boats were beaten against the breakwater...many other boats drifted away to sea.... The very beautiful harvest, which gave so much hope to the Chéticamp farmers, has been almost completely destroyed.[20]

How can the houses resist these storms? With previous knowledge and experience, the houses are now built stronger, often in a sheltered place and with a slanted roof on the southeast side, leaving few openings to the wind.

Trouble comes to him who pays no attention to the suête. When Mr. Toutaint came from Trois-Rivières in 1937 to build the hospital, he was warned of the great strength of the suêtes and was advised to construct the walls stronger and more impervious to these winds. He took the counsel into account up to a certain point, but when the hospital weathered its first suête water entered by the windows and walls with an irresistible force. It entered everywhere. Mr. Toutaint had to return to repair the damage and make the walls more watertight.

There was an experience almost similar to this at the church. Its steeple, one of those made by Morin Company, rose to a height of 181 feet. Was it solidly built? It certainly was—for some other place, but not for Chéticamp. The suêtes decapitated it fifteen or sixteen years later, flinging its heavy iron cross off into the distance. The steeple had to be lowered about fifteen feet, lessening its elegance, and was fastened on the inside by four large steel cables which passed between the arch and the roof in order to be attached to the southeast walls.

Drownings attributed to the suêtes are rather rare these days. Our fishermen learned the hard way not to go out on the sea when there was any sign of danger. But many cruel bereavements must have been experienced by the small colony before they realized the deadly and sudden dangers of the vicious suêtes.

On September 22, 1812, twelve fishermen of the area, of whom seven were fathers of families, were surprised by the storm and swallowed up by it. Four among them were brothers: Cyprien, John, Simon and Lazare Leblanc, sons of Lazare Leblanc and Modeste Chaisson. Again, the Registers mention Isaac Leblanc, François Radoub of France, and Ignace Le Français, a Canadian.[21] John had been married for only eight days. Cyprien's widow had a baby four days after the tragedy.[22] This misfortune threw the population "into consternation," wrote Father Lejamtel to Bishop Plessis.[23]

History relates several losses of large boats on the coasts of Chéticamp, as well as numerous drownings. We will see all this further on. Let us say right off, however, that these disasters were rarely due to the suêtes, but to the winds of the *nordet* (northeast) which, without being as strong, greatly stirred up the sea, rendering it very dangerous.

CHAPTER THREE

Founding of Chéticamp

Before the Deportation

Before and during the French régime Chéticamp didn't exist and had no history. There was no permanent settlement. La Petite Rivière, Le Platin and La Frênière often played host to groups of Mi'kmaq Indians who set up their tents here while on their hunting excursions. However, there are no documents to indicate a permanent Indian community here. Later, some families did establish themselves in this area, such as those of François Chomable and Jean François, but they did not stay.

Jacques Cartier himself, according to one author,[1] visited our coasts on returning from his second voyage to America on June 1, 1536. "We arrived that day," he says, "at Cape Lorraine, which is 46.5 degrees south, from which cape there is a lowland and the appearance of a river outlet, but no worthwhile harbour."[2] To which cape in Chéticamp does he refer? Perhaps to the cape of "La Source de la Montain," from where he could see the mouth of the river of La Prairie and the lowlands of what today is called "Petit-Étang."

Again, in 1758, a map of Île Royale (Cape Breton), according to Le Chevalier de la Rigaudière, places Cape St. Lawrence there which, incidentally, positions too far to the north the whole region of Chéticamp.[3]

Later, in the seventeenth century, another traveller, Nicolas Denys, while making a tour of his domain, would visit Chéticamp.

From Cape North to Chadye is a distance of about fifteen or sixteen leagues. The whole coast is rocky and covered with fir trees, mixed with small birches. We find there sandy coves which can barely shelter a rowboat: this coast is dangerous:[4] Le Chadye is a big cove about two leagues deep; in the back is a bar of sand mixed with pebbles, the work of the sea, and behind is a pond of salt water, and this cove is bordered by rocks on two sides. The codfish are plentiful in the bay, a fact which attracts the boats, though often some are lost, because of a lack of shelter there.[5]

To those who are familiar with these regions, there is no doubt this is Chéticamp.

It is very probable that the Bretons and the Basques built temporary cabins at La Pointe where they came to dry their cod during the fishing season, say the elderly folk of Chéticamp.

Franquet, in his "Mémoire sur la presqu'isle de Chétécan" in 1752, wrote that "the installations of the fishermen are made at this point, as well as their cabins and storehouses."[6] And Holland, in his wonderful document of 1768, in describing Cape Breton Island, said that before the fall of Louisbourg and the French empire in America, the French built many boats in Chéticamp because the forests furnished them with the necessary materials.[7]

It is beyond doubt then, that Chéticamp was a fishing station during the summer a long time before becoming an inhabited village.

After the Deportation

Chéticamp was still uninhabited during the winter of 1780-81. Ensign S.W. Prenties of the Royal Highland Emigrants was sent by General Haldimand of Québec to carry a message to Sir Henry Clinton of the English forces in New York: his brigantine, the *St. Lawrence*, ran aground south of Port Hood [or near Margaree Harbour] on December 4, 1780. He undertook to travel northward around Cape Breton to find some inhabited place; he passed in front of Chéticamp and found nothing.

In Arichat, in 1860, Mr. Rameau de Saint-Père, picked up from an old Acadian coastal sailor named Fougère the following testimony:

When he was 22 years old, about 1782, there were only two families in Chéticamp: Pierre Bois and Joseph Richard, called "Matinal.'" These families were formerly at Port Toulouse [St. Peter's]; then, during the French Revolution,[8] they took refuge in the Bay of Chaleurs area, from whence they came to Chéticamp, rejoining the Jerseys who were already fishing there; later came the Landrys, the Aucoins, etc., etc., from Prince Edward Island.[9]

It is in 1785 that the large contingent arrives, who, along with later newcomers, will populate Chéticamp, Saint-Joseph-du-Moine, and Margaree. These Acadians arrived in Chéticamp after much journeying from place to place. Some of them, for example, Joseph Boudrot, were descended from those deported from Grand Pré, but nearly all had been uprooted from Prince Edward Island or Cape Breton in 1758. Then they were strewn like so much jetsam on European shores, from where they returned to the islands of Saint-Pierre and Miquelon, then to different places along the Gulf, such as Arichat and Remshic in Nova Scotia, to the Bay of Chaleurs, and, finally, to Prince Edward Island, where several people had, earlier on, already intended to build their permanent home.

To get an idea of the wandering of these Acadians, it is enough to read the following testimony acquired from Jeanne Dugas, wife of Pierre

Bois, by Bishop Plessis himself during his visit to Chéticamp in 1812:

Worthy of note is that I met at Chéticamp, on Cape Breton Island, in July of 1812, Jeanne Dugast, aged about 80 years then, and widow of Pierre Bois, who told me she had been born in Louisbourg, having gone from there to Acadia, to a place named Grand Pré (Horton), then of returning to Cape Breton, and later, of living on Île St. Jean [P.E.I.], after that at Remshic, in Acadia, thence again to Cape Breton, from there again to Remshic, then to Île St. Jean a second time, then a third time to Remshic, from there to Restigouche, from Restigouche to Halifax, from there to Arichat, then to the Magdalen Islands, then to Cascapédia, and from Cascapédia to Chéticamp, and of never going to bed without supper.[10]

These wanderings were due to the exactions and vexations they encountered everywhere, as well as to their desire to find a peaceful place where they could finally feel at home. As proof of this statement, let us take another look at our pioneers on Île St. Jean (Prince Edward Island) and the reasons for their departure:

Captain Holland had divided the territory into 67 lots, each 20,000 acres in size; the requests for grants were so numerous that, in May of 1767, they were granted by drawing lots among all kinds of speculators, officials, and officers of the army and navy. Thus, in a few days, the whole island was awarded to grantees, who, for the most part, never lived there, but were speculators only....

During this time, what was happening to the former owners, whose spoils were being distributed so lavishly?...

For a long time after the deportation, the Island Acadians were victims of odious exploitation: they were permitted to establish themselves on any land, they cultivated the soil, pulled down the trees, burned the brush, working, sowing; but, at the time of harvesting the fruit of their hard labor, there would suddenly appear an English-speaking owner who, armed with unknown titles, would claim the harvest or an owner's fee. If the Acadian gave in, he soon found himself doomed to serfdom; if not, he was evicted and often reduced to exile.... As early as 1787, a dozen of the heads of Acadian families from Fortune Bay...complained of never having obtained the promised leases in exchange for the work they had done, and threatened to leave the Island...in October, a large number of these Acadians emigrated to Cape Breton.[11]

Why Chéticamp (and Margaree)?

The Acadians encountered arrogant and greedy English masters nearly everywhere in the provinces of the Gulf. Rich from the spoils of our ancestors and established on the best lands, all-powerful with regard to the Acadians whom they treated as outcasts, the English only sought to exploit them. Our proud ancestors, once masters of the soil, could not get used to such a régime and searched for a free place where they would not have to tolerate these humiliations.

As well, the lieutenant-governor of Cape Breton, Magistrate J.F.W. Desbarres, in fear of seeing the Acadians strengthen the islands of Saint-

Pierre and Miquelon and from there compete with the English trade, tried to attract them for some years with offers of grants of land and food supplies.[12] Finally, there were also the Jerseys, tradespeople in fish, who wanted them there. Already, in 1774, these people had brought over from Jersey to Canso twenty Acadian families to fish for them.[13] These Jerseys had owned a fishing station at Chéticamp since 1770[14] when our ancestors arrived. A good part of Chéticamp Island was already registered in their name and they owned large wharves at La Pointe. This Jersey presence assured the pioneers an easy market for their fish and a sure source of supplies.

Founders

We know that Pierre Bois and Joseph Richard, called "Matinal," were already in Chéticamp in 1782. The latter must have left very soon afterwards for Tracadie, Nova Scotia,[15] for there is no trace of him in Chéticamp, nor would there be any descendants of him if it were not for his sisters, who remained there.

In 1785, some families arrived, relatives of these two pioneers, who had fled with them from Arichat to the Bay of Chaleurs in 1780,[16] during the American Revolution: Régis Bois, aged twenty years and son of Pierre; Maximilien Gaudet, married to Geneviève Bois, and Raymond Poirier, husband of Marie Bois. Geneviève and Marie were daughters of Pierre Bois. There was Augustin Deveau (Justin), married to Rose Richard, sister of Joseph Richard. That same year Anselme Aucoin arrived, twenty-one years old and married to Rose Chiasson, daughter of Paul; Louis Gaudet, sixteen years old (surely a relative of Maximilien); and, finally, Simon Doucet, aged eighteen years. There may have been others, also.

In 1786 another group arrived to join the others: Paul Chiasson, fifty-nine years of age, and Louise Boudrot, his wife, who would go back to Île St. Jean a few years later, never to return; Basile Chiasson, thirty-one years of age, son of Paul, with his wife, Adélaîde Arseneaux; Jean Chiasson, forty-six years old, brother of Paul, and his wife, Isabelle Boudrot; Joseph Gaudet, husband of Marie-Anne Richard, and father of Maximilien Gaudet; Pierre Aucoin, fifty-three years of age, married first to Félicité Leblanc and then to Marie Doucet. Pierre was the father of Anselme Aucoin who had come the previous year. There was Joseph Boudrot, twenty-three years old, with his wife, Anne Chiasson; Lazare Leblanc, thirty-three years old, with his wife, Modeste Chiasson; Étienne Chiasson, twenty-two years old, and his wife Monique Gaudet; Joseph Deveau, twenty-one years old; Joseph Aucoin, forty-two years old, and his wife, Marie Hébert. This last couple brought with them Cyriac Roche, aged two years, born in Nova Scotia of parents born in Ireland.[17] François Cormier, married to Anne Haché, and Joseph Cormier, married to Suzanne Leblanc, arrived in Grand-Étang with one or the other of these contingents.

Some other newcomers arrived in 1788, such as Joseph Leblanc, twenty-three years of age, and probably Grégoire Maillet, fifty-seven years old, along with his wife, Anne Leblanc.

These were the pioneers, the founders of Chéticamp.

Newcomers

For forty years, however, new recruits continued to arrive. These were either relatives, friends or acquaintances left in some corner of the Gulf who decided to join the others; or they were other Acadians, exhausted from the tribulations of which they were the object, as in Prince Edward Island and the Magdalen Islands. A letter from Father Cécil, parish priest at Rustico, tells us "that in the year 1822-1823, thirty-six families from Rustico went to Chéticamp, to Grand-Étang and to Lake Bras d'Or, in Cape Breton."[18]

In 1792 Jean Bourgeois arrived in Chéticamp. He was born in France and was nineteen years old when he arrived here. He married Angélique Poirier and later married Rosalie Maillet. He is the ancestor of all the Bourgeois in Chéticamp. About 1820 another Jean Bourgeois arrived from the Magdalen Islands, but his children were all girls.

Some of the Chiassons, such as Paul, Basile, and their children, returned to Prince Edward Island. Paul died there. Shortly after 1800 Basile came back to Chéticamp with a large group of Chiassons: Thomas, Charles, David, Germain, Polycarpe, Lawrence, Firmin, John and "P'tit" Basile. They settled on Chéticamp Island.

The family of Jean-Marc Romard came from Tracadie, Nova Scotia, before 1809; that of Lapierre arrived early on from the Magdalen Islands; the Larade, Haché and Broussard families came later from Margaree; Jean Camus, son of Jean Camus and Marie Fleuri (Henri?), came from Plaisance, St. George's Bay, Newfoundland. In 1820 he married Marie Deveau of Chéticamp, where he himself had lived for two years. Jean Shumph, son of Christian Shumph and Monique Goie of Québec City, married Anastasie-Angélique Romard on August 7, 1820. He was the first of this name in Chéticamp.[19]

During the same period, from 1800-1815, the Acadians received some French reinforcements, who arrived under strange circumstances. The English had had many occasions to take prisoners of war from the West Indies, as well as from naval vessels. Some of these prisoners escaped in various ways, and the fugitives succeeded in reaching some of the inhabited Acadian villages.[20]

It appears that this number was not made up solely of prisoners of war; a number of French sailors sought nothing more than to flee the inhumane conditions they suffered on the warships and other boats. "Thus it was, that in 1806, five French sailors, Servant and Nazaire Lefort...and their brother, François,[21] as well as Louis Luidée and Pierre Chapdelaine, had deserted a frigate and sought refuge on our coasts...."[22] They left the boat at Cape North and walked from there to Chéticamp. No doubt fearful of bringing more trouble onto themselves, the Chéticantans opposed the settlement among them of these five. These refugees understood the situation and went on to the Magdalen Islands. François Lefort, Louis Luidée and Pierre Chapdelaine later returned to Chéticamp and became the ancestors of all those in Chéticamp who carry their names.

From time to time other Frenchmen were added to the list of those who settled in Chéticamp: François Levert, native of Sarneg, a parish in France,[23] and the families of D'Or, François Radoub, and Étienne Rambeau.[24]

Some Jerseys who worked for the Robin Company, became Catholics, married Acadian women and settled down for good in Chéticamp. There was Louis Breuillat,[25] who married twice, first to Marie Mius and then to Anastasie LeBlanc; Jacques Avy, of Saint Élier, Isle of Jersey, married to Gertrude Poirier. Likely there were others, but the most famous among them, by personality and descendance, was Jean Lelièvre, married to Marie-Angélique Deveau, daughter of Augustin Deveau.

Next to the name of Jean Lelièvre in the parish registers is written the following phrase: "merchant of this parish." After a long training period working for the Robins, he opened a small business of his own at La-Pointe-à-Cochons [Pig Point] where he had his home. Jean Lelièvre seems to have realized the future importance of the Chéticamp harbour. Far from concealing himself in the back areas, he acquired nearly the whole coastline southeast of the harbour. His store was the first one at the harbour (La-Pointe-à-Cochons) and also, with the exception of the Jerseys, the first in Chéticamp.

With the passing of the years some Irish settlers arrived and joined the group. Besides Cyriac Roche, or Roach, born of Irish parents and adopted at the age of two years by Joseph Aucoin, there was James Butler, George Flinn, and the Odle family, all of whom came from Waterford, Ireland. The Harris family was Irish as well. It is reported that James Butler had left his mother in tears to flee Ireland at the age of twelve years and crossed the Atlantic as a stowaway. One thing is certain: immunized against the smallpox that he had already contracted, he became famous for his devotion to Amable Chiasson's family who were victims of that disease.

Close Consanguinity

Among our people, as in all Acadian groups of those days, there was such a close relationship that the marriages caused anxieties to the missionaries and necessitated dispensations which were not easy to obtain in these regions where communication was occasional and, inevitably, slow. We hear it often from the first missionaries—Bailly, Lejamtel and Allain—in their request for powers to the Bishop of Québec:

Being nearly all related, the young people have great difficulty in getting married without facing an impediment beyond my faculties.... Having recourse to authority may take many years and this, often, is not without grave danger to their spiritual and temporal welfare.[26]

It often happened that a brother and sister in one family married a sister and a brother in another family. It even happened that a widowed father married the widowed mother of his daughter-in-law, creating genealogical tangles that were difficult to unravel. These narrow bonds of kinship contributed to make of this isolated group a type of large family that had no other possible link with the rest of the world but the occasional visit of the missionary, the oppressive Jerseys and their own valiant schooners.

Rapid Growth

In 1782 Chéticamp sheltered only two Acadian families; in 1790 there numbered twenty-six.[27]

Some details given to Bishop Denaut of Québec in 1803 by Father Champion, missionary to Chéticamp, are listed below:

Chéticamp: 185 souls, of which there are 101 communicants.
Margaree: 168 souls, of which there are 81 communicants.
Magdalen Islands: 351 souls, of which there are 111 communicants.

Father Lejamtel's census, taken at the end of August 1809, tells us that Chéticamp, with a population of 226, had forty-eight Catholic families and Margaree, with 200 inhabitants, had thirty-seven Catholic families.[28] In 1820 Chéticamp and Margaree together had a population of 784 Catholics.[29] The population of Margaree reached 1,000 souls then remained stationary, while that of Chéticamp continued to grow.

In the autumn of 1879, a part of Chéticamp, Grand-Étang, was created a parish with its own autonomy under the name of Saint-Joseph-du-Moine. Even with this separation, the population of Chéticamp reached 2,500 souls, then it, in its turn, remained stationary, despite its very strong birthrate. Emigration is a continuing problem, even today. It is like a running sore, from which escape all the powers of expansion. In spite of all this, for over thirty years, thanks to the cooperatives, Old Age Pensions and Family Allowances, etc., life has become less difficult, the parish grows and the population increases.

Today the population of Chéticamp is 3,000.

Emigration

As we have seen, there seems to have been a period during the early years when Chéticamp showed signs of population fluctuation. New families continued to arrive; others, already there, left for other Acadian centres like the Magdalen Islands, Prince Edward Island, and even Newfoundland. Finally the population stabilized.

At the end of the last century an increasing flow of emigration, which had been unceasing, began in this region. About 1890 publicity sheets were brought to Chéticamp—no one knows how. These papers seductively propounded the marvellous living conditions of Lac St. Jean, Québec, particularly in Val Jalbert, near Roberval, where a pulpwood business was opening up. Seven or eight families fell for the illusion and set off for Roberval.[30]

About 1895 a number of the men left in the autumn for the lumbering sites in Bangor, Maine. Several of them stayed, married, or brought up their families there.

Then began the emigration to the mining regions of Reserve, New Waterford, and North Sydney. David à "Bichoure" Chiasson, already there, came back to Chéticamp to look for workers for the coal mines. At first the people went for the summer and returned home in the autumn. But little by little entire families, in great numbers, emigrated there. The thousands of Acadians that make up the present French communities in New Waterford, Sydney, and the neighbouring localities came from Margaree, Saint-Joseph-du-Moine, but especially from Chéticamp. In the beginning they were treated like outcasts by the English. Here, one person deservedly stands out and should be remembered by all Acadians: Father Ronald MacDonald, parish priest at Glace Bay, who was their defender, their benefactor, and their friend.

Then there was the emigration to the United States up to about 1930; another to Montréal; and, finally and more recently, another to Ontario where today are found such a great number of Acadians, hundreds of whom came from Chéticamp.

Original Establishments

As the present harbour of Chéticamp was closed by a sand dune which made it impractical, our pioneers had no desire to live there. Besides, the Jerseys were already established at the other end of the island, at La Pointe. It was across from them, on the mainland, on "Le Banc," that our people settled down. The first settlers arrived late in autumn, probably in October, and built homes as quickly as possible.

The winter was hard. Three people died. They were buried close by on the point of Le Banc where a cross was set up; from that comes the name Pointe-à-la-Croix or Point Cross. These graves could still be seen in 1930. Today the cross is gone and the field has been ploughed.

A large number chose to settle in the area presently called "Le Platin." On his pastoral visit in 1812 Bishop Plessis wrote that:

It appears that the inhabitants would have to establish themselves on both sides of this beautiful basin that makes up the harbour. Not at all. If you exclude three or four, all the others, numbering more than forty, have isolated themselves in a horrible valley, bounded on one side by mountains completely covered with woods, and on the other by a hillside which separates them from the harbour by nearly a league.[31]

Why this choice? For the same reasons which, from the outset, caused many of them to settle in Petit-Étang or "Le Chêne," although the bishop does not mention it. First, our fathers felt the need of placing some distance between themselves and the coasts which had been, so many times, an open door to their rapacious enemies, the English.[32] The more distance there would be between them and the sea, the more they would be sheltered from surprise attacks which they could still remember very bitterly. They chose the plains, again because they were very easy to clear, and quite nearby extended the grasslands where they could pasture their animals and gather in the hay. For this reason La Prairie was divided into equal parts of this domain. The wood, close by, was better, also, and easier to reach. Finally, and especially, they settled near the water supplies for domestic reasons: the Platin River, the Petit-Étang Brook, and the river of La Prairie.

Charter of 1790

Learning by experience, our pioneers wished to avoid in this area, what, on Île St. Jean, had caused so much unhappiness to them and their compatriots after the Expulsion. They resolved to procure titles which would give them real possession of their land. This would prevent from hovering over them the shadow of any bird of prey, such as unknown titleholders who, dropping in on them without a moment's warning, would pocket their earnings or would expel from their lands the too-trusting workers who had tilled the land by the sweat of their brow.

By 1790 the settlers had obtained from the government in Sydney a charter, dated September 27, which granted to fourteen among them[33] 7,000 acres of land.[34] On the diagram which accompanies this charter, more than half of the southwest of Chéticamp Island (1,000 acres) belongs to Philip Robin and Company. At La Pointe, this company already owned three large wharves and some good buildings. The other end of the Island was still Crown land. According to this same diagram we see that, in 1790, there were already eight houses at Petit-Étang; eight at the head of Le Banc to the southeast; thirteen at Le Platin; and a flour mill, property of Pierre Aucoin and Joseph Boudreau, up the Platin River.

We also take note that, little by little, the Chéticantins have become purchasers, with legal title, of other Crown lands.

In 1809, when Father Lejamtel wrote his account of the population of these places in order to send the census to Bishop Plessis in Québec, there were five families settled in Grand-Étang, twenty-three at Le Platin, nine at Petit-Étang, and six Acadian families and three English families on Chéticamp Island.[35]

The 1790 charter and several subsequent grants did not assign a lot to each person, but left the sharing to the understanding of the group concerned. The best part of these lands was parcelled out immediately, while other sections were done later. We have seen, preciously preserved in families, old papers duly signed by "les vieux" (the old ones) who settled some of these lots. Here are some examples:

In 1818 fifteen of the old people divided "le platin de la petite rivière," doubtlessly at Petit-Étang. The names of this old document, along with its errors in spelling, are: Joseph Deveaux, Gustain De Vaux, ansel auquin, manavoir Chiasson, Pierre auquin, joseph Le Belanc, Joseph Godes, Rémon Poirier, Joseph auquin, Joseph Boudrot, Joseh à Pole, Syriaque Roche, étienne chiasson, Régis Bois. The document points out that "these shares were drawn by lots," then "Joseph Deveaux and Joseph Godes have la cave a Lou" (these two have Wolf Cave).

In 1825 Le Banc was divided among eight of the old ones of Chéticamp.

Chéticamp—August 29, 1825

division of Le Banc and the shore among eight old inhabitants. Each one marks his lot.

1. to the northeast of Le Banc—the lot to Joseph godes.
2. after that the lot of Pierre auquin.
3. then comes the lot for gustain Deveau.
4. then the lot for Anselm auquin.
5. then the lot of joseph Boudrot.
6. next, the lot for pierre Boi.
7. then the lot of Rémon poirier.
8. then the lot for joseph auquin mondou.

for the shore

1. to the northwest Joseph godes.
2. then the lot of joseph Boudrot.
3. Next, the lot of justain Deveaux.
4. then the lot of Anselm auquin.
5. then the lot of pierre auquin.
6. after that, the lot of Remon poirier.
7. then the lot of pierre Bois
8. then the lot of joseph auquin Mondou.

[on the other side of this document]

Reserved part of Le Banc on the northwest side about 30 paces for the road and also the space for collecting seaweed.

Each one will sign his share, beginning with those who can sign. Those who cannot sign, the witness will sign for them.

	justain	x	Déveau
	joseph	x	Boudrot
Witness	Regis	x	Bois
Witness	Simon	x	auquin
Witness	Maccimilien	x	godes
	joseph	x	auQuin
	Rémon	x	poirier[36]

In the beginning it appears that the decision of the old inhabitants, duly signed or fixed with their mark, had the force of law for the people. But with the passage of time the younger generations did not so readily accept the decisions of these old ones and criticized the earlier choices. This is what seems to be indicated on other documents of these same old persons. Those documents of December 8, 1819, say:

Agreement among the eight old inhabitants on the maple sugar trees. Each one of us shall keep his old maple sugar trees forever, while the younger ones will find maple groves where they can, as long as the owners of the land do not need them and shall not cut trees on them maliciously.

Pierre auquoin	mark x
Augustin Deveau	mark x
Remon Poirier	mark x
Joseph Boudrot	mark x
Regis Bois	mark x
Aselme auquoin	mark x
Joseph Godes	mark x
Joseph auquoin	mark x
Maccimilien godes	mark x

[on the other side of this document]
Le Pré Perdue (The Lost Meadow)

For the lost meadows, the eight old inhabitants have made this agreement to keep them as meadows and want to keep them as meadows and still sign them as meadows and also the alder-groves as meadows.

Signed by the eight old inhabitants those who cannot sign, their witnesses will sign for them.

Joseph	x	auQuin	justain	x	déveau
Rémon	x	Poirier	joseph	x	Boudrot
			régis	x	Bois
			Simon	x	auquin
		Witness	Maccimilien	x	godes
			Peter	x	auquin[37]

The imprecise dividing of the lands later gave rise to many difficulties and quarrelling. The missionaries would complain about them several times. This question would generate so much misunderstanding among the people that Father Blanchet said, in writing to Bishop MacEachern, who shared it with the Bishop of Québec:

A number of misunderstandings exist in his mission in consequence of their not having run each lot at the first settling of it by the Acadian settlers. Many of the old Inhabitants are dead, and the rising generation do not like the divisions made by their fathers.[38]

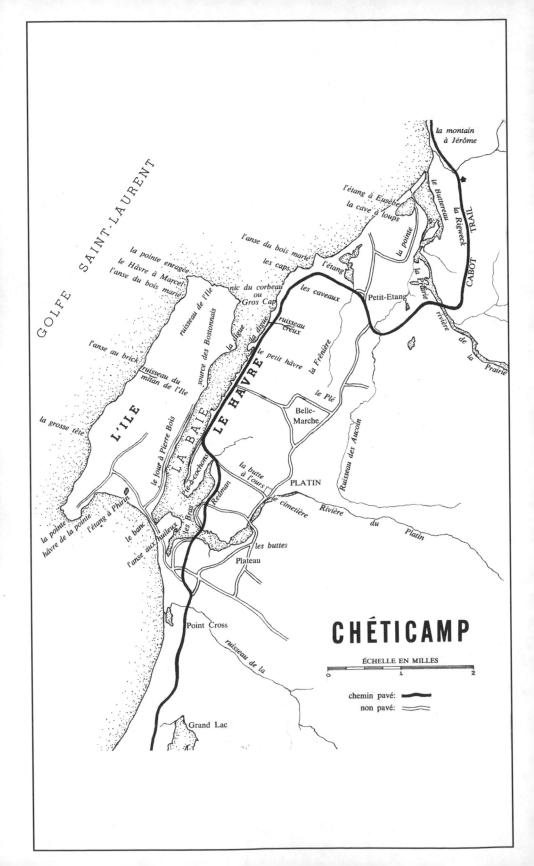

CHÉTICAMP

ÉCHELLE EN MILLES

chemin pavé:
non pavé:

CHAPTER FOUR

Economic Life

MATERIAL LIFE IN THE BEGINNING

MR. RAMEAU DE SAINT-PÉRE WROTE that the Acadians who, on their return from exile, had settled on the islands in the Gulf, possessed more valuable personal belongings and seemed better off than the others.[1] We believe this was true of the pioneers of Chéticamp.

Assuredly, the Acadians were not rich. How could they have been after thirty years of exile and endless wanderings? As the proverb says, "A rolling stone gathers no moss." But the presence of a Jersey store in Chéticamp at the very beginning, the schooners in which the men travelled from one end of the Gulf to the other, even to Québec and the West Indies, as well as their resourcefulness, procured for the Chéticantins, if not comfort, at least a certain degree of affluence which many homes, even those of French-Canadians, were lacking at that time.

In order to convince ourselves of this, we have only to read the account books of the Robins. As early as 1788 we see Anselme Aucoin buying so many things over only a three-month period that we wonder if he wasn't perhaps buying for all the members of his crew. Even for that time, his purchases were considerable. To get an idea of them, let us look at the principal items he bought for those three months, as transcribed, then translated, from the records:[2]

2 iron pots	1 scythe, some tobacco
1 frying pan	1 silk handkerchief
1 barrel of Lard, 1 barrel of flour	1 pair of women's shoes,
1 pair of carding implements	5 yards of linen cloth, 1 glass
4 yards of serge	Some ribbon, thread, coffee, tea
2 bundles of shawl material	A mug (small cup), 2 pot handles
some needles, a pair shears	2 iron pitchforks
1 tin basin, 1/2 dozen knives and forks	1 line, some fish-hooks...

some serge, some cotton goods	1 bar. of fine flour, a piece of silk
1 axe	30 lb. of lard, etc., etc.
1 pair of shoes	[and, evidently, from time to time]
1 doz. gun-flints	a bottle of wine, 1 gal. of rum.

The bill added up to £38 14s. 5p., while the "Credit" on the right hand page gave, for the same dates, £44 14s. 3/4 p. This left in the autumn a balance of £5 19s. 7 3/4 p. Signed: Jean Luce, of Robin and Co., September 25, 1788.

As we examine other pages, we see that he also lacked none of the usual commodities. We go on to see: "1 pair of boots, some sailthread, hooks, butter, blankets, buttons, nails, cord, candle lanterns, candles, papers of pins, petticoats, cutting knives, combs, handkerchiefs, fishing lines, tin lamps, double pulley blocks, herring nets, windows, etc." and, often, rum by two, and even five, gallons.

These early pioneers were not deprived of the necessities of life. When their first missionary, Father Champion, died he left his furniture and money to the poor. Everyone asked Father Lejamtel to use this money for the church, "there being no one among them reduced to begging."[3] So prosperous were they that another missionary, Father Manseau, wrote in 1814, "In Chéticamp, everyone is well-to-to."[4] Other missionaries as well, right from the beginning, could only express their satisfaction with the generosity of the Chéticantins: "They are very generous towards the priests who minister to them," said Lejamtel.[5] "Everything is given to us, including food and clothing," said Father Manseau; "there is no need to spend a cent; which is a great help to us," he added.[6]

The early settlers were resourceful. Upon their arrival, Pierre Aucoin and Joseph Boudrot built a flour mill above the Platin River. They had chosen the place well, since the mill, after having changed hands many times and after having undergone many changes as well as serving other purposes, was still in use up to 1949.[7] There were blacksmiths and carpenters among the group of pioneers. If the blacksmiths had less to do, the carpenters, on the other hand, built everything, from the wooden plough in the farmyard and the furniture in the house to the elegant dories and schooners, proud of their numerous sea voyages.

The cost of clothing was minimal. The women spun and knitted the wool, hacked and wove the flax, and made all the good, homespun materials. It was economical as well as being very strong.

Without a doubt, the people suffered privations just the same. But the charity shared among the neighbours of this growing community was sufficient compensation. These pioneers, so closely related by blood, by the common trials in the past and by a common fate in the future, formed, as we have said, one large family.

It was these same ties of brotherly love, strengthened by faith, which made them rush to the aid of one another, whether it was to build a barn, raise a house, launch a boat, dig a well or a grave, or bury the dead.

The women, who were the spirit behind this charity and unity, set the example. When the men were out fishing and the women at work in the fish-drying yards,[8] it was understood that each one would take her turn in preparing the common dinner. They would hurry to help anyone in need, act as a midwife or doctor, or welcome under their roof the orphans of a relative or neighbour who had been taken too soon from the bosom of his family.

Let us honour, with love and devotion, these strong women, our mothers. That our fathers, old sea wolves that they were, braved the oceans and the storms, loving the risk of new adventures, is not surprising, as long as their wives accompanied them! We salute these women! They were the strength of their husbands, the spirit of joy in their new homes, the sanctuary lamp keeping alive in the hearts of their men and children the faith which inspired their energy and courage.

First Homes

The most important task of each newly-arrived family was to build a house. This was a fairly easy undertaking as there was quite an abundant supply of wood nearby.

There was no sawmill or forge and, as money was scarce and everyone bought as little as possible at the Robins' store, no matter how sufficiently well-stocked it was, the people themselves made everything they could out of wood. The main tools at their disposal at that time were the long-saw, hand-saw, axe, squaring axe, two-handled knife, and penknife. Very few could afford the luxury of buying nails, except for shingle nails. They used oaken wooden pegs for all construction, even sometimes for attaching fence poles or stringers. Even the hinge-pins for the doors were made of wood.

The first homes were built of roughly-prepared wood, log-house style (superimposed axe-squared logs). Some of these homes still remained at the end of the century.

Let us now visit one of these primitive homes.

The house isn't finished on the inside. The floor itself is of squared wood, sometimes even of smaller round logs or *rollons*. The furniture is very rustic, a dining table made of planks, no chairs, just benches for seats. Against the wall there is a *dorsoué* (sideboard or shelving) for the dishes.

The beds are wooden, simple sleeping couches, but with one peculiarity. There are no bedroom or partition walls. The beds serve those purposes. Thus, boards are nailed to the beds, placed in such a way as to make a closed closet, a box from the ceiling to the floor, called a *sac à housse* (covering bag). The sole opening in these beds is not a door, but a curtain.

In the corner of the room is the shelf to hold buckets of water, with the mug or common cup on a nail.

In another corner is the broom—and what a broom! It too is homemade, and sometimes very simply made, like a broom with branches tied together and attached to a handle; sometimes it is the more sought-after *balai à tilleul*, a broom made from the linden tree, still in use in the barns.

Hung on the wall are the ever-necessary musket and powder horn.

On the windowsill are notches, where the sun marks the hours.

In the ceiling, at the edge of the wall, there is an opening, and attached to the wall is a ladder to climb up. This leads to the attic where all supplies are stored (wool, clothing, beans, etc.) and where, often, boys sleep on straw mattresses on the floor.

From very early times, the outside walls of the house were covered with clapboard. The roofs were always covered with shingles, handmade right on the place. These were always made from the fir tree. The trees were sawn into large logs. Then, with a special knife on which the men hammered with an axe, the logs were split into pieces as thick as a shingle. Afterwards, by means of a certain frame, the shingles were finished by hand with a two-handled knife. The shingles were solid, durable and of superior quality.

There were some ovens outside, but they were never greatly in style, probably because of lack of flour and because so little white bread was eaten. Large, square stoves called sows were used, like those in country schools. Ordinarily bread was baked on the stove in a large cauldron called a "big pan." This pot was encircled with big firebrands, right to the rim, and when they were burned out the bread was baked—and "what great bread it was!" the old ones said. Most often, in the absence of bread, it was the *torteaux* or griddle cakes that they baked. The method used was quite elementary: a barrel hoop was placed on the stove, which was then filled with paste, unable then to overflow. It was baked very slowly and was a most delicious morsel to eat while still hot.

Fire

Today, with all the means available to obtain flame from a match or a lighter, it is hard to imagine the difficulties experienced by our ancestors in this regard. Matches were only invented by the French in 1831 and put on the market much later.[9] Up to that time, our ancestors, as everywhere else, had to make use of the flint or gunflint which, when hit with another stone or by the back of a penknife, produced sparks.

But the sparks alone were not enough to set fire to the pieces of wood, not even to the shavings. Everywhere the people used touchwood, called *tonde*, a dry, spongy substance made from a fungus of the oak or other trees. It is believed in Chéticamp that this substance was obtained from the woody part of old, decayed wild cherry trees, well dried out. It was indeed *prime* (easily flammable).

However, the easiest method of having immediate fire was not to let the stove or fireplace go out. If by some misfortune that did happen, one would run to the neighbour's for embers to relight the flame in his own home.

Methods of Lighting Homes

The pioneers used candles for their evening light and in the winter they used the *maçonne* (fireplace) as well. Candles were made with sheep tallow. The lantern was a luxury item. For an outside light they used torches, some sticks from the hazel tree set on fire at one end which were shaken to keep lit. Later would come the candle lantern, then the *lampe à becquillon* (a spout lamp, somewhat like an Aladdin's lamp) which used codfish oil, then the kerosene lamp, and finally and more recently in 1937, electricity.

Water

All the pioneers established themselves near rivers or streams. Their good, common sense made them do this. They wanted to have an abundant supply of water nearby for their numerous domestic needs.

For a long time the new homes would be built along brooks or close to springs. But little by little, wells were dug. Often, three or four families used the same well that they had dug together. However, it wasn't so very long ago that some families were still transporting water by wagon in puncheons, or by foot with a yoke over the shoulders, for distances of a quarter of a mile or more. This was easy to do in the summer, but in the winter when everything was frozen—what misery!

Little by little wells were dug in sufficient numbers, to a depth of fifty or sixty feet in some places. There was no drilling machine at that time. They had to dig a hole large enough to bring them to the desired depth and continue their work there. At that depth, this was very dangerous. A cave-in and that would be the end of the workers! They forestalled this danger by shoring up the well with wood as they descended. When water was found, the wall of the well was faced with stone. It was the work of experts. Even at the bottom of the well, the hole was from ten to fifteen feet wide. The mason would choose his rocks, with which he formed a solid circle having a diameter of about two and one-half feet in the centre of the well at the bottom. Then he raised the circle of stones, gradually enlarging it in such a way that the stones were solidly settled on top of each other with no risk of falling. Rarely, if ever, was mortar used. The space between the rocks and the wall of the hole was filled with earth and rocks removed in the digging. Arriving at the surface, the opening was bridged, and on this bridge was built the cage with the crank-pin for raising the water. Around the well, birchbark was arranged in the form of shingles so that the rainwater or any other water would run outside the well. All this was covered with earth and peat, leaving the well on a low mound.

Today, most of the families possess a handpump on their well or have an electric pump with a pressure tank in the house which brings the water to the taps. This last installation permits the people to enjoy all the modern conveniences like a bathroom, hot water tank, electric washer, or a garden hose, etc.

Laundering

In spite of numerous difficulties, our Acadian mothers took great pride in keeping everything clean. Laundering was always their most important task.

In the beginning, and for a long time afterwards, they knew nothing of the mechanical washer and the latest soaps. Clothes were washed by hand by being beaten on rocks along the rivers or streams. Later, wooden tubs were used, most often a flour barrel or a small puncheon sawn to the correct height, of which two staves were kept longer than the others. Holes were bored in these two staves so they could be used as handles.

The first washboards were made of polished wood. Later came the wavy glass boards, then the *couloir* (plunger washer), and finally the electric washer of today.

Soap

Soap was homemade, using lye or potash from ashes. There were two kinds of soap: Sunday soap and weekday soap.

Lye was made by following the good, old-fashioned method: a quantity of hardwood ash was put into a barrel over which some water was poured; this mixture was left to soak. In only a few days the water would become red and, when it was strong enough to burn, it was, finally, the best lye imaginable.

The barrel of lye was put on a framework. In the lower part of the barrel a small hole was bored and tapped with a peg. From this peg would hang a bag filled with straw which acted as a filter. To use this, one only had to pull out the peg and let the lye run into the bucket of water in varying amounts (and strengths) according to one's needs.

Sunday soap was made in a large iron cauldron with animal fat boiled with the lye. This job was done outside, usually by the women. It was they who knew how to regulate the intensity of the heat but especially, they knew, as is done in the making of fudge today, how to watch the progressive thickening of the liquid and stop it just in time. Taken off the fire and poured into more shallow containers, the liquid would harden and become beautiful grey soap, nearly white, which they now had only to cut into pieces.

Weekday soap required the same process of manufacture. In place of animal fat the rotted liver of the codfish was used, again with the lye. While the liquid was heating to boiling point, the odour was extremely disagreeable. This is why the job was carried on outdoors. This soap, of a more inferior quality than the others, had a yellowish colour. It was called *drâche* (râche) soap (draff soap).

For a long time these were the only soaps in use, for the face as well as for the floor. Today, while each family uses perfumed soaps, and "Comfort" soap for rougher uses, very few families still make the soap from grease, or the soap from *râche*.

Painting and Whitewashing

For these poor Chéticantins, there was no thought of buying paint. There were more urgent necessities. Their ingenuity, spurred on by their desire for beauty, however, supplied them with another manner of obtaining the equivalent result.

They succeeded in making a dark red paint with red clay located in certain streams; with this they painted their houses. It seems, however, that this paint was not very successful. Such was not the case with lime.

The nearby mountains contained an abundance of limestone and gypsum. From earliest days the Chéticantins were familiar with using these to whitewash the interior of their homes and the exterior of their buildings. To give it body, hair from the cows was mixed with the gypsum.

Limestone and mortar were made in this way: Below the home of Den à Lubin Chiasson there was a lime pit. Into this hole wood and limestone were placed, in layers on top of each other: two feet of wood and one foot of rocks alternately in layers. Then a fire was set inside these layers. This would make the quicklime. When wet with water, this would become slaked lime, ready for use. The whitewash, that is the lime thinned with a greater proportion of water, was used to whiten the interior and exterior walls of buildings.

Moistened and mixed with sand, the lime made the mortar which was used for cement. In the construction of the church *du buttereau* and that of the present church, only mortar made in this way, right on the construction site, was used to cement the stones together. This mortar holds well and has never needed any repairs. Today, however, it is no longer used. It has been replaced with commercial cement.

Use of Flax

For more than a century flax was cultivated in Chéticamp. It was used for a variety of things, such as sewing thread, twine, lines, and even as ropes for the schooners. To make these lines and ropes, the flax was twisted by hand.

Shirts, caps, sheets, towels, as well as sails for the large schooners, were woven with flax.

Le butin (Clothing)

Change de butin! Ramasse ton butin! This means: Change your clothes! Pick up your clothes! This is the meaning which has been preserved in the word "butin," the meaning of clothes, as in *habit*, vêtements and *linge* (garments and body linen).

Shoes

For a very long time the people wore only shoes and high moccasins made from hides. It is not such a long time ago that they still wore them, even the women and young girls. Today, except for the children perhaps, this type of shoe has completely disappeared.

To prepare, cut and sew hide shoes was an art. The animal hide was stretched out on the floor, hair underneath; this was stretched as much as possible and nailed down all around to dry out. Once dried, the skin was scraped on both sides with a knife to remove the fat and hair. Elsewhere, the entire skin could have been sent out to be tanned, but here it was tanned by hand, in sections.

In order to cut a shoe, one had to place the foot on a piece of skin. The skin was then cut out all around, two inches from the foot, just enough so that the raised piece would make the height of the shoe. On the toes, and on the front of the foot, a leather tongue was placed which was sewn all around to the skin, while pleating it. It made a nice foot, like the moccasin of today. As for the heel, it required a vertical seam and another horizontal seam, the latter on the lower part of the shoe. The art consisted of taking the correct measure and in making a seam regular and waterproof. Beauty being relative, we can safely say that these were very beautiful shoes!

These hide shoes, for use outdoors in the spring, summer, and fall as well as for indoor use, were as comfortable as slippers. They were less useful in winter because of the snow. The people tried to remedy this situation. Instead of shoes, they made *les hausses* (high boots). This was a type of boot made from the hides, but which came up above the ankle or to the calf. Laces were not used, but a pleat was made behind the calf and attached to the top with a string.

There was another type of footwear, simpler to make and more inventive: *les caristaux* (high moccasins). The skin all around the leg of a horned animal was removed from the knee to the *sotilles* (hoof). Afterwards, the bottom being sewn, it was worn with the hair outside. With this type of footwear, one went to school and to church; even the altar server wore *les caristaux*.

In the summer, as was the case everywhere else, the children went barefoot. This was no sacrifice. Who has not known the haste with which the children rid themselves of their footwear in the spring and the running they do to feel with their feet the fresh grass, the newly-tilled earth, the hay in the loft and the water in the streams!

At this time, the children only wore their shoes to church. Even to school they went barefoot. Today, with the change in economic conditions, no school would tolerate this. Young boys must surely regret it!

One fine day there arrived in Chéticamp the shoemakers who made leather footwear called *souliers français* (French shoes). There was Laurent Thériault, nicknamed "Cap Sable" because he came from that place. He married a girl from Chéticamp, Émélie Deveau, daughter of Charles à Marie-Luce. There was Angus MacGillis, nicknamed *Pied Gelé* (frozen foot). Then some people from Chéticamp learned the trade. Eusèbe à Thomas Aucoin, Dominique Poirier ("la Furie"), and Irénée Christophe Aucoin became excellent shoemakers.

It is likely that the richer families among them had not waited for the coming of the shoemakers to procure leather shoes for themselves, whether they got them from the Robins' store or from Halifax or some other place. But the general population only gradually began to wear them. The first who dared to wear the *souliers français* were accused of being vain. Little by little, vanity won out and the wearing of these shoes became a general practice. Oh, how they were cared for! For a long time they were worn only to go to church and, even then, the people would walk as far as the woods near the church in their hide shoes then change to the leather shoes. The procedure was reversed on the way home. Young girls, especially, did this, while others simply continued to wear their hide shoes.

Other Clothing

Sometimes the people bought flannel to make skirts and bodices, but most often all the clothing was made from homemade material.

The women knitted,[10] and still do knit, stockings, mittens, sweaters, caps, scarves, shawls, underwear and *les manigaux*[11] (hand protectors).

The homespun for breeches, coats, dresses or skirts was loom-woven. These were the main items the people wore. "This simplicity is so great and so severe," wrote Bishop Plessis on his visit of 1812, "that a boy who would dare to wear a bourgeois [middle-class] suit, would find it difficult to get married."[12] But the bourgeois suit, as well as dresses of other materials, have penetrated the area little by little, and the last outfits of the rough, homespun material disappeared over thirty years ago.

Also on the loom were woven woollen blankets, as well as blankets and rugs of *breillons* (rags). The *tapis à breillons* were also woven with scraps—heavier mats, woven by hand.

The men wore beards and long hair in the old Breton way up to the end of the last century. On Sunday they wore coloured woollen wrist bands with a lacy fringe.

The women wore their hair long, naturally, simply braiding it in a chignon, somewhat in the Empire style of the Napoleonic era. There was never a question of their wearing jewellery or make-up before quite recent times.

In the early days of the settlement the women wore a cape or bodice and a skirt. Dresses only came later. They didn't bother with hats. To go out in the summer the women and young girls wore the coif, the beautiful white cap with pleated lace all around it. "J'étions belles!" (We were beautiful!), say the old ones who lived through this time. In the winter they wore woollen shawls.

Today men and women are dressed without extravagant luxury, but with the most modern outfits which they order each season from the commercial catalogues.

Dyeing

There weren't many varieties of dyes on the market in the old days. Our ingenious mothers succeeded in obtaining a multitude of colours from different plant substances.

From the bark of the sap-running alders, mixed with some indigo, they made black dye; from the moss of the wild cherry trees, they got a beautiful yellow; the bark of the white birch trees gave a bluish-grey colour, but hardened the wool. With the urine of someone who had eaten fresh potatoes, mixed with indigo, and *le corvar* (a local shrub called sheep's poison), they obtained indigo-blue.

Tobacco

Each family cultivated tobacco for its own use. This leaf tobacco, chopped and lightly moistened with molasses, had a unique aroma and an excellent taste.

The tobacco pouch, made from the hide of the seal or the moose, accompanied the clay pipe in the pockets of all adult Chéticantins.

A great number of women smoked, too. How can we explain this custom among people otherwise so austere? Smoking was considered a powerful remedy against toothache. Therefore, even the women thought it wise to pick up the habit.

There were also some snuff users in the beginning. Snuff was produced by mixing good tobacco with wintergreen.

The snuffbox is no longer in use, and hasn't been for a long time; the clay pipe likewise has disappeared, as well as the tobacco pouch. Men continue to smoke the pipe and young men the cigarette. Some ladies also smoke cigarettes, even without a toothache as an excuse!

TRAVELLING AND METHODS OF TRANSPORTATION

AT THE END OF THE EIGHTEENTH CENTURY horses were still rare in America. It appears that Chéticamp was deprived of any for more than twenty years.

Oxen were the only beasts of burden. Moreover, at this time, as much pride was placed in a beautiful pair of oxen as is placed today in a luxurious automobile. With oxen, the early people tilled and harrowed the soil and transported the wood in winter.

In winter, the vehicle used was a great sleigh, not even iron-mounted, by which wood was hauled from the mountains.

In the summer, stretchers for transporting hay, fish or flour were used. These stretchers had no wheels. The oxen were yoked in the *menoires* (the shafts), while the other end of the shaft dragged on the ground. Simon (à Lazare) Leblanc owned the first wheeled cart in Chéticamp. These first carts were not much better than the stretcher. With their wooden axle, their huge wheels not fitted with iron, huge rims and hubs, they could be heard creaking and groaning for miles. A can of *râche* (liver of codfish) accompanied every cart so it could be greased repeatedly.

Women, even young girls, drove these teams, especially in the summer when the men were fishing. The ladies, though, were more particular than the men, more vain. Once, the daughters of Élie (à André) Poirier of Petit-Étang went to the harbour by ox-cart. Because the ox was dirty, they drove into the *ruisseau à Médéric* (Médéric's stream) on their way and there, with a linden-tree broom, thoroughly washed their ox before entering the harbour area. In the eyes of many people this was, again, a good example of vanity.

Of course, oxen were not harnessed to transport people; unless helpless, one preferred to walk. It was less tiring. Besides, to leave Cap-Rouge or Grand-Étang, a distance of six or seven miles, to go on foot to Chéticamp was nothing out of the ordinary. Didn't Suzanne Aucoin, wife of Joseph Ryan, walk from Margaree to Chéticamp with a baby (Louise) in her arms to be baptized! And she was not the only one.

Then came the horses. This was luxury. How sparingly they were used! First of all, they didn't replace the oxen. At the very most a horse would be harnessed ahead of two oxen, as leader. The people were afraid to make them sweat.

In the spring the horses were unshod and pastured for the summer. Then they were used as saddle horses. Husband and wife would go to Mass on the same mount. Saddles were made of canvas. Boys rode bareback (no saddle).

After this came the horse wagons (*les caboroits*). The first one was bought by "Gros" Lazare Leblanc. These first conveyances were not attractive looking, nor had they the lightness of later models. However, their first owners took great pride in caring for them. A neighbour, having borrowed one of these wagons to fetch a barrel of flour from the harbour, was warned to be careful of it. He returned, seated in the wagon naturally, with the barrel of flour on his knees! Old Damouk (Damien) Aucoin used to go to Mass, he on his horse, while his wife sat in the *caboroit* (wagon).

Travelling on Foot

Until about 1940 every Sunday during the summer about fifty wagons or more, and as many sleighs in the winter, would arrive at the church, filled with father, mother, and numerous young children. The roads were filled with people on foot. They would walk three or four miles to church with no difficulty. The walk to, and especially the return from church, was an occasion to chat on the way with friends and relatives; as also, for young people, to timidly undertake approaches with those they dreamed of marrying, of creating ties of friendship, or of publicly declaring their love. For no young man would dare walk with a young lady if she was not his girlfriend or if he did not wish to begin courting her. This was taken as a declaration of love.

With the appearance of the automobile these happy return trips from Mass with the people along the highway have also disappeared. No one walks anymore. Everyone owns his own car or pays his way in someone else's.

Bicycles

The bicycle arrived in Chéticamp in 1889. It was the style of that time, a six-foot wheel in front and a much smaller one in the rear. There were steps to climb to the seat. This bicycle was owned by Joseph (à Élie) Mius from Margaree who bought it in the United States. When he came to Chéticamp with his bicycle the people were terrified of it. They believed it was the devil.

Automobiles

The first automobile to make its appearance in Chéticamp was that of Doctor Louis Fiset in 1908. It was powered by an oil engine. Some automobiles were powered by steam.

Horses were terribly afraid of these cars. We have to admit the cars made a hellish racket. Even some people were afraid of them! This story is told: When Bishop Morrison of Antigonish came to Chéticamp in 1911 for the first time, by car, he was accompanied by a few priests. On the road they noticed coming toward them a small boy and his mother in a wagon. The horse stopped but, scared to death, pranced about, trying to turn back. As was often done in those days, the priests got out to take the horse by the bridle and help it get past the car. They found the mother and child as afraid as the horse. The young boy said: "Help my mother pass first, the horse I can look after!"

Today, nearly every family has its own car and it would be of no use to go to Chéticamp to see any old *bagnoles* (jalopies).

Aeroplanes

About 1920 two aeroplanes flew over Chéticamp. This was the first time the people had seen them. Since then, seaplanes have often alighted in the bay to bring a doctor in from Sydney, or a boss from the gypsum mine, or an engineer or a building contractor.

MEANS OF SUBSISTENCE

TOUGHENED BY CONTINUAL TRIALS, tossed about from one shore to another by the vagaries of political and religious sectarianism, our Acadians still retained a nostalgic feeling for the peaceful and calm life of the farmers of Grand Pré or Île St. Jean. The turmoil had brutally uprooted them from their lands. It had lasted a long time, but had not totally smothered their love for the land, especially in the hearts of the old ones. However, these old people had aged and the younger ones didn't know any other methods of subsisting than hunting in the woods or fishing in the sea.

The Land

The Charter of 1790 obliged each of the fourteen grantees to cultivate fifty acres under pain of confiscation of their land. They made admirable efforts. Many among them resolutely went to work, clearing their lands and cutting themselves real agricultural domains. After a difficult beginning, several soon knew a relative prosperity. A pair of yoked oxen, five or six horses, as many milk cows, a good flock of sheep, some poultry and hogs; all of this, with the produce of the land, took on a look of abundance for these Acadians, so long used to the misery of a hard life.

These completely new lands were rich in humus, and the crops, whether grains or vegetables, were plentiful. Only wheat failed to grow. The old people believed that the salty sea air blighted that harvest.[13] So, after trying for several years, they abandoned the growing of wheat.

Both flour mills, built on the arrival of the group, ceased to grind; one became a sawmill, the other a mill for the carding of wool.

The people had to do without flour, which became a luxury item. For a long time in this region, the buckwheat griddle cakes (girdle cakes or black bread) took the place of white bread. Only the Jerseys and some wealthier families used white bread. True, the Jerseys did import some flour, but the price was prohibitive for most Chéticantins. It is said that one autumn four barrels of flour were brought over from Europe. The Jerseys, themselves, took one, "P'tit" Simon Leblanc took the second, while Charles Deveau and Amable Aucoin shared the third. The fourth barrel had to be returned in the spring for want of a buyer.

Later, the people began to eat white bread and make use of the flour, but how sparingly! They never broke open a barrel. This would cause the flour to be used up too quickly. They pierced a hole in the barrel with a drill and put a cork in it. This flour was only used for great feasts, and then only moderately. Even in 1850 it was rationed. When they had other things to eat, such as meat, they didn't eat bread. "Épargnez le pain!" (Don't waste the bread!) was the reminder that followed the blessing at each meal.

Conditions were favorable for the raising of stock. Lands and meadows were vast. More especially, there were mountains close by which, even if everyone there was a woodland owner, would remain pastureland for the animals. Each spring, the farmers would drive to those mountains all the animals for which they had no need at home. In the autumn they would round up these animals, now beautiful and fat, ready for the slaughter and winter meat, or for the schooner voyage to Maritime ports or the West Indies. This organization of pasturelands still remains. Today, as in other days, in order to recognize their own, each animal is marked in a certain fashion on the ear. Each owner has his own personal mark registered with the Justice of the Peace.

Agricultural tools were primitive, as were any other of those times. The two-handled ploughs with steel ploughshare did not exist then. The only ones known and used were those made by Paul Leblanc, Isidore Leblanc and Apollinaire Poirier: all of wood and with only one handle. The harrows, also of wood, are still in use. The homemade shovels and the pitchforks were most often made of wood.

There were vast maple groves with a prosperous maple sugar industry.

Oats were cut down by sickle and tied in sheaves. The grain would be beaten by flailing, then winnowed by hand. Flax was cultivated and pounded as in Québec. Barley was crushed with a pestle. It was not winnowed. Once crushed, it was soaked in water; the chaff would float to the top and would be easily removed.

Cultivation of the barley and flax, as well as the maple groves, has long since disappeared from Chéticamp.

Moreover, in Chéticamp, as in all new Acadian centres after the Expulsion, with the exception of Prince Edward Island, cultivation of the soil would come to be, unfortunately, less and less popular. In Chéticamp it gradually fell to the level of furnishing necessary vegetables to the family and some hay and oats to keep a horse and a cow or two. Today the abandoned farms are too numerous to be counted.

Hunting

In Chéticamp as elsewhere, hunting today has become an excellent sport. Formerly, it was an industry. In the beginning especially, it was a way of surviving, a way to stay alive.

There were two types of hunting, very different from each other, but equally important: seal hunting and moose hunting.

Seal Hunting

Hunting for seals was always thrilling, in spite of the difficulties it presented and the tragedies that followed. This hunting took place in the spring and lasted a month or two, depending on the temperature and the duration of the ice along the coastline.

In Chéticamp, as everywhere else along the Gulf, the ice freezes in the bays, the harbours, and lightly along the coast, but not in the open sea. The Gulf fills up with floating ice-fields coming down from the north. When pushed by the north winds, they reach our coasts in January and February and stay there up to the beginning of May. In the interval, they shift with the winds. The southeast winds sometimes push them out of sight, then the northeast winds bring them back to violently pound the coasts, sweeping the shores and carrying away the rocks, piling the ice up in huge banks with terrible cracking sounds. This coming-and-going of the ice usually begins about the end of March. That's when the seal hunt begins.

Every spring, around March 25, as soon as a passage opened to the

Gulf, about ten schooners from Chéticamp would be ready to leave. But since the schooners were still in the harbour, and the harbour was still frozen, it was necessary to saw a path open to the boats, about a mile long. All crews were employed in this work. They sawed the ice in pieces which they then slid under the firm ice. This would go on quite rapidly. Everyone was happy. The thirst for adventure, the call of the ice, gave a new vigour to these hardy people.

Furnished with enough provisions for more than a month, a change of clothing in case of a fall into the water, and their sticks for the hunt, each schooner would leave on its way to search for seals. They would go great distances, even as far as the Magdalen Islands, when the openings through the ice permitted it.

The boats stopped wherever seals were found. Seals, in the early days, were plentiful. From their boat, using binoculars, the hunters would locate the seal herds on the vast expanse of ice. The men would lower their rowboats from the schooners and thread their way towards the herd of seals. Finally, they would lift the rowboats onto the ice and, from there, go on foot. Armed with large clubs, they would surround the herd to prevent the animals from saving themselves in the water. As these animals are not dangerous, and have almost no means of defense since they can't move very quickly when out of the water, the slaughter was easy. One could knock them senseless by clubbing them on the nose. When a herd was surrounded quickly enough, very few managed to get away. Each herd sometimes held four or five hundred seals. This surprise attack was a thrilling adventure for the men because of the great number of seals killed. After the slaughter they had to dress the seal: that is, skin it and cut up the carcass. The schooner was brought nearby, loaded with all this catch, then the men would go off in search of other herds. In this way they spent six or seven weeks on the search, the hunt, and the cutting up of the animals.

On Sunday the men never hunted, even if there was a seal herd within striking distance. At the very most they would allow themselves to circle the herd, to bring the animals closer together in order to drive them as close as possible to the schooners, thereby making it easier to guard them during the night for the next day's slaughter. But, often, seeing themselves surrounded and unable to flee, the seals would use some strategy, such as piling themselves up, pressing down on the weak point of the ice which would soon give way. Next day, not a single seal would be in sight!

On the return of the hunters, all the schooners would come to berth at L'Anse-aux-Huileux on Chéticamp Island where the fat would be melted down. This is how the area got the name "L'Anse-aux-Huileux" (Oiler's Cove).

This fat had several domestic uses. Mainly it was used in the making of soap. Lamps were filled with the oil, and skins, footwear and harnesses were softened with it. The hides themselves were used in the making of footwear, blankets, hoods and mittens. The people kept enough for their own use and sold the rest.

Other Chéticantins hunted along the coast. This was a hunt for isolated seals, or those in small groups of five, six or, at most, a dozen. Rarely would more of the animals come ashore. The men still used clubs on them, but more often they used the rifle, for the expanse of ice was narrower here, the patches of water closer, and the seals could easily save themselves. This hunt, too, was very thrilling.

One has be an excellent marksman to kill a seal with a rifle. It has to be hit in the head. The other parts of the animal are too fatty, the bullets won't penetrate.

In the water, the seal is difficult to kill. If it sees the flame of the gun it plunges into the water so quickly that the bullet cannot hit its head. With their old muskets loaded with powder—those were the guns of the olden days—some of the men were quite famous for their marksmanship, like Jules (à Jean) Desveaux, for example. The hunters, in small groups of three or four, would move away, sometimes up to five or six miles along the coast, sometimes in the rowboat, sometimes on foot leaving the rowboat behind them. This was just as dangerous as the seal hunt from the schooners, perhaps even more so.

Dangers. Tragedies

The schooners and rowboats that were used to hunt seals were specially constructed for this purpose. The bottom of these vessels was flat. The great danger *aux glaces* (in the ice-fields) was to become cornered between the floes, and having boats of thirty or forty tons crack like an egg. With flat-bottomed boats, when the trenches of water would narrow and the floes touch each other, the boats, instead of being crushed, would rise up and keep their balance on the ice.

However, there were some tragedies.

One year, Jules (à Jean) Desveaux went to l'Île-aux-Oiseaux (Bird Island) near the Magdalen Islands. The floes gripped his boat in such a way that it couldn't lift itself. It was crushed to bits. The crew had to return on foot over the ice, dragging their rowboat and only the most necessary food behind them. This took several days, naturally. The cold was terrible. During the night each man was permitted to sleep ten minutes only, lest he freeze and die.

The winds and currents sometimes carried the ice-fields far away, and the boats caught up by them were dragged along. Lubin (à Jérôme) Aucoin and Clément (à "Monock") Haché were caught in this way with their boat. The wind pushed them, prisoners of the ice, at first up to Cape North; then the wind changed, and so did the ice-fields. They crossed the whole Gulf, up to near the Miramichi, along the coast of New Brunswick. There the men managed to free themselves and, with a great deal of trouble, got back to Chéticamp.

Marcellin (à Jeannot) Deveau was caught in the same way. The ice carried him three times to Cape North. From there, his boat was pushed towards the Magdalen Islands, then back towards Cape Breton. While passing in front of Chéticamp, the crew could see the lights in the houses through the darkness.

Some of the coastal hunters were caught in the same predicament.

On April 5, 1842, five men from Chéticamp—Luc Chiasson, Léonard ("Konock") Chiasson, Fidèle Chiasson, Norbert Aucoin and Janvier-Benoît Aucoin—were returning from the hunt which had taken them about six miles along the coast. In trying to jump from one floe to another, three of the five—Fidèle Chiasson, Norbert Aucoin and Janvier-Benoît Aucoin—fell into the water and were drowned.[14]

Norbert's father, Hubert Aucoin, married to Marie (à Régis) Bois, had previously been the victim of a still more horrible death. Hubert Aucoin was probably the captain of the schooner. He and his companions left for the ice like the others. They did not return. No one had seen them. It is easy to imagine the desperate anxiety of the families involved for months, and even years, afterwards. The boat must have been broken up by the ice. The whole crew was lost. Hubert Aucoin must have clung to an ice floe which brought him to land on Île Saint-Paul (St. Paul's Island) at Cape North. A vessel, some years later, found his bones with this inscription written on a nearby stone: "Hubert Aucoin, son of Anselme Aucoin, dead from hunger and thirst. If you find my body, please bury it."

Let us conclude our tragedies with another adventure which happened to Hyacinthe Chiasson, Placide Boudreau and Hippolyte Lefort. The story was told by Hyacinthe himself, in his last years, and is reported here by Miss Joséphine Aucoin:

It was on January 17, 1874. Early in the morning, I left with two companions to hunt seals on the ice to the west of the Island. All of us carried a strong club and a safety rope. The weather was dry and cold, the ice solid, and we set off, walking happily and without fear. We had already gone six or seven miles from shore, but had seen no seals.... Not the least seal was in sight, useless to continue our search. In returning, we felt that the ice was drifting a little towards the open sea, but, as the wind continued from the northwest, we were not worried, and we walked at a brisk pace. Suddenly, we found ourselves facing a huge stretch of water! We were on some ice floes! It was impossible to find the smallest passage to firm ground, from which we were separated by about a mile. It was about eight o'clock in the evening and we thought of the anxiety of our families. Only the echo of our voices, repeated in the mountains, responded to our cries of distress. About midnight a violent wind arose, accompanied by snow. After many searches, a pile of large pieces of ice gave us shelter from the wind, though not from the cold. As soon as dawn arrived, and in spite of the storm, we began walking towards the east. After a walk of about seven miles, we found ourselves facing Cap-Rouge. Hoping the people would notice us from the shore, we fastened our jackets on the end of our clubs to use as a signal. They were seen, all right, but the wind was still too violent to risk sailing through the ice floes.

Numb with cold, wet to the knees and feeling the pangs of hunger, we had to return, this time towards the west, for the floes were moving out rapidly to the north, towards the Gulf of St. Lawrence. Night descended again, forcing us to discontinue our walking. Once again, hollows between blocks of ice served as our bed. We tried to warm ourselves by pressing against each other, while over there in the distance, our church bell slowly sounded.[15]

With the appearance of daylight, we continued our walk, legs heavy by this time, stomach empty, chewing the bark of our clubs so as not to think of our hunger. Near noon the solid ice was about fifty fathoms from land. But the ice-field ended there. In front of us were only some floes covered with melting snow, which floated here and there. It was high time to try the impossible, to gain land before arriving at Cape St. Lawrence. Our ropes tied together, we went in single file from one floe to another, afraid to see them sink or turn over under our weight. You can imagine the feeling and joy we experienced when we found ourselves on firm ground. But, where were we?[16] Over there in the distance there was a cabin, from which we could see smoke rising. We were saved! Another last effort and we were at the door of a good Scottish fisherman. He quickly understood our predicament; he had no bed to offer us, but a good armful of hay near the blazing fire appeared to us as comfortable as the softest feather bed. Some hot tea, drunk in small mouthfuls, and a bit of food warmed us up again.

Next day, somewhat rested, we were en route for the nearest village, where we found some Acadians, and from there in four days by easy stages, we arrived home, surprising our families, who had already given us up for dead.

Oh, my children! I am now more than eighty years old, but each time the great southeast wind blows, I relive in my memory those terrible hours when, lost on the great moving field of ice, we could hear the sounding of our own death knell.[17]

The seal hunts in Chéticamp lasted for more than a century. They were stopped at the beginning of this century because seals had become too scarce.

Moose Hunting

Another means of subsistence for several families in Chéticamp was the moose hunt. After the Dispersion the Acadians had to hide in the woods and live by hunting. They would continue to do this for a long time yet, even after settling down in Chéticamp, as much by choice, for adventure, as by necessity, or even usefulness. Fifty or sixty years later this hunt had been given up, except in the minds of the old people who relived its memories and enriched the evening conversations with their friends.

This hunt was carried out in autumn, as well as in winter. Preparations for it began some days in advance. Muskets were cleaned, powder horns were filled, and bags were packed with food. In the winter, snowshoes and dogsleds were also carefully prepared.

The dogs were as eager as the men to go out hunting. They recognized the preparations taking place. On the last night they wouldn't sleep and, at dawn next day, they would wake the hunters with one or two yelps, then excitedly run back and forth until departure time.

At that time moose were in abundance. They roamed far away from the settlement, however. It was necessary to go far into the mountains to find them: to the east of "la Montagne à Jérôme" (Jerome's Mountain), also at "Habitations neuves" (newly acquired lands). But once there, one was sure of finding all the game he could hope for.

In certain places cabins that the hunters had built served as a shelter, as well as a storage place for their supplies, ammunition, meat and skins of the animals they killed. Most often, though, they had no cabins. When this was the case, they built shelters of trees and boughs and warmed themselves at outside fires.

The group was usually made up of five or six hunters. One remained in the cabin to do the cooking while the others went out to hunt.

In the winter it was easy enough to catch the moose if one could find its habitat. The moose, like the deer, doesn't travel in winter when there is snow. It traces out a route that it keeps well beaten, a path which crosses the groves of white woods (birch and others)[18] that it feeds on. In these clearings a moose can be alone. Sometimes there are three, four, or even six of them. If there is a great deal of snow, nothing will make them leave these areas. The hunters only had to set the dogs on them, station themselves in a good place, and kill the animals as they passed by.

In the autumn, the hunt was more difficult, also more thrilling, and sometimes dangerous. Knowing well the customs of the moose, the hunters would surprise him in his usual habitat, the swamps, or along marshy streams. Conditions did not always permit the hunters to approach the animals, even when they had located them. It was then that the dogs were brought into play. They leapt to the attack with a furious zeal. The moose defended itself with its paws and its head. Sometimes the dogs were hurt, but would not give up the attack. Harried by the enemy, the moose would decamp. That's what the hunters wanted and, for this, they posted themselves in advantageous places to wait for the animals, ready to kill them as they passed. This autumn hunt demanded much more skill on the part of the hunter. The moose was no longer in a clearing where he would turn round and round and pass back and forth in the same place. It was necessary to get him with a musket shot, sometimes from among the trees, sometimes at an unexpectedly long distance. The animal also had to be killed with the first shot, or else he would become dangerous and go after the hunter who had wounded him. But the musket was not a modern repeating rifle. Fortunately, the dogs were there to harass the animal, giving the hunter time to reload the gun.

Often, instead of the hunters finding the animals, the dogs would pick up the scent and, on a sign from the hunters, would go off in pursuit of the game. A good dog could stay on the scent for hours and even a whole day without stopping. The hunters only had to follow him. When the scent was visibly fresh, the hunters set the dogs off in pursuit of the moose. The dogs, once they had found it, kept it at bay, preventing the animal from taking flight, barking to warn and direct the men.

No matter which hunter killed the moose, the fruit of the hunt was shared equally among all members of the team. The men returned home after a few weeks with meat for several months and a quantity of hides.

The Sea

The Expulsion completely upset the Acadians' way of life. The impossible conditions from 1755 to the end of the eighteenth century made them followers of the sea. Unable to obtain lands where they could settle during this entire period, they lived by hunting and fishing. This was, certainly, a case where one could say: one cannot serve two masters. The Chéticantins would neglect their lands because they served the sea. All the young people had been brought up around the sea, and the sea, more so than the farmland, had become their domain. The endless wanderings to re-establish themselves in Acadia, as well as their stay on the islands of Saint-Pierre and Miquelon where they had lived solely by fishing, had given them a taste of the sea, a taste which was never lost.

Several among them had arrived in Chéticamp in good schooners which they had built on the islands of Saint-Pierre and Miquelon or in Arichat. Others were built in Chéticamp, and what beautiful schooners they were for that time! There were even some famous builders of schooners of thirty, fifty, and even ninety-nine tons. The names of Jean Bourgeois, Joseph (à Cyriac) Roach, Paul Leblanc, Édouard Cormier, the Boudreaus, and others are still famous. Some of the well-known schooners are: the *Dolphinée*, the *Messagère*, the *Three Brothers*, the *Quick*, the *Matagon*, the *Hélène*, the *Saint-Vincent*, and the *Sea Flower*.

The ideal place to build these schooners was at "La Pointe-à-Cochons," a stretch of land surrounded by water. But some boats were built in the fields near the houses, sometimes quite far from the sea. Then they were dragged to the sea by ox team. A labour party was organized, an *halerie* (a hauling party). Neighbours and friends would come with their ox teams. Michel Maillet had built a large schooner at Petit-Étang, a mile from the sea. Seventy-five pairs of oxen, harnessed by the horns, hauled it to the sea. It was a solemn ceremony with numerous witnesses. Before starting out, Michel climbed on the front of the schooner and said: "Don't stop for an ox, I can still pay for an ox!" These schooners were the pride and joy of their owners and captains.

They have never completely discontinued building schooners or fishing boats in Chéticamp. Chéticamp has always had experts in this type of construction. Even to this day, trawlers of about fifty-five feet in length are built there.

Economic Life

Long Voyages

We have no idea of the hardiness of those Acadians. Our ancestors, with sail and oar, sailed from one shore to the other of the Gulf of St. Lawrence. Saint-Pierre and Miquelon, Newfoundland, Anticosti Island, Québec, Halifax, and even the West Indies were well-known places for many of them. They exported codfish and farm animals and imported commodities such as molasses, fruits, flour, rum, clothing and utensils which couldn't be made in Chéticamp. These Acadians were extremely courageous. Gabriel (à Stanislaus) Boudreau, in order to make his first voyage to Bermuda as captain of the *Saint-Vincent*, hired a pilot in Halifax. On his return he spent the winter in Halifax to study navigation. The following summer he left for Bermuda again, this time without a pilot. He often took his bearings, which he noted on a board. During the voyage he met other boats. The captains exchanged observations on the notes taken. There was a noticeable difference. Captain Boudreau maintained that he was right and continued on his way. One evening he said: "If I'm not mistaken, we will arrive before midnight." He climbed the mast and just as he had said, there were the lights of Bermuda. "Lighto!" he said.

They were not all so fortunate.

Early one summer old Michel Maillet, on the point of leaving with a load of animals for Saint-Pierre and Miquelon, fell sick. His son, Théophile, insisted on leaving just the same, declaring he was capable of finding Saint-Pierre. Michel let them go. They only returned late in the autumn after having *gabarré* (wandered) all summer without being able to find Saint-Pierre. All the animals on the boat had perished.

These navigators were deprived of even the most elementary navigational instruments. Under sail and by oar, without even a sea chart, they had only their compass, their sense of direction, their experience, their courage and their resourcefulness. For example, not knowing yet how to use, or not having on board the log for measuring the speed of their schooners, they used the following method: at the bow of the ship a man would throw into the water a chip of wood that he would follow on the deck while walking backwards toward the stern. With his watch in hand, he would calculate the speed according to the number of steps to the minute.

All the schooners, even those which occasionally made these long voyages, were used mostly for fishing. But even for fishing, the long trips didn't frighten the men. They would be away for weeks and months on the coast of Arichat, towards the north of Prince Edward Island, in the vicinity of the Magdalen Islands, especially *au corps mort* (Dead Body), so called because, viewed from certain angles, its shape resembled a dead body in its shroud. They would also sail up to Natashquan and to La Pointe-aux-Esquimaux along the Côte-Nord of Québec.

Every spring, in the month of May or June, two or three vessels from Chéticamp would leave for Anticosti to search for the *boètte*, or bait, for codfishing. Others went there to fish for cod. Herring and caplin were found in abundance there. Caplin would be stranded on the coast and the cod would follow it closely. The fishermen would take a good catch of it in a fathom of water, especially on the fishing bank called "la houle de l'Anticoste" (the surge of Anticosti). In the evening the boats would enter Fox Bay, a natural shelter about fifteen miles from Pointe-de-l'Est.

Some of the men, such as "Gros" Lazare Leblanc, Alex Leblanc, and Placide (à Simon) Leblanc, dried their own cod and sold it themselves in Halifax or elsewhere.

It is difficult to believe that all the people of Chéticamp were so well organized. No, this was the exception, we believe.

The majority of Chéticamp fishermen devoted themselves to coastal fishing, with small boats carrying two or three men. It wasn't so adventurous, perhaps, but it wasn't any easier either. To leave port about two o'clock in the morning, sometimes under sail, often by using oars (there were no engines at that time), and row up to Le Banc-Vert or Le Trou à Couillard to find codfish banks within five or six miles from the coasts was no easy task! "Row, and row again!" say the old fishermen. "Our hands were full of blisters!"

Later, about 1906, came the first gasoline engines. It would take some time before the people accepted them. For a long time yet the fishermen would use the sail or oar, looking on this new invention with a great deal of suspicion. Besides, the first engines were so often broken down. But, little by little, the engine changed fishing, as well as the life of the fisherman. Today, thanks to mechanization, fishing has become an agreeable occupation and, what is more, a lucrative one.

Tragedies of the Sea

Many tragedies occurred, including shipwrecks, with loss of ships and loss of life. In the beginning of the colony, before the people realized the dangers of the terrible suêtes (violent southeast winds), before they learned to watch and prepare for them, there were some cruel disasters.

Father Lejamtel had nearly lost his life at sea in 1799. "I made a resolution never to embark in the autumn, unless it was to save my life which was being threatened in another way," he wrote to the Bishop of Québec.[19]

In 1801 six men, five of whom were fathers of families, were drowned at Margaree, surprised by a storm at sea.[20]

In the spring of 1810 "three boats from Chéticamp were broken up and lost, but the crews were saved," wrote Bishop Plessis in his travel journal.[21]

On September 22, 1812, three other boats "having set sail the night before, were hit by a terrible gust of wind, and all hands have perished— all twelve of them. Seven were fathers of families in this area." [22]

The sea, so alluring to seamen, throughout history has exacted its ransom and taken victims. Still many more perished, swallowed up in its storm-tossed waves. The last disaster took place in 1926. Every year, in August or at the beginning of September, there is always a particularly bad storm which hits the Maritimes, often leaving victims in its wake. This annual storm is known as the "tempête du mois d'août" or August gale. Chéticamp suffered often from this storm. Some of these hurricanes struck with particular cruelty.

The storm of 1873 sadly remains famous. Several boats were out fishing, far out into the Gulf. The sea began to swell; it became terrible. But there was no wind, so it was impossible to gain shelter. Suddenly the hurricane hit. A terrifying storm which hit at first from the east, then from the northeast, then from the south, then from the west, then from the northwest! Appalling! The waves looked like mountains as they flung themselves on the ships. Several schooners were lost. At least four ships from Chéticamp were out in this storm; one of these was lost.

A schooner from Chéticamp, the *Hélène*, whose crew was composed of Élie (à Lucin) Aucoin (captain), three brothers, Fidèle, David and Firmin à Konock (Léonard) Chiasson, John McFarlane, and one other, was surprised out at sea, far out in the Gulf between Anticosti and the Magdalen Islands. The ship was saved, having ridden out the storm by heaving to. Three other ships found themselves to the north of Prince Edward Island.

Calixte (à Charles) Boudreau was the owner and captain of one of these boats. His crew was composed of Jerome Aucoin and his son, Lubin, Charles Aucoin, William (à Isidore) Deveau, Philippe (à Olivier) Luhédé, Constant (à Charles à Jean) Deveau, the last well known for his coolness under pressure. Surprised by this sudden storm, Calixte tacked to gain shelter at Souris, fifteen miles to the south of Pointe-de-l'Est on Prince Edward Island. The boat was in danger of being thrown by the wind and waves onto the shores of Pointe-de-l'Est that they were trying to pass. In fact, this was so threatening that Calixte, in a panic, could stand it no longer and decided to turn around. This would have meant a still more certain death. Then Constant Deveau came forward and took the wheel. The boat, bent under her sails, passed the Point. A perilous adventure which succeeded just in time. They were saved. At Souris, they could take shelter until the storm passed.

The *Matagon*, a boat captained by Victor Aucoin, endured the whole hurricane at sea. The members of the crew believed they would founder at any moment. The wind and sea shook the boat like an empty shell. The boat and the men were at the mercy of the storm with no possible control. After the storm, nothing remained on the deck, even the bulwarks had been carried off. The crew had prayed, seeking God's help and, on their knees, had made promises to have Masses and prayers of thanksgiving said. They always claimed their rescue was miraculous.

The *Fairy Queen* was lost. The crew was made up of William Bourgeois, captain, only son of Laurent Bourgeois, Nectaire (à Pierre) Aucoin,

David (à Timothée) Chiasson, Den (à Mick) Chiasson, and finally, Calixte (à Fulgence) Bourgeois. All were young men, still unmarried with the exception of Nectaire Aucoin who had been married for only six months. Another large boat was not very far away and its crew had seen the *Fairy Queen* perish. They were even able to approach it closely enough to see the captain secured to the wheel. At each gust of wind, the boat disappeared from view. Finally, they could see nothing.

Laurent Bourgeois, father of William, desolated by the death of his son, said to Father Girroir: "If only one had the consolation of being able to say he had had the priest!" "Poor Laurent!" said Father Girroir, "a death like that is the most beautiful confession!"

In 1926 another storm came up to throw Chéticamp into mourning. Two boats from there went to fish near Sable Island. The August storm hit them unexpectedly. One of these schooners, whose crew was composed of Luc (à Charles) Chiasson, Charles (à Théophile) Chiasson, and "Gros" Polite Chiasson, was fiercely buffeted for two or three days. The crew expected to founder at any moment. While waiting, all of them, but especially Luc Chiasson, prayed and made the Sign-of-the-Cross over the huge and furious waves, rushing to swallow them up. These men also made promises to God and always claimed their rescue was miraculous. The storm had stripped the schooner of all its sails and rigging.

The crew of the second boat comprised Stanislaus Mius, Cyrille P. Chiasson, his brother Joseph, and Amédée J. Chiasson, all four from Chéticamp and, except for Amédée, married. They were not so fortunate as those in the first boat, and were lost. Nothing was ever heard of them again. Before the storm they had been seen near Sable Island. Without a doubt, the hurricane threw them into the great banks of sand that encircle that island and in which they were engulfed.

Others, also, never returned, lost, no one knows where. "Gros" Lazare Leblanc, late in the autumn of 1854, ready to leave for Saint-Pierre and Miquelon with a load of animals, suddenly decided to stay put without really knowing why. He let his son-in-law, Jean (à Laurent) Chiasson replace him as captain. Among the members of the crew were Xavier Chiasson, Jean's brother, probably Marcellin (à Thomas) Aucoin, a McKeagney, brother of Father McKeagney, and Michel (à Angus) MacFarlane who, when he had said goodbye to his aunt, Mrs. William (à Nanette) Aucoin, had told her, "I will not be back." No one ever heard of them again. "They haven't returned, yet,"[23] the narrator of this story said to me a century later.

Some single drownings occurred also, due to accidents. Gabriel Aucoin, in turning the sail from the bowsprit, fell into the water at La Pointe-Enragée. He sank like a rock and did not return to the surface. He left to mourn him a wife and five children. Sylvain Aucoin and Nouchon (à Marcel) Odo drowned at the entrance to the harbour when their rowboat tipped over. In January 1948 Paul O. Mius drowned in the bay while crossing it in a rowboat. He and his companion clung to the overturned rowboat, but the freezing water killed Paul Mius before the arrival of the rescuers. John-Joseph Aucoin, his companion, succeeded in holding on and was saved. Both men were returning from the lighthouse on La Pointe-de-l'Île.

One of the stories tells of a man who fell into the water during a storm and couldn't be found and was seen no more. Another, similar case was counted as lost but arrived next day after swimming ashore. In a sudden storm, a man was abandoned in his dory on his dormant line in the open sea. The schooner to which he belonged couldn't come to his rescue, dragged as it was by the storm. Lubin (à Jérôme) Aucoin, at the risk of his own life, left the harbour and picked him up. The survivor was so fear-stricken because of this experience he never went to sea again.

Let us conclude our narrative with the story of another tragedy that illustrates the terrible anguish which sometimes afflicted these fishermen and their families. One frightfully stormy day when the wind viciously swept the sea, Fidèle à Konock (Léonard) Chiasson was returning from the coast of Halifax in a schooner of which he was the captain. He followed *la route de terre*, that is, the route near the land along the headlands, in order to avoid the full strength of the southeast winds. The sea was terrible. Lifted up by the waves and the wind, the schooner suffered such wild gyrations that even the bravest "sea wolves" who made up the crew shivered in fear.

Conscious of his responsibility as captain, Fidèle remained at the helm. The waves swamped the boat and swept away everything on the deck. "Be careful!" cried Fidèle Chiasson to the six crewmen. "Hold on firmly! We can't turn back in such a terrible storm!" Hardly had he said this when a cry of distress was heard the length of the boat: "Man overboard! William overboard!" Fidèle clung to the wheel despairingly. He turned pale as a sheet. It was his own brother. "Say your Act of Contrition!" he shouted, while tracing in the air a large Sign-of-the-Cross.

The schooner, leaning over so much the hatchways could touch water, was running as wildly as the storm. William could be seen struggling in the water, his cries for help came to their ears; then he was lost to their sight. No member of the crew asked him to turn back. This was not cowardice. Seasoned experienced sailors, they all knew that "in such a storm, one does not turn back."

> O waves, you know so many tales!
> Deep waves, dreaded by mothers on their knees!
> You tell these stories to yourself while raising the tides,
> That's what makes you carry such desperate voices
> In the evening when you come towards us! [24]

In 1912, under the government of Sir Robert Borden, a rescue boat was granted to Chéticamp. A lookout was installed at l'Anse du Bois Marié, another on the Island, and any vessel in distress was reported by telephone to the crew of the rescue boat. This service lasted until the war of 1914. It was resumed in 1921 and lasted again until the war of 1939. It must be admitted that this boat had very little work to do and almost no one to save. The members of the crew became fat and stocky and were called *les paresseux* (the lazy ones).

ECONOMIC DEVELOPMENTS

EVEN THOUGH THE CHÉTICANTINS did some tilling of the soil, raising of livestock, and hunting, their economic life was concerned, above all, with fishing and the marketing of fish. Other endeavors, such as the Credit Union, stores, mines, and the rug-hooking industry, also deserve mention.

Fishing
The Robins at La Pointe

Established in Chéticamp about 1770,[25] the Robin Company monopolized the fishing industry for almost a century. Before the arrival of the pioneer Acadians, the company only kept a summer fishing station here, and every winter transported its personnel and belongings to Arichat. But, since it provided a guaranteed market for their fish, the company must have been a strong influence on our ancestors to establish themselves in this area.

This company originated in the Islands of Jersey and Guernsey in the English Channel. These islands owed allegiance to the British Crown but their inhabitants spoke French. On the other hand, the Robins and their staff, although French-speaking, were Protestants or Huguenots. Their language favoured relations with the Acadians; their fealty and, doubtlessly their Protestantism, made it easier for them to get along with the English. So they stayed, for more than a century, the strongest fishing monopoly in eastern Canada.

This business—known at first under the title of Philippe Robin and Company, then as Charles Robin and Company, later as Charles Robin, Collas and Company, and finally as Robin, Jones, Whitman and Company—as well as its staff, was commonly designated according to its place of origin: the Jerseys. That is what it is still called, though Jones and Whitman have nothing to do with the Jersey Islands.

The "Jerseys" had established themselves at La Pointe to the southwest of the Island, around an immense natural amphitheatre called the "Cove" which had an easily accessible harbour sheltered from the winds off the ocean, as well as those from the northeast. Unfortunately, this harbour was without protection against the formidable sweeping blows of the terrible southeast winds.

By 1790 the Jerseys already possessed a great wharf in this area. Large schooners, probably some English "bricks" (brigs) and a number of small boats have used this wharf. The big Jersey store had all the more patronage as, except for Jean LeLièvre's small store at La Pointe-à-

Cochons, it was the sole supply house in the area for the Chéticantins. "La Pointe" immediately became a teeming centre of activity. There were the *graves*,[26] with huge racks or trellises on poles on which the cod was laid out to dry. There was the large *chafaud* (shed) and the small *chafaud* (warehouse) to store the dried cod. The fishing boats which sailed through this bay bumped against the wharf or pitched and tossed at anchor. The fishermen were busy cutting their fish, transporting the gear, singing a song or, their work completed, relaxing with friendly teasing, bantering, or silliness. The employees, especially the women and children, bustled around the *vigneaux* (flakes) to spread out the fish, turning them again and again to let them dry out in the sun in order to pile them up in the warehouses later on. And the masters of all this work were the Jerseys.

Little by little, this appearance of prosperity gave way to harsh reality. Fishing killed off farming and, with agriculture gone, the Chéticantins assisted in the very agony and eventual demise of their economic independence. Furthermore, the arable lands of Chéticamp are quite limited and are not as rich as the lands of Saint Mary's Bay or Prince Edward Island. As far as they themselves were concerned, the Jerseys favoured fishing, their great source of profit. Bit by bit, the life of the Chéticantins organized itself around the fishing industry. And, as the Jerseys were their sole agency in the field of buying and selling in this industry, the Chéticantins were soon at their mercy. Kept in ignorance, incapable of defending themselves, they were victims of tough economic slavery and hardship.

For lack of competitors, the Jerseys paid what they chose for the fish. Even taking into account the market prices of that time, we can see that the Jerseys exploited our fishermen as long as possible.

The day came when very few of the Chéticantins possessed their own boat. Everything, boat and fishing gear, belonged to the Jerseys to whom the fishermen paid a fee, one-tenth of their catch. On All Saints' Day (November 1), all boats were put up for the winter. Today, fishing is continued until later January.

The lot of those who worked for the Jerseys was not any more enviable. Working conditions were terrible. These employees toiled from five o'clock in the morning until late into the night. A half hour was allowed for breakfast and an hour for dinner. Supper was permitted when work was completed, sometimes after sunset. It often happened that it was necessary to return after supper, if there were still some fish to be cut, and continue with the work until ten or eleven at night. And, at what a salary! The trade workers, like the cutters and salters of the fish, received a dollar a day. The others received twelve to fifteen dollars a month, or twenty-five cents a day, plus dinner. And this was at the end of the last century when conditions, supposedly, were becoming better! Imagine what the conditions must have been like around 1820 or 1830!

Those whose salary included dinner had no chance of making up for the poor salary on the food. This was strictly rationed. At the beginning of the week, each employee received seven pounds of hardtack, three pounds of inferior quality meat, a pint of molasses and a half pint of peas. No bread. Those who dared to ask for some were raked over the coals: "There's none! If you don't like it, go back to your mountain!"[27] In the communal kitchen everyone's meat was cooked in the same pot. In order to recognize his own piece, each one roughly marked it by attaching a nail to it, or a piece of string or a peg. By Thursday the food was used up. One could only pay extra for more or go hungry.

Another aspect of this system, well calculated to keep these people in bondage, was that the Jerseys never paid their employees in money. All that a man, employee or fisherman, could gain was credit. All year the people had to buy at the Jersey store. And God knows if they avoided needless expense! In the autumn the Jerseys gave to each worker his statement of account. Most often one would just finish paying the expenses of the preceding year when it was necessary to buy on credit for the approaching winter. This régime continued even after World War I. There is even a song of protestation composed against the Jerseys which shows that the Chéticantins were not fools. A rough translation follows:

1
When you catch some fish
They [the Jerseys] are as nice as sheep.
When you go to their store
They are as tough as lions.
They don't look you in the face.
They turn on their heels.

2
When the autumn comes,
It is necessary to weigh the cod.
They go around with their scale
Their scale and their false weights.
They go from one cod-drying field to another
Collecting what one owes them.

3
In the autumn they go to Jersey
While making fun of the French.
Simple inhabitants of the country
You have no spirit
The Jerseys tell you
That you have none.

4
In the spring they arrive
With their rotten hardtack.
They sell it pound by pound
In order to make more profit.

The Lawrences at the Harbour

In the middle of the last century Sam Lawrence, who owned a business in Margaree, established another fishing business and a store at Chéticamp Harbour. One could have hoped that a healthy competition between him and the Jerseys would improve the lot of the Chéticantins. It did nothing of the sort. The newcomer only rivalled the Jerseys in exploiting the people. The old ones can still recall the swindles of old Walter Lawrence, brother of Sam, who became the sole owner of the Lawrence store in Chéticamp.

The Jerseys and the Lawrences held the Chéticantins in their avaricious grasp. Even if the owners of the large schooners could sell their fish in other markets, thus retaining a certain independence, the majority—the small coastal fishermen—were compelled to sell to the Jerseys or the Lawrences. And woe betide anyone who dared sell his fish to anyone else! These people, so dependent on their masters for their livelihood, would have paid dearly. In fact, many times merchant boats were seen coming to Chéticamp offering double price for the fish and being turned away because the fishermen were not free to bargain with them.

In 1903 the Robins moved their business from la Pointe to the Harbour, where the competition of numerous businesses and strong co-operative organizations succeeded in forcing them to become more flexible.

Matthews and Scott

After the death of Walter Lawrence in 1906, Charles (à Nanette) Aucoin, a Chéticantin, became owner of the Lawrence business which he sold in 1911 to the Matthews and Scott Company from Queensport, Nova Scotia. The latter were much more humane than the Jerseys and the Lawrences in their business and dealings with the people. It seems they were the first to pay the people in cash.

The old Lawrence store burned down in 1927,[28] but Matthews and Scott had moved many years before into the store owned by Sandy Aucoin which they rented.

Dredging of the Harbour (1874)

One undertaking changed the face of Chéticamp and was the origin of a growing economic development. This was the dredging of the present harbour, obtained by the parish priest, Father Girroir.

The mouth of the harbour, so the old people say, was closed by a sandbar, the *platié*, covered by only a few feet of water. Navigation there was impracticable. This was the reason why the Jersey stores and the centre of business were established at La Pointe, access to the wharves being easy there. But, as was noted earlier by Nicolas Denys, the harbour of La Pointe was unsafe and without sufficient shelter. Finally, for Chéticantins on the whole, La Pointe was too far away, while the present harbour was more centrally placed and offered a shelter against all winds. The Lawrences had installed their business there and many fishermen did business with them. Consequently, the present harbour area slowly began to become populated.

But the entrance remained the great problem. Small boats like the dories could easily clear this sandbar, but the large schooners could not. The latter had to remain outside or go to La Pointe. In the autumn the large schooners were beached on the sandbar. The north wind and the heavy seas permitted them to cross over, little by little, into the present bay where they were put up for the winter. All the fishing boats, as well as other types, unloaded their cargoes into dories outside the sandbar. Those which carried fish to outside markets loaded their boats the same way. If their cargo was animals, these were forced to swim to the schooner where they could be hoisted. Some medium-sized boats that went out or came in unladen were hauled by towline onto the sandbar. In a boat, or by wading through the water, the youngest members of the crew would go drop the anchor, which was on the end of the forward cable. Then, from the boat, the others would pull on the cable in order to cause the boat to pass smoothly over the sandy bottom. The whole operation was long and tiresome.

The need to dredge a channel at the entrance to the bay was felt more and more. Father Girroir understood this need. He approached the federal government about it and, in 1874, the channel was dredged. Carefully maintained since then, it is now a beautiful passageway about two hundred feet wide and twenty-four feet deep. Since that date the harbour has not ceased expanding. In 1888 the federal government built a wharf there, while Father Fiset also had a wharf of his own. Finally, in 1890, the government erected lighthouses to guide the boats.

There have been up to twenty large schooners of thirty-five to sixty tons belonging to the Chéticantins in the harbour—an impressive sight. Many times between 1890 and 1910 the people could admire fleets of American schooners from Boston, sheltering in the harbour from threatening storms. Chéticamp has been honoured by visits from hospital ships, such as the *Ville-d'Ys* from France. Finally, during the last working of the gypsum mine from 1936 to 1939, great ocean-going vessels of 9,000 tons entered our harbour without difficulty, thereby adding to the pride of Chéticantins.

On the other hand, La Pointe saw its importance diminish day by day. The Jerseys sold their properties to Father Fiset. However, nothing remains any longer. A wharf, built and maintained by the government, still serves a few fishermen. Today, La Pointe, where there exists only a few shabby fishermen's cabins, is beginning to look like a desolate wasteland.

Lobster Factories

To be marketed, certain fish, such as cod and mackerel, require only being cut open, washed, then frozen or dried. Lobster, however, requires a much more expensive operation. For this business, a lobster factory is essential, including the installation of huge steam boilers with thermal controls and all the technical machinery to strip away the lobster shell and put the meat into cans. It is only lately that the lobster factories were installed in Chéticamp.

The first lobster factory was constructed in Chéticamp in 1876 by a Mr. MacFayden of Pictou. It was built at the harbour, at the end of *La Digue*. MacFayden was in business for only two or three years when it failed. Sam Lawrence then acquired the factory, but after running the business for eight years he, too, had to abandon it. Today the sea covers the whole site.

Again it was another outsider who built the second lobster factory. In

Inside St. Peter's Church, 1953 (built 1892). See building, front cover of this book.

Old churches: at the foot of the "buttereau" (hillock) at Le Platin, and at Saint-Joseph-du-Moine

Corpus Christi procession through Chéticamp, 1950

SOME PRIESTS WHO SERVED CHÉTICAMP

Fr. François Lejamtel

Fr. Augustin Magloire Blanchet

Fr. Hubert Girroir

Fr. Julien Courtaud

Fr. Pierre Fiset

Fr. Patrice Leblanc

Fr. Jules Comeau

Priests at Eucharistic Congress, Chéticamp, 1936

PRIESTS WHO WERE BORN IN CHÉTICAMP

Fr. Louis-Michel Maillet

Fr. Anselme Chiasson, Capuchin

Fr. Théophile Maillet

MORE PRIESTS AND A SISTER BORN IN CHÉTICAMP

Fr. Euchariste Leblanc,
Capuchin

Fr. Arsène Cormier

Louise Boudreau, Mother
Provincial, Les Fille de Jésus

Fr. Ernest Chiasson

Fr. Charles Aucoin, Eudist

Fr. Henri Cormier, Eudist

Fr. David Boudreau,
Capuchin

Fr. Daniel Boudreau,
Capuchin

Br. Hermann Deveau,
Capuchin

Fr. Joseph Roche

Fr. Daniel Deveau

Fr. Paul-Anselme
Boudreau

Conference on the co-operative movement, 1947

Men's and women's study clubs—part of the co-op movement [NFB]

Co-operative fish factory

Old Robin store

Above: The harbour at Grand-Étang. Left: Presqu'île—Cap Rouge, heading from the Highlands south toward Chéticamp. Below: Main Street in Chéticamp, circa 1920.

Hospital, nurses' home, old hall, old convent, church, glebe house

SOME OF THE DOCTORS WHO WERE BORN IN CHÉTICAMP

Edmond L. Aucoin

Edmond D. Aucoin

Daniel (à Placide) Chiasson

Jean Cormier

Henri Haché

Gabriel Boudreau

William Leblanc

Wilfred Poirier

Boat coming in to the wharf

The *Réo*, one of the coastal vessels; a ship loading pulpwood at the gypsum mine wharf

Marie Chiasson—Mrs. Willie D. Deveau—Anselme Chiasson's principal informant for songs and traditions of Chéticamp and the Acadians

Old houses at La Digue

View of Chéticamp Harbour, circa 1925

Alexandre Boudreau, co-op pioneer

Elizabeth Lefort, the hooked rug artist

Harvesting kelp; barrels of salt mackerel ready for shipping; cleaning fish; a spinning frolic

Four men at the lifeboat station—"les paresseux"

Joseph Larade, fiddler

Three fishermen over 80 years old, from the same fishing boat, circa 1930: Michel Romard, Méderic Leblanc and Lubin Chiasson

1898 H. L. Foran of Portland, Maine, opened his establishment at L'Anse-du-Bois-Marié, between the harbour and Petit-Étang. This was in operation until 1921.

About 1900 two Chéticantins opened their own lobster factories. One of them, Charles (à Félix) Chiasson, bought the one constructed by M.W.F. Dawson on the dunes of Cap-Rouge at the "Block," but sold it almost immediately to H.L. Foran. The other man, Fulgence (à Christophe) Aucoin, built his factory at La Cave-à-Loups (Wolf Cave).

Father Fiset bought the lobster factory of the Robins at La Pointe in 1896 and continued the business until 1909. In 1910 Charlie (à William) Aucoin built one on La Digue at the harbour. Shortly afterwards he moved it below his store where it was subjected to all the hazards of his business. It was finally bought by the Leslie Company. In 1912 Georges Lebrun, manager for the Robins, built a lobster factory on the dune of "La Ferme." Five years later it failed and had to close its doors. In 1917 Lévis and Conrad Fiset, who already owned Father Fiset's lobster factory at La Pointe, built another one in the heart of Cap-Rouge, near Maurice's Brook. Eight years later it closed down. Finally, in 1947, the Robins opened another on their wharf which is still in operation. But the two most important lobster factories, of which we shall say more later, were constructed under the aegis of the co-operative movement.

Co-operative Movement
First Co-operative for the Sale of Fish in America:
The Small Factory at La Pointe[29]

In 1915 the wharf at La Pointe was still a beehive of activity, echoing with the footsteps of many fishermen. At this time, though, Chéticamp was very poor. Often heard were these words of a song: "Chéticamp, my little Chéticamp, you have always been poor and you will remain so forever!" The fishermen were poverty-stricken. Fish was sold at a very low price, irrespective of foreign market prices. Great numbers of fishermen could not make both ends meet, no matter what quantity of fish they took in during the summer.

It was about this time that a group of fishermen from Chéticamp, far-sighted and courageous in spite of their lack of education, laid the first actual foundations for their economic liberation. Well before the co-operative movement of Antigonish began, some poor Acadian fishermen from Chéticamp organized themselves and, in 1915, founded the first sales' co-operative in the Maritimes, the first co-operative to sell fish in all America, we believe. Theories of co-operation were already in the air, however, since in 1907 twenty-eight miners from Sydney Mines (at the other end of Cape Breton) had opened a Co-op store. Its growing success made it a household word in every village on the Island.

The founders of "the small factory at La Pointe" were Séverin (à Hippolyte) Lefort, Placide (à Eusèbe) Lefort, Émilien (à Servant) Lefort, his son Pat, Marcellin Doucet and his son Élie. The mainspring, the force behind the movement, was Sévérin Lefort. Others later joined this group: John (à Eustache) Cormier, "Polite" (à Jean) Deveau, and Paddey (à Eustache) Comier. The last one was the prophet and apostle of the growing co-operative movement in our region. He had predicted the future magnitude and the importance of the movement. He spoke of it to everyone with so much zeal that, for the majority of the people, he seemed a visionary. The number of shareholders grew and, one day, nearly all the fishermen of La Pointe, about twenty in number, became part of *la petite factorie* (the small factory).

The method of running the co-operative was very simple: to join together all their efforts, their works and the expenses required for the processing of their fish; to organize, on their own, the sale of the fish on foreign markets; and to share the profits among the shareholders in proportion to their catch. This formula, applied with conviction and tenacity, surmounted all obstacles: the obstructions and blackmail of the tradespeople in competition, the difficulties in exporting the fish, the mental anguish of having certain people laugh up their sleeve at them, and of others using offensive words against them.

The beginning of the movement was quite modest. The government wharf and shed were used by the group. The fishermen themselves canned their lobster. At first a large cauldron took the place of the steam boiler and the cans were welded by hand with a red-hot iron. The fish were sent by boat to Halifax, Charlottetown and Port Elgin.

As the venture looked promising, a small house near the wharves, the home of Philippe (à Odilon) Deveau, was bought immediately and served as a shed and an office. Later a small lobster factory was built, then a larger one, fifty feet by eighty feet, as well as a large shed for the cod.

That co-operative was in business for twenty-five years for the greatest good of its shareholders. Closing its doors in 1940 was not due to bad internal administration, nor through the resignation of its members. It was because the co-operative movement, of which they had sown the first seeds in Chéticamp, was extended at the time to the whole of Cape Breton Island through the stimulus of the Antigonish Movement. Thanks to mechanized transport, fishing and fishing factories were more and more centralized at the harbour and there, from that time on, the fishermen owned their own large Fishing Co-operative. The members of the small factory dissolved their co-operative in order to join up with a more far-reaching co-op.

The success of the small factory at La Pointe had silenced the "smart" mockers and strengthened the courage of the other fishermen in Chéticamp.

The Small Factory at the Harbour

In 1933 some fishermen from the harbour decided to try to duplicate for themselves the successful experience of the fishermen from La Pointe. The most determined amongst them, like Lazare Boudreau, Pat Maillet and Jeffrey Lefort, succeeded in getting more than thirty members. The project became a reality. The first meeting of the future shareholders took place in October and the foundation was decided upon immediately. Right from the time of the first meeting, and without wasting any time on theoretical considerations, it was decided to form a corporation, to take the name "Chéticamp Fishermen Co-operative, Limited," and to immediately build a lobster factory. Each member furnished his share of the work and the supplies, whether this was in materials or money. Begun in November of that same year, this lobster factory was nearly finished by Christmas. It was in operation by the spring of 1934, when a wharf was built.[30] During the summer the new co-op was running at full capacity.[31]

Pat Maillet, secretary-manager, undertook the job of shipping the lobster to foreign markets and of getting the best price for it. On behalf of the Co-operative he also bought, at wholesale prices, the fishing supplies for the fishermen.

In 1935 these fishermen, not content with just buying their fishing equipment at wholesale prices, decided to use the same method for all their purchasing. They then founded (at Petit-Étang) the first co-op store. It was run by the secretary-manager. When another co-op store was opened in 1938 the fishermen decided to sell their small store to the secretary-manager himself.

Naturally, such an enterprise could only really succeed through devoted efforts of their members. Thus the secretary-manager, in spite of his responsibility and his workload, did not accept a cent of salary the first year, just fifty dollars the second year, and one hundred dollars the third year.

The Credit Union

The idea of co-operation was in the air. The Antigonish Movement had been launched since 1930. There were regional study club associations and annual conferences held at the university in Antigonish to which the regions sent delegates. The first credit union in Cape Breton was founded at Reserve Mines in 1933; the one in Chéticamp followed in 1936.

As is true of all great and lasting institutions, it began very modestly— in actual hardship. It was during the Depression. The deposits were not reckoned in the hundreds of dollars; no, not even in dollars, but in poor, thin dimes. On Sundays Joseph Chiasson, who acted as an unpaid manager, would seat himself in the Parish Hall or under the Sacristy to receive the depositors before and after Mass. The founders were Alexandre Boudreau (then an agronomist), Joseph (à Théophile) Chiasson, Arsène (à Hippolyte) Roach, Jeffrey (à Paddey) Lefort, Léo (à William) Cormier, and Dr. Wilfred Poirier.

After buying the co-op store, the Credit Union office was moved into it. In 1949 the Chéticamp Credit Union bought its own building, hired a full-time manager and, in 1956, added the services of a female clerk.[32]

In 1957 the turnover reached $683,000 and the number of members totalled 1,022.

Chéticamp Co-operative, Limited, or The Co-op Store

Keep in mind that, at the time of these foundations, the Depression was at its deepest point. But in Chéticamp a group of men faced it by taking matters into their own hands. The Credit Union was barely founded when it was learned that Léo Bellefontaine's store, closed for many years, was up for sale because of arrears in taxes. The Imperial Oil Company of Halifax, the new owner of the property, was asking four hundred dollars for it. Alexandre Boudreau negotiated the contract and made the first payment. The directors of the Credit Union wished to use the building for a co-op store. The growth of the co-operative movement was beginning to raise serious fears in the minds of the monopolizing merchants, and two days later, a merchant who was told all about the deal, offered a large sum for the store. Naturally the organizer turned down this offer. They sold some shares to pay for the store and immediately ordered some merchandise from Antigonish. While waiting for this merchandise the directors, with their own hands, thoroughly cleaned up the store. The arrival of the truckload of merchandise was solemn. All the directors were present, as well as a crowd of curious onlookers. The store opened its doors in June 1937[33] and by 1956, with a membership of 325, the turnover in sales amounted to $198,500.

In 1938 the directors, in order to provide better service to its members, opened branches in three other localities of Chéticamp: Petit-Étang, Belle-Marche and Plateau. In 1950 these were closed in order to establish a home-delivery service. This practice has proven to be very effective and popular.

The purchase of the Bellefontaine store included the land and a dilapidated wharf. After numerous study sessions, it was decided to repair the wharf and use it in the fishing business. Lobster was not bought, however, since there already existed a co-operative for lobster (The Small Factory at the Harbour). A fish-processing plant was built and in 1942 the co-op store added fish to its business and became, in its turn, a sales co-op for its members who were almost all fishermen.

Union of the Small Factory at the Harbour and
The Chéticamp Co-operative, Limited

The directors and members of the two co-operatives did not remain idle, nor did they cease to study their problems. Given the much more rapid expansion of the Chéticamp Co-operative, Limited, in 1944 the respective directors decided to merge the two co-ops into a single, more powerful business. The lobster factory was moved to the wharf of the co-op store during the winter. Thus there remained one large co-op for the purpose of consumption and production, grouping together all the co-operative forces in Chéticamp.

Famous Conferences of 1947

The small factory at La Pointe and the small factory at the harbour, launched by the fishermen of Chéticamp in 1915 and 1933 respectively, were two businesses that no outside movement had especially influenced.

Then, about 1933, the Co-operative Movement of Antigonish began to spread throughout Cape Breton and the Maritimes. Its influence was felt in Chéticamp, more by the publications distributed on the subject than by personal contacts. Acadians in general, and Chéticantins in particular, are readily on their guard in their contact with newcomers or strangers. To these Chéticantins the representatives who came from Antigonish to speak to them in a language other than their own were strangers. One year Antigonish even wanted to name a representative of the Co-op Movement for the whole of Inverness County, an Englishman from Mabou. Chéticamp and its neighbouring parish, Saint-Joseph-du-Moine, flatly refused to receive him. He was then appointed for the English territory, extending from Inverness to Hawkesbury. Even the publications, in the beginning, were exclusively in English.

Now Alexandre Boudreau, who had played such an important role in the co-operative movement of Chéticamp, had become the administrator and the secretary-general of the United Fishermen of Québec. The great success that he had brought to the foundation and organization of the co-operatives of the Gaspé coast, the North Shore and even the Magdalen Islands had not prevented him from maintaining his interest in the co-operatives of Chéticamp. He understood the complaints of the Chéticantins who wanted to take courses in co-operation in their own language. In 1947 he agreed to go with a team from the School of Fisheries in Sainte-Anne-de-la-Pocatière to give a week's course, organized by La Société Saint-Pierre. The team of professors was composed of Alexandre Boudreau, his brother Patrice, Louis Bérubé and Ange-Marie Bourret.

There were courses given in the morning, in the afternoon and in the evening. Followed enthusiastically by the whole population, the parish hall was not spacious enough to hold all those who wished to attend in the evening.

These courses were very worthwhile for the people of Chéticamp. A number of Chéticantins became interested in co-operation. Afterwards, up to two hundred members took part in the Study Clubs.[34]

This event was also beneficial for the directors of the Antigonish Movement. By the following year, in November 1948, they organized some three-day co-operative courses in Chéticamp, Saint-Joseph-du-Moine and Margaree. To aid them in this work they sent in some notable Acadians, such as Martin Légère, Adélard Savoie, Gilbert Finn, and others. Finally an Acadian from Chéticamp, Mr. Anselme Cormier, was hired as a public relations man for these three Acadian parishes in the County.

Separation of the Consumer's Co-op and the Fishing Co-op

One of the immediate results of the study sessions organized during this week of study was the decision to completely separate the two branches of the existing co-operative: the co-op store and the Fishermen's Co-operative.

This division took place the following year, in 1948. The store took the name "Chéticamp Co-operative, Limited" and no longer occupied itself with fish. The fishermen's co-op took back the name of the small factory at the harbour, "Chéticamp Fishermen Co-operative Society, Limited." Since then the two have not ceased to increase their sales.

Refrigerated Warehouse (Freezer)

Besides the icehouse of the Robins, there were no refrigerated warehouses for the fish in Chéticamp, not even for the fish used as *bouette* (bait). Bait-fish, herring or squid, is not always found in the same amounts along the coasts. It has to be taken when it passes. Then it has to be kept in good condition and Chéticamp was not equipped to do this. When bait was lacking, some had to be imported from the warehouses in Sydney at a very heavy cost or the people stayed unemployed. The co-operators decided to look into the matter.

After intense study, approaches were made to the provincial government's Department of Trade and Industry to try to obtain the construction, in Chéticamp, of a fish freezer which would serve this whole region of the County. The government acceded to this request and the building was constructed on the site of the old *Petite Factorie du havre* (Small Factory at the Harbour) at a cost of $35,000. On May 5, 1949, the official opening took place, along with the Blessing of the new building.

This freezer could hold 300,000 pounds of bait and could freeze 18,000 pounds of it per day. Furthermore, in an annex, there was storage space of 150 tubs of long, baited lines; this eliminated the loss of bait and the necessity to re-bait when the lines were ready but the temperature did not permit any fishing to be done.

This freezer was an immense economic advantage to the fishermen. In 1954 the Fishermen's Co-operative, concerned with its independence in business, bought this freezer warehouse with the aid of a $10,000 grant from the federal government. Since that time the Co-operative has run it themselves.

In 1950 the Fishermen's Co-operative listed 150 members with a total catch of 2,772,648 pounds of fish.

At the other Co-op wharf, that of the store, improvements were made also. Huge warehouses were built and outfitted with the most modern machinery. But on August 11, 1955, a fire started in these warehouses and razed everything, in spite of the desperate efforts of nearly one hundred men. Even the wharf was lost. The value of the loss in money was about $50,000. For less-convinced co-operators, this would have been a complete disaster and the end of the co-operative. But, immediately, the members held a meeting, studied the problem and decided to rebuild. A loan was requested from the provincial Department of Trade and Industry. In a magnificent gesture the Department granted a loan of $200,000 at an interest rate of 4 1/2 percent to be paid off in thirty years.

Since it was necessary to build everything anew, it was decided to build as near as possible to the entrance of the harbour and the refrigerated warehouse. To do this a lot was bought from Paul (à Hippolyte) Chiasson and, first thing in the autumn, construction began. Wise with the experience of many years, and administered by a devoted and competent manager, Mr. Denis Aucoin, the large, modern co-operative was built. There was a department where fish was cut up, another where the product was wrapped and frozen in the least possible time, another where the fillets of cod and haddock (*aiglefin*) were processed, weighed and put into boxes. Finally, to freeze the fish and conserve it until shipped, a second freezer was built.

Fish Meal

Another industry was also launched in Chéticamp. As we know, before placing the fish on the market it must go through a series of operations in which it loses—poor thing!—its most vital parts, its intestines, backbone, head, heart and skin. All these parts are rich in vitamins. Up to now, all this was thrown out, constituting an enormous loss. Someone thought of using these parts of the fish to make food for animals. This required numerous installations but, today, it is the most lucrative industry of the Fishermen's Co-operative. On May 5, 1957, the Blessing of this establishment was the occasion for demonstrations—processions of boats, then speeches suited to the occasion given by important people.

If we add the construction of the wharf, the capital invested by the Fishermen's Co-operative has reached the amount of $255,000.[35] Denis Aucoin, manager of this co-operative, was also manager of the co-op at Grand-Étang, a neighbouring parish. Accordingly, understanding was easy between the two co-operatives and was beneficial to both. Thanks to this understanding, duplication of work was avoided, thus reducing expenses. Chéticamp took care of frozen fish, fish fillets and fish meal; Grand-Étang received all the fish for salting or drying as well as the lobster. In this way about one hundred people, not counting fishermen, worked at the co-op in Chéticamp and nearly as many as that in Grand-Étang.

The two fishermen's co-operatives in Chéticamp and Grand-Étang produce more than two thousand crates of lobster each year. The Chéticamp Co-op alone has a turnover of $500,000.

These two co-operatives are affiliated with The United Maritime Fishermen, whose head office is in Halifax. The fish is sent to the United States in huge, refrigerated trucks.

This improvement and modernization in production is not limited to factories, freezers and transport but is just as evident in fishing itself. Chéticamp can now count about twenty large trawlers of forty-five and fifty-five feet in length in its fleet. These latter, especially, are furnished with the most modern equipment: diesel engines; wireless telephones; electronic apparatus for measuring the depth of the water, the nature of the sea bottom and the fishing banks; machinery for the handling of fish and tackle; electric lighting; gas stoves; and sea charts. In a word, nothing is lacking.

These boats, whether bought or built, are expensive and cost $30,000 at least. But this no longer frightens the fishermen. The time is past when any debt and any loan is considered a shameful thing. The young co-operators of today know that a good loan is often a good investment. Thus they took advantage of federal subsidies begun in 1947 and of loans obtained from the provincial Department of Trade and Commerce. It is now big business.

Let us finish this section on co-operatives with an example which well illustrates the new vitality that characterizes the present fishermen, brought about by the Fishermen's Co-operative. Wilfred (à Johnny) Chiasson, owner of a fifty-six-foot-long trawler named *Stella Maris*, aided by five young fishermen, sailing out up to a hundred miles into the Gulf, sets out up to twenty-two buckets of long lines each day. That is more than 11,000 hooks set out on a line several miles in length. They also fish up to 40,000 and even 50,000 pounds of cod in two days and nearly 100,000 pounds per week. For the mackerel they also use huge mechanically-operated seines which allow them to take up to 30,000 pounds of mackerel each day. This trawler, by itself, has landed 1,094,000 pounds of fish in 1957 alone.

That's a great deal of fish and money! It is to be hoped that an ever-increasing number of young Chéticantins will take up this trade, a trade which has become less troublesome, very interesting and remunerative.

Finally, the Co-op Movement has brought well-being to Chéticamp—its economic liberation.[36] From a poor village with the shabby houses of twenty years ago, it has become a prosperous locality with stylish, bright houses and proud, beaming inhabitants.

Stores

Shortly before 1812 Jean Lelièvre opened his own store at La Pointe-à-Cochons.

Evariste Leblanc, a teacher from New Brunswick who had come to Chéticamp, built a store in 1873. Father Fiset bought this store and kept it opened during the summer for several years. But when Michael Crispo, his clerk, built his own store right beside it about 1890, Father Fiset had his brother-in-law, Timothée Crispo, come from Havre-à-Boucher to keep his store open all year round. On the death of Father Fiset, Conrad Fiset, his nephew, inherited this store and operated it. Michael Crispo's store passed into the hands of Simon, then of Léo Bellefontaine, and finally became the Co-op Store in 1936. The Co-op also bought the store of Conrad Fiset some years later.

About 1891 John (à Men) Leblanc and William Cormier opened a small store which only lasted a few years. The building later became the office of the gypsum mine.

William (à Nanette) Aucoin was one of the first Chéticantins courageous enough to try the field of business. He opened a small store in 1894 where Freddie Aucoin's store is now situated. William Aucoin was, at the same time, in the fishing business. His son, Sandey, succeeded him about 1897 and built a large store about 1900. With the accidental death of its owner in 1917, the store was rented to the Matthews and Scott Company. After the departure of this company in 1927, the store remained closed until 1940 when, thanks to the dynamic abilities of its new owner, Freddie J. Aucoin, it became a magnificent and spacious variety store.

About 1900 Georges Lebrun, the last manager for the Jerseys at La Pointe, opened his own store at the harbour. In 1914 he rented the building to the Royal Bank. Today it contains a beauty salon and doctors' offices.

Charlie (à William) Aucoin, then a teacher, began a small business with his brother, Dougall. They built the present large store in 1906. Dougall separated from his brother in 1921 and built his own store. Charlie, now the sole owner, joined in partnership with his son, Harry. This was one of the most important businesses in Chéticamp. It rivalled that of the Jerseys. It had a lobster factory and bought fish from the fishermen, as well as the cattle they wanted to sell. Charlie Aucoin was always very humane and good to the people. His death in 1932 was deeply mourned. Harry, his son, succeeded him in the business. But about 1933 the entire business was sold to F.W. Leslie Company whose office was in Halifax. The general store was completely destroyed by fire the night of October 24-25, 1958.

In 1912 Didace (à William) Roach opened a business at Belle-Marche that is still prosperous. The same year Joe (à Zéphirin) Boudreau opened a store at the Plateau which no longer exists.

In 1917 it was Petit-Étang's turn to have a store. Joe (à Eussisse) Chiasson was the owner. After having changed owners and belonging to the Co-op for years, this store became the property of Mr. Pépin Chiasson who operated it himself.

Then the number of Chéticantins who entered the field of business increased, Fidèle (à Simon) Cormier in 1917 and Polite (à William) Deveau a short time later. The latter kept, at the same time, a barbershop and a billiard room. Today it is a store for electrical accessories, "Léo's Appliances," opened by Léo Boudreau in 1953. On the second floor were the offices of the dentist, Russell Chiasson, and those of La Société l'Assomption.

In 1921 Dougall-John Aucoin separated from his brother Charlie and opened a business of his own—"D.J. Aucoin"—that his son Alex runs today. Then there was the business, a small store and barbershop, of Mick (à Antoine) Boudreau (1922-48); that of Joseph (à Timothée) Roach at Belle-Marche (1925-30); that of Philippe Lelièvre near La Pointe-à-Cochons (1926); that of Amédée (à Hippolyte) Aucoin (1928); this store, built by Amédée (à John) Mius, after having changed owners often, became the "Harbour Restaurant" and the property of Mrs. Sandey Bourgeois; the Co-op Store, of which we have already spoken, opened in 1936; also in 1936 Philippe Lelièvre opened another business at *Le Pied de la Montagne* (The Foot of the Mountain); in 1936 as well Hubert Leboutellier left the Robins, where he was manager of the Chéticamp store, and opened his own business; in 1938 the Homecraft Shop was opened by Mrs. Marie Lelièvre; Pat (à Marcellin) Maillet opened up at Petit-Étang in 1938; Job (à Lubin) Mius at the harbour in 1946; in 1947 Tom (à Polite) Lefort at *La Farm*; Willie (à Charles) Roach opened a lingerie store called "Ladies' and Children's Wear" in 1949; Job Deveau opened a barbershop and a store to sell souvenirs and crafts, "Foyer du Souvenir" (Souvenir Shop); in 1952 Joseph (à Amédée) Camus built a general store, which was bought in 1955 by Milton Aucoin; in the same year (1952) Philias Aucoin opened a small variety store which also sold souvenirs and crafts; in 1953 Sévérin (à Louis) Aucoin at "Le Lac"; Joseph (à Lubin) Mius at the harbour in 1954; in the same year the Robins opened a hardware store; finally, Padé Cormier opened a small store on the other side of La Prairie. Aside from six specialty stores, the others all offer groceries and general goods for sale.

Mining Industry

During the pastorate of Father Fiset numerous attempts were made to develop the natural resources underground in the neighbouring mountains. Unfortunately, except for the gypsum mine, none of these enterprises succeeded.

The Gypsum Mine

Round about 1897 a prospector from New Glasgow by the name of M.W. Grandin did some mineralogical research in the Chéticamp mountains. In his research he noticed the mountains of gypsum to the southeast of the parish and informed Father Fiset of the riches this find could mean for Chéticamp.

After many studies and negotiations, a company was set up in 1907 called "The Great Northern Mining Company." Father Fiset became president of it. Hubert Aucoin was hired to sell shares at five cents each. All Chéticamp bought some, and when he went to Québec, they were sold by thousands at a time.

Thanks to the funds collected, a gypsum crushing machine was bought and, as early as August 1908, the manufacture of gypsum began.

Thirty-six men toiled there ten hours a day, six days a week for the meagre salary of $1.15 a day.

To ship the plaster to the "Ramsay and Kelly Company" of Montréal, Father Fiset himself bought, in that same year, a large boat of five thousand tons, the *Amethyst*.[37]

In 1911 a railway line was constructed from the quarry to the harbour and a locomotive, to the great wonderment of the parishioners who had never seen one before, drove the line with its boxcars loaded, making a hellish noise.

In this first endeavour, the mine was in use until 1913. After Father Fiset's death, however, difficulties became greater and greater and, in 1913 when the work came to an end, the workers had had no pay for seven months.

This was the occasion for the people of Chéticamp to compose a satirical song about the gypsum mine. A loose translation of this song follows here:

1

A couple of years ago, in back of
/ "Le Petit Plé,"
A gypsum mine has been started.
Since that time, business has been good;
Last year they built a railway line.

Refrain:
Chéticamp, oh, beautiful Chéticamp
You have always been poor
You will be rich sometime. (twice)

2

They began to haul the gypsum by cart
From the gypsum mine to Father Fiset's wharf.
Mr. Grandin was president
I tell you he has "greased his palms" well.
Refrain

3

It was in the year 1910,
They asked for something that resembled
/ a building.
Charles à Félix was to be the driver of this.
At the end of the third load, they overturned
/ it in the bog.
Refrain

4

There were some from Le Moine and
/ others from Chéticamp
And many others who had no money.
When they came for their pay, there was
/ nothing to draw out
Because the gypsum mine had taken it
/ all away.
Refrain

5

Who composed this French song?
Georgie à Joe and the half-wit of Anselme à Pitchet.
They composed it; we must excuse them,
Because they were forced to sing it.
Refrain[38]

The following year a certain James Brodie from Montréal took over the mine on a trial basis, with the idea of buying only if it were successful. He pretended to have a great deal of money. The labourers toiled for three months without being paid, then they went on strike. Brodie then sent a cheque for $1,000 to pay for these months of work. But no funds existed in Port Hood where the cheque was payable. The workers had angrily decided to bring a lawsuit against the company when P.M. O'Neill, who had already advanced $100,000 for the railway track, paid the salaries himself and took control of the mine as its principal shareholder. He did not reopen for work, however, but only kept two watchmen there, Pitre and Lucien Poirier.

In 1923 the International Gypsum Company, having bought this enterprise, sent in MacFarlane to start it up again. Gypsum was again manufactured and was shipped out in bags. The labourers received only $2.00 per day and worked like slaves under the eye of an over-zealous foreman. A year later work ceased again due to lack of funds.

In 1926 the mine was sold to the American company Atlantic Gypsum which began work the following spring. This time, gypsum was no longer manufactured, but was sent out in its raw state. In 1936 the mine was sold to The National Gypsum Company, another American company, with head office in Buffalo. Up to 1939, the date of closure of the mine because of the war, this was its most prosperous period. The gypsum was sent to *Longue Pointe* (Long Point), Montréal, the United States and Europe. One could often see up to three huge cargo boats in Chéticamp Bay at one time, two of which were transatlantic, the *Brookwood* (8,643 tons) and the *Maplewood* (7,900 tons).

Since 1939 the gypsum mine has been closed in Chéticamp. The company has transported its activities to Dingwall, farther north, where it seems the gypsum is purer and easier to obtain. But this operation closed its doors definitely in 1955 to re-establish itself at Milford, Hants County, where the beds of gypsum are considerably greater and the transportation less costly.

We must point out that a Chéticantin, Mr. Anselme Boudreau, was the office manager of this enterprise from 1926 to 1956.

At the Small Spring of the Mountain

At the entrance of Cap-Rouge, at the foot of the *montain à Jérôme* (Jerome's Mountain), there was a deep hole in which the children, in spite of their desire to find some treasure, didn't dare venture for fear of meeting some fairytale monsters or ferocious beasts.

This hole was dug at the end of the last century by some prospectors searching for copper and gold.

At *ruisseau de l'abîme* (Chasm Brook)

In 1898 the Chéticamp Mining Company, a company from Halifax incorporated in 1897 with its head at Brookfield, undertook some work at the Chasm Brook to the southeast of La Prairie with a view to extracting lead. The company spent a great deal of money to install machines and to open up a road suitable for vehicles. It seems that it spent more than

$300,000. Unfortunately, the quantity of mineral was not sufficient to assure them a remunerative operation and the company folded after two years of testing.

At Cap-Rouge

The following year, 1899, another Halifax company, Henderson and Potts, came to make an assay at Cap-Rouge, near the former premises of Mr. Amédée Camus. Fifteen to twenty men worked there for a couple of years, extracting barium. Their salary was one dollar for a long day's work. Transportation was very difficult in these mountainous regions and the enterprise was doomed to failure.

At Plateau

At the same time (1897-99) another company, whose name is unknown to us, spent a great amount of money searching for gold. The site of this mine is at the foot of the mountain in Plateau. To the people of Chéticamp it is *la mine d'or de chez Clément Pinandou* (the gold mine of the family of Clément Pinandou). After some years of drilling the company closed up shop and disappeared without giving any explanation.

In 1926 a group of Chéticantins, intrigued by the silent and almost mysterious departure of this company, wished to try their luck in resuming the operation of this mine. These men did not possess the required knowledge nor the necessary funds, and probably the mine didn't contain any gold in the first place. After some months of work, the project was abandoned.

All these projects were serious and were backed by considerable funds. Unfortunately, it seems likely that the mountains of this region of Cape Breton contain no minerals in sufficient quantity to assure a profitable operation. Even if each generation of Chéticantins speaks of opening the mines, recent prospecting, using the most modern techniques, appears to confirm the results of past experiences and leaves little hope for the future.

Lumber Camps

Every family in Chéticamp, or almost every one, had its *part à bois* (wooded lot) in the neighbouring mountains. They cut the wood for firewood and for necessary construction. But there was never any serious commercial exploitation. Today, several of these *terres à bois* (wooded lands) have become the property of the National Park in the highlands of Cape Breton.

Other Cape Breton centres—for example, Sainte-Anne [St. Ann's] and Petit-Saint-Pierre [St. Peter's]—operated lumber camps and attracted there some of the men of Chéticamp. The number of Chéticantins going there was never great, however. The work was hard, hygiene was completely absent—lice stayed there, permanently!—but salaries were relatively good. Certain years were poor, however. Here is a loose translation of a song composed for the occasion by the Chéticantins to show that hardship did not keep them from joking around:

Life in the Lumber Camps

1

It was in the year 1921.
A famous battalion went up.
Next day after breakfast,
Walter was above the woodpile
Half of them were scared
And the other half was discouraged.

2

But, when Walter had sorted them out,
Luc à Charles said: We have to go.
His son, Joseph, was angry,
They both had to go on foot.
After having had the trouble of going
/ there
They returned feeling ashamed.

3

The men who happened to stay
Were all most anxious to get going.
With the old damaged axes
That Walter had given them to work with
When he sent them to cut wood.
Léon à Charlot was crippled
With an old saw that Léonie had
/ sharpened.

4

On Friday, all the men left
All thinking of making a good life.
Jackson was crazy to give them credit,
Giving each one a pair of boots
That cost eight and one half dollars.
If the Good God doesn't wish to send
/ us any rain,
All of us are going to stay in debt with him.

5

The bravest men were discouraged
About fifteen of them left.
Job à John was not among the last ones
He was going to transport manure.
'Zabeth had said to him: Job, don't go,
It will pay you far better to stay here
/ sleeping with me.

6

The rest of the group who went home
Went because their shoes were unfit.
All began to swear;
Walter had to get angry.
Joe à Placide and Victor à Charlot
Got hit on the back with a broomstick.

7

It's lonesome in the woods so far from home
Joe à Marcellin is completely terrified.
The dams are nearly always closed
Hardly any water to wet your feet.
The bull-cook is usually angry
Because the men continually bother him.

8

One who was there last year
His name was 'Milien à Timothée.
He had gone there to be a driver
He was obligated to start shoe-repairing.
The boots were not badly ruined,
He'll not earn enough to pay his way home.

9

Placide à Placide left this morning.
He wasn't very far on the road when
He thought it wouldn't pay him
To go home to eat bread and molasses.
He promptly turned around, while saying:
There's too much snow on the road.

10

Simon à Fabien without knowing anything
Entered the house of the son of Félicien.
They said to him: Simon, don't go,
There's diphtheria at your father's home.
Soon, Simon was so worried, that
He went up to l'Étang to sleep overnight.

11

Who composed this song?
Léonie à Lubin and Placide Chiasson.
They made it and composed it
While waiting to begin work.
You will have to excuse them
For they were hurrying to get their supper.

Men went there to recover from a bad fishing season or to make the money necessary to raise a barn or a house, but seldom to find a regular livelihood.

For about fifteen years, some Chéticantins had been cutting pulp-wood in the mountains of Chéticamp. They dumped this wood by truck-loads into the bay and a boat from the Price Company of Rimouski came to get it every fortnight.

Hooked Rugs: A Cottage Industry

The introduction of the co-operative movement into Chéticamp made itself felt in an industry which has soared to new heights: the industry of rug-hooking.

Our grandmothers, as far back as we can go in our history, made rugs. These were very simple rugs, most often made with old rags called *breillons*. There were the *tapis à tresses* (braided mats), Catalonia mats made on the loom, the *tapis à breillons* (mats hooked with old rags), the *tapis à rosettes* (mats made with ribbons), the *tapis à franges* (mats made with fringes); and finally, rugs hooked with wool. These last were intro-duced into Chéticamp by the wife of Dr. Napoleon Fiset, an Acadian lady from Arichat who perhaps learned this art at Ancienne-Lorett, her hus-band's birthplace, which she visited several times.[39]

The rugs were made simply for home usage. They were not very pre-tentious, yet these rugs, by their colours and designs, revealed a true art form. Then came the tourist and commercial period.

About 1923 a Miss Lillian Burke came from New York to spend her summers in Baddeck where she sold rugs to the tourists. To increase her sales, she encouraged the making of rugs in several villages of Cape Bre-ton. It was through her that trade in hooked rugs began in Chéticamp. She herself came to encourage women, teaching them to dye the wool and make the patterns. She paid sixty cents a square foot for rugs without flowers and seventy-five cents a square foot for rugs containing flowers in the pattern.

This business made a slow beginning in Chéticamp. But, in 1929, came the Depression.

The cutting of wood ceased; the lumber camps of Cape Breton closed; the gypsum mine no longer operated. There only remained fish-ing—and fish sold at a ridiculous price. Rug-making then came into great style. Each home became a workshop for the making of rugs. Men, wom-en and children worked at it. Miss Burke bought these rugs which she sold to the tourists or sent elsewhere. Some tens of thousands of dollars came to Chéticamp each year through this industry. Even if it was in her own interests that she was doing this work, Miss Burke has nonetheless rendered a great service to the people of Chéticamp.

The initiators of the co-operative movement judged that the industry of rug-making would greatly benefit by the same formula. "Why not orga-nize yourselves to sell your rugs?" insisted Alexandre Boudreau. And, with his help, this was done. Someone had to be found who would under-take the directing of the work of the hookers, of procuring the canvas, and of selling the rugs. It was decided that the salary of this person would be ten percent of sales. Mrs. Charles Aucoin accepted the job and is still busy at it.

Great courage was necessary. Miss Burke, through her agents, was installed in the place and did not look kindly at losing the business. She even brought a suit against the people which was turned to the advantage of the Chéticantins by their lawyer, Alex MacKinnon of Inverness, who had been engaged by Alexandre Boudreau.

Sales were organized quite quickly and merchandise never ceased to flow smoothly since the beginning. The rugs were first sold here in Chéti-camp to tourists and visitors, then to the outside: to the Canadian Hand-craft Guild of New York, the Canada Steamship Lines, and to the variety stores all across Canada, right to Victoria in British Columbia.

It was found, by taking a count, that about two hundred and fifty wom-en at one time were making rugs in their own homes. Prices for their work have risen since the beginning. Workers now receive $2.00 per square foot for their rugs, while the canvas is furnished with the design already imprinted on it. Over $30,000 comes to Chéticamp each year through the rug-hooking industry.

This home industry continues to operate, though it has experienced a slowing down with the return of prosperity.

Several hooked rugs are real works of art. Miss Elizabeth (à Placide) Lefort has completed a tapestry of *The Last Supper* which took 750,000 hooked stitches and is valued at more than $15,000.[40]

Mink Raising

We must not forget to mention a completely new industry in Chéti-camp, but one which is, perhaps, destined for great expansion: mink rais-ing. In 1955 three men from Chéticamp, Jim Roach, David Bourgeois and Louis-Philippe Chiasson, decided to launch themselves in this work. In 1957 they already owned eighty-five mink, full of life and promise.

David Bourgeois and Gerald Aucoin began another mink-raising farm in 1958 with 215 mink.

Tourism

In 1936 the federal government expropriated a corner of Chéticamp called Cap-Rouge and the "Rigwash." Those lands were, from that time on, part of the famous National Park in the highlands of Cape Breton, the most beautiful in the Maritime Provinces. Through this Park crosses the Cabot Trail. With the splendour and vividness of its panoramic views, this part of Cape Breton is a worthy rival of la Gaspésie, whose own name is so well established.

These mountains, which once used to see only dogsleds in winter and men on horseback in summer, are now crossed by wide magnificent roads on which the cars of American and Canadian tourists roll merrily along.

Economic Life

Without taking into account the livelihood created for about fifty men from Chéticamp who work there, this park is also a great source of revenue through the tourists who are attracted there. The following is a very loose translation of a song on the work of the National Park.[41]

1

Oh! Come to hear me sing
What I have composed
After work in the evening.
It's in regard to the work
Being done in Chéticamp
To build a park,
You know it very well,
Will it pay? We don't know.

2

The subject of my song
I'm going to explain it to you
In few words—it won't be long
It's about the Trail
Being made in the mountains,
Following the river
Up to the third salmon hole.
It's for the tourists who will come.

3

In regard to the lodging,
You can be told about it.
Everyone is comfortable,
There is a good bull-cook
Who gets up very early.
He makes up all the cots
It doesn't take long.
It's Jos à John from Petit-Étang.

4

The people of Chéticamp
Work, each in his turn
As do the Moineaux.
William à Arsène is boss.
Everyone thinks he's good.
Pierre à Dominique is the cook.
We absolutely need him,
And little Tommy who marks the time.

5

At the end of the song
You will be well able to understand
That we work for the government.
At the end of two weeks
Or at the end of the month,
We will draw a small cheque,
And we will go home.
The money will all go
To the small merchants.

Finally, to improve access to this park the government built a wide road from Port Hawkesbury to Chéticamp which did away with sharp corners, cleared the valleys and, in the valley of Chéticamp, moved back the houses so as to pass by more easily. The work was completed with the paving of the road in 1947.

With all these advantages, Chéticamp acquired a reputation of being the Queen of Northwest Cape Breton.

The question of tourism never even arose in Chéticamp prior to the opening of the National Park. The boat was the only practical way of getting to Chéticamp because the route from Port Hawkesbury was not yet paved. Chéticamp was the terminal point of the shabby *chemin du roi* (main highway) that stretched along the west coast of Cape Breton.

Today, with wide paved roads, and the automobile eating up the distances, with the route crossing Chéticamp and circling all of Cape Breton, and with the Cabot Trail at the very limits of Chéticamp crossing one of the most picturesque national parks in Canada, Chéticamp is becoming a more and more frequently visited tourist centre. We must add here that the number of Chéticantins who emigrated to other places in Canada and the United States perhaps surpasses the present population of Chéticamp. Several return in the summer to spend their vacations with their families or other relatives.

In order to answer the needs of the tourists, many restaurants, hotels, cabins and motels have sprung up.

The oldest restaurant in Chéticamp dates from 1917. This restaurant, the Acadian Inn, also became a hotel and still enjoys a fine reputation for its excellent cuisine, its cleanliness and the friendliness of its owners, the family of Marcellin Aucoin. Recently, three other restaurants have opened: the Harbour Restaurant, Albert's Restaurant, and the Parkway Restaurant.

The first hotel in Chéticamp was "The Royal Hotel," opened in 1907 and owned by Mrs. Donathilde Doucet. It later became "The Evangéline Hotel" and was owned by Willie C. Aucoin when it was devastated by fire in 1931. Then, between 1920 and 1930, there were opened "The Cormier House" and "The Ocean Spray Hotel," which later became "The Cabot Hotel." Much later "The Rialto Hotel" and "Chez Pierre" were opened for business, then some cabins: Laurie's, Arm Bridge, Fraser's, Mac's, Parkview, and others still under construction. Taking into account the private homes which rent out rooms, Chéticamp, at this time, can accommodate about one hundred travellers overnight. This is no longer sufficient during the beautiful days of the summer season. We need more motels and a large hotel. The Chéticantins fear tying up such a large sum of money because the tourist season, lucrative though it is, is very short and is almost limited to the two months of July and August. But thanks to the growing popularity of the National Park, this season will come to be lengthened from June to October.

With this influx of tourists, Chéticamp itself has discovered some charming tourist attractions: incomparable beaches; delightful countryside; thrilling trout-fishing and salmon-fishing in its river, and organized deep-sea fishing; hunting; the attractive simplicity, the shyness of its inhabitants; the rich folklore; the archaic seventeenth-century language; and, finally, the remarkable craftsmanship of its own people.

There are still other interesting possibilities to develop: canoeing, existing sailboating, horseback riding, tennis, perhaps a golf course, rifle range, archery and water skiing. We hope that the Chéticantins are clear-sighted enough not to wait for the coming of strangers to organize tourist services in Chéticamp and, in so doing, let them drain off all the profits from our village.

Economic Life

Public Services

Transport Service

As the railroad will never come to Chéticamp despite the repeated promises of politicians, transportation is organized in other ways. Formerly, all transportation to the outside world was done by schooner.

Boats

The first steamboat which came to Chéticamp was propelled by paddlewheel and was called the *Powerful*. This was in 1886. The following year a regular service was established between Chéticamp and Pictou, with stops at Port Hood, Inverness, Margaree and Grand-Étang. The boat, the *Beaver*, made the run once a week. Shortly afterward, the *Beaver* was replaced by the *St. Olaf*, which also served the Magdalen Islands. Afterwards, the *Lunenburg*, property of Leslie and Company, carried out this work until it was lost at sea. In 1900 the *Amelia* undertook the same service, then the *Malcolm Cann* of The Cann Steamship Company. Finally, since 1909 it has been The North Bay Steamship Company of Pictou which has maintained this service using the following boats: *Magdalen* (1909-1913), from Mulgrave to Chéticamp twice a week; the *Kinburn* (1914-1936), covered the same route but also went to Pictou twice a month. Her captain was Cyrille Bourgeois of Chéticamp. This boat was flung onto the shore behind Chéticamp Island during a severe storm in 1936 and was smashed to smithereens. Up to then, these boats were outfitted to handle passengers also. In future, they would no longer do this. Another *Kinburn* was put into service from 1936-1939, then was succeeded by the *Playmaid*. Today, the *Réo* has undertaken the twice-weekly trip from Pictou to Chéticamp, but without going to Mulgrave. An Acadian from Chéticamp, Cyrille Bourgeois, was the captain of all these boats from 1918 until his death in 1958. He was succeeded by his son Wilfred.

From 1905 to1913 a Mr. Beatty, Captain and owner of the boat *Electra* and, later, of the *City of Ghent* after the loss of the former in a storm, assured the people of regular service between Chéticamp and Pictou.

In 1909 a service which still endures was inaugurated between Halifax and Chéticamp. The boats used were: *Strathlorne*, from 1909-1917,[42] which was lost at sea; the *Réo*,[43] which took over this service in 1934; then it was replaced by the *Joseph K*,[44] still in service.

For several years a similar service was established between Sydney and Chéticamp. First there was the *Aspy*, then in1913 the *Bras d'Or*,[45] which passed by Cape North. These boats arrived in Chéticamp every Tuesday. This service lasted until the loss of the *Bras d'Or*, which burned at sea in 1936.

Trucks, Buses, Taxis

Nothing has diminished the importance of water transportation as has the construction of modern highways.

Today, most of the transportation of goods is done by truck. The Fishermen's Co-operative sends out all its fish by truck, even to the United States. There is also a regular truck transportation service between Chéticamp and Sydney, begun in 1935. Wilfred (à Charlie) Aucoin began it and still runs it.

For travellers, a daily bus service between Chéticamp and Sydney, then between Chéticamp and Inverness, was inaugurated in 1943.

In the present village of Chéticamp a bus service connects the other areas of the parish to the village.[46] Finally, we must mention the service of at least seven taxicabs.

Customs Office

As Chéticamp was always a fishing port and, from its very beginning, exported fish to Europe from where much merchandise was brought back, the need to establish a customs office was very soon felt. We see that as early as 1770 the Robins solicited and obtained from The Lords Commission of the Treasury of His Majesty, the King of England, a customs office for Chéticamp.[47]

Post Office

The first post office was installed at La Pointe in 1868. It was later moved to Walter Lawrence's store at the harbour. Today we can count six post offices in Chéticamp, one in every section.[48]

Telegraph Service

Father Fiset obtained telegraphic service for Chéticamp in 1891. This service was installed at the home of Conrad Fiset. In 1905 it was moved to the home of Charlie W. Aucoin, and in 1912 to the home of Moïse S. Aucoin. This service ceased in 1959.

Telephone Service

The first telephone service began in 1906, but only in the village itself, with no communication with the outside world. It was only during the war of 1914 that Chéticamp was linked to the exterior by the Maritime Telegraph and Telephone Company, Ltd.

The people of Cap-Rouge were too far from the centre and their region too mountainous for the company to be interested in installing a telephone line for them. That didn't hold them back! The people themselves installed it, right up to Pleasant Bay, in conjunction with the Scottish people of that place. This was the first rural line in Chéticamp. In 1936 the inhabitants of Cap-Rouge saw their lands expropriated by the federal government for the establishment of a national park and this telephone line disappeared. In 1939 part of this line, for which the posts were still standing, was put to use again by about thirty men from Petit-Étang and the other side of La Prairie. The owners of this line administer it according to the co-operative formula. They maintain it, sharing the costs and paying the rent for the services to the "Maritime" to which their line is connected.

Banking Services

In 1914 the Royal Bank of Canada opened a branch in the Georges Lebrun building. Closed in 1926 for a year, it opened its doors again the following year on the re-opening of the gypsum mine. In 1954 it was moved to a modern and spacious locale at the home of Paul Cormier.

Electrical Services

For a long time the fish markets and large stores possessed their own electrical installations. It was only in 1937 that the Nova Scotia Power Commission continued the transmission line for electrical energy from Inverness to Chéticamp.

Since that date, each home in Chéticamp has been able to provide itself with all modern conveniences.

Garages

Thanks to the progress of the co-operatives, economic expansion was felt advantageously in several ways.

There had never existed any garages in Chéticamp before 1937. True, there were automobiles around, but every owner was his own mechanic or, in more difficult cases, had recourse to a friend more knowledgeable and more experienced in matters of repair than he himself.

The Robins, who up to now had concentrated all their efforts on fishing, saw that business was escaping through the work of the co-operatives. Immediately they bent their efforts elsewhere: a wholesale store with a travelling salesman for different Cape Breton centres; a hardware store; a butcher shop with home delivery of the meat. In 1937 they built the first garage in Chéticamp.

Today, in 1957, there exists in Chéticamp seven large garages with modern equipment and competent mechanics.[49]

Theatre

Up to now the priests or the parish associations brought in films which were shown at the Parish Hall. Then certain individuals who earned their livelihood from this work went from parish to parish in Chéticamp to show films several times a month.

Quite particularly remembered are the performances shown by the curate, Father Samson. During the week he would photograph scenes of Chéticamp taken on the spot and by surprise. He didn't ask permission of his subjects and continued to film them notwithstanding their feelings in this matter. Some let him do it willingly; others were offended by it. Still others, embarrassed, absolutely refused, struggling like devils caught in Holy Water. Their gestures were all the more comical. These films formed a parade of scenes, laughable and hilarious, taken in the area. On Saturday evening there would be a crowd in this improvised theatre.

In 1947 a Chéticantin, Mr. Joseph Lelièvre, built Le Théatre Évangéline, with a capacity of 225 seats. Since then, this theatre is open every evening and does well financially.[50]

Other Services

In 1957 Chéticamp had three barbershops, two beauty parlours, three or four small billiard rooms, four or five butchers and sellers of meat, some vendors of pharmaceuticals, a small printing shop (Chéticamp Printing Service, begun in 1935 by Joseph-Luc Chiasson) and finally, a bakery and a laundry at Petit-Étang.

Volunteer Firemen

A fire department is closely related to the economic sphere. It effectively protects real estate against fire and saves people who were too careless to insure their property from total ruin.

It was only about 1940 that a group of men from Chéticamp organized themselves as a voluntary unit to form a fire brigade for Chéticamp. Before that date, when a fire was really bad in a house or barn these were irremediably lost. The owners, as well as the neighbours, remained helpless witnesses of the disaster.

In 1953 these volunteer firemen procured their first mechanical pump. Today they are outfitted like the most modern fire stations in our largest towns: a vehicle with ladders and hoses, bought in 1957 for $12,000, gas masks, uniforms, alarm systems—nothing is lacking.

When a fire starts anywhere, only a telephone call is necessary. The fire truck starts off as quickly as possible towards the fire. At the same time, by an agreed alarm, the siren guides the volunteer firemen in the same direction. The houses saved from fire by this brigade of volunteer firemen have already reached a goodly number.

FUTURE POSSIBILITIES FOR CHÉTICAMP

EVEN TAKING INTO ACCOUNT the distance from major centres, the economic possibilities for Chéticamp are great. First of all, modernized fishing, which has become interesting and remunerative, must attract the young people more and more. Too many good lands are totally neglected or even abandoned. Actually, there is no market garden produce in Chéticamp, no raising of pigs or other animals for slaughter, no dairy-farming industry and no poultry farming.[51] If a little of this is done, it is for domestic use only and very little for commercial purposes. There are, however, many areas where competent people could find it profitable to work. Perhaps La Société Saint-Pierre will be able to steer certain young people who have the inclination towards an agricultural school to take some practical courses, then to return to Chéticamp to operate one of these agricultural domains. Besides the small lumberyard for furniture and boats belonging to "Fraser and Chiasson," there does not exist any factory in Chéticamp. It would be necessary to begin at least a few of them.

The economic future of Chéticamp is of the greatest importance. The young men and women emigrate to Toronto or elsewhere. They do this not by choice, but by necessity. All agree that if they could earn their living in Chéticamp without too much hardship they would gladly return. This is a problem about which the Chamber of Commerce, the associations and the people who enjoy a measure of prestige must think seriously.

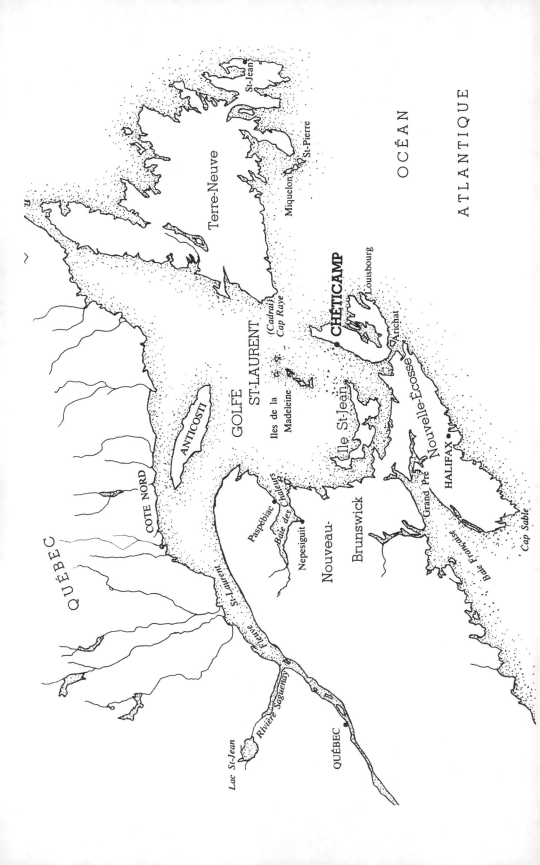

CHAPTER FIVE

Religious Life

MISSIONARY PERIOD

AFTER THE EXPULSION, the wanderings of the Acadians and the short-age of priests made it very difficult to organize any religious ministry. For a long time the only priests to whom the Acadians, settled here and there, could have any recourse were the missionaries sent to all Acadian missions by the Bishop of Québec.

White Masses. Hymns

In all Acadian villages where there were no "live-in" priests and where the visit of the missionary was made at long intervals, some trusted men appointed by ecclesiastical authority took over the direction of religious ceremonies where the power of the priesthood was not required such as in baptizing the newborn or receiving, before witness, the mutual consent of those who wished to marry. There was Louis Robichaud for the region of Boston in New England,[1] Jean Doucet for all of Prince Edward Island,[2] and Charles Hébert for the Magdalen Islands.[3] In Chéticamp this position was occupied by Joseph Aucoin.[4]

Every Sunday the faithful went to church, for Mass when the priest was making his visit in the area, and for the "white Mass" when the priest was absent. During the times of the priest's absence, prayers were said and hymns were sung. Some hymns, adapted to liturgical times or to special feasts, enlivened the ceremonies and sustained the religious fervour of the people. At the *messes blanches* only Joseph Aucoin read the Gospel and recited the prayers reserved for the priests. Out of respect, he omitted the words of the Consecration.

Joseph Aucoin presided again at the evening Rosary, as well as for the Sunday afternoon service. Nearly everyone went to church. Faith and piety were strong among the people. One does not undergo the suffering of martyrs for generations without acquiring a soul of sterling steel character. Nothing was permitted to disturb the people during their prayers. The story is told that one day during the recitation of the Rosary, one of the old people saw through the window of the Church one of his creditors, no doubt trying to steal one of his cattle. He didn't budge, but waited for the completion of the Rosary before running after the thief.

Hymns were sung in church on Sunday, and in the homes during the evenings. Who can say what great influence the hymns had on this young colony? The singing of the hymns was a prayer and maintained an atmosphere of piety and contributed to the elevation of the soul. It was an expression of community life and a connecting link to the past. Finally, this was the most popular way the people knew to practice their faith, to safeguard it and pass it from generation to generation. Some collections, such as the "Cantiques de l'Âme dévote" or the "Cantiques de Marseille," were, for them, invaluable treasures. These hymns described the religious ceremonies to the last detail. A typical example is the canticle of the Mass with its thirty-two couplets that were sung every Sunday and which is still sung in certain families. All the mysteries of the Faith, the life and Passion of Our Lord,[5] the main facts of the Old and New Testaments, the lives of the Saints, the conditions of prayer, "The Last Things"—everything was included. These hymns, according to the Preface of *Le Dialogue de l'âme chrétienne avec son Dieu*, "represent in a good, easy manner, the principal mysteries of the Faith, and the virtuous principles of the Christian religion." These hymns that they sang in church, and no doubt in all the families for more than a century, that many knew by heart, constituted an astonishing amount of religious knowledge, the best of catechisms and the best theology for the use of the Faithful.

The Missionaries

The first visit of a missionary priest in Chéticamp was that of Father Ledru, Dominican, on June 1, 1787.[6]

The Chéticantins, finally settled in one place, suffered from the absence of a priest. Very quickly they went about the business of trying to acquire one, either to stay with them or in the region nearby. Father Jones, o.f.m. cap., Vicar-General of Halifax, sent their fervent request to Bishop Hubert of Québec. He replied on March 19, 1791, that it was impossible at the moment to send a priest into these regions: "no help for the Acadians of Tracadie, Chétican and Arichat." There were too many parishes in the centre of the Diocese which were in need.

However, the Bishop of Québec was very much interested in these dispersed sheep who were without shepherds. It was with the greatest of joy that he welcomed into these missions some French priests who had been driven from Saint-Pierre and Miquelon or France by the French Revolution.

Father François Lejamtel de la Blouterie from Arichat

This priest[7] was the kindest missionary in Cape Breton and one of the best in all of Acadia. There were few who were as understanding as he to the Acadian soul, few who could understand it and love it as he did.

Father Lejamtel was born in France near Granville, Normandy, in the Diocese of Avranches, on November 1, 1757. He was ordained priest on June 14, 1783, and was missioned to the islands of Saint-Pierre and Miquelon. The French Revolution chased him, along with a companion, Father Jean-Baptiste Allain, from this area because both refused to take the Oath of Allegiance to the Civil Constitution of the Clergy.

Father Lejamtel took refuge in Halifax where he was warmly welcomed by Father Jones. The latter, deeply impressed by the sterling qualities of this young priest, immediately entrusted to his care the missions of Cape Breton, along with several villages situated along the coast of Nova Scotia.

For twenty-three years, from his residence in Arichat, Father Lejamtel tended to his flock throughout the vast area entrusted to his care by religious authority. At least once a year this great apostle visited his widely-separated missions, crossing the whole island of Cape Breton over land and through water with Indians as guides. In 1793, on one of these trips, Father dislocated a leg. In 1799 a storm at sea just missed drowning him. But nothing stopped this tireless priest. After Father Allain retired from his work in the Magdalen Islands, Father Lejamtel added this area to his other "parish," in order to bring the consolations of his ministry to the people.

This priest inspired love and respect in all who met him. After his first interview, Father Jones recommended him to Bishop Hubert: "having found Fr. Lejamtel a pious and gentle man of 34 years of age...in case of accident or death, I beg you to replace me...by this Fr. Lejamtel. He is a prudent man...."[8] Having met him at the time of his pastoral visit in 1815, Bishop J-Octave Plessis himself wrote of him: "He is a man of great simplicity, having a broad-enough knowledge of Holy Scripture, of ecclesiastical history, of the speculative and practical Theology, with a spirit of mortification, which manifests itself in spite of him, and an angelic fervour, a zeal for the salvation of his sheep, and, neither fear, nor the seasons, nor terrible voyages are permitted to prevent his visits to his people: these are the qualities well-suited to make a pastor extremely dear to his flock...."[9]

In 1819 Father Lejamtel was named Parish Priest at Bécancourt where he died, venerated by all, on May 22, 1835.

The first visit to Chéticamp of this saintly priest took place in the autumn of 1792. In returning from the Magdalen Islands to Arichat, "I have ministered to the inhabitants of Chéticamp, who still had not made their Easter Duty. I sent the Census to Fr. Jones immediately after" by names and surnames.[10]

He returned often after that first visit. While the Chéticantins were deprived of a missionary of their own, Father Lejamtel did not miss making an annual visit to them.

Like the first missionaries, Father Lajamtel held the people of Chéticamp in very high esteem. While he might complain of the people of Little

Bras d'Or, and while he might suffer the Acadians of Arichat, he had only praise for the courageous people of Chéticamp. In return, they appreciated his work among them and loved him deeply. In Chéticamp his memory is still honoured, even to this day.

Father Jean-Baptiste Allain from the Magdalen Islands

Along with Father Lejamtel, Father Jean-Baptiste Allain had to flee Saint-Pierre and Miquelon where he was apostolic vice-prefect.

He was born in France in 1738 and was ordained priest on September 24, 1763.

Bishop Hubert of Québec welcomed him with open arms and offered him the comfortable position of looking after a beautiful parish in the Diocese, but the humble apostle asked for the favour of being allowed to devote himself to the remote missions of the Diocese. He looked after the missions of the Magdalen Islands, of Chéticamp and Margaree. He established his residence in the Magdalen Islands to accede to the wishes of his Bishop.

Father Allain's first visit to Chéticamp was made in 1794. The crossing from the Islands to Chéticamp tired him greatly. He was already fifty-six years old and his health was failing.

After his second trip in 1795, he wrote to Father Grave, Vice-General, his desire to retire close to Father Lejamtel because of the great fatigue of travel, infirmities of age and his weakened constitution.[11]

Actually, in the autumn of 1797 he was en route for Arichat. He stopped in Chéticamp where he spent the winter.

Father Allain was attached to the Chéticantins. Soon after landing in Arichat he showed his desire of returning to them. He insisted. On July 26, 1799, he wrote to the Bishop: "Last summer I mentioned to you my wish to return to Chéticamp, because of the affection I have for the people there...if no missionaries come to minister to them, I still feel the same way."[12]

The response of the Bishop was most favourable. Father Allain wrote those people immediately, placing as a condition that they first build a chapel.

The First Chapel

Up to this time, during a missionary's visit religious service took place in the home in which the priest was lodged. Usually this was the home of Augustin Deveau. Naturally, this place no longer suited the needs of the parish.

The Chéticantins, in answer to the request of Father Allain, immediately set to work building the church. It was built in the winter of 1800. This loghouse church was very primitive, put together "piece by piece," "not according to any plan," wrote Father Lejamtel in 1809, and already "too small," said Bishop Plessis during his visit in 1812.

This church was situated behind Le Platin on the property of the Aucoins (Eusèbe à Thomas). The ruins were still visible at the end of the last century.

Later on a small glebe house was built, very poor, you can be sure. Bishop Plessis was lodged there during his 1812 visit.

With the arrival of spring, delegates from Chéticamp and Margaree went to Arichat to fetch Father Allain. However, Father had had no answer from them to his autumn letter. There had been a disagreement. The people wanted a younger man. Father Allain got wind of this. Finally, the people decided to go get him and bring him back, but with certain conditions: that he would serve Chéticamp and Margaree with an equal length of stay. That meant more expense and painful travel.[13] He refused to go with the delegates and the conveyance returned without him.

The disappointed Chéticantins decided to write to the Bishop on their own asking for another priest. This letter, "signed by three of the leading inhabitants of the parish, speaking for all the others" (written in the margin), permits one to suspect there was some bitterness on the subject of the refusal of Father Allain:

Chétican, second day of June, 1800

My Lord Bishop of Québec
My Lord

after having done our best last Summer with you, to have a priest here we are again without one we are a flock which has been abandoned That is why we throw ourselves on your mercy so that you will do your best to procure for us a priest. Father Allain wrote to us that he had received a letter from the Vicar-General of Québec telling him to come minister to us he had us build a chapel during the winter in the bad weather and he made us go get him and he did not wish to serve the whole parish he only wished to serve half of it and he always asks for the tithe offered by the whole parish which is the sum of 1,000 pounds.

My Lord

We recommend ourselves to your prayers
Salutations and Blessings
Benony Le Blanc
Joseph Boudrot
Régis Bois[14]

Father Allain had informed the Bishop of the facts after being asked for an explanation. As the latter requested further information on the matter in a letter to Father Lejamtel, indiscreetly read by Father Allain, the anger of the old missionary knew no bounds and was given free rein in a letter to the Bishop the following August 16: "If it has cost them something," he said of those people who came to bring him to Chéticamp,

it cost me four times as much as they altogether...my pride is hurt at seeing myself imputed to have such an odious trait, while I served these Louts free two years out of six, about whom I was never completely satisfied. This is the first word I have said on this matter, and concerns the people of Margaree, of which

81

you have seen one of the chiefs of the group, though the greater number are good people, among whom a few bad apples spoil the barrel. God's will be done.[15]

This little quibbling should not diminish the reputation of this great missionary. He was quite elderly and full of infirmities, and the Acadians were not entirely blameless. In order to have a good idea of his worth, let us remember what Bishop Plessis wrote of him during his voyage to the Magdalen Islands in 1811: "Nothing was more correct than for him to hold [the Acadians] in this estimable simplicity worthy of the most beautiful age of Christianity, in this innocence of manners, in this union, this harmony and this integrity in every trial, that we still admire among them."

Father Allain made a last visit to Chéticamp in 1808 during his voyage to the Magdalen Islands, where he returned to live with one of his nephews.

In 1812, aged seventy-four years, exhausted by his infirmities and fatigue, Father Allain entered the General Hospital of Québec where he died a month late, in July.

Father Gabriel Champion of Chéticamp

The letter from the Chéticantins to the Bishop of Québec seemed to bear fruit. By the following year a great joy was announced to them. They were going to have their own missionary who would reside among them. His name was Father Champion.

This priest had been chased from France in 1790 by the French Revolution. He had spent the winter of 1800-01 with the Acadians of Fortune Bay on Prince Edward Island.[16] He came to Chéticamp during the summer of 1801. He was the first priest to establish his residence there. He had to serve both Margaree and the Magdalen Islands as well.

In one of his first letters to the Bishop of Québec, the newcomer described his civil state: "My former Diocese...is that of Avranches.... I was born on December 17 in the year 1748.... I was ordained priest in the year 1778.... My name is Gabriel Champion...."[17]

Father Champion was immediately noticed for his good character, a character which never wavered. Father MacEachern, missionary to Île Saint-Jean (P.E.I.), said of him the first time that he had met him: "He is a worthy character."[18]

Father de Calonne said the same: "He is very strong," he wrote to Bishop de Canath,

very zealous, and a man of excellent conduct. The bark is a bit rough because he has always lived among country people, but, for this reason, perhaps, he is better, though ill-fitted to lead them in the way of perfection, which is not required for the multitude. Moreover, his feelings are very good in all aspects.[19]

"The fine missionary," as Father Burke called him, lived six years in Chéticamp, making frequent and, naturally, prolonged travels to the Magdalen Islands and Margaree. These were six years of peace and happiness in both places, interrupted only by a terrible accident at the end of Lent 1805: Father Champion suddenly became blind. "In less than a second, I lost, totally, my sight, to the point of only being able to get around in daylight with great difficulty," he wrote to the Bishop of Québec on May 7, 1806.[20] He had to go to Halifax for medical treatment. "The nerve...was attacked" and only "The Great Specialist could cure it," wrote Father Burke.[21] However, Father Champion was able to say Mass at Saint-Pierre and return to Chéticamp before winter, to the great joy of all, for "the loss of this fine man," Father Burke wrote, "cannot be mended very soon."[22]

The beloved missionary would remain afflicted with this malady until his death, which wasn't long in coming. He felt his death approaching. He notified the Bishop of Québec with these touching words:

I am in the Magdalen Islands...always bothered by the same infirmity. It seems to threaten my life sooner by causing shortness of breath...which bothers my sight and depresses me, sometimes making me feel that I may not be able to complete the Sacrifice of the Mass without an accident, which had already happened once or twice.... Then, a dizziness, caused by the new-fallen snow on the ice of the bays, on which I was obliged to spend the day...going to minister to a sick person, who was in danger of death.... I greatly fear that this will not last long, because of this breathlessness which is added to my other infirmities, and probably warns of an early death....[23]

By the autumn of 1807 Father Champion didn't dare stay alone on his missions. He went to live near Father Lejamtel in Arichat. He died there January 18, 1808.

This death was a great loss for the mission of the Gulf. "It leaves an emptiness," wrote Father Burke to the Bishop of Québec, "that Your Grace will fill with difficulty."[24]

Even in death, this man of God continued to show a generous soul. After all his debts were paid, and one hundred pounds had been left to his nephew in France, he left the rest of his possessions and his money to the poor of Chéticamp; to this beloved mission as well, he left his vestments and things he used at the altar.[25]

This missionary, simple and modest, was not a scholar; he was probably not a builder; he was happy with the primitive chapel and poor glebe house. We owe to him, however, the founding of Chéticamp's first school. He was not hard to please: "He always found everything going well, the people said of him, and he did not wish to leave them with any expenses." Without doubt, he was not a liturgist nor an eminent canonist: at his death, the church and glebe house "are not in very good order...things are not in a good state." There were still no Parish Registers in Chéticamp. Finally, as soon as possible after his death, the people had to think of procuring "the things necessary for Divine service."[26]

But this priest had a generous heart. He never asked for anything. On the contrary, he gave all he had and, especially, he gave of himself. Too, he received much in return: the esteem of his confrères in the priesthood and the unbounded devotion of his parishioners. In addition to the tithe, these people furnished the wood, gave him meat, more than he could eat, "and many other things, from the goodness of their hearts." Especially, they gave him their affection, their love. The sadness they felt on his death was great: "They mourned him deeply," wrote Father Lejamtel to his Bishop.[27]

Again Without a Priest

We saw that Father Allain made a short visit to Chéticamp in 1808 on his way to retirement at the home of his nephew in the Magdalen Islands.

And again the people of Chéticamp were without a priest, with all the hardship and worry which this condition means.

The working conditions of missionaries obliged them to make long, hard voyages to visit their missions, or more often, to carry the comforts of religion to those in danger of death. This was done through enormous sacrifices and heroic devotion. But let us not forget that the lot of the poor people in these regions was not any better. In Chéticamp one often speaks of those days of great hardship when the men would leave for Arichat in their light boats to fetch the priest for someone in danger of death. One can imagine the anxiety running through the thoughts of the dying person who is, perhaps, facing eternity! Would the priest arrive in time?

The following year, 1809, it is again Father Lejamtel who makes the trip and arrives in Chéticamp. The letter of praise that he writes to the Bishop on the subject of the Chéticantins gives evidence that the kindness of Father Champion had produced excellent fruit:

These are people who cannot be more charitable towards one another; they have much piety and it would be a shame not to assist and nurture their zeal. They are very generous towards the priests who serve them, and have a great regard for them; the treatment I have received from them soon made me forget the fatigue of my voyage. I went to them by land and by water, in crossing Cape Breton with two Indians. The people didn't want me returning by the same method, as they felt it was too difficult for me; and they equipped themselves, at their own cost, with a boat to take me by sea to Arichat, where I have now returned....

The last Sunday that I was in Chéticamp, the people were all assembled with the deputies from Margaree, and they agreed to pay three dollars per family to a missionary who would come for them, and even four dollars, if necessary. He would not incur many expenses while among these people, for they would furnish him with firewood and give him meat, more than he could use, and many other things, gratis, as was the case with the late Fr. Champion, whose loss they regret so much....

Fr. Champion left his belongings and his money to the poor.... All have asked that his sum be used for the church, as being the poorest in their area, there was no one among them reduced to begging. I have agreed to their request...all asked this with a unanimous voice, and knowing them all inclined to assist the needy.[28]

It was on this visit that Father Lejamtel made another complete account of the Catholic population of Chéticamp and Margaree. "In general, all these families have many children," he wrote.

After this visit he especially reported the following impression: "I have found the people desolate at having no missionary." Some days later he returned to this subject with the Bishop:

A priest would live at ease in these lands, although the situation can, at first, appear a bit disagreeable to those who are not used to it.... These people often sing High Masses, and have other services, the fees would be sufficient, so to speak, to pay any expenses the priest would be obliged to make.[29]

As for a missionary, none came. And in the summer of 1810 old Father Lejamtel had to take to the road to these missions once again. He had all the people make their Easter Duty and gave First Communion to the children. The same idea preoccupied him: to get them a priest. "I have informed the inhabitants of Chétican and of Margaree of the feelings of Your Grace in this respect.... They rejoice to see that they are not abandoned, and console themselves with the hope of having a priest sooner or later."[30]

The Second Church

Father Champion was always satisfied with the primitive chapel, opposing all improvements to it that would be at the expense of his flock. After his death, and in the hope of more easily getting another priest, the Chéticantins decided and promised, on the advice of Father Lejemtel, to build another church as well as better lodgings for the missionary. They kept their word and the construction of the church began in 1810. It took two years for the people to build it. When Bishop Plessis paid them a visit in 1812 he wrote in his journal that it still only had its first covering, but should be finished in the autumn.

This second church was built on *la part* (the lot of land) of Joseph Boudrot who was happy to cede the land to God. It was again situated at Le Platin, at the foot of the *buttereau* (hillock) to the southeast of the road. The remains are still visible. This church was built of wood and was very well constructed, with a bell-tower surmounted by a beautiful, tall, iron cross.

The first church had not been named. The second was. The Bishop himself, during his voyage of 1812, "named it for Saint Apollinaire, martyr, because he had opened his mission among them on the date the Church honours this saint."[31]

In 1955, the year of the Acadian bicentenary, the parishioners of Chéticamp raised a monument to their ancestors on the actual emplacement of the second church; and on the plaque of the monument is printed the names of the *quatorze vieux*, the fourteen names on the Charter of 1790, the fourteen founders of Chéticamp.

The Old Cemeteries

Beside the first primitive chapel was also, perhaps, the first cemetery.

This is not certain, but if there was a cemetery, it was already moved before the construction of the second church. The new cemetery was located on the *buttereau* (hill) descending the slope across from the new church. The site was very badly chosen since half the land was wet by springs. This area is what we today call the old cemetery. It was in use up to 1868.

There rest the remains of the founders of Chéticamp. With the exception of some who, perhaps, were buried behind Le Platin in the first cemetery, they are all buried here.

The Parish Registers

In 1811 Father Lejamtel faithfully returned to make his visit to the Chéticantins, still deprived of a priest. It was on this occasion that he began his Parish Registers of Chéticamp—the date was September 22, 1811. The first item recorded in the Register is a marriage at which he himself had officiated during his first trip to Chéticamp in 1792. The second item in the Register is the baptism of Philippe Lelièvre dated September 22, 1811. Of the baptisms, marriages and deaths between these two dates, none are written in the Register.

Episcopal Visits to the Missions of the Gulf.
Visit to Chéticamp of Bishop Joseph-Octave Plessis,
Bishop of Québec

For a while the bishops of Québec had shown their intention of making a pastoral visit to these regions of the Gulf. The missionaries were happy to spread the word to the people: "This would be a great honour for us, and, at the same time, a blessing for our people," replied Father Lejamtel.[32] They permitted themselves to hope that this dream would become a reality, a dream which was not unmixed, however: "The too-great distance from these places," wrote Father Champion, "the undependability of the winds, weather and sea, make me fear that we will not be fortunate enough to enjoy your presence in this wild country."[33]

By 1803 Bishop Denaut undertook this long, painful trip. He reached Arichat. He hesitated a long time about going on to Chéticamp. On the advice of Father Lejamtel and Allain, he decided to have Father Champion come to see him at Arichat.

Bishop Plessis, successor to Bishop Denaut, undertook the trip to the Gulf missions in his turn.

In his first voyage in 1811 he visited the Gaspé region and went on to the Magdalen Islands. By the following spring, on May 20, he embarked again in order to go farther on and complete his pastoral trip. He made his way to Chéticamp.

The Bishop travelled with Captain Aimé Dugast in the *Angélique*, a thirty-two ton schooner. He was accompanied by Father Maguire, Parish Priest of Saint Michel de la Durantaye; by Father Beaubien, a priest destined for the missions of the Gulf; by Father Xavier Côté, the Bishop's chaplain during his voyage; and Louis Lemieux, servant for the group. Fathers MacEachern and Macdonnel, one a missionary on Prince Edward Island and the other in Nova Scotia, embarked at Prince Edward Island to travel with the Bishop.

Arrival in Chéticamp

Having left from Fortune Bay or Rollo Bay "where 26 Acadian families can be found,"[34] they arrived at Chéticamp two days later on June 22. As war had been declared with the Americans, terror was widespread in all the colonies along the Gulf, so exposed to the corsair raids. However,

There did not appear to the eyes of the travelers, any vessel of which the sight would cause them alarm; but, without wishing to do so, they, themselves, would spread terror to those of the faithful they were going to visit in a spirit of charity and Christian peace.

Three rowboats which had left on Wednesday morning from the harbour of Chétican, were fishing for cod a short distance offshore. Captain Dugast, who was not familiar with the entrance to the harbour, approached one of the three boats a short distance from the others. His intention was to take one of the men on board to act as a pilot for him. The brave men thought his intentions were hostile, and, convinced we were Americans, began to talk among themselves concerning what course of action they should take. One wished to fight to defend themselves, though they were not armed; the second wished to cut the anchor cable to save themselves; the third agreed to be taken, without arguing. His advice carried the day. On the schooner's approach, their fears doubled. The Bishop was standing near the mast of the foresail. Although he was wearing his black soutane, they took him for an officer of the crew, and no longer doubted their coming captivity. They were only reassured when they heard someone calling them in French, and they recognized Fr. MacEachern, whom they had previously seen at Île Saint-Jean. In their relief, all three at once would have come to pilot the *Angélique*, if we had wished it. We only needed one; he happily jumped on board and told us of the fright they had had. But, at the same time that these men were being reassured, a poor Irishman, named Dudley, whose house was in sight, seeing what he thought was a wretched American privateer, escaped into the woods with his wife and children, taking away with them their most precious belongings and probably burning others. When he saw the Bishop and his companions disembarking peacefully with their luggage and taking the road to the church, he was ashamed of his mistake, and believed the least he could do to make up for it, was to acknowledge it to them. He did this on his approach.

Description of the Places

The harbour of Chétican is formed by a peninsula about two leagues in length, which runs northward parallel to the mainland of Cape Breton. The isthmus which joins it is only a sandbar, washed by the sea on both sides, without ever being completely covered by it. It seems that the inhabitants would have had to settle on the edges of this beautiful basin. Not at all. Excepting three or four, all the others, more than forty, are confined to a frightful valley, bounded on one side by mountains completely covered in woodland, and on the other side by a hill which separates them from the harbour by about a league. The glebe house and a very small church are also buried here in this type of vast tomb,[35] as a larger one still has only its first covering and has to be completed in the autumn. A small stream, the kingdom of frogs and bullfrogs, meanders disagreeably around the glebe house and entertained the Bishop, who spent his resting hours listening to a concert of croaking bullfrogs for the four nights he spent there.

Piety of the Chéticantins

On the other hand, if the valley occupied by the Chéticantins is made disagreeable by its marshlands and by the winds from the south and southeast, which exercise a control about which it would be difficult to give you an idea, one is abundantly compensated by the kindness of its inhabitants, by their respect and their affection for their priests. These feelings were shown in a very consoling manner on the arrival of their primary shepherd. They had never seen a bishop among them, their joy was inconceivable, each family came to within two or three acres to greet him and receive his blessing, then joined in the procession making many offers of service to him and his companions, whom everyone was anxious to welcome among them and lodge in their homes. These good, faithful people spoke only with the greatest praise of the priests who had, up to now, spread the Good News of the Lord and administered the Sacraments to them. The voice of a priest is so powerful among these people, that it is considered like that of an angel, because they are incapable of suspecting that a priest can say anything less than the truth, or expect anything of them other than what God commands. They only speak to an ecclesiastic with their hats removed, even in the rain that washes their hair or the sun which burns their heads; they can continue an hour of conversation with him without daring to cover themselves, if they were not repeatedly ordered to do so. These people have only been served by a roving missionary, Fr. Lejamtel, since the death of Fr. Champion in 1807. Nothing is more fervent than their desire to have a priest who can stay among them, or, at least, can stay several months at a time. Fr. Lejamtel cannot do this, burdened as he is with several other areas. The people here would consider themselves to be happy if they had a priest who was to serve them and the faithful of Margaree and the Magdalen Islands.

Ministry

Margaree is about five leagues to the south of Chétican, and on the same piece of land. The population of this place is only about thirty-eight families spread out on both sides of a river, where they can only occupy the flatlands. The Bishop did not have the time to go among them. Fr. Macdonnel, who had very little to do in Chétican, was given the job of notifying the people of Margaree to come to Chétican, on his way to hear the confessions of the Scottish people of Margaree Cove, continuing on from there to Justico. He then left on Thursday morning, only leaving behind with the Bishop Fathers Maguire and MacEachern, who were kept busy hearing confessions for four days, which were just enough; to relieve them, the Bishop, with the chaplain, undertook all the instructions of the morning and evening, made up the list of all those from Chétican, and heard the confessions of the children who hadn't yet made their First Communion, as well as those of a dozen persons, for whom he, himself, celebrated their six marriages before leaving this place, on the express condition that the marriage festivities would not begin until after his departure. This order was faithfully executed.

After having described the weddings (see page 181), Bishop Plessis continued:

Chétican and Margaree are generally inhabited by Acadian families, although there can be found there some foreigners, French, Irish and Jersey, all very strongly united and zealous for their own religion. They did not cease giving proof of this during the stay of the Bishop among them, renewing every day their entreaties to have a priest who can have a more stable residence among them, than they have had for five years.

Chapels

The name of the chapel in Margaree is called Saint-Michel. That of Chétican having none, the Bishop named it after Saint Apollinaire, Martyr, because he had opened his mission among them on the day the Church honours this saint. The Bishop left Chétican on Sunday, July 26th, Feast of Sainte-Anne, after having anointed 154 persons.

Departure

On the afternoon of the same day, the Bishop took his leave to return to the schooner; most of the inhabitants wanted to escort him to the boat, which was to receive him above the harbour; to get there it was necessary to walk a league; this distance did not stop the men or the women from accompanying the Bishop. The Bishop found it impossible to resist a feeling of tenderness brought about in his heart by the sight of this crowd of good souls on their knees on the shore, asking a last blessing and wiping away their tears, while recommending themselves to his prayers. This spectacle, repeated in several other places, inevitably recalls the one which the faithful of the church of Milet gave to St. Paul, and gives place to some parallels and comparison, in which the modern apostle feels how much he is inferior to that of the nations.

The group embarked about five o'clock in the evening. Their intention was to reach a harbour called Justico or Justaucou or Justaucorps, for no one agrees on this name.

During this visit Father MacEachern performed three baptisms and Father Maguire fourteen. Those of our ancestors who had the honour of being married by the Bishop were: Charles Boudreau and Luce Aucoin, André Poirier and Anastasie Devaux, Hubert Aucoin and Marie-Madeleine Bois, Frédéric Deveaux and Marguerite Romard, all eight from

Chéticamp, and two other couples from Margaree, Paul Doucet and Marthe Haché, and Jean Etchevery and Henriette Larade.

No priest was named to Chéticamp during his visit. Father Lejamtel came faithfully in September of that same year to make his visit.

Lost Hope: Drowning of Father Dufresne in 1812

The Bishop retained such a good impression of the people of Chéticamp that he could not put off attending to their problem. In the autumn of 1812 he gave them their heart's desire in the person of Father Antoine Dufresne.[36] This priest, furnished with the necessities of religion and with extended powers, embarked for his mission. "Never had a priest left...with more joy, more speed, and more edifying projects than Fr. Dufresne," wrote Bishop Plessis.[37]

Unfortunately it was well into the season; sailing was difficult and the captain drunk. The captain missed not only Chéticamp, but even Cape Breton Island and, aiming too far north, attained the Atlantic. A storm surprised their schooner and tossed them, along with their belongings, onto the rocks of Mocodome Island where they all perished on November 14, 1812.[38]

Just imagine the desolation of the Chéticantins who had waited such a long time for a priest: "The loss of the priest who was being sent to them, threw them into dismay," wrote Father Lejamtel.[39] The following winter, while Father Manseau was with them, they had one or more services a week celebrated for the soul of this priest whom they had not known but who "had perished on his way to them."[40]

Touched by the profound trial which overwhelmed them, Father Lejamtel spent six weeks with them the following year. On his return he sent to the Bishop, in very delicate and respectful terms, the entreaties of the inhabitants to have a priest.

This elderly missionary returned again in August of 1814. At one time he believed he had found a candidate for the priesthood:

I have in view, another young man from Chéticamp, who seems to have much more of a disposition and a desire for the ecclesiastical state than young Hureau. The sole objection in his respect, is that he is the oldest in his family, and that his parents, who are poor, are having trouble consenting to his absence, seeing that he is a good child, and they look to him as their support.[41]

That was the last voyage of Father Lejamtel among these people that he loved so much. He was approaching his sixties. The fatigue he suffered on so many trips, and the rheumatism which tormented him, made the job far too difficult for him. A younger man was necessary.

Father Antoine Manseau of Tracadie, Nova Scotia

This young priest, born at Saint-Antoine de la Baie-du-Febvre, a region of Nicolet, on July 12, 1787, had been received into the priesthood on January 2, 1814, in Québec. At first he was assistant to the pastor of

Sainte-Anne de la Grand-Anse, but at the end of August 1814 he was named "missionary of Tracadie, Pomquet and Havre-à-Boucher, in Nova Scotia, and also, of Chétican and Margaree, in Cape Breton."

Having arrived in Tracadie, where he was to live, the new missionary found still there, Fr. Pichard, a French priest, who had resided there for several years. As it was then November 10th, and there was no way for this old and venerable priest to leave for Québec where he was called by his Bishop, Fr. Manseau decided to spend the winter in Chéticamp, which is about thirty leagues from Tracadie. He sent word to the inhabitants of this Mission through a Negro who had to make the trip on foot, for which the priest had to pay dearly.

At the news that a missionary was going to reside among them, the good Acadians launched a schooner, set up the rigging, and were soon en route for Tracadie, where, twelve days later, they arrived under full sail.

Since the small amount of luggage of the missionary was completely ready, he did not keep them waiting. They were under way without losing any time, and by the evening of the next day, they dropped anchor in the harbour of Chéticamp.

It was November 28th,[42] and a most opportune time to arrive in port, for, by the following night, winter had set in for good with a severe wind accompanied by snow, in one of the most furious storms one can see on that beach.

However, it is not surprising that this storm did not become so violent until after the arrival of the missionary, for all the devoted Acadians had made a Novena for a safe and happy voyage; and, on the last day of this pious exercise, the vessel entered the harbour, an occurrence never seen before in a season so advanced.

As well, the good Acadians were very anxious for the safety of everyone concerned, in seeing the boat exposed so late to all the furies of the winds and sea. How great was their joy in learning of the fortunate crossing of their missionary. From the harbour to the chapel, a distance of half a league, was a continual procession of these fervent Christians who hurried to meet him and prostrate themselves at his feet to receive his first blessing. "Dear Father," they said to him in their unsophisticated language, "we are very pleased to see you arrive. We were very worried, because of the weather, that you would not be able to take to the sea so late in the season."

It was the first Sunday of Advent that the missionary found himself in the region of his new parishioners. It was a truly touching and very emotional scene.

The purest joy shone on all their faces; and there was nothing lacking for the happiness of this shepherd who, for a long time afterward, was still so impressed with it that he admitted that in that moment, he was perfectly happy. It is so true, that a good people make the happiness of its pastor!

He spent six months with these fine people, who, by their docility, their faith and their piety, made things easier for him, and even made him forget the pain of his position. He found himself situated between two mountains, only seeing the sun from ten o'clock in the morning to two o'clock in the afternoon, since these mountains were only five or six acres from each other.

Margaree, where he found the Christians just as fervent as in Chéticamp, is situated about six leagues from Chétican. Fr. Manseau had to visit this mission at least every three weeks in order to have Sunday services, to teach Catechism to the children, to minister to the sick, and to have the people make their Easter Duty. All these trips had to be made on foot, accompanied by only one or two men.

The winter was spent in traveling in this way from one mission to the other, instructing the children, administering the Sacraments to the adults and in giving singing lessons to fine young people who became, for their missions, excellent cantors.[43]

The manner in which they welcomed me, and the treatment they continued to give me well confirms the good opinion Your Highness gave me about these wonderful inhabitants. Everything is free here, food and clothing, both; there is no way to spend a cent; something which suits me fine.[44]

Father Manseau returned to Tracadie in the spring, but returned to spend the following winter with those fine Cheticantins. He would again make another short visit of about a month's duration in 1816. In 1817 he was named pastor of Les Cèdres, Québec, where the difficulties he would meet "in the exercise of his ministry, made him miss the fine missions of the Gulf, and several times he repented of having left them so soon."[45]

Later, Father Manseau became Vicar-General at Montréal, and even refused the mitre with the post of co-adjutor of Bishop Lartigue.

After having become pastor of Saint-Charles de l'Industrie (presently Joliette) in 1843, Father Manseau founded the Collège of Joliette, as well as the Convent for young girls.

Father Joseph Cécil

During his first winter spent in Chéticamp, Father Manseau was accompanied by a seminarian who had discontinued his studies for a while due to poor health. This young man set himself the task of teaching Catechism and school lessons every day. "The people of Chétican wished, absolutely, to keep him in Cape Breton in order to have prayers with them and to teach school," wrote Father Manseau.[46] Father Cécil returned to Québec to be ordained in 1815, and then to Prince Edward Island, where he remained as a missionary for six years.

Father Rémi Gaulin of Antigonish

On his third voyage to the Gulf missions, Bishop Plessis was accompanied by a young priest ordained four years previously who was intended for these missions. He was placed at St. Ninian's, or Antigonish, with the added duty of Chéticamp and Margaree where he was to reside two months each year "in two visits, one in the spring, the other in the autumn. You will levy a dollar from each communicant." This would be the Spanish dollar.[47] This priest was Father Rémi Gaulin, born in Québec on June 30, 1787, and ordained October 13, 1811.

By the end of September 1815 Father Gaulin made his first visit to Chéticamp. Faithful to the instructions of Bishop Plessis, he returned there every year up to 1819, the date of the arrival of Father Joseph Moll in Chéticamp.

Father Gaulin had some complaints about the people of Chéticamp. "I am a bit tired of the habitual drunkenness of many of the Chéticantins," he wrote to Father Beaubien of the Magdalen Islands, whom he hoped to succeed in this mission.[48]

The difficulties he met in Antigonish were of such a nature, however, as to make him wish to be recalled to Québec. "You have abandoned yourselves to impurity and drunkenness; quarrels are frequent among you.... Sundays and feastdays have been changed into days of dissolution, etc...," wrote Bishop Plessis in a pastoral letter of August 21, 1816,[49] to the inhabitants of the missions of Saint Margaret of Antigonish. As a result, by 1817 Father Gaulin requested his recall to Québec "to provide for my poor old father."[50]

He wrote to the Bishop in English, although his Registers were kept in French. His four years in the missions having run out, the Bishop, during the year 1817, offered him work in Canada for the following year. Father Gaulin only replied to the Bishop's offer the following spring and was forced, to his great regret, to refuse: "I had the imprudence (I might say foolishness) to undertake the building of a presbytere in Chéticamp, which undertaking caused me to run into debts the last year's penny deranged all my projects."[51]

He then asked permission to prolong his stay in these missions to pay off his creditors. He remained there for this purpose until 1822. Later he became co-adjutor for the Bishop of Kingston, then Titular-Bishop for the same See on January 14, 1840.[52]

Religious Chant

Father Manseau, and the seminarian Cecil who spent the winter of 1814-15 with him in Chéticamp, endeavored to teach the basics of plain chant to a group of men and young people of Chéticamp. Father Rémi Gaulin continued the work already begun. Plain chant, with knowledge of the note, was faithfully transmitted until the arrival of the Sisters in 1903, the *Filles de Jésus* (Daughters of Jesus), who took over the direction of the choir and later adopted Gregorian Chant in obedience to the directives of Pope Pius X.

To be master-cantor was always considered a great honour in Chéticamp. Besides directing the group and choosing the chant of the Offices, his especially important role was that of intoning, alone, all the chants: hymns, psalms, and antiphons.

One favorite story told, which appears to be true, occurred in the second church. Upon the death of the master-cantor, there were four other cantors left. One of the four knew the note, but hadn't the voice necessary for the chant. Another didn't know the note, but possessed a very beautiful voice. The other two had neither advantage, since the story does not mention them. The dispute took place between the first and second cantors as to which one of them would take over the place of the dead master-cantor. The priest had to intervene and he decided in favour of the second, the one with the beautiful voice but no note. The following Sunday at Vespers the new master-cantor intoned the Laudate on the fifth tone, but he missed the attempt, went off pitch and stayed in trouble. Another tried, but also failed. The first began again, but without any more success than before. Then the one who knew the note got up and sang very strongly on the fifth tone:

"There are three cantors in the choir who do not know the fifth tone!"

New Episcopal Jurisdiction

Up to this point all of eastern Canada was under the ecclesiastical jurisdiction of the Bishop of Québec. In 1817 papal bulls established an apostolic vicariate of the whole peninsula of Nova Scotia with Bishop Edmund Burke as Titular-Bishop. Cape Breton and the rest of the Maritimes were still under the direct jurisdiction of Québec.

On January 12, 1819, Father Bernard Angus MacEachern was named Suffragan-Bishop and Assistant to the Bishop of Québec for the provinces and islands of the Gulf. In 1820 he established an episcopal See in Charlottetown, Prince Edward Island. Cape Breton was included in this new ecclesiastical division.

The Bishop of Québec, in agreement with the Suffragan-Bishop, would continue to care for their priests who were already working in the French missions of this region. They would continue to grant them their powers,[53] but would keep the right to rule on particularly difficult matters of conscience, of sending out to the priests their decision on these matters[54] and of also sending out pastoral letters to them.[55]

On August 11, 1829, bulls from Rome established the Charlottetown bishopric, with New Brunswick, Prince Edward Island and the Magdalen Islands as its territory. On September 4 of that same year the whole of Cape Breton Island was annexed to the ecclesiastical province of Halifax, as it had been united politically to the peninsula in 1820. It then came under the jurisdiction of Bishop William Fraser of Halifax.

Finally, on September 21, 1844, the Holy See established a new bishopric at Arichat, suffragan of Halifax. On August 23, 1886, the See of this bishopric was transferred to Antigonish by Bishop John Cameron.

Father Joseph Moll[56]

Since the death of Father Champion in 1808, the Chéticantins were only visited on rare occasions by a missionary who lived elsewhere. Finally, with Father Moll they once again had a missionary of their own, one who actually lived among them. He probably served Margaree and the Magdalen Islands as well, but his residence was established in Chéticamp.

Father Moll took over the position in September 1819. He didn't even stay the four years, the length of time expected of missionaries[57] who were sent to these remote missions. By the spring of 1822 he left these places, which he did not like, and which, it is highly likely, did not favour him either. He was named pastor of Sainte-Anne-de-la Pérade.

He is the first missionary to complain bitterly about the people of Chéticamp and especially those of Margaree. It seems that this priest fooled himself on the life and difficulties in these missions: "I have suffered many more setbacks in the first six months that I would have thought possible."[58] His criticisms, though justified, seemed tinged with a touch of bitterness cause by his overly-high expectations:

The glebe house, which was only begun, and which was still to be completed, the dances and the drunkenness which it was necessary to try to abolish, and which are beginning to give way, were difficult changes to make, accustomed as the people were to being accepted with all their bad habits. Now I feel a bit more consoled. Dancing has become quite rare, drunkenness less frequent. It is true that several people have become more virtuous by necessity, drink being scarce this winter, and I very much fear that those people will again begin their usual debauchery, on the arrival of the Merchants.[59]

It seems that Father Moll never got used to Chéticamp. He was not happy there. By 1821 he speaks of returning home at the first opportunity, "for it is not every season," he said, "nor even every year, that one can find occasion to leave this lonely place."[60]

He departed Chéticamp without waiting for his successor, who had not yet been named.

Father Vincent, Trappist

Chéticamp was again without a priest and its spiritual help again had to come from the outside. Father Gaulin returned for a short visit in the autumn.

It was also that summer that Father Vincent, a Trappist monk stationed in Tracadie, made a visit to Chéticamp. It seems he was only passing through since the Registers contain only one act of his, dated June 14.

PASTORS OF CHÉTICAMP

Father Augustin Magloire Blanchet

By August of 1822 Bishop Plessis conferred missionary powers for Chéticamp, Margaree and the Magdalen Islands on a young priest whom he had ordained in Québec on June 3 of the preceding year. The first record written by him in the Registers of Chéticamp dated from October 20, 1822. He was the first priest to sign "curé de Chéticamp"[61] (pastor of Chéticamp).

Nothing very remarkable would have happened under his reign if it were not for some difficulties among his parishioners on the subject of successions and division of lands. Father Blanchet wished very strongly to keep peace among his flock and did not hesitate to write, with his own hand, several wills for the elderly. These papers are still preserved by the families involved.

Father Blanchet also had certain cases of injustice to set right, about which he consulted Bishop Plessis. One of these cases concerned a merchant who had placed some salmon nets at the mouth of the Margaree River contrary to the regulations passed by the inhabitants of that place. The people were furious. They ordered him to remove his nets within twenty-four hours. The merchant decided to do this, but during the night one very angry and over-zealous inhabitant cut the nets. Because of the serious damage the merchant brought an action in court to make the one who had threatened him the most pay a fine. But that one was innocent.

Into the midst of these very ordinary difficulties, Father Blanchet was warmly welcomed. No doleful stories or sharp complaints from him. He understood that the missions were not heaven on earth and, with humility, only regretted his inexperience.

I would not want to complain about my situation, but it is not less sad for a young man like me, who has such a great need for advice, and who finds himself so far away from those who could give it to me, both for my own needs and for those of the sheep entrusted to my care. The sole thing that reassures me: I believe it is God's will.[62]

Father Blanchet had to make the trip from Chéticamp to Arichat to go to confession.[63] Bishop Plessis answered him:

It is easy to realize that your loneliness has its inconveniences, but it also has its consolations, even if it were only the removal from occasions of backbiting and other sins, to which one is exposed in society. Besides this, you are in the right place, since you are where Providence has placed you. When your four years are finished, you will be free to return here, but you must let me know six months in advance.[64]

In July of 1825 Bishop MacEachern, who had been in charge of Cape Breton since February 1820, came to confer the sacrament of Confirmation on 222 persons. This appears to be the first visit of a bishop after that of Bishop Plessis in 1812. A good Scotsman, he administered the sacrament to all those who were not yet confirmed, even infants at the breast. When he heard of this, Bishop Panet, who had become Archbishop, asked Bishop MacEachern not to do this again, "were it only to please me," he said to him.[65] That action could be done formerly when there was no Bishop,[66] but not now.

Father Blanchet returned to Québec in 1826, his four years of obedience having run out. In 1846 he became Bishop of Walla-Walla in the state of Oregon. His stay in Chéticamp, if not spectacular, was carried out well and left memories. He was a noble person with a kind heart whom Chéticamp could well honour.[67]

In looking back, it must be said that if Chéticamp was often without a priest, and if these came only at rare intervals, they were nevertheless personalities of exceptionally moral character.

Father Champion was outstanding for his goodness and his poverty; Father Lejamtel was a very holy man; Father Manseau was a superior man who, out of humility, refused a bishop's mitre; Fathers Gaulin and Blanchet, especially, were two great men who would become bishops.

Hence, a deep veneration for priests took root in the hearts of all Chéticantins. From that veneration came an unswerving faith, repaid even by some miracles. This faith sometimes goes a little too far. The Chéti-cantins have always believed, and many still do believe, that every priest enjoys the power of making miracles as he possesses that of administering the sacraments and blessings. They have difficulty in accepting that, in his domain, he has only the power of intercession, more or less efficacious according to his saintliness and the faith of the people.

Father Julien Courtaud

Father Courtaud was the successor of Father Blanchet. He was born in Deschambault on September 12, 1787, and was ordained on February 24, 1812. From Rivière-Ouelle, where he was curate for two years (1825-26), he was sent to Chéticamp on September 4, 1826. He only arrived, however, at the beginning of November.

A letter from Father J.B. Maranda, pastor of Arichat and a Canadian, to Father Charles-Félix Cazeau, paints a picture for us of this new missionary who was going to Chéticamp. "I have finally seen Fr. Courtaud," he said. "He is likeable because he has many Canadian ways; but mixed with some pronounced peculiarities that he brought from Deschambault, and has kept up very well among the Acadians. In Canada, one has to conform. Yet, he is well-nigh the precious stone of the clergy," he said, sarcastically.[68] And in 1842, in another letter to the same person, he said: "I have Courtaud for a neighbour; I am more convinced than ever that he is not one of the Seven Wonders of the World. Good, as far as morals are concerned, but eccentric...."[69]

Father Courtaud's first contact with his mission made a good impression on him: "As I had expected, I found everything in order, and I have nothing to complain about: the people are zealous enough according to their means; for they are very poor, more so than I thought; their finances are ever decreasing."[70]

But he quickly changed his tune, and by the following year he wrote:

I thought that I would find the people more zealous for their missionary than I have found in actuality, principally the people of Margaree, who, from what I had been told, caused much anxiety to Fr. Blanchet, and who are prepared to treat me no better, by their lack of obedience and the difficulty they have in following the right path, because of their dishonesty and their disobedience.... I warned them that I would inform Your Highness of this; it seems to have made them somewhat more docile.[71]

In 1828 things seemed to be going no better:

As for my mission, everything has been going well for a while, except for some small fusses with Acadian heads, swelled with pride, as can be found in several missions of the Gulf. My glebe house must be repaired, I asked them to do it before I leave, and I found only a little opposition, less than I would have imagined.[72]

We feel that Father Courtaud imagined many things, and that he was awkward in his dealings. So much so that the people, full of respect for their other priests, seemed to have no confidence in his judgements.[73] Thus, when he speaks of telling the Bishop about them the people are immediately "more docile," and even on the questions of litigation, ready to submit themselves to the Bishop's decisions.[74] One subject under litigation illustrates this. The government gave bonuses to the fishermen, so much per ton of fish. The schooner captains wished to keep these bonuses for themselves without sharing them with the fishermen whom they hired at so much a line or at a certain percent. Without making an absolute judgement on the matter, Bishop Panet believed they were right. Father Courtaud wanted the captains to share the bonuses with their fishermen, which they refused to do. Then the missionary lost his temper: "I beg Your Highness to send me some written words to force them to do this; for I do not want to be led by some dunces, such as they are, nor to go against my duty, in order to agree with them."[75]

He returned to his project six months later. About the advice he gave them on this matter, he said: "Nothing can get through to them; once the Acadians have taken a path, they cannot change their minds, in spite of very good reasons." His own reasons were, perhaps, not so good either, since he added: "But, I could be mistaken; they tell me that if Your Highness orders them to give it, they will do so willingly...the people only want to hear the decision of the Bishop."[76]

Unfortunately, if Father Courtaud had not the stability of Father Manseau, nor the patience of Lejamtel, the Chéticantins and the people of Margaree, for their part, had lost much of their innate honesty, and their sense of morality left much to be desired.

Two vices in particular seemed to have caused much damage to these friendly populations, according to the missionary:

The most deplorable vices here, are drunkenness and injustice.... I would be so pleased if Your Highness would strongly reprimand them, by letter, on these two vices, but, especially, on drunkenness.... And I am certain that this scolding would be of great benefit to them, along with the threat of not granting them a missionary, because they fear nothing so much, as to be deprived of a missionary again.[77]

And certainly, schooners loaded with barrels of liquor did not land without this entailing social and moral degradation.

Father Lejamtel, it seems, did not have too much to complain about. Father Manseau was quite concerned. In a letter of 1814, after having spoken with admiration of the people of these places, he added: "It's a great pity that in both places [Chéticamp and Margaree], rum is held in such high esteem."[78] The use of it, as so often happens with drink, quickly became an abuse which inevitably ended in misery.

Subsequent missionaries would complain about the intolerable abuse of drink and the poverty of these same people. While the first missionaries insisted on sufficient revenue to take care of their needs even in the first years of the foundation, the attitude changes with the growing abuse of drink. In 1827 Father Courtaud could write: "The people...are very poor, more so than I thought; their finances are ever decreasing."[79] He returned to the same topic on June 4, 1828, in a letter to the Bishop: "The poverty of my mission is extreme and, it necessarily follows, I have only a very small revenue."[80] While in 1809 each family was ready to pay three dollars to the priest and furnish him with wood and meat freely,[81] twenty years later "the people neglect to pay their debts, as well as the tithe; if we ask them, they seem upset.... I am in dire circumstances."[82]

The Bishop of Québec threatened to take away the priest if they did not mend their ways: "You can warn your people for me," he wrote to Father Courtaud, "that, if they are not more careful in honouring their obligations to their missionaries, and if they do not renounce their debaucheries, I will withdraw you and leave them without a priest."[83] A bit further on in that same letter he says:

I did not send them a missionary, so that he could die of hunger. I have too great a need for my priests in other areas of my diocese, than to leave them to perish in their work. It is the unfortunate love of drink which, perhaps, leads a great number to quench their thirst and lose their souls, rather than to take care of the needs of the one who works to save them.[84]

The reprimand solicited by Father Courtaud finally arrived:

Bernard Claude Panet, by the mercy of God and the grace of the Apostolic Holy See, Bishop of Québec. Dearly Beloved, Parishioners of Chétican, Salutations and Blessings in Our Lord.

It is with the greatest sorrow, Dearly Beloved, that in place of the excellent reports we are accustomed to receiving about you, we have learned that you abandon yourselves, almost continually, to the excesses of drink. What a sad spectacle for those whom God has entrusted with the care of your souls, that of seeing Christians abandon themselves to such loathsome excesses. Unfortunately, that is not the only reproach we have to make to you. The injustices that you permit against each other are another subject of affliction for us. Oh, be fearful, Dearly Beloved, that the Lord, angered at seeing so many offenses taking place among you, will not strike you with the forces of His anger! If we, of necessity, are making similar reproaches to you as are your priests, realize that our affection for you has not diminished. Nothing would please us more than to hear you have put to good use the paternal advice we give you today, and that it has made a lasting impression on your souls.

This pastoral letter will be read and published from the pulpit at the Parish Mass the first Sunday after its reception.

Given at Québec under our sign, the seal of our arms, and the countersign of our secretary, on July 9, 1830.

Bern Cle Bishop of Québec

By Monsignor

C.F. Caseau, Priest-Secretary[85]

Chéticamp, apparently, was not an earthly paradise for Father Courtaud. He had written to the Bishop on September 12, 1829: "Your Highness will remember that, next year, it will be four years that I have been in purgatory, and sometimes, in hell; that I would like to have my successor arrive before I leave the place…he should know a bit of English, and he should be capable of making them mind; for fear, among the Acadians, is the best motivation of keeping them to their duties." In spite of everything, Father Courtaud remained in Chéticamp until 1841, and one can say, to his credit, he did not lessen his devotion to the people or his duty towards them. Moreover, the memory that he left in Chéticamp is that of a good priest, somewhat eccentric, sometimes awkward, but well-intentioned and a real apostle.

Besides ministering to Chéticamp, he also served Margaree and continued his apostolic trips as far as Broad Cove and even Baddeck.[86] These travels tired the missionary: "My health becomes poorer," he wrote, "because of the necessity of making long trips on horseback."[87]

Father Courtaud was replaced by Father Paddey McKeagney and sent to L'Ardoise to "correct the blunders" of that priest in this region.[88] He died on May 6, 1869.

Father Paddey McKeagney

Father Paddey McKeagney, successor to Father Courtaud, was born in Clogher, Ireland, to Patrick McKeagney and Catherine McCarney. He spoke and wrote French well, having done his studies at a French institution.[89]

Father McKeagney arrived in June of 1841. Since his lack of tact had already left something to be desired in L'Ardoise, his coming to Chéticamp was not promising, for there "would soon be spoiled what Courtaud had done well," wrote Father Maranda, pastor of Arichat.[90]

Like Father Courtaud, Father McKeagney had chosen to live in Chéticamp but also had to serve Margaree. The neighbouring pastor was Father Alexander MacLeod of Broad Cove. In 1843 when Father McKeagney was sent to Meteghan, where he remained eight months, it was the pastor of Broad Cove who visited Chéticamp and Margaree, now without a priest. Father McKeagney returned to Chéticamp in June 1844 and stayed there until September of 1854.

The memory he left us is that of a priest who did not measure up to the standards of his predecessors. He was satisfied with the old church below the *buttereau* (hill), now no longer sufficient. The most outstanding deed of his sojourn in Chéticamp was his departure, at which there was an unforgettable scene.

Realizing that his ministry had been somewhat lacking, Father wished to make a public act of reparation. He left on a Sunday. First he celebrated Mass, then, with a large white cross painted on his back with whitewash, he asked pardon of his parishioners who had come in a crowd to say goodbye to him and who were moved to tears at this act of humility.

There was in Father McKeagney a large dose of eccentricity mixed with an evident desire to amaze people, as was seen in his parting words: "I would have destroyed this place, if there had not been so many good people here." He was leaving his pigeons behind. When asked what he wanted done with them, he replied: "Leave them. They will follow me."

Father left not only Chéticamp, but also the diocese. In 1854 he was incardinated in the diocese of Saint John, New Brunswick. He died in 1860 in Madawaska, pastor at St. Leonard's Church.

Father McKeagney had spent thirteen years as pastor in Chéticamp. It seems that, in spite of his great deficiencies, he was looked upon sympathetically by the people because of his simplicity, his easy manner and, especially, his devotion to the sick.

Ten Years Missing from the Parish Registers

The worthy successor to Father McKeagney does not appear in the Parish Registers. Ten years are missing from these records. One volume must have been lost. The last act recorded was by Father McKeagney on January 2, 1846; the next recorded act, October 19, 1856, is signed by Father Jacques McDonagh, P.P. But we know that between Father McKeagney and Father McDonagh there was Father Chénal.

Father H.J. Chénal

At this time the Bishop of Arichat, Bishop Colin Francis MacKinnon, conscious of his apostolic duty, multiplied his efforts to obtain French priests for his Acadian parishes in the diocese. With the same apostolic zeal, he tried to obtain French nuns for Arichat. To this end, he wrote to the Cardinal-Prefect of Propaganda, Superior of the Seminary for Foreign Missions, in Paris. Finally, he sent Father John Cameron, future Bishop of Antigonish, to Paris to carry out the necessary arrangements on the spot, thus hurrying things along. More or less well-received in Paris, Father Cameron was given little encouragement. Just the same, he returned with a priest, Father H.J. Chénal.[91]

Father Chénal was an eccentric too. He was more unstable than Father McKeagney, and did not have the same zeal. Negligent of his ministry, even of the sick, it was necessary to prod him along just to make him administer the Sacraments to the dying. Rough-spoken and arrogant, he battled with the church wardens on the subject of church property. The Bishop had to intervene to calm things down at first, then again to set them right. He had to threaten Father Chénal in order to force him to admit into the religious services people the priest had excluded,[92] and to make sure he did not continue to harass them.

In his wagon, pulled by his horse, "Steamboat," Father Chénal would stop for no one. Even if one had a load of hay or wood, it was necessary to give him the whole road. He would cry: "Clear the road!" and everyone had to get out of his way.

Father Chénal wasn't any more moderate from the pulpit. The story is told that one Sunday he was preaching against the game *au loup* (a card game played for money). Pointing his finger at the wife of a parishioner, he cried out: "Face of the Devil!" The husband immediately got up and said: "Father Chénal, that's a lie!" Father Chénal leapt into the aisle and ordered him to leave the church. The husband, remaining calm, told the priest, "Go back to the altar, Father Chénal. I'll leave when I'm ready!" He left shortly afterwards.

Father Chénal's stay in Chéticamp was a short one, about a year or two. We do not know where he was sent.

Father Jacques McDonagh

Father McDonagh was in Chéticamp during the winter of 1856-57. He wrote in Latin and signed "parochus," pastor of Chéticamp. Afterwards he was sent to Mulgrave where he became the founding pastor of that parish.

Father William Chisholm

The son of John Chisholm and Margaret Chisholm, Father Chisholm was born in September 1830 in Glassburn, Nova Scotia. He was one of the first students at the College of Arichat. In 1854, after some months in the seminary in Québec, he had to return because of his health. He continued his studies at the University of Antigonish where he was the first student with Father Thomas Sears. Ordained priest by Bishop MacKinnon on September 21, 1856, in Antigonish, he was immediately named pastor in Margaree.

Father Chisholm was trilingual in that he was fluent in French, English and Gaelic.

On May 9, 1857, Father was made pastor of Chéticamp while still looking after Margaree. Two years later he undertook the job of building a new church at Margaree, the third for that place. He didn't have time to finish it himself, but Father H. Macdonald, who later became pastor of Margaree, finished the job.

In Chéticamp Father Chisholm, or *le gros Chisholm*, as the people still call him, left among the population the memory of a serious man, a stable apostle and fearless builder.

The Third Church (1861)

Scarcely freed from Margaree and the cares of the church he had undertaken to build there, Father Chisholm began to build one in Chéticamp. It must not be forgotten that, at that time, the parish of Chéticamp included all of the present-day parish of Saint-Joseph-du-Moine. Its boundary was Patrick Delaney's brook which separated it from the sister-parish of Margaree. On the other side the parish extended as far as Cap-Rouge where the families of Maurice Aucoin and *Warrec* (Joseph) Leblanc were situated.

With time, the tiny wooden church in Chéticamp was quickly becoming too small. It was about fifty years old when it was demolished.

The third church left Le Platin, "that vast space, like a tomb,"[93] Bishop Plessis had said of it. Instead, it was raised, proud and gleaming, on the *buttereau* from which it took its name: *l'église du buttereau* (church on the hill). It was situated to the northwest of the present cemetery, but near the main road, with the entrance facing it.

Built of stones with grooved joints, it was proud of its two belfries. Two large steps, also of stone, raised the entrance. One of these, a single piece, is none other than a large stone of the steps of the present church, found in front of the main entrance doors. A cut stone, in which Le P'tit Clerc[94] had chiselled keys, embellished the façade below the large rose window. This same stone and the same rose window are found in the façade of the present church.

This third church was built in 1861. Bishop MacKinnon of Arichat placed the cornerstone on May 29, 1862, Feast of the Ascension. The architect was Enée Hamel. Ronald and John Gillis of St. Rose were the contractors. The interior was completed by a Chéticantin, Mr. Félicien (à Basile) Chiasson.

The high altar is the same one used in the sacristy today. The old pews are still used in the Parish Hall. Finally, the pulpit, a pulpit on wheels, was also used for a long time in the present church, as well as the railing and the three altars.

Ten years later, in 1871, Father Hubert Girroir procured a beautiful bell which he had installed on a high bell tower beside the church. That bell is the very same one pouring out joyous and powerful notes from its high bell tower today. Its name is Marie.[95]

The Present Cemetery

The cemeteries, like the churches, were too small. The old cemetery, besides being very limited in its usable space, was full; another one had to be opened. The whole pinnacle of the *buttereau* was assigned and set up as a spacious yard for the church. This is the present cemetery, somewhat enlarged later by descending the northwest side.

The first person "buried in the new cemetery,"[96] was Marie Larade, wife of Cyprien Deveau (Sépultien, the people say), on June 27, 1868.

This story is told about her: Marie, it seems, was bad, even terrible. Her very timid husband, naturally, became the victim of her tirades. One day when she was using the broom handle on him Sépultien hid under her bed. Marie beat on the bed and poked it, ordering her husband out from there and accompanying her orders with worse threats. "Get out from there!" He bravely answered, "No I won't come out! There is nothing like a man who has courage!" Imagine anyone hiding under a bed considering himself courageous!

The first funeral service in the church of the *buttereau* was that of Agatha (à Konock) Chiasson.

Father Chisholm was a builder. He was not satisfied with simply building a church. He also built a beautiful glebe house. Later he built another church and glebe house in Heatherton where he was sent as pastor. Still later, he completed the interior of the church in Pomquet and also built a glebe house there.

Father Chisholm left Chéticamp for the parish of Heatherton in the spring of 1866. He had been nine years in Chéticamp and had accomplished great works there. His memory is still held in reverence by the people. He died in Pomquet on February 15, 1884.

Other Gaps in the Registers

The Registers have no entries for a two-year period from 1864 to July 1866. Moreover, during his whole stay in Chéticamp, Father Chisholm kept no records of burials in the Registers. He only recorded Baptisms.

Father Louis-Romuald Fournier (1866-67)

Father Fournier, pastor of Margaree, was also named pastor of Chéticamp on the departure of Father Chisholm. He was born in Vaudreuil, Québec, on August 24, 1828. Father Fournier spent only a year in Chéticamp. From there he went on to take over the parish at Arichat, where he died on April 10, 1870.

Father C.A. Chisholm (1867-68)

Father Hubert Girroir, who was then named pastor of Chéticamp, had obtained permission to make a visit to Rome before coming to take possession of his new parish. It was during Father Girroir's trip to Rome that Father C.A. Chisholm spent the winter in Chéticamp. The records kept by him in the Parish Registers are filled with spelling errors.

Father Hubert Girroir (1867-75)

Father Girroir compares favorably with the first missionary, Father Lejamtel, in being one of the most devoted of all the priests who came to Chéticamp. He was born in Tracadie, Nova Scotia, on July 18, 1825. He first took his ecclesiastical studies in Halifax, then in Québec, where he was ordained priest by Bishop Turgeon on February 18, 1853.

In the beginning, Father Girroir was made pastor in Arichat, a post he held for ten years (1853-63), and immediately showed his great devotion to the cause of French Education. In 1856, strongly supported by his Bishop, he obtained a few Sisters from the Congregation of Notre Dame in Montréal, as well as some Brothers from Les Écoles Chrétiennes. Unfortunately, school laws of that time doomed this work to failure and these two religious teaching communities had to leave Arichat. Father Girroir was named pastor at Acadiaville in 1863 and during his stay he built another convent there.[97]

In 1867 Father Girroir was named pastor of Chéticamp. After such frequent changing of its priests, and especially after having been served by such types as McKeagney and Chénal, the parish of Chéticamp left much to be desired. Father Girroir was equal to the task. "I was sent to lead the parish, and I will lead it," he said in his first sermon without beating about the bush. He would lead his people with wisdom, for the greatest spiritual and temporal good of the parish.

On his arrival, Father busied himself with the question of schools. Profiting from the advantages in the school law of 1864, he began to fill the parish with new schools, of which two big ones were "the large school at the harbour" and "the large school at Plateau."

Thanks to the wise direction and the overflowing charity of that energetic man, the abuse of drink, as well as other vices, was quickly suppressed and good will encouraged. The Parish felt a renewal of the intense religious fervour and moral integrity of its former best days.

A strong man of great girth, Father Girroir was interested in the economic future of Chéticamp as well as the spiritual advancement of his sheep. He realized the importance the harbour of Chéticamp would have if it was made navigable by the dredging of an entrance channel. He doubled his efforts to this end and obtained the dredging of this channel from the federal government in 1874. A tangible result of this action was that the bay of Chéticamp soon became one of the most beautiful harbours of the Maritimes, assuring a shelter against every wind. Little by little, La Pointe, at the other end of the Island, was abandoned as a fishing harbour and centre for trade. The demographic geography of Chéticamp had completely changed and the present harbour has become one of the most important and most populous in the country.

In those days, when information was more difficult to acquire and the people less informed on important political questions, the pastor became the great counsellor of his flock. Most often the parish voted according to the wishes of its pastor. In the federal election of 1872 Dr. Hugh Cameron of Mabou presented himself as a candidate for the County against Samuel MacDonnell. Canadian Confederation was still a hot topic among the people at that time. Cameron led his electoral campaign against Confederation, while MacDonnell supported the new regime. Father Girroir took up the cause for Mr. Samuel MacDonnell. But Dr. Cameron, it seemed, was cousin to the co-adjutor Bishop and therefore had *his* support. The result of this affair was that Father Girroir was named to another parish in another county.

The Camerons had the nickname "Red."[98] In his last sermon Father Girroir said to his people, "I am sorry to leave you. But, I'm leaving because of a redhead, red like a red ox." And he cried.

Once out of the harbour on old Prudent Chiasson's boat, which carried him and his belongings away, Father said, "I would give all I've got, to return to the people of Chéticamp." Father went on to take care of Havre-à-Boucher. He lived there until his death on April 25, 1884.

Father Pierre Fiset (1875-1909)

The first act recorded in the Registers by Father Fiset dates from May 30, 1875. The last one dates from February 26, 1909.

Father Fiset was born in Ancienne-Lorette, near Québec, on May 28, 1840, issue of a beautiful and numerous family of which the father and mother were Joseph Fiset, farmer, and Marie-Adelaïde Gauthier. He was still a seminarian when he responded to the call of Bishop Colin Francis MacKinnon, then Bishop of Arichat, who had invited French-Canadian priests for the Acadian parishes of his diocese. Father Fiset was ordained on December 3, 1864, at Antigonish (1864-65), then pastor at Havre-à-Boucher (1865-75), and in 1875 he was named pastor of Chéticamp to succeed Father Girroir. He stayed there thirty-four years, until his death in 1909.

In his first sermon Father told the people: "If you have any sick ones in your families, come get me. [He had no horse at that time.] If you have no horse, come tell me about the sick and I will go on foot anywhere in the parish."

Father Fiset was a man of exceptional works. More than any other, this great man helped to put Chéticamp on the geographical map by his vigorous actions and the importance he has succeeded in giving it. He was one of the finest characters among the numerous French-Canadian priests who gave themselves to the diocese and who contributed so much in saving the Acadians from being anglicized.

Division of the Parish

On his arrival, one of Father Fiset's first concerns was to create the Parish of Saint-Joseph-du-Moine, up to that time considered part of Chéticamp. The southern limits of the parish of Chéticamp extended beyond Grand-Étang and Cap-du-Moine, ten miles or more for certain parishioners to travel to attend the Chéticamp church. The creating of the new parish had to be accomplished, and soon.

In 1824 Bishop Plessis of Québec had written to Father Magloire Blanchet who had consulted him on this matter:

There is nothing to stop you from building a small chapel between Chéticamp and Margaree, for the reasons that you gave. Take St. Norbert or St. Claude for its patron.[99]

However, it was only on September 8, 1879, that this project was completed; the new Parish was named after St. Joseph. From that we get Saint-Joseph-du-Moine.[100] The church was built the same year and blessed on November 16. The first pastor was Father Guillaume Leblanc. Father Joseph Marinelli is the present pastor there.[101]

This Acadian parish, totally homogeneous, has a population of eight hundred. The people make their living by farming and fishing.

The Fourth Church

The church *du buttereau*, built in 1862 by Father Chisholm, had become too small, even after the founding of the parish of Saint-Joseph-du-Moine. Besides, it was no longer central. The population was clustering more and more at the harbour since the dredging of the channel had made a magnificent seaport.

It was Father Fiset who carried out this feat of strength, this bold strike of building a new church while the still-solid stone church *du buttereau* was only thirty-one years in existence. As the materials in the old church had to be used in building the new, it had to be demolished. The last Mass was celebrated there on December 11, 1892.

We have to admit that this construction raised a great deal of opposition. The parishioners preferred to build a chapel at Petit-Étang and to repair the roof of the church, badly in need of it, than to face the task of a new construction. As often happens in these circumstances, a few individuals mounted a resistance and came well-nigh into drawing others into regrettable extremes.

But Father Fiset was the man of the hour and succeeded in convincing the people with telling facts. He bought François Chomable's house which was on the spot of the present Convent. He said Mass during the week and received visitors there to get the people used to directing their steps in that direction. In 1888 he built a spacious glebe house nearby.[102] He bought the land for the future church from Moïse and Pierre (Mitouk) Poirier. When the idea was set sufficiently in everyone's mind, Father announced his decision to build.

Five years before beginning work on the church, a levy of six dollars per family was established in the parish. When the five yeas were up, Father invited the parishioners to continue to pay the six dollars each year on their own, or to give a day's catch of fish which he, himself, would sell on his own for the benefit of the church.

Father Fiset wished to build a large and beautiful church. He called the architect, D. Ouellet of Québec, to make plans for it and entrusted the construction to Hubert Morin of Trois-Pistoles. The Robins, owners of the Island from which the stone was brought, gave this building material freely. The parishioners furnished the mortar, wood and manpower. Some years before this, the stones were transported over the ice from La Pointe-Enragée on the Island. The ice during those winters, according to the people, stayed miraculously firm. Even in the spring when it was weakening, it was still possible to transport the stones, protected by the invincible faith in the word of the priest who had said: "Haul, haul, no one will go under." And, indeed, there were no accidents to weep over.

The land for the church became a great building yard where each one expended himself without counting his time or his sweat. The people still speak with pride and emotion of those months of intense labouring where, encouraged by this ball of fire, Father Fiset, everyone gave of himself heartily and joyously.

The Morins built solidly. The Chéticantins still recall with astonishment the length, depth and width of the ditches destined to hold the foundation of the huge edifice.

The work, begun in 1892, went forward quickly. In the autumn the walls of the church were up to the window ledges and the sacristy was sufficiently completed to celebrate Mass. The first Mass took place December 18. Afterwards the church *du buttereau* was demolished for the use of its stones.

Construction, at that time, did not reach the frightening prices of today. Morin asked $27,850 to build the church and sacristy, finishing the sacristy on the inside as well . For the interior of the church he was content with $11,000-$12,000. In all, about $40,000 for a church that would cost $500,000 today. As well, it was built practically without debt. When Father Fiset undertook to collect the funds to complete the interior there remained $3,000 to pay on the church. He himself paid this debt from his own pocket, simply telling the people from the pulpit: "Someone paid it. I leave you to guess who." The interior of the church was finished in 1900.[103]

That church, built by Father Pierre Fiset with, and for, fishermen, could not be dedicated with a better patron than Saint Peter the Apostle, fisherman of Galilee. From this we derive the name of the church of Saint-Pierre of Chéticamp.

The church measured 212 feet in length and 74 feet in width. Its belfry, originally raised to 181 feet in height, had to be lowered about fifteen feet after it had been decapitated by a *suête*.

The church is a monument to the memory of Father Fiset whose body is entombed in the vault. It is also a memorial to the courage and the spirit of the Chéticantins.

Finally, this church is the glory of Chéticamp. From its elevated position on a small hill it overlooks the village and the bay. By the beauty of its Roman style and the fine workmanship of its woodwork, this church is one of the most beautiful religious edifices in the Maritime Provinces.

Teaching Sisters

One of Father Fiset's most important interests was education. Later on in our story we shall see how instruction was given in a haphazard manner. Father Fiset immediately took on the task of organizing existing schools and building others. But he had bigger dreams than that for Chéticamp; he wanted to bring in Religious teachers.

By 1900 three Religious from the Sisters of Providence of Montréal arrived in Chéticamp. Father Fiset immediately began the building of a large convent.[104] While waiting for the convent to be ready to receive them, the Sisters lived in the glebe house. Difficulties arose and the three Religious left to make a Retreat in Montréal, never to return. The facts seem to indicate that Father Fiset appreciated Sister Superior, Sister Antonin, very much, and knowing something was in the wind and that the nuns would likely not return after their Retreat, he wrote to their Mother General asking for Sister Antonin to continue in her post. "Sister Antonin, or nothing," he wrote. Mother General answered, "Nothing." The Sisters never returned. In 1903 the Filles de Jésus of Kermaria (France) came in their place and are still present in Chéticamp.

First Doctor in Chéticamp

Attentive to anything that could better the lot of his flock, by 1875 Father Fiset had convinced his brother, Napoléon Fiset, a doctor, to move to Chéticamp. Dr. Napoléon Fiset was the first doctor in Chéticamp.

Efforts at Economic Freedom

Determining on his arrival the pitiable slavery in which the Chéticantins were held by the Jerseys, Father Fiset resolved to devote himself to their economic freedom.

Ever since they had settled in Chéticamp, the Jerseys were powerful people. All the pastors up to now had not missed paying a courtesy call on the Jerseys shortly after their arrival. Father Fiset did not bother to go see them. This worried the Jerseys, so they came to visit the priest. Without beating about the bush, Father told them: "I am going to devote my life to chasing you out of Chéticamp. I have a certain amount of money to do this, and if it isn't enough, I can get more." We are sorry he let himself, later on, devote so much time to trade and business, but we must not forget the charitable and completely apostolic thoughts which led him in these pathways.

With the required permissions and the blessings of his Bishop, Father completed a gigantic task, the kind that the newspaper *L'Évangéline* could, at his death, write about: "a real easing of circumstances has replaced the straitened conditions that reigned there until the last half of the nineteenth century."[105]

Father Fiset's first enterprise was the buying of a store in 1883,[106] which he entrusted to the care of Michael Crispo, then later to Timothée Crispo, his brother-in-law, both of whom he had encouraged to come to Chéticamp from Havre-à-Boucher. This store became one of the larger stores at the harbour.

To the store he added trading in fish and animals. The huge stretch of land above the church and glebe house was covered with *vigneaux* (wire netting on posts to dry the fish). Father Fiset bought the fish at the harbour and at La Pointe, just as he did the cattle for resale on the outside market.

Later, in 1888, Father Fiset built a large wharf at the harbour, then another at La Pointe in 1904. He himself became the owner of the lobster factory that the Jerseys owned at La Pointe. He bought the flour mill situated at the head of Le Platin and gave it new life.

Father Fiset also owned a large farm with five barns, eight horses and more than a hundred cattle. He taught the people respect for the land and wished to give good example to the Chéticantins, for whom fishing had always been an obstacle in the advancement of agriculture. He himself worked long days in his overalls, breaking new ground, sowing and gathering in the harvest. With the intention of encouraging his parishioners to do as much, he preferred that the tithe be paid in produce.

Father's business was increasing, as were his properties. The Robins, having closed their business at La Pointe about 1893 in order to concentrate themselves at the harbour, no longer attached any importance to the Island. Father Fiset bought the entire Island, except for the stock on it, from them for $10,000. It was a vast territory that he pulled from the hands of the Jerseys.

As well, Father Fiset had made gigantic efforts towards exploiting all the types of mines which were opened in the nearby mountains. We have seen in the chapter on economic life the important part he played in the operation of the gypsum mine, of which he was president.

All these works and all this progress made it more and more imperative to have a transport service between Chéticamp and the outside areas. In 1886, thanks to Father Fiset's efforts, the regular service of steamboat, the *Beaver*, was obtained between Chéticamp and Pictou, thus connecting Chéticamp to a railway system. Later, Father Fiset would have his own 5,000-ton boat, the *Amethyst*.

In all this work, Father Fiset had one goal: to favour the economic expansion of Chéticamp and permit its people to live more comfortably and more humanely.

Character of Father Fiset

Father Fiset was always of a proverbial simplicity in his person and in his belongings. In spite of his great administrative qualities, of being a "mixer and shaker" of affairs, he lived within the reach of the people and easily mixed with the small and humble folk by whom he was much loved.

Father regularly invited parishioners to dine with him. The poor, as well as those most deprived of knowledge of etiquette, were quickly put at ease. Social conventions were never Father Fiset's forte. If any of his colleagues found him a bit unpolished, his humble parishioners loved him.

He greatly enjoyed a good laugh. On Sunday morning there was always a gathering at the glebe house. The men met there to tell stories, make jokes or tease one another. Father Fiset, pipe in mouth, would urge on the conversation, then roar with laughter. The time for the Mass would pass and they would continue to talk. The women would gossip in groups around the church while waiting for Father and the men. Suddenly, sometimes an hour late, Father would say: "Fine! I believe we are going to say Mass now." There was never a fixed time for it. This was a happy time when one was not rushed. Happy the parishioners whose priest was so close to them!

Father Fiset, though engrossed in a multiplicity of affairs, was a profoundly religious priest. It must be said that, at this time, the ministry was less time-consuming than it is today. The people went to Confession once a year. The most devoted went two or three times. On Christmas Day perhaps only one person would receive Communion.

Attributed to the pastor was a special power of intercession with God. It is still recalled with reverential fear, the infallible realization of his predictions, sometimes accompanied with threats. There were then, just as always, a few strong-willed people who made fun of religion and the priests. Some of them even plotted to make him travel to Broad Cove to appear before a representative of the Apostolic delegate, Bishop Sbarretti. "He has forced me to trek in the mud; he will die face down in the mud! He makes fun of the priest! One day he will greatly desire to have the priest, but it will be too late!" These are words among others Father Fiset is supposed to have uttered against some of these irreligious people. Is this the obvious scolding the Good God ordinarily inflicts on scorners of priests? Whatever it is, everyone agrees that not one of Father Fiset's utterances failed to take place.

All this encircled Father Fiset with a halo of majesty which attracted to him the respect, admiration and complete devotion of his parishioners. This was well noticed in 1901 on the occasion of his dispute with the federal deputy, Dr. MacLennan, called *la grande barbe* (long beard), who had brought Father Fiset before the tribunal of Bishop Sbarretti. The latter had delegated the Bishop of Antigonish who, in his turn, was replaced by his Vicar-General. Father Fiset and his parishioners were completely ignorant of the charges against him and the name of the accuser. But from conjecture to conjecture, the people never doubted that *la grande barbe* was responsible. Immediately a group of men organized themselves. A cavalcade of twenty-two vehicles filled with men from Chéticamp, Saint-Joseph-du-Moine and Margaree accompanied Father Fiset to Broad Cove. All were determined to defend him and be a witness if need be.

At Broad Cove the Vicar-General announced that, seeing their large number, six only, chosen by their own group, would be witnesses. Charles Broussard, William Cormier, Placide Boudreau, Patrice Cormier, Sévérin Leblanc and Joseph Deveau were chosen. This is the story told by one of the group on the subject of that inquiry:

Question: Had Father Fiset made any threats in his sermon on the preceding Sunday? *Answer*. No.

Question: Do you know So-and-So? (Two Chéticantins who went to Broad Cove as witnesses for *la grande barbe*.) *Answer*. Yes.

Question: Are they considered practising Catholics? *Answer*. They don't even make their Easter Duty.

This was enough. The group returned home in triumph with Father Fiset in the lead. At Grand-Étang a group of fifty persons awaited the news. It was night time. Even so, a great shout of joy came from the people at the good news.

Father Fiset's authority was great in the parish, not only from the point of view of religion, but also from the civil and political points of view. Many differences among the families were settled by him. As was the custom then, he played an important part in the political life of the area. Too much so, probably. He wanted the parishioners to vote as he thought they should. He even asked it from the pulpit. It was not easy to vote against him. Those who dared were afraid afterwards, though wrongly so, to fetch him for the sick. At first he was a Conservative. But in 1896 the federal deputy, Mr. Cameron, and the Prime Minister of Canada, Sir Wilfrid Laurier, being Catholics against two Protestant adversaries, Father Fiset mellowed somewhat and mixed less in politics afterwards.

Sometimes he had outbursts of temper, easily explainable. A parishioner refused to pay his tithe and wouldn't go to church. Then his wife had a baby. Old Damase Deveau, brother of the mother of the child, came to have the child baptized. "Whose child is it?" asked Father Fiset. "Germain's," replied Damase. "Get out! I'm not baptizing him!" Damase couldn't believe it. "Get out! " repeated Father Fiset, in a determined tone of voice. Damase left. He had scarcely gone when Laurent (à Delphin) Aucoin arrived in his wagon to get some nails. "Hurry, hurry," Father Fiset said to him, "take your horse and run after Damase and tell him to come back."

"When he worked in the fields or on clearing the Island, it was sometimes difficult to disturb him, even for the ministry," say the people. But this impression in the minds of the parishioners arose more from their own timidity than from the attitude of Father Fiset.

Unfortunately, great men age just as do others of lesser stature. He, who was so courageous, so interested in works of which he was the instigator, felt himself weakening in the autumn of 1908. He was sixty-eight years old. He wrote to a member of his family on November 25, "I am kept at home by weakness.... I don't feel any pain, but I have no taste for anything." For Father Fiset to admit that much, it was clearly the end. The weakness persisted. He died the following April 18, 1909.

Father Fiset remained great right up to his death. His will, written in his own hand and dated December 14, 1908, begins thusly:

Being of sound mind, I wish to dispose of my goods in the following manner:

1. To cancel all debts against Église Saint-Pierre of Chéticamp.[107]
2. I confirm the donation of the Convent to the Sisters.
3. I am transferring $5,000 to the College in Antigonish as payment for room and board for the members of my family.
4. Four hundred dollars for the Souls in Purgatory.

The rest of his goods—farms, store, Island, wharves, as well as a large sum of money—were left to his nephews and nieces.[108]

Father Fiset's body is entombed beneath the church in Chéticamp. In the actual church a tombstone commemorates him. The whole church is a monument to his memory. But the most beautiful monument of all still remains all the good he accomplished and the lasting memory he left in the hearts of his parishioners. It is with pride and emotion that the old folk still speak of "Father Fiset's time."

Father Patrice Leblanc

Father François Broussard had been sent to aide Father Fiset at the first sign of weakness of the latter. Father Broussard waited for the successor then went on to be pastor at Saint-Joseph-du-Moine.

On July 13, 1909, Father Patrice Leblanc arrived to take over the direction of the parish in Chéticamp. He was born in Margaree on January 8, 1868, son of Abraham Leblanc and Margaret Thompson. His mother was an Irish lady who had been rescued from the ocean at the age of five years on the débris of a doomed boat, the *Lady Smith*.

Father Leblanc had been ordained at an age older than usual. It was after being a schoolteacher for about twelve years that he decided to become a priest. Ordained in 1900, he was named immediately to the parish of Ingonish, remaining there nine years before being transferred to Chéticamp.

At Ingonish, Father Leblanc had built a glebe house, a parish hall, and partly completed the interior of the church. His experience came in handy in Chéticamp. Here too he built a large beautiful parish hall in 1916. The convent having burned on February 26, 1924, Father Leblanc immediately put to good use the generosity of the people and had another convent built by summer on the ruins of the other. The glebe house was renovated, the church interior was painted and its bell tower repaired. He also arranged for the building of the present high altar and the pulpit. In 1949 he had loudspeakers installed in the church. Finally, thanks to his encouragement and his kindness, the Religious of Les Filles de Jésus were able to build a beautiful, modern, forty-bed hospital in 1936.

From the national point of view, Father Leblanc, without seeming to do so, did much to give Chéticamp a French look. At this time the Post Office did not recognize any French name in Chéticamp. It was Eastern Harbour, Little River, etc. In future, thanks to Father Leblanc, the true, original French names have been put back in place: Chéticamp, Petit-Étang, La

Pointe, Plateau, etc., telling the world that Chéticamp is a French parish.

In the religious domain, the stay of Father Leblanc has also been marked by some consoling facts. First, a great number of religious and priestly vocations, as we shall see; two ordinations in Chéticamp of children actually from the parish—that of Father Ernest Chiasson on June 24, 1931, by Bishop McDonald of Vancouver, and that of Father Paul-Anselme Boudreau and Father Anselme, O.F.M. Cap.,[109] two cousins, on June 11, 1938, by Bishop Guy, O.M.I., of Gravelbourg.

The culminating point of religious demonstrations was, unquestionably, the Diocesan Eucharistic Congress, which took place in Chéticamp on September 9, 1936. Bishop James Morrison was present, along with about forty priests and a huge crowd of diocesans. Father Leblanc was well-known for his particularly difficult character, or rather, for his crotchetiness. This is the reason why the parishioners, on the whole, were never much at ease with him.

However, his devotion to ministry, particularly to the sick, was boundless. On being called to the sick, day or night, there was no storm nor any road bad enough to prevent him reaching his destination, even if the distance was six or seven miles, as it was to Cap-Rouge.

His charity towards the poor was well-known. He himself never had a cent. Besides his car, a necessity in which he took great pride, he was satisfied with very little in the way of material goods.

In 1953, at the age of eighty-five years, forty-four of which were consecrated to the parish of Chéticamp as its pastor, Father Leblanc was forced to realize he was weakening. He was wise enough to ask for help from the Eudist Fathers. Father Louis-Philippe Gagné, C.J.M., spent the winter with him. In the spring, during Sunday High Mass on May 24, Father Leblanc said his goodbyes as pastor of the parish. He retired to the hospital of Chéticamp, which he had encouraged so much to be built. He died there on September 5, 1956.

The Eudist Fathers

In the religious history of Chéticamp, one of the most important events, if not the most important, is the coming of the Eudist Fathers.

The age and health of Father Leblanc had, for a long time, no longer permitted him to respond to the needs of the parish. Unfortunately, he didn't realize this sufficiently soon enough. Some sensible parishioners realized that the situation could no longer endure and on February 23, 1953, sent a delegation to Bishop John McDonald of Antigonish to ask for the resignation of Father Leblanc and to beg His Excellency to invite a Religious community to take over the direction of the parish. His Excellency received them paternally and understood the merit of their presentation. In his accustomed manner, His Excellency did not hesitate in acceding to their request. The following March 22 Father Leblanc resigned and Father Gagné, C.J.M., was named administrator of Chéticamp. The parish was entrusted to the Congregation of the Eudist Fathers. During the summer, Father Jules Comeau was appointed pastor. On his arrival on August 1, 1953, dozens of automobiles from Chéticamp went to welcome him to the parish.

Father Jules Comeau, C.J.M.

Father Jules Comeau, born August 1, 1899, at Saulnierville, took his studies at Collège Sainte-Anne-de-la-Pointe-de-l'Église and was ordained priest on August 5, 1923, at Bathurst. At first he was a teacher for nine years and later became Superior at Collège Sainte-Anne-de-la-Pointe-de-l'Église (1937-43); after that he was rector at l'Université du Sacré-Coeur de Bathurst (1943-47). He had been pastor in each of the important parishes entrusted to the Eudist Fathers—Pointe-de-l'Église, Chandler, Chicoutimi—and assistant-pastor of the Sacré-Coeur-de-Marie parish in Québec. He was well prepared to take into his hands the guidance of the parish of Chéticamp.

The happy changes and improvements brought into the parish since the arrival of the Eudist Fathers are beyond reckoning. The glebe house has been transformed, renovated and made hospitable. The church itself was given a good going-over. To begin with, Father Gagné had already begun the improvements in changing the place where the stairs rose to the choir loft. In place of dark tunnels, favourable for wasting time, the large, open stairway no longer descended to the porches but led directly into the church. No one, the pastors even less than the parishioners, likes a church with no central aisle. Chéticamp church was one of this type. For marriages, solemn entrances and departures were impossible; for funerals, the whole ceremony took place in the back of the church. Also, as the floor of the church was old and needed repairs, Father Comeau took advantage of this to cover it with fine rubber tiles. While putting back the pews that had been taken up at this time, he had them replaced in such a way as to leave a large centre aisle.

During spring cleaning in 1957, when the interior had been freshly painted and decorated, Father Comeau had the workmen put in stained glass windows which, by their richness and colour, gave to the whole church an atmosphere of piety and contemplation. Thus the Chéticamp church is one of the most beautiful in Nova Scotia, and the numerous tourists who pass through here would not think of not visiting it.

Spiritual life and parish works have experienced a new awakening. Before, Communion was distributed on certain days, like Ash Wednesday, while today the number of Communions distributed each year surpasses 70,000. Religious ceremonies have increased; there are solemn Masses, processions, the blessing of the fishing fleet, the erection and unveiling of a monument dedicated to the pioneers of the parish, as well as a special demonstration each year for the national feast of the Assumption. All in all, these activities contribute greatly to the spiritual reawakening of the people of Chéticamp and give them a deeper pride in being French and Catholic.[110]

PRIESTLY AND RELIGIOUS VOCATIONS

WITHOUT WISHING TO ASSUME THE HONOUR of counting among her sons Bishop Patrice-Alexandre Chiasson, future Bishop of Bathurst, and Father Lubin J. Gallant (though both were born in Grand-Étang before the creation of that locality as a separate parish), Chéticamp can, just the same, boast of having given thirteen priests to the Church. Their names are:

Father Arsène Cormier
Son of Patrice Cormier and Isabelle Delaney, he was born on December 25, 1883, and was ordained priest on May 30, 1909. At first he was a professor at the College of Antigonish, then pastor at Larry's River. In 1918 he became pastor of the parish of Margaree. He died there on March 7, 1948.

The Very Reverend Father Euchariste, Capuchin
Born Médéric Leblanc, son of Placide Leblanc and Catherine Lefort, on July 16, 1884, he was ordained priest on June 10, 1917. He was missionary for ten years in Ethiopia (1917-27) and for ten years in India (1939-49). He now lives at the Capuchin Fathers' Monastery of Réparation, Montréal.

Father Théophile Maillet
Born on February 4, 1898, son of Polycarpe Maillet and Marie Romard, he was ordained priest on February 19, 1922. He died November 20, 1941.

Father Ernest Chiasson
The son of Marcellin Chiasson and Henriette Broussard, he was born on November 24, 1905, and was ordained in Chéticamp on June 24, 1931. He is presently chaplain of St. Rita Hospital in Sydney.

Father Henri Cormier, Eudist
The son of Daniel Cormier and Luce Cormier, he was born October 16, 1909, and ordained on March 31, 1934. He was, successively, rector of the Collège du Sacré-Coeur at Bathurst and of the Collège Saint-Louis of Edmundston. He presently holds the position of Assistant-Provincial.

Father Charles Aucoin, Eudist
The son of Moïse Aucoin and Mathilde Leblanc, he was born on February 19, 1911, and ordained priest on February 9, 1936. After having been the Superior of the Seminary in Halifax for several years, and rector

of the College du Sacré-Coeur of Bathurst, he is now professor of moral theology at Charlesbourg.

Father Louis-Michel Maillet

The son of Polycarpe Maillet and Marie Romard, and brother of Father Théophile Maillet, he was born on September 29, 1911, and ordained on June 24, 1936. He offered himself to the diocese of Bathurst where he is pastor-founder of the parish of St. John Bosco in Dalhousie.

Father Anselme Chiasson, Capuchin

Born Charles Chiasson, son of Timothée Chiasson and Colombe Boudreau, on January 3, 1911, he was ordained priest in Chéticamp on June 11, 1938. At present he is Superior of the Capuchin Fathers' Monastery in Moncton.

Father Paul-Anselme Boudreau

The son of Placide Boudreau and Esther Broussard, he was born on October 23, 1912, and ordained in Chéticamp on June 11, 1938. He offered himself to the diocese of Gravelbourg where he is pastor of the parish of Shaunavon.

Father Joseph Roche

Born on January 16, 1915, the son of William Roche and Louise Chiasson, he was ordained on June 7, 1941. He too offered himself to the diocese of Bathurst where he is pastor-founder of the parish of Notre-Dame-du-Rosaire in West Bathurst.

Father Daniel, Capuchin

Hector Boudreau, son of Placide Boudreau and Esther Broussard, was born on June 14, 1917, and ordained on June 17, 1945. He has been a missionary in India since 1949.

Father David, Capuchin

Brother of Father Daniel and of Father Paul-Anselme Boudreau, Alphonse Boudreau was born on April 18, 1921, and ordained on February 27, 1949. He is presently Master of Novices in Cacouna, Québec.

Father Daniel Deveau, Holy Cross Father

The son of Francis Deveau and Catherine Arsenault, he was born on December 12, 1933, and ordained on June 29, 1960. He is presently in Rome where he pursues his studies.

Another child of the parish, Joseph Deveau (Brother Hermann), is a Brother with the Capuchin Fathers.

About ten other priests, whose parents were born in Chéticamp, are scattered all over the country in other dioceses.

Finally, sixty-six Religious, natives of Chéticamp, have been counted already; some are with the Sisters of Providence and others, the larger number, are with Les Filles de Jésus.[111]

So many vocations cannot help but call down blessings from Heaven on the parish, and even on other Acadian groups of the diocese, so long deprived of Acadian priests.[112]

LES REVIRÉS[113]

WITH THE EXCEPTION OF THE JERSEYS, the Lawrences and the Matthews, the population of Chéticamp was always homogeneous; that is to say, Acadian, Catholic and French.

But towards the end of the last century some young people, having been attracted to Protestant colleges in the United States, lost their faith. Afterwards one from among this group lived in Chéticamp for fifteen years. He and his associates, who returned from time to time, worked artfully to undermine the faith of the people.

Other Chéticantins who left about 1930 to work in the United States met some Jehovah Witnesses and, inspired by the role they were offered to play there, returned some years later and became propagandists of this strange sect. Helped by agents on the outside, they were able to seduce some malcontents and the ignorant. For twenty years these fanatics have constituted a threat to the faith of the Chéticantins. Before having a meeting hall of their own, they took advantage of the absence of the men to introduce themselves, nearly by force, into the families, and there played their records and distributed their propaganda. There were some scuffles and legal proceedings. Today, especially since the arrival of the Eudist Fathers, not only is their recruiting at a standstill, but these groups are losing ground. In 1958 there were no more than seventeen families, and the other parishioners mock them for their ineptitude. Haven't they believed in the second coming of Abraham? Haven't they preached that none among them would die? Naturally, Abraham never came back! The Witnesses now have their own cemetery. But the survivors continue to hold on to other illusions.

Neglected soil becomes favourable ground for the growing of weeds. In Chéticamp religious instruction has been wanting for a long time. Error has found good ground to grow, which ignorance has well fertilized. But the test will prove, perhaps salutary, all things considered. If about ten people, influenced by this atmosphere of propaganda, have ceased to practice their religion without joining the Jehovah Witnesses, the rest of the population took notice of the necessity for a more fervent and more convinced faith. Finally, catechism is taught better in the schools of the parish, and the Eudist Fathers, since their arrival, give a sound and suitable teaching in their sermons.

CHAPTER SIX

Field of Education

Instruction in the Homes of the Pioneers and the First Schools

The governors and the missionaries of Acadia, especially the Capuchin Fathers, were deeply involved with the education of Acadian children. About 1632 the Capuchins had founded "the first regular school in all of Nova Scotia." Father Joseph du Tremblay wrote: "We place the education of our youth among the most profitable works of apostolic zeal."[1]

Provided with school staffed by Religious teachers for boys and for girls, both at Port Royal and Louisbourg, the Acadians received an astonishing education during the whole of the seventeenth century, which was quite enviable for the times, in spite of frequent attacks by the English pirates. Father Lionel Groulx wrote: "We have to ask ourselves, in what corner of the world one can find another group, at that time, capable of offering such above-average people, knowing how to read and write."[2]

The Treaty of Utrecht (1713) brought under the English flag the most important part of Acadia. From that time grew the anxiety of the Acadians, the uncertainty of the next day, the emigration to Île St. Jean (P.E.I.) for several, the terrible deportation for more than ten years, the endless wanderings without homes for the survivors, then the persecuting laws which tormented and still harass our Acadians in their native land.

The Chéticamp pioneers were children of the "Great Turmoil" during which they were born and in which they lived. Nearly all, deported youths or sons of the deported, did not even know how to sign their names. Who could reproach them for the lack?

A school law of 1766 prohibited all Catholic schools in Nova Scotia: "If any adherent to popery, or professing the religion of the Pope, is bold enough to establish a school in the province, such delinquent, for each violation, will remain in jail for three months, without privilege of deferment or bail, and will pay to the King a fine of ten pounds."[3] This law didn't bother the Chéticantins, and for good reason! Their primary concern was to subsist, to live. For a long time there was no question of schools in Chéticamp, and by the time the people were preoccupied with building any, the laws had changed.

In the very beginning, it appears that Régis Bois was one of the few who knew how to sign his name and write a little. Tradition reports that he was the primary clerk of the village. It is probably he who, in 1800, wrote the letter from the Chéticantins to Bishop Denaut asking for a priest. Several old family papers seem to be written in his hand.

About 1812 other papers appeared, written by more unskilled hands, and some of the sons of the pioneers began to be able to sign their names.[4] From where does this indication of instruction come? The missionaries.

Father Jean-Baptiste Allain, as all the missionaries of that time, spent some time giving instruction to the children. But it was Father Gabriel Champion who founded the first school in Chéticamp. Father Antoine Manseau, who had already established schools in Tracadie, and Father Cécil, still a seminarian, consecrated the winter of 1814-15 to the teaching of Catechism and plain-chant and having school classes in Cheticamp.[5] In October of 1814 the missionary, Father Lejamtel, found a young man of Chéticamp ready and willing to enter the Seminary in Québec,[6] which leads us to believe that this young man had already received an elementary education. Father Rémi Gaulin and his successors continued this worthwhile work.[7]

Each missionary of that time, although living in Chéticamp, had to serve Margaree and Baddeck as well. Their load was heavy and the time devoted to teaching greatly lessened. As soon as they could, they entrusted this job more and more to lay persons.

Among the new-arrived recruits in Chéticamp, some men knew how to read and write: for example, François Lefort, Louis Lehuidée and Jean Bourgeois from France, Jean Lelièvre and John Cartret, converted Jerseys, and others. There were probably some among them who acted as itinerant teachers, of whom tradition has kept the memory without giving us the names. We know that in the beginning the teacher went from house to house where he gathered the children of the neighbourhood and taught them the catechism and the rudiments of reading.

John Cartret must have been one of these teachers. At first an ambulant teacher, it seems he was the first person to teach school in Chéticamp. A Jersey in the service of the Robins, he left them after being converted to Catholicism, and devoted the rest of his life to teaching. Jean Bourgeois, as well, would have taught at his home and in other houses. Urbain Cormier from Chéticamp was also one of the first lay teachers. At first he taught in his home, then later in the first school for many years. He was lame, from which comes his nickname "Urbain, le Croche" (The Crippled One). The children brought him to school by sleigh in winter and by cart in summer.

All these people only taught what they themselves knew, and this amount was quite rudimentary. Urbain Cormier only taught them to read with block letters; others showed them how to read and write a little using cursive letters, as well as a bit of mathematics and Catechism.

Then came teachers from the outside, probably invited by the pastors of the parish. There was Sophique Beaudin (others say Boutin), Joséphine Thériault and Charles La France. Finally, again from Chéticamp, there were Paddy à Christine, Laurent à Suzanne Chiasson, and others whose names are forgotten.

The Books:

There was no instruction manual and very few books in these early Acadian settlements. Only the odd hymn book or religious book was to be found, preserved most carefully by the families or received from the missionaries. For a long time after having built some schools, the sole books they would have at hand would be a Bible, a "Nouveau Traité de piété," "Les Cantiques de Marseille," and others of the same type.

The First Schools

A law of 1786[8] eased the injustice of that of 1766 by granting to the Acadians some of their rights. In 1811 the government recommended the building of schools throughout the province. In 1826 it "made it obligatory to erect a school in all the important villages. Another law in 1832 provided for a provincial grant for the upkeep of each of the schools."[9] It was only after the adoption of the law of 1826, it seems, that the people of Chéticamp built their first school.

The School at Petit-Étang:

Apparently, the first school in Chéticamp was that of Petit-Étang. It was built on the property of *Pitch*, near the home of the late Patrick (à Warreck) Leblanc, at the head of the present road coming from La Prairie. This school had to serve all of northeast Chéticamp.

Later, in order to make it more central, this school was hauled to a spot near the Petit-Étang Brook.

The School at La Petite Source:

The second school, built at almost the same time as the Petit-Étang school, was that at "La Petite Source." It served all southwest Chéticamp. Later it too was hauled to a more central location, near the home of Willie (à Hélène) Aucoin. A new school has replaced it.

These schools were neither spacious nor luxurious. They were cabins in comparison with the schools of today: a single room fifteen feet by fifteen feet, with a plank along the inside wall as a bench for the students and a simple table for the teacher.

Evolution of the School System

Even if Catholic schools had been recognized and accepted at that time, nothing in the laws passed officially recognized the teaching of French. The Acadians experienced this joy in 1841: "Let it be decreed that every school, where the daily instruction could be in French, Gaelic or German in any district of this province, will have the right to an equal proportion of public money as the other schools, where instructions would be English."[10]

Up to then there did not exist any official school programme. No special degree of competence on the part of teachers was required under the law, nor specified hours for teaching either. All was left to the judgment or caprice of the teachers at the time. In Chéticamp, if anything, the teachers sinned by their overzealousness. Class began early in the morning and continued all day, without any recess, until night was coming on. The only stop was for dinner. And there was no vacation during the year, not even in the summer.

The government wished to remedy this state of affairs and put some order in teaching throughout the province. To this end, in 1854 it founded the Normal School in Truro. However, it was not obligatory to possess a certificate from this school before teaching. By the School Act of 1864 the government established a single programme for all the schools of the province, imposed its manuals and required official diplomas of the teachers.

The Free School Act

On May 10, 1864, Dr. Charles Tupper, then head of the government in Halifax, imposed the system of public schools, neutral and obligatory, throughout the province. From then on, parents would no longer pay the teacher directly for the education of the children entrusted to him. Every homeowner would pay a school tax according to the evaluation of his property. Unfortunately, by this law English became not only obligatory, but the sole language permitted in all schools. French was only tolerated from ninth grade on and was still only optional. Teaching of religion would only be tolerated during class hours with the unanimous consent of the parents. For the Acadians of the province, this was the tolling of the knell for the acquired school freedoms: their language and their faith were in danger. Finally, the régime of a unilingual body of inspectors was established—English, naturally.

In mixed areas where Catholic and Protestant, French and English, had to attend the same schools, the situation became extremely serious for the Acadian people. In Chéticamp, a totally homogeneous milieu far from the English and Protestant centres, the unanimity of the parents for the teaching of religion in the schools was not even put in question, and the teachers continued as before to teach Catechism in the schools. As for French, it continued to be taught on the edge of the law. The spelling book of the Frères des Écoles Chrétiennes and the series of readers of A.N. Montpetit were used. We honour the inspectors of that time who, although English and Protestant like John Ygunn, John McKinnon and others, understood how to temper the injustice of the law by their broad outlook and their spirit of tolerance.

The great difficulty was to find teachers with diplomas who were familiar with the situation. French teachers of the time were inept in earning their diplomas and the only teachers who could be hired with their papers were English. It was necessary to depend on this latter group while waiting for Acadian teachers with diplomas to relieve them. There was Francis MacRae of St. Rose, who later became a priest; Jim Doyle, Scottish and Catholic; John MacLeod, about 1881; Alexander MacLellan of Broad Cove; Moses Coady, future priest; Moses Doyle, future priest; Pit Coady, who became a doctor; Maurice Tompkins, a famous teacher who later became a priest; and Jimmy Tompkins, also a future priest.

These English teachers, nearly all candidates to the priesthood, were well known for their intellectual qualities and outstanding morals. Their kindness and patience are still remembered. Unfortunately, they didn't know one word of French! And the students were totally ignorant of the English language. One can easily guess the difficulties that had to surface. As an example, the teachers taught the students to ask permission to go to the privy in the following words: "Please, can I go out?" While the older students pronounced the sentence reasonably well, the younger ones crucified it until it sounded like "Piss, can I gout?" One can easily imagine the poor pedagogical results this system had to produce. The system was somewhat remedied by giving to the English teachers some Acadian assistants, taken from among the oldest students, who taught French and Catechism.

Father Girroir succeeded in obtaining the services of two Acadians from New Brunswick, Paul and Evariste Leblanc, who taught for some years, Paul at Petit-Étang and Evariste at the school of Blaise. Paul later returned to college and became a priest with the Holy Cross Congregation while Evariste had to abandon teaching for reasons of health.

During these years a large group of Acadian students from the region were qualified, obtained their official diplomas and became teachers in our schools. Among the first were Charles (à Félix) Chiasson; Alexandre Chiasson, future Bishop of Bathurst; Henri Haché, future doctor; "Petit" Lazare Leblanc; future sheriff, Joseph Doucet; future judge, Thomas Gallant; Patrice Leblanc, future pastor at Chéticamp; and others too numerous to mention who kept our schools amply supplied with teachers from the end of the last century.

Other Schools

Following the School Law of 1864 Chéticamp wished to benefit from the government grants and furnish themselves with schools more appropriate to their needs. They built, about 1866, two high schools, one at the harbour called "la grande école" and the other at Plateau, near the home of Blaise. Other, smaller schools were built at Petit-Étang, Le Lac, on the Island, and at the home of *Caniche* at Le Plé; in time came all the other schools in Chéticamp.

Religious Teachers in Chéticamp

Father Fiset, pastor of the parish, who dreamed great dreams, was always greatly concerned for his schools and the quality of his teachers. Encouraged in this by his Bishop, Bishop Cameron, he dreamed of attracting a community of Religious teachers to Chéticamp. In 1900 three Sisters of Providence of Montréal, responding to his invitation, disembarked at Chéticamp. Two years later, following some difficulties, they left. The "Filles de Jésus," a community from France, replaced them the next year (1903). They arrived on August 15,[11] yet it was only by mid-September that they were able to move into the large convent Father Fiset had built for them. Since their arrival, these Religious have attracted abundant blessings from Heaven on the region of Chéticamp. Having conquered the heart of Chéticamp by their joyous simplicity, their charity and their devotion, they have accomplished up to this time an immense good. Responding to all the needs of parish life, they have been the "right arm" of the pastors, often supplying what is lacking in these latter. Occupying themselves with training altar boys, looking after the Sacristy and the altars, singing Masses, playing the organ, directing the parish choir, directing all the women's associations in the parish, teaching Catechism for the solemn First Communions, receiving parishioners in quest of advice but too shy to go to the glebe house to see the priest, visiting the sick and consoling the afflicted are just some of the areas where the Filles de Jésus devoted themselves with a boundless zeal, responding to the requests of the pastors and the needs of the parish. Who can guess what great influence these Religious had on the people of the parish when the pastor was too old to be effective and the curates...English?

However, all this devotion was added to their principal work of teaching. Here, naturally, they played their most beautiful role and accomplished the greatest good. With a little difficulty, Father Fiset had succeeded in obtaining the closing of the large school at the harbour in order to have the pupils attend the convent school. As the other schools of the parish usually only included a single class with one instructor to teach all grades, little by little the pupils of these schools who persevered to the eighth grade enrolled at the convent for the ninth or following grades. In this way the Religious molded every generation of those who are somewhat educated, from 1903 to the present day; they have influenced all the professionals who have come out of Chéticamp; they have formed all the schoolmasters and teachers of the parish, and raised, by this fact, the teaching level of other schools; they have fostered about sixty religious vocations and more than a dozen priestly vocations. Heaven has blessed their work in granting them many vocations among the young ladies of

Chéticamp; more than fifty coming from the present Chéticamp have entered the Congregation of the Filles de Jésus.

It can be said, then, that the Filles de Jésus have markedly contributed to the safeguarding of the Faith and the French language in this corner of Acadia. As for the teaching of French, there were difficult periods of adjustment. For several years the Sisters accepted boarding students from different regions of Cape Breton. A good many of these boarders were from English families. They followed classes at the convent and, because they didn't understand French, their presence, by necessity, influenced teaching, forcing it to turn to English, to the detriment of French. Fortunately, this system of boarders has definitely ceased. There remains one danger: the still-present tendency to content oneself with the obligatory school programme and to only consider French as a way for the young to learn English. It is the temptation of easy successes and immediate results. Other Religious congregations have totally failed in their mission to this subject among the Acadians and have betrayed the French cause. The Filles de Jésus, in spite of occasional weaknesses, have reacted against the too-easy tendency to flow with the current and have been well repaid for their devotion to the French cause. There was a time when their students entered the classical colleges in the province of Québec on an equal footing, and succeeded without too much trouble. The success of their students in the international competitions of French composition, organized by the Comité Catholique des Amitiés Françaises during the year preceding the war, has earned them praise in high places. As Bishop Beaupin wrote:

> The students from the Academy of Chéticamp, who are directed by the Filles de Jésus…have always shone at our gatherings. We have received from this institution works of value…. We can state that Chéticamp maintains its reputation, acquired at our gatherings, from this shining centre of excellent French culture.[12]

There remains only to say that we hope the Filles de Jésus maintain this reputation, both for themselves and for Chéticamp.

French Inspectors and More Favourable Laws

In 1902, after a study led by a government commission on Acadian schools, a more humane law corrected, in part, that of 1864.[13] It permitted the use of French readers and the use of French in the first five grades in Acadian schools. In 1908 a French visitor, Louis d'Entremont, was named specially for bilingual schools with a "special function…to help the inspectors and superintendent in making those schools in French areas more favourable in all the reports."[14] The English inspectors, however, kept their jurisdiction over the Acadian schools. In 1926 d'Entremont was named inspector of Schools. Today there are two French inspectors in Nova Scotia: Mr. Rémi Chiasson, for Richmond County, and Mr. Alphonse Comeau, for the Counties of Clare and Argyle. Moreover, the former is an inspector for all Acadian schools in the east of the province, while the latter carries the same title for the western part. In Chéticamp itself an assistant inspector, Mr. Alphonse Saulnier, is busy looking after all the Acadian schools in Inverness County under the authority of the English inspector, Mr. Lent.

In 1939 an improved French programme was put into force:

1. For the elementary course, that is to say, up to the seventh grade, all subjects are taught in French, except for Arithmetic and English.

2. From the seventh to the tenth grade, the teaching of French and English is going on in the two languages. The history manual must be French, and that of Geography will be, too, as soon as one is found which gives a suitable summary of the Maritime Provinces. The other manuals, although drawn up in English, can be explained in French by the instructor.

3. For the academic course (10th, 11th, and 12th grades), the subjects are the same as in English schools, except for French Grammar, of which the teaching is continued until the 10th and 11th grades.[15]

This school system is difficult to apply in a mixed milieu, but that is due more to the nature of these areas than to the system itself and depends a great deal on the inspectors. It still involves for the latter the temptation to neglect French in order to go for the easy job and the immediate result. In Chéticamp, a perfectly homogeneous milieu, the present school law would allow an excellent bilingual education, if the teachers only knew it and wished to make use of it. The absence of sufficiently enlightened patriotic convictions often leads them to consider English as the magic key to all success, thereby not giving to French the level of importance it should have. However, it has been seen for some years that an encouraging new spirit has arisen in the parish schools. The inspectors and parents, as well as the teachers, must see that the young Acadians of Chéticamp fully profit from the advantages of the School Law and that, while learning English sufficiently, they learn even better their mother tongue and live proudly French.

Consolidated School

After an inquiry by the Pothier Royal Commission, on January 1, 1956, the Government of Nova Scotia approved a piece of school legislation of great importance: the consolidation of rural schools in the province and special grants to help carry out this consolidation and maintain these schools.

For a homogeneous milieu like Chéticamp, this law held only advantages. In anticipation of this law and before its promulgation, Father Comeau, supported by far-sighted parishioners, had the School Board buy the convent, the new school and the land owned by the Religious. The convent became the consolidated school, under the direction of the Sisters, for all pupils of the parish who made it to the seventh grade. A bus transported the children to and from school at the expense of the Board. The resulting benefits are already being felt. The small schools are less crowded and the teachers can give more attention to the low classes they still retain. The number of students who pursue their studies to higher levels has grown appreciably.

Up to that time, each school was administered by its own commissioners; from then on a single school board was to govern the nine parish schools. As a result, there would be more uniformity in the administration of each school and the choice of the teachers and their salary.

Since 1926 we can say that the government of Nova Scotia has applied itself with admirable energy and success to improving the school system within the province, to encouraging the building of modern schools, and of rendering justice to the French minority. Chéticamp, more than any other area, understood how to profit by these encouragements. Within the space of five years, from 1945-50, all schools were enlarged and renovated or newly constructed.[16]

In 1950 the report of the Superintendent of Education to the provincial Legislative Assembly gave to the Acadians of the Chéticamp region the following testimony:

The area that has made most progress is the northern end of the county [Inverness]. The people here are mostly of Acadian origin. With the completion of the 1950 building program this rural area in a space of ten years will have provided twenty-two new classrooms. Even a cursory survey of such development in a fishing area of this province must lead to the indication of a strong, gradual educational development.[17]

Home and School Associations

The parents themselves, pioneers in the co-operative movement in Canada, already used to taking part in their own economic affairs through numerous study clubs, could not fail to take an active interest in their schools. Some associations of parents and teachers have existed in Chéticamp for about thirty years. Each school has its own Home and School Association, and that of the convent school even had its own newspaper, *École et Famille* (Home and School), during the years 1939-40.

La Société Saint-Pierre

The New Brunswick Acadians and those from southwest Nova Scotia had an Acadian Education Association for many years. Those of Cape Breton had none.

Too far away from the group in southwest Nova Scotia to join them, a group of men, all from Chéticamp or natives of Chéticamp, decided to found an Acadian Association of Education on their own and in 1947 laid the foundation of this society. The name of this society, whose head office would be in Chéticamp, would be that of the patron of the church, La Société Saint-Pierre. The goals of this society (legally constituted in 1948) are: "to constitute in an association the Acadians of our region, that is to say, eastern Nova Scotia and Cape Breton Island, to develop among them a spirit of solidarity and fraternity, to work to conserve their heritage, to promote their intellectual, social, and economic interests, especially by encouraging by all possible means, education in subjects of descendance, or of Acadian or French origin, to all those who have the aptitudes and necessary qualifications."[18]

This society grants bursaries of $250 a year in the form of loans without interest to Acadian people "who wish to pursue college, university or specialization studies" in a French institution. In 1957 it permitted forty-seven Acadians of this area to follow their courses in higher French institutions. Disbursements in loans reached $12,000. The funds were gathered through an annual subscription in Acadian areas. Unfortunately, each year the directors have to refuse several requests for loans to some deserving students due to insufficient funds.

La Société Saint-Pierre organized an annual French contest in Acadian schools and distributed prizes to the winners. The society was concerned with all questions pertaining to life, survival, and the development of Acadians of the region: schools, adult education, founding of French parishes and requests for French pastors for these parishes. In brief, nothing was too much for this society to take on. It is the spokesman for the Acadians of the east and the sentinel guarding their interests.

Professionals and Notable Men Who Came from Our Schools

A general view of the history of Chéticamp impresses us with the dynamism and organizational sense of the inhabitants. In spite of unfavourable conditions in the past, as far as school life or economic life were concerned, they have, just the same, the most beautiful church in the diocese; they were pioneers of the co-operative movement and credit unions in the Maritimes; they profited well from the governmental programme of building schools; finally, a large group of men succeeded in becoming priests or professional men, or in establishing worthy institutions.

Other than the thirteen priests and five doctors of whom we speak elsewhere, Chéticamp was the birthplace of nine other doctors, some of whom are worthy of special mention.

Dr. Edmond D. Aucoin:

Born in Chéticamp in 1887, Edmond (à Didier) Aucoin was one of the first, along with some future priests, to overcome almost insurmountable obstacles for that time in order to follow the classical course of studies. Aided and encouraged by Father Mombourquette of Arichat, he pursued his studies at Collège Saint-Anne-de-la-Pointe-de-l'Église. When his philosophy course was completed, Edmond didn't have the means to go on to university. Being a very energetic man, he worked for the tramway company of Montréal and succeeded in this way to complete his studies in dental surgery.

In Montréal where he followed his profession, "he was the power, the driving force behind all Acadian interests...." He consecrated "even his slim financial resources to this end." He was one of the founders of the Assumption Society—"Abbé Casgrain" branch—and its main spokesman. In 1917 he founded *La Revue Acadienne*, a monthly publication whose purpose was "to have the élite of Québec know the beautiful qualities and noble origins of the Acadian people."

In 1920 the University of Montréal recognized his worth and his capacities and awarded him the new seat of Acadian history that it had opened.

"Unfortunately, Dr. Aucoin's health began to break down due to the hardships of his lifestyle, his overwork and the mishaps he suffered."[19] He developed tuberculosis. In 1923 he had to leave Montréal with his family to go to Glace Bay, Cape Breton. He died there on July 16 of the same year.

Dr. Edmond L. Aucoin:

The son of Lazare Aucoin, Edmond was born on October 12, 1893. The winner of a bursary from La Société l'Assomption, he obtained his Arts degree in 1912 from Collège Sainte-Anne-de-la-Pointe-de-l'Église. His medical studies, begun in 1912 at the University of Montréal, were interrupted by military service and not completed until 1920. After winning a bursary from the Comité France-Acadie de l'Alliance Française, Dr. Edmond left for Paris to study under the French masters Drs. Lubut Barbon Laurens, Sébileau, Bourgeois, Hautant and Lemaître to become a specialist in otology-rhinology-laryngology. He was a student from 1925-30, then an assistant of Professor Chevalier Jackson of Philadelphia, the great master of broncho-esophagoscopy. On his return to Montréal in April 1931 he became chief of the broncho-esophagoscopy services of Notre-Dame, Sacré-Coeur, and Sainte-Justine hospitals, as well as doctor-consultant of other hospitals affiliated with the University of Montréal.

In 1924, on the request of his tutor, Lemaître, Dr. Aucoin acted as liaison between the laryngologists of Paris and Drs. Sheehan and Smith of the United States in order to organize, in Paris, a teaching centre for English-speaking doctors, particularly those from the United States, and thereby introduce French clinics to them. Dr. Lemaître retained the services of his bilingual assistant, Dr. Aucoin, as interpreter in French and English for the courses given to his students from several different countries.

Functioning as liaison and interpreter led Dr. Aucoin to translate two works of Chevalier Jackson: *Maladies de l'oesophage* and *Bronchoscopie et oesophagoscopie*. Finally, his own competence allowed him to publish some studies that were very much appreciated by specialists.[20]

Unfortunately, a fatal accident put an end to the brilliant career of this Dr. Edmond Aucoin and permanently removed him from medical science. He drowned on July 19,1931, at Côteau-du-Lac (Soulages, Québec).

Dr. Jean Cormier:

Son of Guillaume (William) Cormier and Catherine Roche, Dr. Jean Cormier was born October 4, 1899. After he completed his classical studies at College Sainte-Anne-de-la-Pointe-de-l'Église, he enrolled at the Faculté de médecine de l'Université Laval in Québec. When his studies in general medicine were completed, Dr. Cormier decided to specialize in ophthalmology-otology-rhinology-laryngology and, for this, he went on to continue his studies in the world-famous universities of Chicago, Paris and Vienna. On his return from Europe he established himself in Sydney, Cape Breton, where he practices his profession among the people of eastern Nova Scotia.

Besides his medical competence, which benefited the people of Chéticamp, Dr. Jean Cormier has another role, particularly recognized by the Acadian population of Cape Breton. After his arrival in Sydney, rather than secluding himself in an enviable personal security, he has been the unobtrusive but tenacious spirit behind the Acadian survival in the diocese of Antigonish. Without fanfare but with determination, he is not afraid of hitting the bull's-eye when necessary or taking the lead in delicate matters. He has played an important role in actively collaborating in all the works of survival, such as the founding of La Société Saint-Pierre, the awakening of La Société l'Assomption, and the founding of the Acadian Club Champlain in Sydney. Dr. Cormier also took steps to obtain French parishes where there is a sufficient number of Acadians. His perseverance in devoting himself, even in apparently hopeless circumstances, is an example and an encouragement for the too-rare leaders among the Acadians of Cape Breton.

Other Doctors

Two children of Chéticamp have recently completed their medical studies at Laval University in Québec. These are Joseph-Daniel Chiasson, son of Placide Chiasson and Hélène Lefort of Petit-Étang, and Didace-Charles Bourgeois, son of Calixte Bourgeois and Annie Aucoin from the harbour. The two pursued their classical studies at Sainte-Anne-de-la-Pointe-de-l'Église and are presently resident doctors at Hôtel-Dieu in Chicoutimi.

Other Chéticantins, having left Chéticamp at an early age, became doctors in the United States but did not return. They were Tim (à Laurent) Chiasson, Johnny (à Lazare) Leblanc, brother of Dr. William, and, finally, a son of Germain (à Konock) Chiasson. Timothée (à Hippolyte) Leblanc became a veterinary doctor, also in the United States.

Notable Men in Other Fields

Alexandre Boudreau:

Son of Placide Boudreau and Esther Broussard, Alexandre Boudreau was born February 9, 1910. A particularly brilliant student at the high school in Chéticamp, he worked for two years as teller and accountant at the Royal Bank of Canada after completing his course. He resigned this job in order to benefit from a bursary from the College de Lévis where he took his classical studies. In 1930 he went to l'École d'Agriculture of Sainte-Anne-de-la-Pocatière where he obtained his Science degree in Agriculture *magna cum laude* in 1933. In 1934 he became an agronomist in Inverness County for the Nova Scotia Department of Agriculture. Immediately he worked in direct collaboration with the Department of People's School Studies, newly begun at the University of Antigonish. Mr. Boudreau took special courses in adult education and in organizing co-operatives. He founded several credit unions, as well as some producer and consumer co-operatives in eastern Nova Scotia.

In 1938 Mr. Boudreau accepted the post of professor of the education of adults and the organization of co-operatives at the High School of Agriculture and Fisheries at Sainte-Anne-de-la-Pocatière, Québec.

He founded the Social and Economic Services of Sainte-Anne. Director of Adult Education in all fishing regions, he organized six-week courses to create local leaders for education of adults; more than 1,100 students have taken his courses.

It is he who completely organized the Pêcheurs-Unis du Québec, a federation of thirty-eight fishing co-operatives with more than 4,000 members. During the war these co-operatives had an average turnover of $3,000,000. Mr. Boudreau has been, in turn, organizer, secretary-general and director-general of that organization, while still carrying out his work of teaching and directing the People's School courses.

In 1942-43 Mr. Boudreau benefited from a Littauer bursary from the School of Public Administration for university graduates of Harvard University. He obtained his Masters Degree in Public Administration and specialized in adult education. He then returned to continue his work at Sainte-Anne-de-la-Pocatière.

In 1948 Mr. Boudreau was invited to Paris by UNESCO as an expert advisor on the basic problems of education in underprivileged countries. In December of that same year he became a member of the Civil Service Commission of Canada.

On the occasion of his departure from Sainte-Anne-de-la-Pocatière, and his resignation as secretary-general and administrator of Pêcheurs-Unis du Québec, one of his closest colleagues wrote in the newspaper *A Pleines Voiles*:

His departure left such a great emptiness among the organized fishermen that we cannot, no, we will not let him go without telling him how much he will be missed by the fishermen who owe him so much, and by all those whom he has directed, encouraged, and inspired for ten years, in the pursuit of a liberating work, fraught with numerous difficulties.

Mr. Boudreau's name is, henceforth, linked more than ever to the historical relief of the fishermen of the province. For ten years he undertook the arduous task of lifting the fishermen out of their misery to the level of desiring to be leaders of their own destiny. A gigantic task. He undertook it with a conviction and an enthusiasm which bridged all obstacles. We can hardly imagine, with the progress made since that time, the farsightedness, the tenacity, and, especially, the powers of persuasion that he had to use to succeed. Only those who were at his side know how often his many talents saved the situation.

And for those who were his associates in the fields of education and organization, Mr. Boudreau will remain in their minds, a leader of the first order, a clear-sighted counsellor, a widespread organizer and a social apostle of outstanding merit.[21]

In 1951 Mr. Boudreau directed a three-member UNESCO educational mission to Pakistan. Over a period of four months he did a complete study of educational problems for adults in Pakistan and drew up a detailed report containing his recommendations for UNESCO and the government of Pakistan. In 1955 he led a United Nations mission of technical aid on public administration in Cambodia.

With all that, Mr. Boudreau continued to give courses in public administration at the universities of Laval and Ottawa. On March 15, 1957, he was named Consul-General of Canada in Boston.

His dynamic and ready-to-work personality was always badly suited to the role of official, despite the important work he accomplished. The diplomat's role pleased him even less. Thus, after a year as consul in Boston, he tendered his resignation.

In September of 1958 Mr. Boudreau accepted a post more to his taste—that of Professor of Public Administration and Director of the Extension Department of the University of Sudbury, Ontario. Finally, in 1960 he returned to Acadia as Principal of Extension Services at the University of Saint-Joseph in Moncton.

William Lefort:

Born on May 9, 1908, son of Baptiste Lefort and Marie Broussard, William Lefort took his classical studies at Sainte-Anne-de-la-Pointe-de-l'Église and from there to Sainte-Anne-de-la-Pocatière for his Bachelor of Science degree in Agriculture. An agronomist representing the Nova Scotia Department of Agriculture in the northern part of Inverness County from 1938-55, he directed his devotion, not only to helping our farmers, but also to all our Acadian causes in Cape Breton. It was with deep regret that we saw him leave in 1955 to accept a more advantageous post in Weymouth as agronomist for all of Digby County.

Léo Chiasson:

Son of Ephrem Chiasson of Chéticamp, Léo Chiasson was born on May 14, 1918. After outstanding studies at Chéticamp high school, he entered the university at Antigonish in 1934 and received his Arts degree *summa cum laude* in 1938, and his Science degree in 1940, with the highest marks ever given by that university.[22] After receiving a bursary from the National Research Council, he continued his studies in Biology, especially in genetics, cytology and pathology of plants, at the University of Toronto. He graduated with his Doctorate of Philosophy (Ph.D.) from the University of Toronto and is now a brilliant professor at St. Francis Xavier University in Antigonish.

And others

Several others have taken their classical studies or occupied honourable positions in their respective fields. We mention, in passing, Joseph (à Charles) Boudreau, District Manager at Trois-Rivières, Québec, for Mutual Life Insurance Company, and whose daughter, Thérèse, won the Prince of Wales Prize in 1944; Patrice Boudreau, who took his studies in France and was one of the founders of the newspaper, *Le Lien*,[23] in Montréal; Amédée Aucoin, who was Inspector-General of Customs at the port of Montréal, two sons of whom are priests, Father Pierre Aucoin, Congregation of White Fathers of Africa, and Bishop Louis Aucoin, pastor of the Cathedral in Montréal.

Finally, seven or eight children of Chéticamp are presently following their studies at the university in Antigonish, and a dozen more are attending College Sainte-Anne-de-la-Pointe-de-l'Église.[24]

A Reverend Mother Provincial

Since 1958, a daughter of Chéticamp, Louise Boudreau, Sister Marie Laurentia in Religion, has directed the destinies of the Acadian province of her congregation, Les Filles de Jésus, as Mother Provincial.

CHAPTER SEVEN

Health

FOLK MEDICINE

WE LIVE IN AN AGE of highly developed hygiene. We pasteurize milk, wrap food in cellophane and sterilize everything possible. We wonder what our grandparents did to avoid germs. It is likely that the salty sea air had a salutary effect on everything, explaining the vitality and longevity of our people.

At eighty years of age, and even eighty-five, some people still continue to fish, and walk miles with a lively step from their homes to church. Some of them still do the haying and cut grass with a scythe up to the age of ninety-three or ninety-five years.

For a whole century after their arrival, the people of Chéticamp were without a doctor. This makes it easy for us to understand the importance of folk medicine in their lives.

Today we rely on the medical profession for anything to do with illness, remedies, cures, and even death. But in the beginning of our community everyone had to be self-reliant. Each family knew by heart and preserved in its memory a list of remedies for the most common milder illnesses, such as fevers, boils, asthma, stomach aches, cuts and burns. For the more difficult cases there were practitioners of folk medicine, experts in whom the people had complete confidence, often well-deserved. We can still remember old Bastienne; Julienne (Mrs. Blaise Deveau); Clothilde Chiasson; Marie MacKinnon (called *Marie docteur*) and her mother; Donathilde Ryan, wife of Marcellin Deveau; the wife of old Romuald Doucet from Le Moine who was famous; Jules Deveau, whose panacea for all ills consisted in making one sweat. There were some *emmancheux* or *rebouteux* (bonesetters) who could set bones or dislocated limbs so well there would remain no trace of a break. The people still speak of Cécime Deveau and old Timothée Chiasson. The latter also possessed the art of relieving the *estomacs à bas* (dropped stomachs).

135

On the whole, remedies were natural ones. That is to say, they were based on medicinal herbs and the bark of certain trees, most often given in the form of concoctions or *sirouanes* (plasters) of various kinds. Many of these remedies were just as well known in other regions, for example, the Gaspé.[1] Some are still widely and effectively used. On the other hand, other remedies relied heavily on superstition, accompanied by magical rites, without any connection to cause and effect, such as rubbing an aching tooth with a nail which is driven into a tree, or rubbing warts with small stones that are put into a bag and thrown behind one without looking, or spitting under a stone to make signs of fatigue disappear after a race. Superstitions are tenacious. Though the people no longer believe in them, these practices still exist.

Catalogue of Folk Medicine

It is impossible to give here a complete list of popular remedies known and used in the early days of Chéticamp. The list would be too long. Even though the basic elements in each were often the same, the preparation of these remedies frequently varied from one family to another. Just the same, we believe this short list will give an idea of types of remedies used.

Aphte (Aphta) (Ulceration of the Mouth): Boil small yellow roots[2] and drink the juice. – For open sores on the lips, use a poultice with roots not crushed or boiled. – For ulceration of the gums, chew the bark of the black spruce tree or the bark of the larch tree. Good for strengthening the gums.

Appétit (Appetite): Drink a concoction of the bark of the wild cherry tree[3] or of the cormier tree (mountain ash) steeped in hot water.

Asthme (or "courte haleine") (Asthma): Drink a concoction of roots of boiled burdocks, or the roots of the sarsaparilla, or one of boiled fern (*Athyrium angustum*). – Take the height of the sick person. Cut a lock of his hair. Go into the woods, find a hidden tree and drill a hole in it at the same height as the sick person; put the lock of hair into this hole. When the patient grows past this mark, he is cured.

Bronchite (Brochitis): Put on a camisole of red flannel.

Brûlures (Burns): Rub with oil of Saint Thomas (an industrial oil from Dr. Thomas). – Place leaves from the beech tree on the burn. – Put on the burn the birchbark that can be found under the first layer of thick bark. – Apply some bluing for washing clothes. – Apply a salve prepared according to the following method: scrape a branch of the elder tree; to this scraping add one-half pound of butter, one-half pound of shortening and a small lump of borax. This salve is also good for cuts, scratches and heat rash. – Linseed oil can also be used: place a small cloth on the wound and put oil on the cloth, which soaks it in, releasing just the right amount to the wound. – Apply melted chicken fat. – Apply a poultice made of grated potatoes. – Apply a poultice made up of Minard's Liniment, baking soda and vanilla.

Health

Calvitie (Baldness): Every day, comb strongly whatever amount of hair you have. – Rub head often, and roughly, with a cloth.

Cassures (Fractures): Boil some catkin bark until a thick residue is left and make a poultice. Renew it every three days.

Chancre (Cankers): With a small rag apply to the sore some very thick and strong detergent made with ashes from the hardwood tree. Sophique, wife of Benjamin Poirier, and her daughter Marie still remain famous for their ability in this field.

Choléra (or "corps changé") (Cholera): Drink a concoction of boiled root of raspberry canes. – Milk boiled with nutmeg can be used. – Eat a thin, soft paste. – Chew a piece of newspaper. – Drink a glass of brandy containing pepper. – Take a drink of strong ginger.

Coliques (Colic): Drink ginger water. – Drink peppered water. – Drink anise syrup. – Take nutmeg. – Apply hot compresses. – Flour softened in water with salt added: one spoon of flour, two spoons of water and some salt.

Coqueluche (Whooping Cough): Apply hot flannels. – Take syrup made of molasses and sheep fat. – Apply a poultice of yeast (hops). – Take an infusion of baume (balsam plant found along streams; *Mentha arvensis*, garden mint). – Take a mixture of kerosene and sheep fat. – Drink onion juice, steeped in water and sugar. – Drink the juice of linseed grain soaked in lukewarm water. – Drink a syrup made of brown sugar and the juice of lamb droppings.

Cors (Corns): To make it easier to remove them, cover them with castor oil.

Coupures (Cuts): To stop the blood, apply a flattened puff-ball to the wound. – Apply spider's webs to the wound. – Apply some *herbe à la coupure* (*Sedum Roseum*, pink stonecrop). – Apply a poultice of turpentine (liquid oil and skin from the fir tree). – Apply chewing tobacco spittle. – Wash with a liquid made by boiling the bark from the larch tree. – Apply sawdust. – Apply heavy thick cream, the older the better. This is good for all kinds of bad wounds.

Crevasses, gerçures (Chapped Hands, Cracked Skin): Apply poultices of turpentine. – Apply urine.

Déplacement (du bébé dans le sein de sa mère) (Wrong Position of Baby in Womb): To the mother, who must stay in bed for nine days, apply a covering of garlic mixed with the ends of green ribbons.

Dent, Mal de (Toothache): Put soda or a clove in the tooth. – Apply a hot flannel to the jaw. – Soak feet in lukewarm water. – Carry a pumpkin stalk in your pocket. – Rub a nail on the tooth, then go drive it into a tree out of sight of others. When the bark of the tree passes above the head of the nail, the tooth falls out. – Rub a grain of salt on the tooth and throw it into the stove, but run away quickly, so as not to hear it crackle.

Eczéma (Eczema): Wash with borax.

Empoisonnement (Poisoning): Drink milk or a mixture of milk and mustard. – Eat dry bread.

Empoisonnement à un membre (called "la marine") (Infection of a Limb): Place a poultice of seaweed on the infected part (dangerous if too strong). – Poultice of rolled oats boiled in milk with two or three leaves of ground plantain and linseed oil. Completely cover the infected limb with this poultice and change it once a day.

Enflures (Swellings): Wet with warm vinegar. – Wash in hot water. – Mustard poultice. – Poultice of large onions. – Poultice of tansy. – Poultice of rolled oats softened in cold water.

Engorgement (Congestion): Boil the bark of the catkin to a syrupy consistency and make a poultice of it. – Wind some marline, dipped in oil, around the wrist three times. This oiled line is called *rupianne*. – Wind an eel-skin very tightly around the wrist.

Enrouement (Hoarseness): Drink kerosene mixed with molasses. – Drink boiled peppermint (peppermint, *papermane*, bought in small squares or pulled from a plant that grows along streams). – Drink liquid made from molasses and onions. – Poultice of yeast on the stomach. – Drink hot milk containing a pinch of grape and some brown sugar.

Entorse (torsaillure) (Sprains): Boil to a syrupy consistency the bark of the catkin and make a poultice. – Wash with hot vinegar. – Wash with hot water. – Wrap the sprained limb with packing material. – Wash in salted water or pickling brine. – Wrap the limb with eel-skin.

Érysipèle (Erysipelas—fever and severe skin inflammation caused by an acute bacterial disease): Wrap around the neck a stocking worn that day on the left foot. – Put hot ashes in a stocking and wrap the stocking around the neck.

There were two types of erysipelas with appropriate remedies for each: *red rash*—a poultice made with hot flour; *white rash*—a poultice made with cold flour.

Estomac, Maux d' (Stomach Ache): Chew the gum of the *pruce blanc* (silver spruce). – Take soda; a teaspoon in half a glass of water.

Estomac, Brûlures d' (coeur à son) (Acid Stomach, Heartburn): Light a match, extinguish it and chew the burned end. – Eat charcoal from the stove. – Drink sweet milk. – Take soda.

Estomac à bas (estomac descendu) (Dropped Stomach): A poultice of resin gum, sprinkled with sulphur and pepper and heated with a poker.

Faiblesse (Weakness): Go to bed. – Wash with cold water.

Weakness after a birth—take the *médecine de chien-dent:* a liquid made from corn and couch-grass.

Fatigue, Points de (Signs of Fatigue): Lift up a stone, spit under it and replace the stone. – Spit on a stone, then throw it as far as possible into another field.

Health

Femme qui allaite (Woman who is Breast-Feeding): A tonic for this is one or two glasses of liquid made from allowing corn to boil for three hours in a gallon of water into which has also been put a *brichetée*[4] (a fistful) of roots from the couch-grass plant and three pieces of bark of shrubs. As the water boils and tends to evaporate, add more water in order to always maintain the very same amount. Then it is necessary to strain the liquid and add to it a lump of ginger about the size of a pea, and a teaspoon of cream of tartar. Drink two bottles of this as quickly as possible. Afterwards, take a purge; then drink the rest of the remedy.

Feu Sauvage (Cold Sores): Chew small yellow roots (coptis, probably the savoyanne).

Fièvres (Fevers): Boil turkey plant root and drink the juice. – Drink the juice made from burned bread. – Put *tailles* (slices) of onions in one's stockings under one's feet. – Place slices of onions on the *bancs de chassis* (window ledge). This draws out the fever. – Put two spoons of cream of tartar in a half-glass of water, stir it and drink the liquid as you feel thirsty.

Furoncles (Boils): Put on these a poultice of plantain and lard. – A poultice of bread scalded in milk or sour cream. Some would add lard to this. – To pull out the core of a boil, a suction system was used: Fill a bottle with boiling water, empty it quickly and immediately apply the hot neck of the bottle to the boil. This pulls out the heart of the boil. – Apply large onions to the boil. – Scald cabbage leaves and place them on the boil. – Put a poultice of soap and molasses on the boils. – Use a poultice of leaves from the tops of the larch tree. – Apply bacon rind to the boil.

Gale (Scabies): Apply a grease made of tar, salt, sulphur, lard and soot from the stove.

Gorge, Mal de (Sore Throat): Swab the throat with kerosene. Rinse with alum soaked in water. – Rinse the throat with brine or salted water. – Wrap a stocking full of ashes around the neck. – Wrap a stocking containing onions around the neck.

Grippe (Flu) (see *Rhume*): Drink the liquid made by boiling bark from the black spruce or the larch tree in water.

Hoquet (Hiccups): Drink seven mouthfuls of water without taking a breath, i.e., without inhaling. – Say seven times without taking a breath, "I have the hiccups. God gave them to me. They are gone."

Jaunisse (Jaundice): Scald lice and drink the juice. – Soak milk-weed from the fields[5] in warm water and drink three glasses a day.

Oreilles, Mal d' (Earache): Soak feet in warm water. – Blow smoke in the ear. – Put into the ear fresh hot milk. – Put into the ear warm drops of olive oil. – Use drops of water from the ash tree (water which drips from the logs one has put into the stove). – Drop of boric acid.

Purger (Purges): Eat some pimbina berries (flat red berries that grow in a boggy area, as do cranberries). – Eat rhubarb root.

Reins, Mal de (Lumbago): A poultice of sap from the white spruce tree, with sulphur and pepper.

Rhumatisme (Rheumatism): Rub with kerosene and butter. – Rub with vinegar and hot water. – Wash with hot, salted water. – Keep warm with bags containing oats. – Keep warm by using packing. – Apply a poultice of tar on the feet. – Drink a cup of spirits of turpentine. – Drink vinegar. – Drink three eggs.

Rhume (Colds): Drink egg yolks sweetened with brown sugar. – Drink lemon. – Eat garlic. – Melt sheep suet and add molasses; drink it or rub oneself with it. – Drink molasses containing pepper.

Rompu, Enfant (Ruptured Child): Using wedges, split an ash tree lengthwise, without cutting it down or killing it, and open it enough so that the child can pass through; have the child pass through this hole, then close the ash tree, wrapping it all around to cure it. When the tree is cured, so is the child.

Roses (Measles): Poultice of warm flour. Leave it on for a long time without removing it. When the flour covers all the skin, the measles are cured. Don't expose the infected part to the air. – Wash with urine and vitriole.

Sang: Arrêter le sang, voir Coupures (Blood: to stop the blood): see *Coupures.*

    Nosebleed—Place a paper cork on the palate of the mouth. – Throw water on the neck by surprise.

    To strengthen the blood—Boil branches of the *sapin-trainard* (*Taxus canadensis*, trailing yew tree, box-pine, yew tree from Canada), save the liquid and drink after very meal. It can be drunk hot or cold. This remedy was good for pregnant women, but could bring on an abortion if the dose was too strong.

Scorbut (Scurvey): Scald the seeds of the *haricots* (*Tsuga canadensis*, hemlock trees, spruce) and drink the liquid when it is lukewarm.

Tête, Mal de Tête (Head, Headache): Rub pieces of potato and some pepper into the hair. – Put white liniment on the head and encircle the head with blue paper. – Wrap the head in a kerchief. – Wash the head in hot water.

    Tête ouverte—"When the children cried a great deal and turned their heads backwards, they were said to have *la tête ouverte,*"[6] a type of meningitis. Remedy: Wrap a green ribbon around the head of the child in the following way: a circle of green ribbon all around the head with two green ribbons crossing each other on top of the head in the form of a cross.

Tuberculose—maladie crachante (Tuberculosis—a spitting illness): Take a drink made from the bark of the larch tree, to which maple syrup has been added. – Some honey in rum.

Ver solitaire (Tapeworm): Eat pumpkin seeds.

Verrues (Warts): Rub the warts with brook-weed before sunrise and after sunset, then hide this brook-weed somewhere. – Rub the warts with a grain of salt and have another person throw the salt into the stove, so as not to hear the salt crackle. – Rub each wart with a bean, put the beans into a bag, then leave the bag along the roadside. Whoever picks up the bag catches the warts. – Rub with the beans, which are then thrown far away. When the beans decompose, the wart disappears. – Rub the wart with a piece of meat that is then buried. When the meat decomposes, the wart disappears.

Vessie, Maladie de la (Illness of the Bladder): Drink the juice made by boiling bean pods. – Drink the juice made by boiling the herb patience (*Rumex Crispus*, crisp patience plant).

Yeux (Eyes): Poultice of tea leaves. – Wash the eyes with tea. – Wash the eyes with saliva.

Epidemics

About 1795 an epidemic caused the death of many children.[7] In 1817 a terribly contagious fever settled on Chéticamp and the surrounding region. At least two-thirds of the population was bedridden with it. Several of them died.[8] There were other epidemics, such as smallpox, the Spanish flu and a few cases of typhoid fever.

The lack of hygienic conditions has allowed tuberculosis, called in this region *la maladie crachante* (the spitting illness), or *consomption* (consumption), to make frequent attacks on the area. When it occurred in a family, all or nearly all of the members of the family caught it. Tuberculosis was an illness against which folk medicine was helpless. It was the same for illnesses like appendicitis or advanced cancer.

Midwives

From the very beginning of the settlement, as well as for a long time after the arrival of the doctors, there were midwives in Chéticamp. Jeannette Dugas, wife of Pierre Bois, and probably the first white women to put her foot in Chéticamp, was a midwife. These midwives were probably competent in their work, as were all professional midwives. But at this time hygienic conditions left a great deal to be desired. Also, the mortality rate after a confinement was higher than in our day. About 1830 we see in the Parish Registers one or two deaths each year of a mother in childbirth. These deaths were likely due to puerperal fever.

Veterinary Medicine

Chéticamp had never had real veterinarians. However, one can still remember a type of veterinarian, Israel Mercure, called in this area *docteur à cheval* (horse doctor), whom one willingly consulted for humans as well. He emigrated to Cadré, Newfoundland. Today, for the worst cases, a veterinarian has to be brought in from elsewhere. The Chéticantins did not neglect their animals, however; for sick animals, as for humans, folk remedies were used. Following is a list of some illnesses with corresponding remedies:

Les barbes (Barbs): A more or less long mucous growth, more or less flat or conical, existing in the mouth of all bovines; they are susceptible to inflammation, especially in the winter.[9] Cut these barbs with scissors and rub the wound with a doorknob.

Bosses sur le dos (Humps on the Back): These humps are caused by maggots (blowflies) that lay their eggs on the surface of the skin. These maggots pierce the skin under which they lodge. Put sewing machine oil on the hump. This kills the larvae which can then be easily removed.

Cornes, Mal de (Illness of the Horns): Pour a spoonful of oil of St. Thomas (oil from Dr. Thomas) into each ear of the animal.

Entorse (Sprain): Wash the affected limb often with cold water, for a long time.

Farcin (Farcy): Rub the piglet with buttermilk; or with kerosene oil and a bit of black poison.

Le flo (fléau) d'une vache (Plague of a Cow): Lumbago is the nature of this illness. Cut the skin seven or eight inches in length on the back of the animal and put soot made from the hardwood tree under the skin.

Gourme (Nasal Drip): When a horse has nasal drip it is necessary to put a few spoonfuls of tar in his oats.

Méchant, Ôter le (removing the evil): When the animal, especially the horse, had bad blood, a bloodletting was done on him.

Poux (Lice): Brush the animal, while dipping the brush in the following solution: linseed oil, kerosene, and black poison, or simply use electric oil from Dr. Thomas.

Purgation (Purging): Make the animal take Epsom Salts with molasses, soda, and a small amount of ginger in a bucket of water.

Remeuille (pis, mamelle), Mal de (Illness of the Udder): Rub udder with water from a whetstone, i.e., water from the whetstone after it has been used to sharpen an axe.

Ringe, Ronge, Rumination (Loss of Cud-chewing): When a cow ceases to chew her cud, she is made to chew a salted herring to make her begin chewing her cud again.

Rognons, Mal de (Kidney Ailment): Give an enema.

Vartigo (Vertigo, Dizziness): The animal with this illness has a tail that is withered and dry. Split the tail, put tar on the wound, then bandage it.

Vêlage (Calving): If a cow is late in calving, put a bag of oats or hot water on her back. When she has calved, purge her with boiled tansy.

THE DOCTORS

Dr. Napoléon Fiset

It was due to Father Fiset that the first doctor was invited to Chéticamp. While serving Havre-à-Boucher, he succeeded in convincing his

Health

brother, Dr. Napoléon Fiset, to set up his practice in Arichat. When Father Fiset went on to work in Chéticamp in 1875, he took his brother with him.

Dr. Napoléon Fiset had married an Acadian girl from Arichat, Maria Forest. All the Fisets in Chéticamp are descended from them.[10] Dr. Fiset was paralyzed for many years before his death in 1900.

Dr. Henri Haché

The son of Clément Haché and Félicité Leblanc of Chéticamp, Dr. Henri Haché took his studies in Louisville, Kentucky, and later in Baltimore, Maryland. After arriving in Chéticamp in 1894, he only practiced his profession there for three years. He then emigrated to Somerville, Massachusetts, where he died in 1918. Dr. Haché had been married twice—the first time to Henriette Leblanc, daughter of Lazare Leblanc of Petit-Étang, and secondly to a widow from Somerville.

Dr. Louis Fiset

Because Dr. Napoléon Fiset had become incapacitated, his brother, Father Fiset, invited one of his nephews, Dr. Louis Fiset (son of Louis), to come take over his uncle's practice in Chéticamp. Dr. Louis Fiset accepted the invitation and served Chéticamp for twenty years, from 1897 to 1917. He then emigrated with his whole family to Sainte-Luce-sur-mer in the province of Québec. In 1926 he moved on to Limoilou, Québec, where he died in 1934. He had married Marie East of Saint-Augustin, near Québec.

Dr. William Leblanc

In 1908 a native of Chéticamp completed his medical studies at the University of Chicago (and at Baltimore) and arrived to set up his practice in Chéticamp. He had married Veanie Gay of Boston. Dr. Leblanc, born in 1876, was the son of Lazare Leblanc and Résine Leblanc of Petit-Étang. He was a brilliant and devoted doctor. Unfortunately, it was thought that he had lost his faith. On the doctor's departure in 1923, Chéticamp regretted the departure of an amiable doctor, devoted as he was, and particularly competent. He went on to Ochelata, Oklahoma, where he has practiced medicine ever since.

Dr. Léo Leblanc

The successor of Dr. William Leblanc was Dr. Léo Leblanc. The latter was born at Margaree Forks in 1890. An alumnus of St. Francis Xavier University in Antigonish, he was a teacher for five or six years before enrolling at Dalhousie University in Halifax as a medical student. Dr. Léo Leblanc practiced medicine at Belle-Côte, Margaree, for a few years. He had only been set up in Dominion, near New Waterford, for a month when he was invited to take over Dr. William Leblanc's place in Chéticamp. Dr. Léo married Marie-Louise Thériault of Arichat, with whom he had three daughters, Claire, Patricia and Edith, and a son, Edgar. Dr. Léo Leblanc, like his predecessors, was outstanding for his great devotion to his patients. At this time, in the winters, roads were not kept open for automobiles as they are today. Storms, the *suêtes* especially, often closed the roads. Our doctors from Chéticamp had to cover the huge territory from Inverness to Pleasant Bay. From Chéticamp to Pleasant Bay the route wound twenty-five to thirty miles through the mountains and, in the winter, the roads were often impractical to travel, even for horse and wagon. Dr. Léo Leblanc, day or night, never refused a call, no matter where he had to go. When the horse couldn't go any farther, the doctor went on by dog-sled or snowshoes, sometimes risking his life to save that of others. He died on the job. In 1943 he had taken a patient to the Inverness Hospital and was returning quickly to answer an emergency call to Pleasant Bay when another car forced him off the road at East Margaree. He was fatally injured. Dr. Léo Leblanc was swiftly brought to the hospital in Chéticamp and died there a short time later.

Dr. Linus Doiron

In 1926 another doctor arrived to set up his practice in Chéticamp, Dr. Linus Doiron, son of Daniel Doiron and Agatha Boudreau of Pomquet. After taking his classical studies at Collège Sainte-Anne-de-la-Pointe-de-l'Église, and his medical studies at Dalhousie University in Halifax, he established himself in Chéticamp in 1925. Five years later, in 1931, he left Chéticamp for Petit-Ruisseau in Digby County. A specialist in illnesses of the head, he practiced his profession in the town of Digby itself for several years. He married Marie Thériault of l'Anse-des-Belliveau.

Dr. Wilfred Poirier

Born in Chéticamp on November 2, 1896, Dr. Wilfred Poirier was the son of Marcellin Poirier and Marguerite Leblanc. Having taken his classical studies at College Sainte-Anne-de-la-Pointe-de-l'Église, and his medical studies at Dalhousie University, Halifax, he practiced his profession at Mulgrave, Inverness, and New Waterford. In 1932 he established himself in Chéticamp.

Dr. Poirier was a good doctor and a competent surgeon. He was also a charitable man. How many poor patients he had, of whom he asked nothing, from whom he refused any payment, and for whom he often opened his own purse! How many times have tears been seen in his eyes for the hardships of his patients! How many times has he left a confinement case in poor families and returned immediately with a suitcase of clothing, sheets, blankets, towels, and all kinds of food!

His good heart, however, did not prevent him from seeing ahead and using his energy in certain other matters. He encouraged all social and economic works capable of bettering the lot of the people. Thus it was that he was one of the strongest supporters of the credit union and co-operatives in Chéticamp.

Charitable, heart in hand, teasing and jovial with all that, Dr. Wilfred Poirier was loved by everyone. On his death in 1947 everyone shed tears for him and his funeral attracted such a large crowd that the great church of Chéticamp could not hold them all.

Dr. Poirier married Yvonne Doucet of Grand-Étang. She survived him.

Dr. Gabriel Boudreau

Son of Charlie Boudreau and Marie Aucoin, Dr. Gabriel Boudreau is a son of Chéticamp. An alumnus of College Sainte-Anne-de-la-Pointe-de-l'Église and of the Faculty of Medicine, Dalhousie University, Halifax, he practiced his profession at Port Hood for a year and at Margaree for five years before setting up his practice in Chéticamp in 1942.

Nearly infallible in his diagnoses, a very good doctor and highly esteemed by the people, Dr. Boudreau is even more likeable because of his charming simplicity. Dr. Boudreau married Hélène (à Calixte) Boudreau.

Dr. Léo J. Doucet

The adopted son of Den A. Doucet of Chéticamp, Dr. Léo Doucet took his medical studies at the University of Mexico.[11] He practiced medicine in the West Indies until his arrival in Chéticamp in 1948. He was a doctor in Chéticamp for ten years. He died there, quite suddenly, in 1958.

Dr. Harold Andrew Ratchford

Dr. Ratchford was born in Halifax in 1899, the son of John and Margaret Ratchford, but moved to Sydney with his parents when he was very young. After his studies at St. Francis Xavier University in Antigonish, he took his medical studies at Dalhousie University, Halifax, completing them in 1925. He was a surgeon at the Inverness Hospital for three years, then in 1948 was invited to succeed Dr. Wilfred Poirier as surgeon at the Chéticamp Hospital. In 1930 he married Marie Mahoney of Westville.

Dr. Russell Chiasson, Dentist

Our ancestors were not familiar with the delicacies with which we stuff our children today. As a result, they had better teeth. Until recently it was usual to see elderly nonagenarians in possession of solid and sound teeth.

But let us not exaggerate. Everyone did not have such beautiful teeth, and several suffered from toothache. There were some practical remedies against pain, but when the pain was too strong, the sole remedy was to extract the tooth. Here as in all localities of that time, there were famous *arracheux de dents* (tooth pullers). Later the doctors took on this job.

Before 1931 a dentist would come occasionally, sent by the Department of Health especially for the schoolchildren. It was only in 1931 that Chéticamp had its own resident dentist. It was at this time that Russell Chiasson, having received his diploma in dentistry from Dalhousie University, Halifax, came to open an office in Chéticamp. He is still there. Son of

Henri Chiasson and Annie Pembroke of Reserve Mines, he married Yvonne Cormier.

THE HOSPITAL

FOR A LONG TIME THE NEED FOR A HOSPITAL had been felt in our region. The nearest hospital was in Inverness, about forty-five miles away. This long trip involved serious inconveniences and sometimes ended in tragic circumstances, especially in the winter when the roads were not open to motor vehicles as they are today.

Father Leblanc had dreamed of establishing a small hospital in Chéticamp. The Filles de Jésus, who had taught there since 1903 and who also took care of the sick, were part of the plan he had in mind. With the help of Drs. Egen and Calder of Sydney, he was instrumental in opening the first hospital in Chéticamp on November 24, 1931. It was a twelve-bed hospital. Three Sisters ensured excellent quality service. Dr. Louis Fiset's old home, which had become the property of the Sisters, had been set up as the hospital. This house became too small and plans were soon made for a more spacious building.

In 1937 the Congregation of Les Filles de Jésus undertook the building of a modern hospital with a capacity of forty beds. This is L'Hôpital du Sacré-Coeur, whose construction cost the Religious $95,514. Its doors were opened in May 1938. Already its personnel include three doctors and ten nursing Sisters.

This hospital, from that time to this, serves the whole region from Cape North to Margaree. Also, in 1956, to once again answer the need, it was enlarged by adding twenty-two beds.[12]

This hospital, built of fireproof materials, is equipped to take on all modern services: an operating room, maternity section, x-ray department, a laboratory, and a pharmacy.

CHAPTER EIGHT

Civil Life

PUBLIC ADMINISTRATION IN CHÉTICAMP was always, and still is, reduced to its simplest expression. Since 1820, the date when Cape Breton was politically and definitely linked to the peninsula of Nova Scotia, Acadians vote in the elections for representatives to the Legislative Assembly of Nova Scotia in Halifax and, since 1867, they vote for representatives in the House of Commons in Ottawa.

The Acadians of Inverness County have only succeeded in having one of their own elected to Halifax twice: Moïse J. Doucet, Liberal, 1897-1906, and Hubert Aucoin, Conservative, 1925-28. No Acadian in the history of the County has yet been elected to Ottawa. Elections to the provincial Assembly would be possible, perhaps even easy, if Acadians could only put aside their political differences and unite to present a candidate and have him accepted (by the non-Acadians). But Acadians are sons of France; and is there any place in the world where the French are not divided in politics?

County Magistrates

Until 1880 the government appointed County Magistrates in all the most populous centres, in numbers sufficient to answer the needs of the people. These magistrates were vested with the powers of our justices of the peace.

Commissioners and Justices of the Peace

Today there are commissioners of the Superior Court of Nova Scotia, five of them in Chéticamp, who enjoy the powers of administering oaths and officially signing legal documents and wills.

Justices of the Peace, less numerous and with more powers than those of commissioners, can judge minor contentious cases (excluding major contentious cases and all criminal cases).

Sheriffs and Deputy-Sheriffs

In Port Hood, shire town of the County, resides the Sheriff, who is appointed by the Crown and entrusted with major contentious cases, as well as criminal cases, for the whole County.

Deputy-sheriffs, called constables, formerly represented the Sheriff in the villages or communities of the County. They delivered summonses and arrested the guilty. Since 1930 the Royal Canadian Mounted Police have replaced the constables and are entrusted with maintaining law and order.

Councillors

In 1878, by the "County Incorporation Act," a County Council was organized for the administration of the whole County, except for villages erected in municipalities, such as Inverness. Since then, every three years Chéticamp elects two councillors who sit on the County Council and, while taking part in the general administration of the County, still see to the particular interests of Cheticamp.[1]

CHAPTER NINE

Different Events

FORMERLY, IT WAS USUAL among the people to recall the date of such-and-such an event that had become a landmark by saying, "It was two years after the *raque à Moïse* (the wreck of Moïse)"; "it was the year of the *grande été* (great summer)," etc., etc. These outstanding events often had some connection with the sea, whether it was a tragedy, a year of abundant fish or a scarcity of it. Some of these events follow here.

The *raque à Moïse* (Shipwreck)

About 1861 some Chéticamp schooners, having gone to the fishing banks near Anticosti Island, had to take shelter in a harbour during a week of bad storms. One of the schooners was owned by Moïse Poirier. The captain of it was Bernard Mius. On board were the sons of Moïse, Gratien and Onésime, as well as other members of the crew. The schooner was named the *Three Brothers*.

When this schooner finally left the harbour,[1] the men noticed new clothes and a quantity of all kinds of objects floating adrift in the water. While picking up these things they saw, in passing around a point, a large boat broken in two, of which only the front part remained trapped on a rock. The sea washed over the hold and carried off all the goods contained therein. Our fishermen gathered up a full load, then approached the boat which some of the men succeeded in boarding. They found a man who spoke a foreign language left there, probably, as a watchman.

The men returned home with their cargo. There were all kinds of things in the load: clothing, blankets, thread, flannelette, etc. Everything was wet. Moïse Poirier's wife dried her share at La-Pointe-à-Cochons.

Old Philippe (à Fulgence) Bourgeois said the boat was a transport of immigrants from Europe who came to settle in our country. Were they Irish immigrants, perhaps?

The owners of the wrecked boat set the law to the heels of Bernard Mius. He had to flee to Prince Edward Island, where he later died.

For a long time people calculated the date of different events from the year of *raque à Moïse*.

The Year of the Militia

On the occasion of the war against the Fenians, the Lieutenant-Governor of Nova Scotia, on March 17, 1866, ordered obligatory military training for all men in the province who had reached the age of twenty-one years. The first spring courses in military training of a few days duration were held in Chéticamp for all the men of Chéticamp. Another such exercise took place in the autumn or early the following spring. A Mr. Blancpied was the instructing officer.[2]

The Year of the Shipwreck in Marcel's Harbour

In 1870 a schooner named the *Brilliant Star*, loaded with green cod-fish, was thrown on shore in Marcel's small harbour on the other side of the Island when surprised at night by a storm. Before running aground it struck a rock. One of the crewmen, believing this was the shore, jumped into the water and drowned. The others were all saved. These people were Englishmen who had come from fishing on the Côte-Nord.

The Year of the Ice

In 1871, and again in 1898, Chéticamp and the surrounding region endured a terrible storm accompanied by thunder and, though well into the month of August, hail and ice fell, doing a great deal of damage.

The Year of the Flour

One certain summer evening in 1874 the people saw a boat on fire passing in the distance. A few days later the fishermen noticed several barrels of flour in the water. Everyone was able to save three, four, or even seven barrels by boat.

Next day the fishermen decided to return to the spoils. But this was the day of *débauche* (hurricane), with high winds from the northwest. The flour came up to the shore, but the barrels were broken on the rocks. At "La Source de la Montagne" at Cap-Rouge, "Petit" Martin Deveau and his children waited. The barrels ran aground and broke up. But, finally, the flour thickened the water and calmed the waves on the shore. "Petit" Martin was able to save thirty-eight barrels. For the people in such straits it was manna from Heaven. They used it to cook *torteaux* on the stove.

The Year of the Butter

Some years after this episode with the flour, and even though no one saw any ship in distress, the waves washed up on the shorelines of Chéticamp about 1,000 pounds of butter, in tubs.

The Year of the Brick (1875)

A two-masted brig, the *Hilda*, still new, left Prince Edward Island late in the autumn, about Christmastime, loaded with oats for England. It was surprised by a snowstorm and the freezing cold of winter, accompanied by terrible northwest winds. Well into the night, the brig ran aground in the middle of the Island at the cove, called since then "l'Anse du Brick" (Brick Cove).

Next morning, Emilien (à Luc) Chiasson, who still lived on the Island, was taking a walk around the shore to see if the storm had brought in any wood. He noticed the brig. While searching through the descent to the headland, he came upon two frozen bodies above the headland. After fetching two companions, he followed the footprints of a third man. Farther on they found his frozen body too. This one had walked far enough to reach some houses, if he had been heading in the right direction. But it was nighttime and he couldn't see where he was going.

The rest of the crew had drowned. They must have taken to the water without knowing where they were, and the three who had reached shore froze to death. If they had stayed on board, they would not have died. The rough sea had tossed the boat onto the shore where it remained resting on its side without completely breaking up. In the spring other bodies were found on the shore.

The Great Summer

The summer of 1884 was a year of extraordinary abundance for the fishermen. During the whole summer cod was plentiful on our coasts. The fishermen caught it in the vicinity of La Pointe-Enragée at the end of the Island, taking in two loads a day.

Families Chased from the Island by the Jerseys

At the beginning of the last century four or five families were established in Chéticamp Island, without attempting to obtain clear title to their property. Later the Robins, who were already owners of La Pointe de l'Île, proceeded to acquire the whole Island. There was an agreement between the Robins and the families concerned. By a contract signed June 22, 1845, these families obtained a lease for thirty-four years for the lands they farmed, but agreed to return them to the Robins by January 1, 1879.

On May 20, 1879, the Robins expected the surrender, not only of these lands, but also the homes, barns and all buildings constructed on them. The following is the notice sent to each of the heads of the families:

Sir: Take notice that you are hereby required to quit and deliver up to us or our Agent on the first day of September next, possession of the lot of land, messuage and premises situate at the east end of Chéticamp or Robin Island (so called), with all the improvements thereon or thereto in any way belonging, which land you held from us under and by virtue of a lease, signed and executed by you thereon (?) bearing date the twenty-second day of June 1845 and which terms expired on the first day of May A.D. 1879.

Raulin Robin, Philip Gessett (?), James H. Robin
by Edw. Briard, their attorney.

All this was to be done with no compensation.

The heads of the families who lived on these lands at this time were Luc Chiasson, "Konock" (Léonard) Chiasson, Amable Chiasson and Joseph ("Tiouette") Cormier. The attorney for the Robins in this matter was their manager in Chéticamp, Mr. Edward Briard.

The Acadian families refused to comply with the demands of the Robins. The case was put before the tribunal at Port Hood and was won by the Acadians. The Robins appealed to the Superior Court at Halifax, where the second trial took place. Unfortunately the Chéticantins did not present themselves at this trial. Probably they didn't have the wherewithal to get there. The Robins won the case.

Even so, these families refused to leave their homes without being compensated for them, but the Robins forced them out. They brought in brawny Scotsmen from North East who made the people leave, strong-arm style. The population rose up against them. Some resolute men marched to La Pointe. They were going to make it tough for Captain Briard when he jumped onto a schooner and fled Cheticamp.[3]

The Year of the Rum

On October 25, 1931, it was rum, in several dozen barrels, that the sea washed ashore at Chéticamp. A rum-running schooner, probably the *Catalogne,* was found days later overturned in the sea with two drowned men aboard.

Expropriation of the Lands of Cap-Rouge

About twenty families lived as well as could be expected from the products of fishing and farming in the mountainous region of Chéticamp, called Cap-Rouge. Since the beginning of Chéticamp, these families were attached to their land from one generation to another. But about 1930 a great threat hovered over these people. The federal government wished to expropriate these lands to make a national park in the northern part of Cape Breton. The expropriation took place in 1936. Were the payments enough? Several former owners refused to leave. They were forced out in 1939. With considerable help from the government, the majority of these families took refuge at the harbour; others settled on the Island. Little by little they got used to it and thanked God for the ordeal which had uprooted them from their shores and their misery.

CHAPTER TEN

Social Life

MORALS

THE EXEMPLARY LIFESTYLE of the pre-Expulsion Acadians has been immortalized by poets and written about by historians.

The long period of trials which followed 1755 and 1758 when, with neither schools nor priests, the Acadians fought for survival, could have led them to live as savages. However, if the Expulsion marked them or changed them in any way, when they re-grouped and established themselves anew, thirty or forty or even fifty years later, these Acadians remained steadfast in their religious convictions and honest in their dealings with their follow man. This was particularly the case with the founders of Chéticamp.

In the beginning the missionaries had only praise for the Chéticantins. "These are the people who cannot be more charitable towards each other...all are inclined towards helping those in need...they are very pious...they are very generous to the priests who serve them and have great respect for them," wrote Father Lejamtel.[1]

Bishop Plessis, on his visit of 1812, was much moved by the "goodness of the inhabitants, by their respect and affection for the priests.... The word of a priest, among them, is as respected as if it were the word of an angel."[2] He admired their perfect simplicity and their faith, and compared them to the Christians of the early Church.

Drinking

Father Antoine Manseau, during his stay in Chéticamp in 1814, heaped the same praise on the people. However, for the first time a reservation appeared. "It's too bad," he wrote, "that in both places [Chéticamp and Margaree] rum is so plentiful; otherwise, they would be the faithful, worthy of the highest level of Christianity."[3] He asked his Bishop "what test must [he] expect of the people who get drunk several times a year, before admitting them" to the Sacraments?

This last complaint would be amplified over several decades with the history of Chéticamp. The contact maintained by the Acadians with the islands of Saint-Pierre and Miquelon where several of their people had lived, their frequent voyages to these islands and to the West Indies, the very liberal sales made by the Jerseys, all contributed to the Chéticantins never being deprived of drink, and even to abusing it.

This state of affairs lasted up to the end of the last century, until the time when the government of Nova Scotia brought in prohibition. With the prohibition law, all manufacturing, all importation, and all sales of alcoholic beverages were forbidden. For Chéticamp, this law only partially remedied the evil, for the secret manufacture of adulterated drinks, and smuggling, were substituted for open trade. Finally in 1929 the government replaced prohibition with controlled usage and permitted the establishment of liquor stores. There were still some abuses, but the presence of the Royal Canadian Mounted Police helped in keeping them less serious and less numerous.

Honesty of the People

In a pastoral letter to the people of Chéticamp in 1830, the Bishop of Québec, Bishop Panet, reproached them for their intemperance and their dishonest dealings. These severe reproaches on the part of the Bishop would be very surprising if one didn't know that they were repeatedly solicited by the missionary of that time, Father Courtaud. As we have already noted, it appears to us that the complaints of this missionary are manifestly exaggerated.

The division of the lands which took place amicably among the pioneers left the following generation an inheritance filled with problems. There was probably some obstinacy in the quibbling that arose in the subsequent boundary disputes, as well as in other problems between neighbours. But we strongly doubt that there could ever have been any obvious and deliberately serious injustices. Aside from poor people who took their firewood from someone else's property, indeed openly and to everyone's knowledge, one can say that, in general, stealing did not exist in any form in Chéticamp. No one locked his doors, and even today many still do not do so. Each person can leave his tools and his clothes in full view with no fear of their being stolen by Chéticantins.

Profanity

Blasphemy doesn't exist in Chéticamp. Some individuals make use of swearing, but very rarely of blasphemy. Again, this swearing is done in the English language. "Goddam" and "Jesus Christ" are about the only known swear words. The sole French swear word is *maudit* (damn). Also, how many times has one not heard our people, on their return from the lumber camps, relate their horror and fear before the blasphemy they had heard used by the French-Canadians: "It was enough to make one's hair stand on end."

Social Life

The first missionaries of Chéticamp were all particularly outstanding priests. Later on there were some, like MacKeagney and Chénal, who left something to be desired, but their brief stay in Chéticamp hardly disturbed the faith of the people. Later, Chéticamp had the privilege of being guided for many years by great men like Father Girroir and Father Fiset. Such men immunize a population, especially when it is protected by its isolation, against all evil influences from outside its boundaries.

Also, up to these later days the faith remained unsullied and strong. Unfortunately, religious ignorance in the homes of too many has created, for nearly half a century, a favourable ground to receive the seeds of the religion of the Jehovah Witnesses. But, by a healthy defensive reaction, the rest of the population is now acquiring a more enlightened and, consequently, a firmer faith.

Before the reforms of Pius X, in Chéticamp, as in other areas, Communion was not received very often. Because of the Jansenist influence, priests did not encourage frequent receiving of Holy Communion.

Religious Practices

Blessed Bread

Sacramental Holy Communion effectively unites us to Our Lord and constitutes a marvellous symbol of unity and love among Christians. But, at a time when this Communion was rarely received, blessed bread replaced it as a symbol of unity in the parish community. In fact, formerly, the ceremony of the blessed bread took place every Sunday.

Each family in its turn furnished the bread, cut it in small pieces, and brought it to the Communion rail in a large basket. At the beginning of Mass the priest came down from the altar to bless this bread. The trustees then distributed it from pew to pew, to all those assisting at Mass. Each one took a tiny morsel of it, then put the rest away in his pocket for the children of the other members of his family who had not been able to come to Mass.[4]

The Crucifix, Holy Pictures, Holy Water, Palms

In a place of honour in every home in Chéticamp, one finds a crucifix, holy picture, and often a statute of the Blessed Virgin Mary, in front of which the family says the Rosary and night prayers. Blessed palm is over the door frame and the bottle of Holy Water and a blessed candle are in a cupboard.

During a thunder and lightning storm the candle would be lit, and outside, all around the house, Holy Water was sprinkled on the ground to make a protective belt; the Sign of the Cross was also made with Holy Water on each window from the inside of the house. At each flash of lightning the people blessed themselves. If the thunder became too fierce everyone knelt down and said the Rosary, often adding to it: "Saint Barbara and Holy Flower, protected by the Lord" or "On the Cross of my Saviour, where the thunder will go, Saint Barbara will lead it away from us."

At the head of each bed a small bottle of Holy Water was hung and each evening, before going to bed, each one blessed himself with the Holy Water, while saying: "Holy Water, I'm taking you now, if death surprises me during the night, you will be to me as a sacrament" or "Holy Water, I'm taking you now, I use you to anoint my body, in the name of the Holy Spirit, if I die suddenly, you will be to me as a sacrament."

FEASTDAYS AND SEASONS

IN ORDER TO PAINT A COMPLETE PICTURE of the life and traditions of the Chéticantins, let us follow the classical cycle of feastdays and seasons of the year and the stages of life, from the cradle to the grave.

Advent

The liturgical year begins with Advent. This is a time of preparation for Christmas and was kept with great austerity. In union with the mind of the Church, everyone abstained from all exterior rejoicing. During this time one permitted oneself, at most, some quiet socializing and card parties among family friends.

Christmas Rosaries

At the approach of Christmas many children, and some grown-ups as well, would undertake the recitation of special Rosary. On each bead, instead of the Our Father and Hail Mary, this prayer was said: "Sweet Babe of Bethlehem, come and take birth in my heart." It was necessary to recite sixty-seven Rosaries of this type, sixty-six before Christmas and the sixty-seventh during Christmas night, preferably during Midnight Mass. Recited in this way, the Rosaries unfailingly obtained a favour for the person involved. The favours asked for were as different as the needs of each person. Children asked for a toy for Christmas, a sled, or the health of a member of the family; young girls asked for a boyfriend; mothers, for moderation in the drinking habits of their husbands and older sons, or some other favour dictated by an immediate need. This tradition still exists, but is beginning to disappear.

Christmas

One legend told to the children stated that the animals speak among themselves during Christmas night. Once, continued the story, a man wished to listen to what the animals said on Christmas night. He went to his barn and on the hour of midnight, this is what he heard: "Tonight is Christmas," said the ox to the horse. The horse replied, "Yes, and tonight the Divine Child is born." The ox asked, "Tomorrow, what are we going to do?" The horse answered, "We will carry our master to his grave!" The master really did die.[5]

Christmas night possessed all the charm of the departures for the

Midnight Mass in the *carriole* (an elegant sleigh with raised and perforated runners) or in the sledges, the jingling bells heard on all the roads, the bouncing lanterns of the pedestrians, as well as the shout of "Merry Christmas!" sent from one group to another throughout the night. In church the *crèche* (stable scene of the birth of Christ), the same one used every year, the old hymns whose verses were sung by the most beautiful voices in the parish, the sixty-seventh Christmas Rosary that everyone recited; all this prepared the heart for the great moment of the personal reception of the God-Child in Holy Communion.

When Mass was over each one re-lit his lantern and all left the church with the last hymn ringing in their ears. Outside everyone wished a "Merry Christmas!" to one another, then went home to bed without any more ceremony. In the homes there were no decorations, no cribs and no Christmas trees. In the afternoon the young married people went to pay a visit to their parents and remained to socialize. If they had too many children and couldn't leave their homes, their parents came to visit them and the grandchildren instead.

Today, automobiles replace the sleighs and lessen so much the charm of those days. But the Mass and the crèche scene are more beautiful than ever. Several homes are decorated for the event.

In early times there was neither Santa Claus nor the Christmas stocking, but by the end of the last century the children were hanging their stocking and waiting for the arrival of Santa Claus. Santa Claus was poor and only brought an apple and a few candies. Little by little he added toys—a small doll, a kazoo, *une musique à bouche* (harmonica), *une trompe* (Jew's harp), and often useful articles such as stockings, mittens, skates, etc., most often bought at Eaton's by means of this company's catalogue.

For the meals, goose replaced the traditional turkey of the Canadians. It appears that turkey never existed in Chéticamp, and geese have disappeared. Today the best beef or pork is cooked with cabbage, or even a delicious raisin *poutine*[6] (pudding). In the early days only the most well-to-do families had pies or cakes. Today every table is loaded with succulent pastries.

New Year's Eve

A unique tradition in the region—no one knows from where it comes—is called *battre la vieille année*[7] (beating the old year out).

On the evening of December 31, if one was outside and the weather was calm, strange noises could be heard rising up from all around. Inside, everyone would be on watch and would move away from the corners of the rooms. Young girls were nervous, but not afraid. With hands clasped to their bosoms so as not to be too startled, they waited nervously, even though they wanted people to knock often on the corner of the house (with huge clubs) during the evening, for they knew it would be mostly for them that one would knock. They would feel the windows full of eyes that evening, watching them from the outside.

This is what would happen: Armed with sticks, the youths would venture closer in the darkness. Through the windows they would peer inside to see in what corner of the house the girls or womenfolk were to be found. Bang! Bang! "Aïe!" would cry the womenfolk. With blows redoubled the young people would beat the outside corners of the house with their long sticks. The dishes would dance in the *dorsoué* (sideboard, dresser), the lamp would blink and the holy pictures on the wall tremble for a few minutes in their shaking frames. One was hardly over the surprise when the racket would begin again. The four gables (corners) of the house would be attacked, blows from the sticks rhythmically descending on them. "For heaven's sake!" the man of the house would cry menacingly, worrying about his shingles. But the blows would continue to rain down and double in speed. With a bound the owner would fly out the door. "Save yourselves!" would cry the one who surveys the interior of the house from near the kitchen window. Before the owner could put his hand on the door latch, the group would fade away. A short time later the same time would be repeated at another house. This was how the young people *battent la vieille année* (beat the old year out).

New Year's Day

The father's blessing on New Year's Day was an unknown practice in Chéticamp. On the morning of the first day of the year the parents and children, in the order in which they got up, exchanged greetings with one another and wished everyone "Happy New Year now and Heaven at the end of your days." For a few days these wishes would be repeated among relatives, friends, and anyone else one met during this time. It was accompanied by a simple handshake. One strange thing about the people of Chéticamp—they were not much known for embracing each other. Aside from lovers who would hug each other, though always out of the public eye, in Chéticamp one never embraced another, nor for New Year's Day, nor at one's departure, even for a considerable length of time, nor at one's return. The usual gesture was to simply shake hands. Contact with the outside world has resulted, little by little, in bringing this custom of embracing one another to Chéticamp but, to tell the truth, is only practiced by those who live in Québec and Ontario when they return to visit their parents.

If someone received a gift or procured for himself an article of clothing—stockings, socks, shirts, etc.—he wore it for the first time on New Year's Day in the hope it would bring him good luck.

Feast of the Kings

Some families made the cake *des Rois* (of the Kings) which contained a broad bean, kidney bean and a button. Those who found the broad bean and the kidney bean were named King and Queen. The one, male or female, who found the button would remain a bachelor or spinster for the rest of his/her life! For the majority of the Chéticantins, the celebrations of *des Rois* had no other purpose than that of being another festival in the *temps des fêtes* (festival season). In other regions this celebration ended the period of festivity; but not here.

The Chéticantins have always lived by fishing. In earlier days fishing finished early in the autumn and during the winter the people had only to carry out their daily tasks of taking care of the animals in the barn and of cutting and hauling home their firewood. Aside from that, the men had nothing to do. Thus the long period of leisure, of a vacation which, for the adults was the *temps des fêtes*, and easily prolonged from Christmas to Mardi-Gras. One travelled from one family to another, to the homes of relatives or friends, who organized the social gatherings. The meals on these occasions were quite substantial. Favourite foods were meat pies,[8] raising pudding, *fricots* (soups made of meat and potatoes), fish chowder, pancakes and various pastries.

Social Gatherings

This was a time when people danced a great deal in Chéticamp. These were the old dances like *la patate longue* (the long potato), *les moutons* (the sheep), and *la boulangère* (Paul Jones). Later on, towards the end of the last century, these old dances were supplanted by more modern and more active dances such as the *sept* (seven) and the *huit* (eight), types of quadrilles danced to violin music and prompted by a *câlleux* (caller). Even today the waltz is not well known; still less, the foolish modern dances.

Unfortunately, the dances were often marred by too much drinking and disorder, quarreling and even fighting. Because of this the priests always sermonized against dancing. Because of the abuses it brought on and because of the prohibition of the priests, dances have always been clothed with an illegitimate character in Chéticamp. Only the least scrupulous families or those least respectful of religious authority organize these dances. The more religious homes opposed them, even the dances among their families. However, dancing was always tolerated at wedding parties. Then, one had a good time dancing all night—or even longer.

Dances were rare and social gatherings took place most often without them. There were card parties, parlour games, songs, tales and funny stories which helped to enliven parties. The senior folk talked of the Expulsion, of the hardships in the beginning of Chéticamp, of hunting parties for moose or sea-wolves, of tragedies at sea, of ghosts and sorcerers.

Candlemas Day

On February 2, besides the liturgical ceremony of the candles in church, Chéticamp celebrated this day with a quite typical social festivity:

La Chandeleur. In the evening there was a great dancing party in each district of the parish. It was necessary to prepare this party some days in advance and, especially to procure the food for the supper. This activity was called *courir la Chandeleur* (to run La Chandeleur). It was run through each sector in groups of twenty to twenty-five young people. All were dressed in rags. Only the leader of the group wore his Sunday best.[9]

The leader, carrying a large be-ribboned cane, led his group to the house and knocked on the door and asked: "Are you going to furnish any food for La Chandeleur?" If the answer was affirmative the leader turned towards his companions and said, "Enter!" If the people in the house refused to give any food for the party the group continued on to the next house. Except for the houses where the children were in bed, nearly all the families gave. At these homes the group was invited to enter and dance the Escaouette Dance.

One behind the other and hands on the shoulders of one another, everyone danced in a circle around the leader while jumping with both feet at the same time. The leader, in the middle, hitting the floor with his cane in time to the music, sang:

L'Escaouette

It is the married gentleman and the married lady (twice)
It is the married gentleman and lady (twice)
Who have not yet eaten. (twice)
A small windmill on the river,
A small windmill to ford the river.
Fire on the mountain, boy run, boy run,
Fire on the mountain, boy run away.
I've seen the wolf, the fox, and the hare,
I've seen "Grande" 'Cité jump.
I've milled my blanket, blanket, 'ket, 'ket.
I've milled my blanket, covered to the feet.
Aouenne, aouenn' your rags,
Ah! Rescue your rags,
Aouenne, aouenne, aouenne, nippaillon!
Ah! Rescue your rags.
Tibounich, nabet, nabette!
Tibounich, naba![10]

Song finished, the house furnished everything imaginable to make a feast: meat, flour, butter, sugar, tea, and sometimes anise.

The *coureux* (runners) asked the questions: "How many of you are coming to La Chandeleur?—Three or four.—Three or four!!! You haven't given half enough for eaters such as you are! More butter! More sugar!" etc. The people gave according to the number of persons attending the party. The same scene was played out in each house.

The runners carried cowbells, jingle bells, *borgos* (bugles), and anything else that could make an infernal racket in order to announce their coming and keep the people awake until their home could be reached.

Previously, the organizers made arrangements with a family to have the food cooked at their house and to have the party there. In order to have the food at this house and make the necessary preparations, the food was picked up on January 30. On February 2, at the designated house, people began to gather about four o'clock in the afternoon. As soon as enough had gathered, dancing to violin music began, as it would be for a wedding. About 6:00 p.m. supper was eaten. Dancing then continued until 11:45 p.m. At this time, exactly, everyone knelt down for evening prayers, bringing the party to an end about midnight.

In earlier days the priest always came to the party to eat and socialize with the people. He played cards with the older men. Supper would hardly be finished when Father Fiset would say, "Quickly! Clear the table so we can play cards!"

For a long time everything went well with no abuses. But, with the passage of time drinking was introduced, dancing continued until 2:00 a.m. and quarreling began. Father Girroir had to forbid La Chandeleur. Father Fiset, who permitted it again, also had to cancel it because of the same abuses. The last Chandeleur party was run in 1907 in Belle-Marche, at the home of William (à Isidore) Deveau.

Candlemas Pancakes

In several families pancakes were the traditional supper for the day of La Chandeleur. Not everyone could eat them, however. The batter was prepared by the cooks, but each person had to flip over their own pancakes when cooking them. Whoever could not flip over their pancakes without dropping them on the floor was not permitted to eat them.[11]

St. Valentine's Day

The custom of sending valentines has existed in Chéticamp for a long time. Formerly, these valentines were nearly always anonymous and were sent by mail. They were always satirical, sometimes crude, though not always funny. They consisted of a drawing done by hand or a cut-out of some printed matter, to which was added a few biting words caricaturizing a physical or moral defect, a blunder, or an ambition of the receiver of the card. It is related that certain individuals, like Jean Chiasson (Petou), wouldn't open his valentine letter "for all the tea in China" but threw it on the fire without so much as a glance at it. Today, many more valentines are sent. They are store-bought rather than homemade, lovable, and are signed by the sender.

Meat Days

Meat days were times of great festivities. Everyone took a holiday on these days. Bad luck to the imbecile who would have worked. He would be criticized by the whole parish.

These were days when everyone visited everyone else. All those who could went out, in carts or on foot, stopping for a while at the homes of all their relatives or friends. In the evenings it was endless socializing. Unfortunately there were many abuses in the past. Several played cards for money and had the liquor jug on the table. Some played *petit-loup*, meaning they only gambled for very small amounts; others played *gros-loup* where the sums gambled were large. Some gambled away their property, such as their pig or their cow, and lost everything. It was not without good reason that the priests spoke out so strongly against gambling for money.

On the day of Mardi-Gras, everything stopped at midnight. It was the closing of all festivities. Lent then began.

Lent

Lent was a time of penance. In addition to fasting, one abstained from all rejoicing. There were no social gatherings and suitors wouldn't even go visit their girlfriends.

Every Sunday during Lent and every evening in many families the "Passion of Our Lord"[12] was sung. One would not miss this service during Holy Week especially. This canticle was piously sung by all the members of the family. Those who couldn't sing listened religiously in silence. "Les cantiques de Marseille" was also sung during Lent.

Another tradition of Lent which is still remembered was the gathering of several neighbouring families in one house for the reciting of the Rosary, with the chanting of the Mysteries as an evening prayer, along with several canticles. This ceremony lasted about an hour.

Mid-Lent

The Thursday of the third week in Lent is called *mi-câreme* (mid-Lent). The children and the youth of the parish, boys especially, though often the girls too, run the *mi-câreme*. Formerly, each person made his mask out of a woollen stocking, a sweater sleeve, a box, some rough material or some linen. Each one dressed in the most original way possible with the intention of remaining anonymous. Sometimes during the day, but especially in the evening after supper, alone or in small groups, one left home all dressed up to visit the neighbouring families in the district. It was the task of the people in each family to guess the identity of the mi-câremes and for these to try to hide it by changing their voice and their mannerisms so as to mystify the hosts. The success and the pleasure were that much greater when the mi-carêmes succeeded in chatting, dancing and making many gestures without being recognized by their close relatives or friends.

Today the mi-carême is more in style than ever. From Thursday, the day on which it was celebrated in the past, it now extends to the whole week. Many more people, even those of an older age, participate. Masks are bought at a store. Costumes more carefully made than in other days, often represent people such as a policeman, a religious, a nurse, or even an Evangeline. The mi-carêmes travel by car and have enlarged the circle of their visits. For the occasion groups of amateur singers, dancers and musicians organize themselves and, dressed as mi-carêmes, travel around bringing happiness to as many homes as possible.

Palm Sunday

In Chéticamp palms brought in from elsewhere are unknown. Each person brings his own palm to the church to be blessed. It comes from the cedar (thuya), from the sévigny,[13] from the chenave,[14] from the colombe,[15] or is even a simple one made of spruce or pine gathered in the mountains and made in the form of a Cross. On returning from the church, these palms are distributed in all the buildings, even the barn, as well as in every room in the house, including the basement. Today they are even placed in automobiles.

Easter Sunday

Easter, the feast of the Resurrection of Our Lord, marks the end of the penitential season.

Easter Eggs

Until later times, the people were not rich and food was simple. The man who left in early morning or at night for a hard day's fishing would have pancakes for breakfast, but often the rest of the family would have to be satisfied with bread and molasses. However, on Easter Sunday the tradition was that there were eggs for breakfast and that one could eat as many as he wished. Hens began to lay eggs late in the season. All these eggs were carefully preserved and on Easter morning everyone feasted on them. Men would eat up to ten or twelve, while children would eat five or six. It was fun to see who could eat the most. The next day, simple breakfasts began again.

The Sun Dance

Popular belief says that the sun dances while rising on Easter morning. At least once in his life everyone rises early to admire this phenomenon.

The Québec custom of gathering Easter water is unknown in Chéticamp.

April Fool's Day

The first of April is the day when one "fait pêcher le poisson d'avril" (plays April fool jokes on each other). Someone will ask another, who is not on his guard, to go look for something. On his way to fetch the object someone will yell at him, "Jette ta ligne! ça mord!" (Throw our your line! They're biting!) or, again, someone will send one who doesn't know how to read to a neighbour's with a paper on which is written, "Faites-le mor-dre" (Make him bite, i.e. try to fool him). The neighbour will say "I haven't any; go to so-and-so's house." This latter will continue the strategem and the following will do the same, until the victim realizes the joke is on him.

May Water

The Chéticantins watch for the first snow that falls in May. They col-lect enough of it so that when it is melted it will give a few bottles of water. This was "May water," which possessed medicinal properties against sore eyes, earache, or some other similar trouble.[16]

Feast of Corpus Christi

The procession on the Feast of Corpus-Christi was a great parish cel-ebration. As everywhere else, ensigns and banners, the veils of the Chil-dren of Mary, and the white dresses of young girls were well displayed. Flags decorated the church, the church yard and the whole route of the procession. For the length of the route along the road and in the fields, spruce trees were placed every five or six feet.

What was unique, we believe, was the improvised guard organized for the occasion. Volunteers, men and youths, dressed in traditional cos-tume, blue trousers with red stripes, white shirt and red cummerbund. Be-fore Mass a captain, usually a veteran solider, would have the group do a few exercises. Between twenty and thirty men, formerly armed with mus-kets but later with rifles, accompanied the Blessed Sacrament. On arrival at the Repository they spread themselves in a semi-circle in front and when the priest raised the monstrance for the blessing, they saluted it by firing a salvo of blank cartridges.

These soldiers would always keep a few extra cartridges. After the ceremony, on return from the church, they would choose the right mo-ment for their surprise discharge, making the men jump, the ladies cry out and the horses rear. This was the custom.

Today the Air Cadets have replaced them.

The Feast of Saints Peter and Paul

Saint Peter was a fisherman and is the patron saint of fishermen. Those of Chéticamp would not forget his feast day which has now be-come theirs. Every summer, on June 29, they beached their boats, then washed and painted them. In the evening, there were, here and there, salmon suppers in the fishing cabins. Unfortunately for several, these too often ended in a bout of drunkenness.

First Three Days of August

During the first three days of August people would go wash their feet in the ocean. Parents especially sent their children to do this. The water was thought to be particularly healthful on these days.

Dog Days

Dog days, they say, correspond to the peak of the summer heat; scientifically, July 22 to August 23. Chéticamp mothers, who worried so easily when their children went swimming, prolonged the period of the dog days. Popular opinion tells us that the water of the lakes and rivers, as well as that of the ocean, is very unhealthy during the dog days. This was a convenient excuse for worried mothers to forbid their children to go swimming and to make this period last as long as they wished.

All Saints' Day

One tradition very well known in earlier times in Chéticamp was that of stealing cabbages on the eve of All Saints' Day so as to have them to cook next day. Popular custom agreed that stealing cabbages on that day was not a sin. Owners of the vegetables had to watch over their property, otherwise they would leave themselves wide open to this rascality. All Saints' Day was a festival celebrated somewhat like the Feast of the Kings (Epiphany) and that of the Meat Days (Shrove Monday and Tuesday, the two days before Ash Wednesday).

All Souls' Day

It is still not very long since there was a general belief that the dead returned to earth on November 2, from midnight to midnight. It was felt in the atmosphere, like a reverential fear, even by adults. On that day children had an unholy fear of going to the barn alone or into any isolated areas.

Chéticantins pray a great deal and have Masses said for their dead. Formerly they had the *criée des âmes* (auction of souls). A parishioner would donate sacks of potatoes, a lamb or a pig. This would be auctioned off on the steps of the church after Mass and the receipts would go to the pastor as an honorarium (offering) for Masses for the souls of the dead. This custom no longer exists today.

Several Chéticantins also have a devotion to the souls in Purgatory. Not only do they pray for them, but they pray to them, asking them for favours, promising prayers or certain sacrifices in return for these favours. Thus, some people ask the Holy Souls to wake them at a certain hour in the morning. They are certain to be awakened at that precise time.

Feast of Saint Catherine

The Feast of Saint Catherine passes totally unnoticed here in Chéticamp. The *coiffer Sainte-Catherine* (celebration in honour of ladies who have reached their twenty-fifth year without marrying) is not spoken of, nor does one recognize this saint as the patroness of single girls. The story of Saint Catherine is not even known in this region.

STAGES OF LIFE

A REPORT FROM FATHER LEJAMTEL to the Bishop of Québec in 1809 tells us that "all these families [in Chéticamp], in general, have many children."[17] This hasn't changed since then. Our families are large. Unfortunately the young people do leave home, and in great numbers.

The Birth

Women of Chéticamp enjoyed good health and, ordinarily, the birth of a baby would not greatly inconvenience them. A pregnant woman would continue to work and busily run the household until the last minute, then start in again very soon after the birth of her baby.

If a pregnant woman was in danger of losing her child, folk medicine would see her through. The classical remedy consisted of a paste of flour and water into which had been put green ribbons cut into pieces with scissors. After having poured this paste several times back and forth into two cups, the mother had to drink it. Another remedy, efficacious, if for no other reason than the tranquillity it called for, involved a long rest on her back for the pregnant woman, with a saucer of garlic on her abdomen.

Parents were, and still are, the soul of discretion on the origin of babies. One does not speak of it. If children showed themselves too curious and asked questions on this subject, they were told that the doctor brings babies, or that they are found in the barn, in the hay, or in the woodpile. The story is told that Léonie (à Lubin à Suzanne) Chiasson, when as a small boy learned that his newborn baby brother or sister had been found in a woodpile, pulled apart all the wood to see if any others were to be found.

For the baptism of the child there is no formal rule in the choice of godfather or godmother. They are most often chosen from among relatives, an older brother or sister. But these people would not complain if someone else were chosen. The ones who carry the babies ordinarily are the grandfather and grandmother. The baptism ceremony takes place with the greatest simplicity. The custom of ringing the church bells for the baptism has not yet taken hold here. There is no organized celebration at the house, and the habit of giving gifts to the child or to the mother is not known in this region. Afterwards, however, on the anniversary of the child's baptism, his godfather gives him a small gift.

In the early days of Chéticamp we notice that the children would often receive, in baptism, the name of the saint whose feast day it was that day. From that practice come names like Barbe, Eulalie, Euphrosine, Félicité, Perpétue, that we meet often and have shortened to 'Lalie, 'Phroisine, 'Cité, etc. Often used are biblical names such as Abraham, Élie, Moïse, Samuel, Judith, Esther, Jérémie, and even Christ.

Since the end of the last century a tendency of giving English names to the children has crept in, names like Walter, Mick, Charlie, William, Tommy, and other similar ones. The pastor, Father Leblanc, did not like this growing use of English names for the newborn Acadians. He would always write the names in French for the baptismal records, but too often the parents would call their child Willie or William, Charlie or Patsy, even if

Father Leblanc had written Guillaume, Charles or Patrice. Some of these names are so common and so long in use that the people believe them to be French. A story is told that after a baptism a wife would say, "Clifford! An English name! Why not give him a French name, like Charlie!"

In Chéticamp family names are very seldom used, except in writing letters and for the sake of outsiders. Among the Chéticantins it is not necessary to say Placide Poirier or Joseph Chiasson, but simply Placide à Lazare and Joseph à Henri. As it often happens that a boy is given the same name as his father, to distinguish him from his father he is called "le petit" (the younger or junior), as in "Petit" Placide à Placide, a name he will keep all his life, even if he grows bigger and taller than his father.

In earlier times after the birth of a baby the mother would not wash herself for several days for fear of catching cold. She was put on a strict diet. For several days she could only have some very clear rice soup with unbuttered toast.

When the time came to *détriller* (wean) a child, the mother placed a poultice of warm cotton and white liniment on her breasts. In place of this poultice, some women used old headgear warmed in the oven.[18]

In view of protecting their fragile limbs, babies were tightly bound in their clothing and well-secured in their cradles. As the Blessed Mother had rocked the Infant Jesus, it was necessary, according to popular belief, for the Chéticamp mothers to also rock their babies. Babies were rocked so much so as to almost make them ill. Today babies are no longer bound and hardly ever rocked. They are all the better for it.

Because of the poverty, certain families could not buy baby powder. To prevent chafing, formerly powder from the spruce tree (found between the bark and the dead tree), then later browned flour, was used.

The baby was breast-fed for at least three months, sometimes for a year or more. Afterwards, a bottle capped with a *tétouche* (nipple) was used, then porridge in milk, and little by little, *bouchées molles* (mouthfuls softened in the mother's mouth before giving them to the baby).

The presence of doctors since 1875, the hospital of today, the conferences organized by health services, the economic prosperity and more advanced education, have banished all the bizarre, often unsanitary habits and permit the mothers of Chéticamp to be perfectly up-to-date in the field of sanitation.

Childhood

The older children help their mother in taking care of the baby. They can play with the child but must not tickle him for that would cause him to stutter later on.

On the subject of children, we have only found this axiom:

When a child has his teeth early,/ Another child will soon arrive.

A seventh son or a seventh daughter in consecutive order has a gift.

It is believed that a simple touch of the hand by one of these can cure all manner of illnesses, such as arresting bleeding, curing toothache or burns. The same gift is attributed to a child who was born feet first.

All parents want intelligent children. They always find them charming, but until proof of the opposite is shown they are afraid the children might be mentally defective. To avoid this calamity, the child's nails and hair are not cut, nor is he permitted to see himself in a mirror before he is one year old.

The Second Stage of Childhood

At the age of one year the child begins to understand and take pleasure in the games one plays for his amusement. His father, his older brother or his grandfather will seat the child astride his foot and, leg crossed, will make him jump while saying:

To Paris, to Paris, – On the tail of a small grey horse, – To Rouen, to Rouen, – On the tail of a small white horse, – Walk, walk, – Little trot, little trot, – Big trot, big trot, – Little gallop, little gallop, – Big gallop, big gallop!

Begun slowly, this movement accelerates with the speed of the horse one is imitating.

Some other games and childish rhymes used to amuse the children:

Lark, lark, small lark! – Run, run, run. – It went that way (rub the bare arm of the child gently). – It made its nest there (in the hollow of his hand). – It is caught there (the thumb). – It is plucked here (the index finger). – It is cooked here (the second finger). – Here it is eaten (the third finger). – And now the small bird has all gone away (little finger)!

There is a game to help the child distinguish parts of his body. While pointing his finger at each of the parts being taught, one says:

Stomach of lead, – Throat of pigeon. – Cleft chin, – Silver mouth, – Boiled cheek, – Roasted cheek, – Tiny nose, – Small eye, – Big eye, – Hit the forehead!

With these last words, the child is lightly tapped on the forehead.

At three or four years of age the child can be very amused by the following game. The child, with both hands joined and fists closed, is made to hold a small stick on his thumb. While pretending to take the stick, one recites the following jingle:

My father had a small dog, – Whose name was Biztaque. – He ran into the forest, – With his tail as stiff as a board. – Biz—iz—iz—iz .... (continue this as long as one wishes) – Taque!

While saying "Biz—iz..." one comes close to the stick, ready to seize it. On the word "Taque" the stick is grabbed quickly in order to tap the fingers of the child who must try to avoid the blow by opening his hands as soon as the other has grabbed the stick.

Another very simple little game: while touching, in turn, the end of each of the child's fingers, count up to fifteen by this simple rhyme,

Pint over pint, – I will bet a pint – That the fifteen's are there.

At each syllable, it is necessary to stress word and gesture.

School Years

This is the chapter on Social Life. Since we have devoted a special chapter to schools, it is unnecessary here to return to school life as such. What interests us here is the life of school-age children.

Today the children begin school about the age of six years. The school bus service permits the children to attend school regularly despite the distances and the weather. In the past many parents did not appreciate formal education, even to the point of distrusting it, considering lazy those who wished to get an education. Naturally the children of such parents were not interested either and did not stay very long in school, and while there very often learned nothing. Many parents, however, understood the benefit to their children of the instruction of that time. As soon as schools were sufficiently organized from about 1875 onwards, we see a large group of children grow up to become schoolteachers, open businesses, or go on to take further classical studies. Today, generally, all parents highly appreciate education and their children enjoy school.

Outside of class or study hours, the spontaneous life of the children shows itself, especially in their games at home and during recreation periods at school. The small boys on one side and the young girls on the other frequently have their own games to play, but since the makeup of families nearly always includes both boys and girls, and as boys and girls in Chéticamp go to the same schools and are in the same classes, it often happens that they play games together, whether this is done without the knowledge of the teacher, gone for dinner, or in his presence and with him during morning and afternoon recess.[19]

At that age, children's games are quite numerous. We will try to mention some of them. There are games for the boys alone, such as the following. In the summer there are the barrel hoops, small carts, boats, ball games and, today, marbles in the spring. Climbing in trees and over roofs, whittling, making whistles, and fishing in the brooks are also some favourite pastimes. In winter there are games in the snow, such as building forts, castles, snowmen, tobogganing and skating. Up until 1930 hockey was unknown. Since then, an arena has been built and hockey clubs have been organized.

For the young girls there are dolls, skipping rope, hopscotch, numerous group games, such as "les clefs sont dans la mer" (The Keys are in the Ocean), and others. A more detailed description of these games follows.

Les clefs sont dans la mer (The Keys Are in the Ocean): This game, ordinarily played by very young girls, is known in parts of Québec as "Les cloches sont au fond de l'eau" (The Bells Are at the Bottom of the Water) and is played in the same way.

The players choose two companions in the group. These two girls choose the name of an object to designate her side; for example, knife and fork, gold and silver. The two join hands in the air in order to permit the others to pass under the bridge. The others pass under while singing:

> The keys are in the ocean
> 0 guai! o guai! o guai!
> Three times you will pass through,
> The last, the last,
> Three times you will pass through,
> The last will stay.

At these last words, the two girls who fall from the bridge let their arms fall around the one who, at that moment, is found under the arch. She is asked "Which do you choose, gold or silver?" She makes her choice and takes her place behind the one represented by the gold or silver. The game continues until all are caught and have made their choice. When everyone is finally on one side or the other, they begin to pull back and forth and the battle lasts until one side carries the victory over the other.[20]

Couper le cou des moutons (Cut the Neck of the Sheep): A child from the group stirs up the ground. The others question him and he replies:

What are you making there? – A small fire. – Why are you making a small fire? – To boil water! – Why are you boiling water? – To sharpen my knife. – Why are you sharpening your knife? – To cut the neck of my sheep.

He then tries to catch the other players who flee to save themselves.

C'est mon beau château (This Is My Beautiful Castle): All the players except one hold hands and dance around in a circle. Outside this circle another dances alone, while turning and singing:

> This is my beautiful castle.
> My aunt lure, lure et lure,
> This is my beautiful castle,
> My aunt lure, lure, lo.

The others respond:

> Ours is more beautiful,
> My aunt lure, lure et lure....

The singer who is alone continues:

> We will destroy it,
> My aunt lure, lure et lure....

The group:

> Which one will you take?
> My aunt lure, lure et lure....

The singer:

> We'll take this young lady,
> My aunt lure, lure et lure....[21]

While the singing is going on, the girl who is singing alone outside the group chooses a child from the group to join her and dance with her.

Then the song is begun again and another girl is chosen. The game continues until the whole group, except one, has passed over to the side of the one who began the singing. Then, the one who is now alone begins the song all over again and rebuilds a following on her side in the same manner.

Où vas-tu boiteuse ermite? (Where Are You Going, Lame One?): All the girls in the group hold hands and form a circle. Then they go around while singing:

> Where are you going, lame one?
> Je t'y pli, je t'y plais.
> Where are you going, lame one?
> With you I am happy.

While they turn and sing, another girl, limping, walks counter to the others in going around. Suddenly, the circle stops, while the lame person continues walking and singing:

> I come to get one of your girls,
> Je t'y pli, je t'y plais.
> I come to get one of your girls,
> With you I am happy.

The circle begins to turn again and continues to sing, while the lame person walks around:

> You will take the ugliest,
> Je t'y pli, je t'y plais....

The circle stops turning each time the lame one sings, while the latter walks on all the time. Here, she answers:

> I don't want your ugly ones,
> Je t'y pli, je t'y plais....

The group continues:

> Then take the most beautiful,
> Je t'y pli, je t'y plais....

The lame one sings:

> Miss Julie, that's you,
> Je t'y pli, je t'y plais....

The lame one chooses a girl from the circle and that one chooses the next and so on to the last, who then becomes the lame one; and the circle begins all over again, the game lasting as long as the group wishes.

Le cercle (The Circle): All the children hold hands in forming a circle. One child runs around on the outside of the circle. While passing, he taps one of the group making up the circle. The one touched must immediately run in the opposite direction and try to regain his place before the one who has touched him. If he arrives first, he keeps his place; if not, the other takes it. The loser must then run around and tap another child until he finally does recover another place in the circle.

Jeu des souris et du chat (The Cat and Mouse Game): All the children form a circle and slowly move around. These are the mice. Outside the circle, standing still, is the cat. While passing by the cat, one of the mice taps him. As soon as this happens the cat must go after the mouse and follow wherever she goes. The tapper goes through the circle and between the other mice. The cat has to take the same route and catch the mouse who tapped him. If he doesn't catch her, he is dead. If he catches her, he becomes a mouse and joins the circle with the others. The tapper then becomes the cat.

Le jeu du bélier (The Battering Ram): A circle is formed with all children holding hands very tightly. In the centre is one child from the group. He is the battering ram; he looks tough and charges with all his strength in an attempt to break through the circle and pass through to the outside. If he succeeds, he escapes and all those forming the circle chase after him. The one who succeeds in catching him becomes the next ram.

La chatte-maigre—Quatre coins (Puss-in-the-Corner): The game Puss-in-the-Corner is played with five players, four of whom each stay in a corner while the fifth, the puss, is in the centre of the square. The point of the game is for the four in the corners to change corners with each other without letting the puss steal one of their corners, momentarily left free during a change. The one who loses his corner to the puss becomes the next puss in the centre searching for a corner.

Le jeu du loup (The Wolf Game): One child from the group hides. This is the wolf.

The others, holding hands, walk around and sing: "Let us walk in the woods while the wolf is not around." Then they ask the wolf: "What are you doing?" The wolf replies: "I'm putting on my shirt."

They ask again: "What are you doing?" He answers: "I'm putting on my pants."

They ask: "What are you doing?" He answers: "I'm putting on my stockings." (And so on, according to how long the wolf wishes to prolong the game.)

What are you doing?	I'm getting ready to leave
I'm getting up.	What are you doing?
What are you doing?	I'm leaving!

He starts after them. They flee. The wolf then has to catch one of them who, in turn, becomes the wolf.

L'anguille brulée (The Button Game): While half of the group stays in one room, the other half hides an object in another room. The first group begins to hunt for the object. If one of this group approaches it, those in the second group say "You're getting warm" or "You're hot!" The voices get consistently stronger, according to how close one is to the object. If one moves away from the object the expression is said less strongly, and if one moves too far away the expression is no longer said. While being guided by these words, the game is won by the person who first finds the object. This is also a fine game for adults.

Jouer au truc—cache-cache (Hide-and-Seek): One child covers his eyes and counts to twenty, thirty, or whatever number gives the other children time to hide themselves. The one who has his eyes covered and is counting loudly, yells the last number to indicate he is beginning the pursuit. Those who then succeed in avoiding the searcher run to touch base (the place where the counter had been with his eyes closed) and say, "Free!" These people are safe. If the searcher sees them in time and recognizes them, he runs to touch base and says, "You're caught!" and names the person. That one is then considered dead. The game ends when all the players are caught.

Jouer au bouche-z-yeux—Colin-Maillard (Blindman's Buff): With his eyes covered by a band, one of the group, the blindman, tries to catch someone and recognize him. If he guesses his identity, this latter person takes the bandage and the game continues with him as the blindman. If the blindman doesn't recognize the player he has caught, he has to keep his eyes covered and continue as blindman until he does recognize someone he has caught.

Jouer au chat (The Cat Game): This is a mixed game that can be played by adults, but is played especially by older students. Each of the boys takes a seat in class, sitting in such a way as to leave a space at the end of the seat for a girl. All the girls go into another class. The liaison officer between the two groups is called the cat and carries a large woollen stocking in which he makes knots. He approaches one of the boys and asks him in a low tone for the name of the girl he would like to sit beside him. Then the cat goes off to fetch the chosen girl. The girl is led back and must guess the name of the boy who asked for her. If she guesses correctly, she sits down and remains with the boy who asked for her. If she guesses incorrectly and sits at another desk, the cat chases her back into the class from which she came while hitting her with his knotted stocking.

After a short time, roles are reversed. The girls are seated at the desks and the boys take their chances on guessing correctly.

Jeu au bouton (Button, Button, Who's Got the Button?): All the children while forming a circle, join their hands as if in prayer. Someone in the center of the circle, passes his hands, in which he hold a button, over the hands of all the others. To each one, he makes it seem as if he's letting go of the button but, in reality, only gives it to one, who must avoid letting the others see that he has it. The one who passed the button asks someone in the circle, "Peek-a-boo, old pal! Who's got it?" If this one guesses incorrectly, he must take a punishment. If he guesses correctly, it is he who is next passing the button.

All these games of which we spoke were often played by mixed groups of boys and girls. Now we write of some which, by their roughness, were only played by boys. It was only occasionally that girls would take part in these games.

Jouer au trône (King of the Mountain): A hill of well-packed snow with one steep side was used as a throne. The boys separated equally into two groups: one group on top of the throne and the other at the bottom of the hill of snow. The group below tried to dislodge the ones above while the group above defended itself, violently repulsing those who were climbing the hill. Anyone from above forced down the hill in some manner was considered out of the game. The goal was to see who could stay longest on the throne. This was a test of strength for the boys, as well as for their clothing. But the strong homespun material was equal to the test and escaped without too many rips.

La barrique à Lima (Catch the Runner): The children form two rows facing each other from about fifty or more feet apart. Each child has to run from one row to another without being caught by the guard standing in the centre between the two rows. Those who are caught become catchers with the original guard and the game becomes more and more cautiously played as the catchers become more numerous. In this game, catching someone consists of giving him three light blows on the back while saying, "Un, deux, trois, la barrique à Lima!" ("One, two, three, you're caught!")

Jouer à béguer (Game of Tag Played with a Ball): In this game the players placed themselves in a row. About twenty or twenty-five feet on each side were two pitchers. In his turn, each pitcher tried to hit someone in the row with the ball. Anyone touched by it was considered dead, that is, out of the game. Each pitcher tried to kill off the greatest number of boys; for the boys in the row, the object was to stay untagged as long as possible.

For a long time neither softball nor baseball were known in Chéticamp. At the very most, some owned blown-up rubber balls, but these were rare. Besides, preferred over these were *les pommes*, homemade balls from the yarn of old, worn-out stockings tacked tightly together by weaving the needle and yarn back and forth through the ball of yarn until the ball was sufficiently hardened. Sometimes cork was placed in the centre and the wool wound around it to make the ball. Those who took greater care in making these balls covered them with hide taken from old boots. These balls threw well and hit well, without any danger to the boys who were hit by them. They were well adapted to the tag game and the type of baseball game played in Chéticamp.

Jouer à la pomme (Type of Baseball): The only ballgame known in Chéticamp somewhat resembled that of the present-day baseball, but with many differences. There are four bases. The point for the batter is not a point for the runners. The batter stays at bat as long as he has not hit the ball. As soon as he has hit the ball he must run to first base, then to the second, third, and even to the fourth if he can and in this way arrives "home" and scores a point. The batter is only dead (out of the game) if a player from the opposing team catches the ball as it flies through the air or if he tags the batter as he runs between two bases.

Comptines (Rhymes): In most of these games, a player must be chosen. He hides himself or covers his eyes or is "it," etc. To this end, the children used rhymes that they recited while pointing to a player at each stressed syllable. The one on whom the last word or syllable falls is eliminated.

A rough translation of some rhymes still in use follows here:

1. Small knife of gold and silver, — Your mother calls you at the end of the field, — To eat some curds – That the mice have trampled – For a whole hour – Scram!

2. Good morning, Monday, and you, Tuesday – Go tell Wednesday – That we will go on Thursday – To fetch Friday – So we can go on Saturday – To eat on Sunday – At "P'tit" Damase's – Wearing a white tie.

3. *First Version:* It is noon – Who said so? – The small mouse. – Where was she? – In the chapel. – What was she making? – Some lace. – For whom? – For that lady.

Second Version: It is noon, – Who said so? – The tiny Mouse. – Where is she? – In the chimney, – What is she making? – Some bonnets, – For whom does she make them? – For the Bostonians.

4. Annie, Anna, – The woodpecker, – The iron harrow, – The wolf passed – Through the desert – Four paws raised in the air; – Broke wind, – For whom? – For you.

5. Piqueti, piqueta, – Hen on the wall, – Who picks at hard bread. – Piqueti, piqueta, – Lifts her rear end – And jumps down.

6. Tales of tales, – My uncle's tiny she-dog, – Went behind the woodpile – And made a small mess – For whom? – For you.

And here's a rhyme with local flavour:

7. I bless you, – I consecrate you, – I place you in a small bag, – I throw you over the cliff, – On Polycarpe's land.

8. One, two, three, etc.... nine, apple nine.

9. My small cow has sore feet. – Drag it by the tail. – Perhaps it will get better.

10. My father has built a small house. – How many nails did he use?

A number is chosen, then someone begins to count while pointing a finger at one of the group with each number. The one on whom falls the chosen number is out of the game, and the counter continues. The last one in the game becomes the person chosen to count off.

It seems that the following verse also appeared as a rhyme:

Monday, Tuesday, feast days. – Wednesday, I will not be able to be there. – Thursday, Feast of St. Thomas. – Friday, I will not be there. – Saturday morning – The week will be nearly over.

Verses and Expressions

The people of Chéticamp passed down the verses, of which some are very well known in other regions.

1. Once there was, – A woman of faith, – Who was selling liver – In the town of Foix. – Once she said to me: – On my word of honour, – This is the last time, – That I sell liver – In the town of Foix.

2. If you have business to take care of, – Never carry your business – To those who have business of their own to take care of, – For those who have to take care of their own business, – Will not leave the business they have to do – To take care of your business, – And the business you have to do – Will still be left to do.

3. Rain, rain, paradise. – Everyone is under shelter – Except my younger brother and I – Who are under the eaves.

Repeat: Rain, rain, paradise. – The baby birds are under shelter. – Except my younger brother and I – Who are under the eaves.

4. Are you hungry? – Eat your hand. – Save the other for tomorrow.

5. One, two, three, – I'm going to the woods. – Four, five, six, – To gather cherries. – Seven, eight, nine, – My basket full of eggs. – Ten, eleven, twelve, – All my cherries are red.

6. What I like, – Is cream. – What I hate, – is porridge. – What I love with all my heart, – Is a *girl* my age.

Finally, also in Chéticamp, the children ask grasshoppers for their syrup in this rhyme:

7. Grasshopper, grasshopper, – Show me your molasses. – Or I will surely break your neck.

As in France, they sing:

8. It's my Aunt Philomena – Who hurt her belly, – On the rim of the cauldron – While making soap.

Social Life

Some people substitute the next two lines, probably of local composition, for the first two lines:

This is my Uncle Timothy, – Who broke the tip of his nose.

Tongue-Twisters

At this age, one likes to learn tongue-twisters, expressions which must be pronounced without stammering over the words and, also, to have others try to repeat them. Some of these tongue-twisters follow here in rough English translation.

1. Three large rats, – In three large holes, – Munch three crusts.
2. Three small, slender pipes in a bag.
3. My fine little man, fancy clad, – When will you remove your fine clothing?
4. Does one grind wheat? – Does one sew a suit? – If one grinds the wheat, – One also sews the suit.

Or: Does one sew a suit? – Does one grind the grain? – If one sews the suit, – One grinds the grain.

5. Promise that it will be well joined, well turned, – well circled, the hoop well tapped down. – If it is not well joined, well turned, – well circled, well trapped down, – I will pay for the joining, the turning, – the circling and the tapping down of the hoop.

6. Good morning, Mr. Original, – When will you unoriginalize yourself? – I will unoriginalize myself – When all the original ones – Will all be unoriginalized!

7. A hunter, knowing how to hunt, – Knows how to hunt without his dog.
8. Three full plates of pancakes – Cut out on the head of a priest.

Enigmas

9. Lath removed leaves a hole.
10. Felix killed a pig, did not salt it, pig spoiled.
11. If Pendi-Pendette had not – Awakened Dormi-Dormette, – Veni-Venette would have killed – Dormi-Dormette.

12. *(or again)* If Pendi-Pendant had not – Awakened Dormi-Dormant, – Veni-Venant would have eaten – Dormi-Dormant.

Response: A man asleep under a tree – Is awakened by the fruit – That falls on him at the moment – When a wild beast turns up to kill him.

Riddles

13. Four paws climb on four paws – Four paws wait for four paws, – Four paws don't come – Four paws go away.

Answer: A cat climbing on a chair to wait for a mouse.

14. In death the living come there. – Six there are, seven there will be – And perhaps that will save me.

Answer: Safe life is promised to a condemned man if he finds an unsolvable riddle. His riddle: A nest of birds in a dried-up skull. There are six little ones and there will be seven, for there remains one egg.[22]

15. Vincent put the ox in the meadow. – (twenty hundred thousand…) – How many feet and how many tails are there?
Answer: Four feet and one tail.

16. What comes and goes, yet cannot enter the neighbour's house?
Answer: A door.

17. What goes around the house and only makes one track?
Answer: A wheelbarrow.

18. What has neither circle nor rings, – And is filled up to the brim?
Answer: An egg.

19. How is it that the wife of a widower cannot marry?
Answer: She is dead.

20. If the sister of your aunt is not your aunt, who is she?
Answer: Your mother.

21. Two blind people go to the wedding of their brother. – But this brother has no brother. – How can we explain this?
Answer: The blind people are his sisters.

22. What eats its intestines and drinks its blood?
Answer: An oil lamp.

23. What enters church standing upside down?
Answer: Nails in shoes.

24. What wears dresses over dresses, made without seams?
Answer: An onion.

25. What goes out dry and comes back wet?
Answer: A water bucket. It is empty and dry going out and full and wet on the way back.

26. The more there are the less it weighs.
Answer: Holes in a plank.

The Life of Youth

Formerly, small boys wore short pants until they passed to the level of youths, about sixteen or seventeen years of age. Young girls wore their hair long. The distinctive sign of the boy who has become a young man was the wearing of long pants; that of the young lady was the wearing up of her hair, replacing her braids.

Age was not an automatic marker. Temperament, maturity, work, salary, and circumstances were taken into account. For the one in question, all these things together made this transition quite an event. It is with anguish and embarrassment that one crosses the threshold between childhood and youth. Would he be accepted by the grown-ups?

Today there no longer exist any distinctive signs of that transition. Young boys wear long pants and young girls wear their hair in any manner they prefer.

This is also the time when girls begin to notice boys, when the boys reach the age of puberty, when boys and girls begin to eye each other and make tentative gestures towards dating.

Courtship

Today in Chéticamp, as everywhere else, there are no evenings set aside for dating. In former times these evenings were well spaced and, whether one liked it or not, one had to be satisfied with that.

Young men would socialize once a month with their girlfriends. That evening was official, even solemn. The boy arrived and could sit down anywhere at first and chat with the people in the house. But, at a certain moment, he got up under some pretext, to go for a drink of water, for example, and, while passing by his girlfriend would touch her on the shoulder. This was the usual signal. The girl would get up and go sit somewhere, apart from the others, most often on a chest or bin. The young man, on returning from getting himself a drink, would join her. Another custom practiced was the throwing of a small piece of wood to the girl, a match or some such thing. This was the signal for the young girl to go sit apart from the others, where the young man would soon join her.

Even off to the side where they chatted in low tones, these lovers stayed under the watchful eyes of their parents.

On these evenings it was the custom for the young man to bring along a bag of brown sugar. During the evening the two would eat spoonfuls of it from the same bag. If any remained the girl would keep the rest and the next time they met in this way she *aouindait le sac*[23] (would take out the bag and they would finish off the sugar).

On Sunday the two would walk home from Mass together. By this action it was now made public that they were courting.

Practices

As in all countries of the world, the young girls of Chéticamp are familiar with certain practices to which they, jokingly, have recourse in order to know their future husband. Some of these practices are listed here. There are certainly more than these few.

1. Putting a mirror under the pillow. The one of whom she dreams will be her future husband. If one is destined never to marry, she will dream of a coffin.

2. With matches, make a bridge on a plate. If you dream of falling into the water the one who comes to save you will be your future husband.

3. Eating a salted biscuit: the one who brings her a drink of water in a dream will be her future husband.[24]

4. Pass a piece of cake through a wedding ring of a bride; then put the cake

under one's pillow. The man of whom she dreams will be her husband.[25]

5. Peel an apple in such a way that the peeling remains in one piece; hold this peeling by one end between the thumb and the index finger, turning it three times around one's head and letting it fall behind one. If a letter is formed, it will be the first letter of the name of one's future husband.[26]

6. Pass a hair through a wedding ring. Wet the ring three times in a glass of water. The third time hold it above the water. If the wedding ring does not ring against the glass one will remain a spinster; if it rings against the glass, count the blows, for this tells the number of years before one's marriage.[27]

7. Many people believe in the following philtre: Put a drop of one's blood in a fruit and have the fruit eaten by the person by whom one wishes to be loved. He/she will fall madly in love.[28]

The Engagement

Even today the young people of Chéticamp ignore all forms of engagement parties. However, when courting is well advanced and marriage is in view the gentleman buys a ring for his intended.

The Proposal

When marriage is decided upon by the two lovers there must be *la grande demande* (the actual proposal). Formerly, this was carried out in solemn fashion. The groom-to-be was always accompanied by a friend. They would arrive one evening and during the visit, after the children had gone to bed, the companion would invite the parents of the bride-to-be into another room. The future groom would join them there to request the hand of their daughter. Today the young man alone makes this request after an ordinary social visit.

The future couple also ask permission of their respective godfathers. One godfather describes the request made of him thusly:

Yesterday Marie had her banns read in church. I am her godfather. Friday evening, they came to see me, she and her sister. She was rather shy with me! I felt so sorry for her! Besides that, the house was full that evening. I was listening to her sister, who was speaking in a low tone, telling her: "You will have to take him into a room or outside." Finally, the others left. As soon as they had gone, I said, "Now sit down here. Don't worry, they're gone." She was so bashful![29]

For the final arrangements the parents of the groom would pay a visit to the parents of the bride in order to discuss the relationship and the marriage. Then, together, the two fathers would go visit the priest concerning having the banns read in church.

The Wedding

On three consecutive Sundays before the wedding the banns were published in church. Weddings always seemed to take place on the Tuesday after January 6. During the time of Father Fiset weddings were celebrated only in winter, and all on this date. Up to twenty-two couples have been married on the same morning. It was a most suitable date in Chéti-camp since it occurred during the festival season.

On the eve of the wedding the groom-to-be and his best man would pay a visit to the home of the future bride. If they lived too great a distance to return home, they would spend the night at the home of a neighbour. This was done because on the next morning the procession would leave from the bride's home, in the following order: in the lead wagon would be the best man and the bride; in the second wagon would be the groom and the maid-of-honour; then would follow the other wagons containing par-ents and friends. It was always the best man and the maid-of-honour who served as witnesses. Returning from the church the bride and groom would occupy the lead wagon with the best man and the maid-of-honour following in the second.

In the church the bride and groom would take their places in the first pew rather than at the priedieu as is done today. They approached the al-tar rail three times, first for the marriage at the beginning of Mass, then for two special blessings given during Mass. Today the wedding couple as well as the two witnesses occupy the priedieu in the Sanctuary.

Bishop Plessis, during his episcopal visit to Chéticamp in 1812, de-scribed weddings of that time thusly:

In all these places wedding displays are reduced to very simple things. The bride is covered, on all sides of her head, with red ribbons hanging to her waist, while the groom has a bunch of ribbons of the same colour attached to one of the boutonnières of his vest, as well as a cockade on his hat; his two attendants have similar cockades; these ornaments are worn throughout the entire wedding day; on the next day they no longer appear, and each one goes to church in his usual clothing and continues in his simplicity. This simplicity is so great and so severe that a girl who would try to put a pleat in her mantlet (for the use of dresses is still entirely ignored) would be considered worldly, and would not find herself getting married; it would be the same for a young man who would dare to wear a bour-geois [middle-class] suit.[30]

During these times the clothing of grooms was only their ordinary Sunday clothes, made of rough homespun material. Later came the bour-geois or middle-class suits. Since several people didn't have any clothing of the newer style the practice spread of borrowing these bourgeois out-fits from those who did posses them. One pair of trousers served more than twenty grooms. Today grooms are dressed in the latest style.

Naturally, any parishioner could assist at the marriage Mass in the church. But only those who were invited would go to the wedding party. From this practice sprang the following expressions: "Are you invited to the wedding?" "I am waiting to be invited," "I have been invited," "I'm invit-ing you to my wedding party," the sole method of sending out invitations.

The dinner took place at the home of the bride, the supper and social evening at the home of the groom's parents, or vice versa. Only the parents and intimate friends attended the dinner. The menu was usually a goose fricot and rice pies. Those invited to the party would arrive in the afternoon, for if they were invited it was understood to be for supper and the social evening. As those invited arrived, certain ladies chosen for this position would serve a light lunch of biscuits, as well as homemade liqueur made of water, vinegar and molasses. There were no carbonated drinks at this time. For supper there were all sorts of meats and pastries. At this time the Bride's Song would be sung, a rough translation of which follows here.

The Bride's Song

I came to wish you a happy marriage, (twice)
To your husband
As well as to you.

It is today, my girl, that you are joined, (twice)
With a golden tie
Until death doth you part.

Today, my girl, is a memorable day, (twice)
It's a blessed day!
Your two hearts are one.

You have understood well what I come to say: (twice)
You will love your husband
As you love yourself.

Today, my girl, you take a husband. (twice)
All your beautiful colours
Will pass like the flowers.

You will no longer go to dances and gatherings at games. (twice)
You will stay home
While we go.[31]

In the evening a lunch would be served. Next day a meat pie was served for breakfast. Several of the guests would even stay for dinner the next day when the rest of the meats and pastries were reheated and served.

At the party, dancing began before supper and continued again immediately afterwards. It continued all evening and often throughout the night: *la boulangère* (Paul Jones), *la patate longue* (the long potato), and the dances called *le sept* and *le huit* (square dances). In Father Fiset's time, and for a long time afterwards, these dances were forbidden, probably because of some abuses that crept in. Everyone contented himself with the dance called *le quatre* (stepdancing), which entailed no bodily contact.

At midnight the whole racket stopped for evening prayers. Then the married couple would shake hands with everyone and retire for the night.

This was really upsetting for them, for the bedchamber, next to the large room in the house where the party was being held, was only a bed partitioned off with curtains as a door. This is likely why the newlyweds on this evening would sleep in their clothes. The next day someone would awaken them. They would shyly leave their "room" and again shake hands with everyone.

Before noon, seeing that everyone was quite fatigued, the guests would begin singing, telling funny stories and playing parlour games.

When many marriages were celebrated on the same day the number of violin players was not sufficient for so many parties. Then one had recourse to the singers for the dance tunes. Still remembered are 'Polite (à Bandet) Roche, Fabien Deveau, Marcellin (à Romuald) Doucet, Johnny Lelièvre, and others.

As an inheritance the groom received a piece of land from his father. The bride received five blankets, a cow, three or four lambs and a spinning wheel from her parents.

Today the curtained-off bedchambers have disappeared, automobiles have replaced the wagons, clothing is completely in style, and there is no longer a fixed day for weddings. Yet, even with all this, wedding parties have still retained all the flavour of the parties of earlier times.

Amusements

Young men paid an official visit to their girlfriends once a month, but this didn't prevent them from going to the girls' homes more often, especially if there were other boys and girls in the family. At these times, though, "they would not pay any more attention to their girlfriend than they would to the others in the family."[32] All enjoyed themselves together with songs and parlour games.

Some of the principal parlour games brightening these evenings follow here.

Haler aux renards (Tug-of-War): (1) This is the familiar game in which two equally strong groups pull on a rope against each other. The group succeeding in pulling down the other is the winner. (2) Two young men would pass a single rope around their necks and, at a distance of four paces from each other, and facing each other, would each pull backwards, trying to force the other down.

Haler au bâton (Stick Pull): Two men sit on the ground facing each other. They take a broomstick, hold it crosswise between them and, feet against feet, pull to see who can raise the other end and haul him towards himself.

Tire à la cuisse (Leg Pull): Two men lie down on their backs beside each other, the head of one next to the feet of the other. Each one raises the nearby leg of his adversary by hooking his own leg around that of the other person and, thus pushing from the leg, tries to overturn the other.

La charrue à chiens (Dog-plough): A group of five or six young people, backs bent forward, each one in front of the other in single file and touching each other, would shake themselves, while another, on all fours, climbed over the backs of the others trying to thread his way from the first to the last without falling.

Au "Guil-guil" or "Fesse-tout" (Strike Him All): This is a game where all the players except one form a circle, sitting on the floor with legs slightly bent but extended towards the centre of the circle. One player places himself in the middle of the circle and must try to capture the shoe/rubber that the other players pass quickly under their knees. While waiting for him to grab it, the players who can *le paunet* (hit him) with this rubber. When he himself succeeds in taking it from one of the players he uses it to hit this latter person who then takes his place in the circle.

All these games were rather rough and, for this reason, were reserved for the men and youths. Several other games were for mixed groups and could be quickly adjusted somewhat for this type of group.

Enfiler l'aiguille (Thread the Needle): The girls line up on one side, each holding a piece of thread in her hand. The boys, in equal numbers, line up on the other side facing the girls, each holding a needle. When the leader cries "Go!" both groups approach their opposite partners and the winner is the one who first threads the needle. To do this, though, the boy must not touch the thread nor the girl with the needle.

La chaise honteuse (The Shameful Chair): This game, which is not exclusive to Chéticamp,[33] is played thusly: Someone sits in a chair in the centre or a corner of the room. Another, in a very low tone, gathers from each person a descriptive word or phrase, whether it be a word of praise or, more often, something funny in reference to the one who is seated in the shameful chair. Then the one who has received the remarks from the others advances and says: "There is one here who said that you have a face like a pumpkin," or "There is one here who said you smell like a small herring," etc. When everything has been said the person in the shameful chair chooses the gibe which has most impressed him/her and the one who said it then takes his/her place in the chair. Then the game begins again.

"Ti belonne toubi": Everyone joins together in a circle. Someone lights a wood shaving then extinguishes the flame leaving only the glowing ember at the end. The stick is passed from one to the other. Each one must say, while holding the firebrand in his hand and before passing it to his neighbour: "Ti belonne toubi; if you *corves* (burn out, that is if you are extinguished) on me, you will bear a good load." The one who holds the firebrand when it is extinguished must lie down on the ground on his stomach. Someone puts an object on his back that he must identify. The object is continually changed for as long a time as he cannot identify it.

Le tison (The Firebrand): The whole group forms a circle. Attached to the bottom end of the rope suspended from the ceiling is a firebrand. One of the group blows on the firebrand, making it swing from one to another in a menacing fashion. No one can protect himself in any other way than by blowing on it.

Jouer au plomb (Lead-selling Game): Everyone lines up in a row. Someone passes by, asking each one: "How many pounds of my lead are you buying?" The others reply two, three, according to the number of pounds he wishes. The one who is going by says to him: "You will say neither 'sir' nor 'madam', 'yes' or 'no' to me." He says the same thing to each one of the group. Afterwards he questions them and tries all kinds of tricks to get them to say these forbidden words. The one who forgets himself and says "yes," "no," "sir" or "madam" is declared out of the game. Each person must answer the questions. The last person to remain in the game without getting caught begins the game again by taking his turn in asking the questions.

Le jeu de l'assiette (Forfeits): The method of playing this game is described by Sister Marie-Ursule: "Each person receives a number. The mistress of ceremonies make a plate turn while saying, 'five, eight, or ten....' The boy or girl who has this number must seize the plate while it is turning or else must pay a forfeit: a ring, a watch, anything. The game continues until all members have been called. Then the punishments are given out; there was always someone in the group who excelled in making up these penances. For instance, the mistress of ceremonies takes a watch and says: 'What is the penalty for the owner of this watch?' 'She must sing!' Then the girl must sing a song to recover her watch. The game continues until each person recovers his/her forfeit or forfeits."

Le roi et la reine (The King and Queen Game): Two chairs are placed near each other but with one chair space between them. A blanket is placed over the chairs. The King and Queen sit on the chairs. When one arrives to pay homage to the royal couple he is asked to sit down. Just at the moment when the visitor is about to sit down the King and Queen rise and the visitor falls to the ground. Sometimes a pan of water is placed under the blanket.[34]

Faire voir la lune (The Moon Game): A naïve participant is made to lie down on the ground while being assured he is going to see the moon. A jacket is placed over his head so that he sees nothing. The sleeve of this jacket is raised above his eyes like a telescope and he is asked whether he sees anything. While he is trying to see the moon, a full cup of water is poured into the sleeve.

Jeux d'élimination (Elimination Games): (1) The whole group dances while the music plays. The music stops suddenly and everyone in the game must also stop. Those who don't are eliminated. (2) The same game, but played with a small rug on the ground. When the music stops those who find themselves on the rug are eliminated. (3) Chairs are placed at one side of the room for all the players, except one. The leader, who is singing, is in the centre. When he stops singing all the players run to take a chair. The one who doesn't get a chair is out of the game. The game continues with one chair being removed each time the music stops.

Finally, certain of the children's games also amused the grown-ups, such as the Button Game, the Cat Game, and Button, Button, Who's Got the Button? all described above.

Other Amusements

In spring and autumn a ball game was played from time to time. In winter, when the ice was safe, skating took place on the bay, the rivers, and the lakes. Often in the evening large fires were lit on the ice and young people skated all around them. As we have mentioned before, at this time hockey was unknown.

Just the same, there were never any organized sports for the young in Chéticamp. It is only lately that there are organized clubs for hockey and baseball.

This lack of organized leisure time during the long, quiet periods of autumn and winter easily brought on regrettable consequences: the too-frequent use of liquor, with accompanying fighting and quarrelling. That, too, perhaps explains the following practice, long since disappeared.

Repasser les châssis (Passing by the Windows): Formerly, though much less frequently today, it was generally accepted that the young men could approach the homes of their neighbours and friends and, through the windows, watch what was happening inside during the evening. This was done especially where there were girls in the house. Next day a boy could tease a young girl about what she was doing the night before at such-and-such an hour, openly indicating by this that he had gone to look through the windows. This did not offend the girl. We must add that the people lived then, and still live somewhat in the same way today, in a completely patriachal simplicity. Thus, even today, no one knocks to enter the home of a neighbour or the homes of those whom he knows well. Knocking is only done to enter the home of strangers.

We should add here that many narrow footpaths cut through the fields and passed alongside the houses. The people of the neighbourhood used these paths when the need arose, day or night. Incidentally, the windows of the houses were low; the people lived in the kitchen of their homes and, in the majority of cases, there were no curtains. Anyone could look inside, just as one could enter without knocking.

Practical Jokes

It is rarely wise to be idle. During these leisure times young people would often become mischievous. There was a time when many practical jokes were played. And, naturally, the young people delighted in playing tricks on those who got angry about it. Gates, wide or narrow, were removed from their hinges, carried off and deposited hundreds of feet away; carts were dismantled; and piled up in front of one's door would be all the loose objects found near one's building. Some of these tricks are still famous.

One time, Ganasse (Charles Poirier) was sound asleep in his fishing cabin. Some young people forced Jim Lawrence's cow into the cabin and pushed her near Ganasse's bed. Calixte Boudreau took a gaff and through a hole pulled the blankets off Ganasse. Ganasse struggled to stand up and jumped...onto the cow! Oh, the screams!

At the home of "P'tit" Martin (Deveau), a pudding was made for the celebration of La Chandeleur. At that time every house had a stone fireplace. The chimney, just above the stone fireplace, led straight up to the roof. That evening the pudding had been left in its bag inside the large pot above the fire in the fireplace to keep it warm. A group of youths, whose leaders were Lubin (à Martin) Mius and Nectaire (à Charles) Deveau, came to steal the pudding. Nectaire climbed to the roof of the house with a gaff. But "Pointu," Martin Deveau's son, suspected something and was keeping a close eye on things. As soon as Nectaire had hooked the pudding, "Pointu" seized the gaff. Nectaire pulled back as strongly as he could. But "Pointu" would not pass through the chimney. So Nectaire let everything go…right into the fire!

One day, molasses candy was made at the home of Paddey (à Edward) Aucoin. After having stretched it the required length of time it was cut into small pieces, put on plates and allowed to cool off in the porch. Some hidden youths, watching for the right time, escaped with several plates of candy after barricading the house doors on the outside so as to prevent the people from going after them.

It must be well understood that these actions were not a question of stealing, but one of simply playing tricks on one another. The victims of these practical jokes always accepted them as such and often were the first to laugh at them…while awaiting their revenge.

P— swore often, it seems. One day he was away at sea, fishing, and swore more than ever—he even called on the devil—and a terrible joke was played on him because of this. Making good use of a moment when P— had gone down to the forecastle of his ship, his fishing companions pulled in his line and attached to it his own oilskin coat into which they stuffed all kinds of things, then put the whole thing back into the water. When P— returned to his line he thought he had a fish on the end of it and began to pull it in. When he noticed this bundle climbing out of the water he believed it really was the devil and cut the line. Everything sank to the bottom!

Another day a boat was being coal-tarred[35] when a Scotsman passed by with an old nag hitched to his wagon. He asked them:

"Why this tar?"

"To make the boat go."

"Will it be swift?"

"Frighteningly so!"

"Can it make a horse go?"

"Certainly!"

"Put some on my horse."

Our fishermen applied a burning, tar-soaked rag under the tail of the horse. With a bound, the horse leaped ahead, the fire on his rear. And, so long as he was in view, the Scotsman was making great signs with his hands and yelling, "Thank you, Sir! Thank you, Sir! Thanks…" His horse died in Margaree Forks.[36]

"P'tit" Bruno Poirier must have had a great liking for rum. During a sociable evening at the home of Philibert Gaudet, the sons of old Anselme Aucoin said to him, "We'll give you a pint of rum, if you wish to win it. You must drive a nail into the great Cross in the cemetery." This was the old cemetery. It was then becoming very dark. "P'tit" Bruno was afraid, but he did go. It was a bit windy that night and, in his nervousness, he attached the bottom of his jacket with the nail, without being aware of what he had done. When he tried to leave he felt himself held back. He believed it was being done by one of the dead. Panic hit him. He shook free and took to his heels! On his return, pale as death, he related that a hand from the dead had seized him. But the next day a piece of his jacket was seen, still attached to the cross.

Radio

During this era there was no radio and even less television. The first radio to make its appearance in Chéticamp was one bought by Charles W. Aucoin in 1925. Each one envied the privileged whose turn it was to put on the earphones. The following year Father MacNeil, curate of the parish, purchased a radio with a loudspeaker. Today each home has its own radio. Programmes from Antigonish and Charlottetown are heard very well in Chéticamp. The French programmes from New Carlisle, Québec, are heard even better, the Gulf placing no obstacles to Hertzian airwaves. So this French corner of Cape Breton has been able to enjoy French programmes at the same time as the Québecois of Gaspésia.

Television came to Chéticamp as well. This was not a good move since the sole broadcasting station in the vicinity (Sydney) is unilingual and English.

Picnics (Fairs)

Having no leisure-time organization at their service, Chéticantins are fond of all parish activity. Hence the success of parish fairs (called picnics) which, besides attracting the people of neighbouring parishes, brought in former parishioners from the mining centres of eastern Cape Breton and often the Scotsmen of Pleasant Bay and the Northeast.

The young parish of Saint-Joseph-du-Moine organized the first of the parish bazaars, about 1881. These picnics began in Chéticamp in 1902, their purpose being to pay off the church debt. These picnics have continued on down to the present day at irregular intervals of two or three years.

For the occasion booths are built on the church grounds, displaying wheels of fortune, bat games, ring games, a game of quite rudimentary bowling, and platforms for dancing, decorated and draped with bunting of vibrant colours. During the picnics meals are served. Every family helps furnish the food: meats, vegetables and pastries. Because of this all receipts are clear profit.

These fairs have become great parish festivals where everyone amuses himself decently in the shadow of the church steeple and to the sound of the music, in the noise of the games in action, and of the hawkers who compete from one booth to another in selling their wares.

Working Parties and Seasonal Jobs

In Chéticamp the people do not use the generic term to designate work done by teams. They are ignorant of the word *corvée* (working party). Here, work of this type has its own particular name—it's an *halerie* (firewood-hauling team), a *bûcherie* (wood-cutting team), an *arracherie* (a team for digging out potatoes), a *filerie* (a spinning party), etc. Nevertheless, no place in the world has known more of this type of work. Small tasks were done by each person, individually or by the family. But all the important seasonal work was carried out in collaboration with others in the parish. The mechanized life of today has relegated these customs to the past of old things and old people.

Roads: It would appear that Chéticamp's first roads were all built by working parties made up of the people who used these roads or by the owners of adjacent properties. This is certainly how the old Redman Road[37] came about, as the following typical document shows:

Chéticamp, June 21, 1826
The sharing of the Redman Road among fifteen inhabitants of Le Platin, each his share

1. to the southeast Pierre Anselm — 2. "le vieux" jean Bourjois — 3. Marie Au-Quin — 4. Charles Boudrot — 5. frèdrique Deveaux — 6. Loui Godes — 7. jean Bourjois de Lille Dela Magdailaine [The Magdalen Islands] — 8. jean Godes — 9. Loui Briard — 10. joseph Godes — 11. joseph auQuin — 12. Toumat auQuin — 13. Charle Chiasson a etienne — 14. Maccimilien Godes — 15. Magdailaine auQuin —

Each one's share is defined and three overseers will inspect it before and afterwards. They are named here below:

joseph auQuin
jean Bourgois vieux [old]
loui Godez

The road must be made and completed by the first of August and those who will not make their share will be forbidden the use of the road until they do make their share and those who will not make their share will be forbidden to use the road for a year, with no excuses accepted for anyone, in the presence of witness signed by the fifteen who have a share of the road,

Louis Breuillat — toumat auquin — Charles Boudrot — Regis Bois — joseph Godes — fabrique Deveau — Louis Godes.

Afterwards, and until the coming of our modern snowploughs, roads were taken care of in the same way, at least in winter. After a snowstorm one man in each section had the responsibility of clearing the roads. To do this he would go to every home and call out the necessary manpower.

When there was too much snow on the road he could decide to make openings through the wooden fences and permit traffic in adjacent fields.

Work on the roads was compulsory. All other chores were left to one's initiative, but all those who were invited to take part in this one considered it a point of honour to be there. In examining the work carried out season after season, we have an idea of the number and variety of these working parties.

Les fouleries (Fulling Cloth Parties): We have already mentioned elsewhere in this work that the period extending from Christmas to Mardi Gras was considered the holiday season in Chéticamp. It was especially during this season that the fulling cloth parties were organized, always accompanied by an evening of fun.

Throughout autumn and a part of January the ladies had woven on a loom a long roll of homespun material. Made of wool, that roll could measure from thirty-five to forty feet in length. Before cutting it for clothing it was necessary to "full" the material (to keep it from shrinking later). To do this a *foulerie* was organized. Friends were invited for that evening. In the largest room of the house tables were installed end to end. On these tables was placed the length of material to be fulled, with both ends of it sewn together. Men and women placed themselves around the table. The first operation consisted in soaking the material in soapy water. Then the fulling began. To the rhythm of a song the material was raised to arms' length and slapped down on the table to the beat of the music. While those on one side of the table lifted the material, the other side slapped the material down in a circular motion. The song gathered liveliness, as did the rhythm of the fullers. Joyous cries were heard on both sides of the table, and teasing began. There was a great deal of pleasure among the group and the material was quickly fulled.

After a few hours the material was fulled enough. Then a lunch was served. The songs, teasing and fun continued into the night.

Bûcheries, haleries et scieries (Wood-cutting, Hauling and Sawing Parties): During the months of January and February men brought the firewood down from the mountains. They had to cut the trees down on the spot and lop off the branches, then haul the wood home and saw it in lengths to fit the stove and, finally, split it. Often a work party was organized to carry out all these jobs, especially for the cutting of the wood (*bûcherie*), taking it out of the mountains (*halerie*), and sawing it (*scierie*).

These work groups always called for hearty meals and often a fun-filled evening at the home of the one for whom the group was working.

Les "attrapes à homard" ou "sougner les attrapes"[38] *(Lobster Traps or Tending the Traps):* When the wood was split and well corded in front of the door the men began to prepare their equipment for lobster fishing. This was in the month of March. Into the kitchen of the house the men would bring their old lobster traps, one by one, and repair the damages of the previous season. If need be they would build new traps. In a corner women and children would make the dragnets to put on the end and sides of the traps. This work of the traps completed, the men touched up the painting of the buoys. Then all was ready for the opening of the lobster season.

Each region of the Maritimes has a season fixed by the government for the fishing of lobster. In Chéticamp this season begins the first day of May and ends at the end of June.

Every fisherman is ready for the opening day of the fishing season. The traps are in the boat with the necessary gear. As soon as dawn breaks, everyone leaves for the lobster grounds. All are in a hurry for they want to get the best grounds. The rules say that the first person to reach a fishing area has the exclusive right to set his traps there. Then, one throws out a *picasse*, a large stone encircled by a yoke of wood, which serves as an anchor to a series of traps that are dropped at regular intervals up to another anchor, a few hundred feet from the first. Above each *picasse* or anchor floats a buoy on which is printed, in large letters, the initials of the owner. Each fisherman owns from two hundred to three hundred traps laid out in lines in this fashion on different fishing grounds. Every day he will come to raise these traps, taking out the lobsters and rebaiting the traps.

These traps, out in the ocean, are left in the safe custody of the seventh commandment of God. No one has ever been heard to say that a fisherman has raised the traps of another. Another remarkable thing is that poaching has never been a problem in Chéticamp. When the lobster fishing season is over the fishermen finally take in their gear and bring it ashore until the following season.

Les semailles (The Sowings): The sowing season offers nothing noteworthy to the reader. Each family manages the planting and sowing by itself. As two horses are used to do the work and each family has only one, the horse of a neighbour is borrowed when necessary and one's own lent in return.

Les écarderies (Wool-carding Parties): When the heat of the summer began everyone sheared his sheep. Then, outdoors in huge cauldrons, the wool was boiled in order to clean it. After letting it dry out in the sun it was shredded so as to card it more easily. It was now ready for the carding party.

The neighbour women and other friends were invited over with their carding tools and their apron. With ten or twelve ladies carding, the wool was quickly finished. After a few hours of work, in which chatting also played a great part, the wool accumulated in front of each carder in silky rolls ready to be spun.

Les fileries (Spinning Parties): The same system of working party was organized to spin the wool. The women brought their spinning wheel instead of their carding brushes.

After the spinning party, as after the carding party, depending upon the hour work was completed, lunch or supper was served and, as usual, the ladies willingly stayed late for endless chatting.

La pêche à la morue (Cod Fishing): We have spoken sufficiently of cod fishing as a means of subsistence. Not everyone went lobster fishing but, aside from a very few farmers, there was a time when everyone fished for cod. There is no designated fishing season for this fish so, beginning early in the spring, it continued until the very cold, stormy days of autumn.

For lobster fishing the fishermen did not move to the harbour; having no need of a wharf for the small boats used for this work they left their traps on the closest dune to their homes. However, the wharf at the harbour was necessary for cod fishing. Every fisherman whose house was not situated at the harbour owned a small cabin there. As soon as spring arrived they moved their gear to this place. These were real cabins that never saw paint! Nor did they often see the scrub brush or soap.

The fishermen stayed all week at their cabin and only returned home on Saturday. On Sunday evening they were seen on the roads walking back towards the harbour, carrying their week's supply of bread and butter in a sack on their backs. No conveniences in these cabins. Food was most frugal, potatoes and fish, bread and butter. Nevertheless, the fishermen loved the life of the cabins. On returning from their day of fishing, when the fish had been cut up and sold, after a tasty dinner of fresh cod, and after a good nap, the fishermen gathered in a group in one cabin or another. In these groups would always be some witty men, who were always ready with comical repartee, who joked about everything, and who amused the others with their funny propositions. There exists in Chéticamp a type of friendly teasing called banter or foolishness. In similar groups this becomes a most enjoyable social entertainment. One can recall many years later such flashes of wit or funny repartee of some of these people, long since dead. Even today this is an agreeable pastime in family gatherings. To give you an idea of this type of banter, there follow some stories that people like to relate.

Charlie à Hélène Poirier had no home and lived from one house to another. One day he was bragging among a group of fishermen of being able to speak in the French, English and Scottish languages. One of the group teasingly asked him, "How would you say in the Scottish language, that one has no home?"

•

As everyone knows, Lubin à Venant Boudreau was a very strong man. But it seems that he always had black hands, they were so dirty. After dinner one day, at the gypsum mine, the miners were talking about strong men and their feats of strength. Someone asked him, "Lubin, at your best! How much could you lift?" Lubin answered, "I have already lifted a large barrel of tar." "It was leaking!" said Henri à Stanislaus Roche, meaning to say that he (Lubin) still had very dirty hands from the tar.

•

Philippe had crippled arms; Marcellin had a simple-minded brother who had drowned in the harbour. His body was washed up on the shore.

Not very long afterward Marcellin met Philippe who was wearing a fur cap on his head. "What do you have on your head," asked Marcellin, "un foutreau [a mink]?" "Hm!" retorted Philippe, "le fou de trop [one fool too many], they found him washed up on shore!" "Yes, but if he'd had crooked arms like yours, he would never have washed up on shore," replied Marcellin. "He would have stayed caught in the seaweeds!"

•

Marcellin à Ben often carried his gun with him, especially into the woods. At this time guns were old flint muskets. One also had to carry along a powder horn and a bag of lead shots.

One day, when "Carawish" was in the woods to cut some linden for the making of brooms, he felt the call of nature and went behind a bush. Marcellin, passing close by—with his rifle, naturally—believed he saw a bear. He would have shot it but he had forgotten his lead shots. After having dug into his pockets, searching to see if he had something he could use as a bullet, he prepared to use the beads of his Rosary when "Carawish" stood up. On noticing the gun he began to yell, "Don't shoot! It's me!"

"You did well to stand up," said Marcellin, "I was ready to spray your rear end with a hail of Our Fathers!"

•

Charles à Lubin was a convinced Conservative in politics. He also pretended to know a great deal and, moreover, to be a pillar of the church choir.

One day before Mass a discussion had taken place between him and Henri à Stanislaus who was pretending to be a staunch Liberal. "Ah, yes," he said, "your Bennett! What has he done as Prime Minister? Absolutely nothing. He's a thief, like the others!" "Hah!" says Charles, somewhat piqued. "What do you know about it? What would you do if you were prime minister? I'd really like to see you in there!" Henri answered him. "I would change the members of the choir!"

The fishermen indeed loved the life in their cabins. Too much perhaps, for they neglected their farms. In effect the fishermen, with few exceptions, stayed in the cabins even if they returned from fishing early in the forenoon, even if it was *débauche*, that is, if the weather did not permit them to go out on the ocean. A fisherman often makes a poor farmer.

Life was hard at sea, but out there men were courageous and did not fear hardship. They rose at 2:00 or 3:00 a.m. and left to fish for *la bouette* (bait), *le squid à la turlutte*,[39] then as dawn was breaking made their way towards the great fishing banks.

Cod doesn't bite equally well everywhere. From generation to generation fishermen have discovered cod-fishing grounds where the catch is usually good. To reach these grounds the fishermen guide themselves by landmarks visible along the coast and in the mountains. Here are to be found the best-known fishing grounds. Their names are taken from the landmarks one used to reach them, or from some configuration of grounds itself.

Along the coasts (in order of distance):
Gratien's Fishing Grounds – The Rough Grounds (i.e. bad weather) – The Fishing Grounds of the Shaft – The Mitten Fishing Grounds – Pousnette's Fishing Grounds – Edwards's Fishing Grounds – The Fishing Grounds of the Jumping Brook – The Rocky Fishing Grounds (a line of water, 150 feet) – The Indians' Fishing Grounds – Basile's Fishing Grounds (landmark in the middle of the Island) – Paddey's Fishing Grounds – The Fishing Grounds of the Barn – "Gros" Louis' Fishing Grounds.

Out on the ocean:
The Fishing Grounds of the Square (five miles from land) – The Fishing Grounds of the House – Raymond's Shoal – The Stump – Placide's Fishing Grounds – Mesmin's Fishing Grounds – Balo's Fishing Grounds – The Sandbar – Couillard's Fishing Hole – The Round Bar – The Green Bar.

Mackerel: Autumn brings the thrilling mackerel fishing season. Mackerel is a migratory fish. When it arrives on our coasts in the autumn it is like manna passing by. It must be taken, and taken quickly, because it only passes occasionally. It travels in schools of hundreds of thousands at a time; it stays near the surface and ripples the top of the ocean, sometimes for an area of some square miles. Fishermen hurry to launch their boats into these moving banks of mackerel. With mincers they grind up some fish, usually herring, that they spread on the water to keep the mackerel near them.[40] Then the mackerel wriggle up to the edge of the boat. The excited fishermen hurriedly bait their lines and throw them into the water. Each fisherman watches two lines. The fish-hook has not descended two feet into the water when a mackerel has seized it and vigorously ploughs through the water with the line. Quickly the fish is pulled into the boat. With a twist of the hand it is unhooked; the line is re-baited and back into the water it is thrown. The other line goes through the same operation. It's like a running fire while the manna lasts. Exciting fishing times, the memory of which is retained by old retired fishermen until death comes to claim them!

The Weather Forecast
It can be readily understood that, in a place like Chéticamp where work parties are most often held outdoors and where the men made their living on the sea, forecasting the temperature assumed great importance for the people. Thus Chéticantins in general, and fishermen in particular,

have a very well-developed flair for forecasting the weather. For these latter, especially, the sky is an open book that they can read and predict the temperature and winds of the next day.

Without recording all the signs of good and bad weather, we do, however, give a partial list below.

In the Evening: When the sky is clear in the west but to the north of the sun: beautiful weather. When the sky reddens in the west and to the north of the sun: beautiful weather. When the sky reddens to the southwest of the sun: wind and rain. Ring around the moon: bad weather. It is from the same side that the ring begins to break up that the bad weather comes. When there is a bull's-eye on each side of the sun: bad weather. The wind will come from the side where the bull's-eye lasts the longest.

In the Morning: When the southeast sky reddens, wind and rain are forecast.

In the Winter: When the fire crackles: sign of snow.

At Any Time: When the sky looks like a mackerel skin: rain. When horses yawn: bad weather. When spiders are active or agitated: bad weather. When hens peck themselves under their wings: bad weather. While hens remain outside in the rain, the rain will continue to fall. When cats are playful it will be windy. A rainbow in the morning is a sign of good weather on the way. A rainbow at noon brings on rainy weather. A rainbow in the evening brings on nasty weather.

Gathering in the Harvest

Today many fishermen have their own cars and can more easily return to work on their land. The greater number of them no longer stay in the cabins. The cabins are disappearing more and more along the harbour, an occurrence which does a great deal to beautify the area.

But even formerly the fishermen returned to their homes to make the hay, to cut their oats, and to gather in the vegetables. For the vegetables, however, the women often managed these with only the help of the children.

Les "arracheries" (Potato-digging Parties): All the people had substantial fields of potatoes. In earlier times these were picked *à la tranche* (by spade). It was a long, tiring, tedious job. To make the work more agreeable, work parties were organized, *des arracheries de patates* (parties to gather in the potatoes). When there was an *arracherie* all the potatoes were picked in one day. What a relief this was! Working in this way a group of friends and neighbours made the day very pleasant. The next day, or another day, it was the turn of another farmer for his *arracherie*.

Les "déserteries" (Working Party to Clear the Land for Cultivation): When land was being cleared in the past the Chéticantins found a way to do this work together. To prepare the land for cultivation is to make it appear deserted. From that comes the Chéticantins expression *déserter* (to clear out) a piece of land and *déserterie* for this work done by a party or group.

Les éplucheries (Corn-husking Parties): When the corn was dry, it was husked and, often, corn-husking parties were organized. These were always small parties, for no one had much corn.

Les boucheries (Slaughtering Parties): It was in the autumn as well that everyone killed his pig, a head of cattle and perhaps a few lambs. Often it happened that an owner was too soft-hearted to kill his animals himself. He would ask his neighbour to do this service for him. But most often there was someone in the neighbourhood who was skilled in this trade and would willingly take on the job.

It is worthy of note to mention that, in all these slaughterings, there was always *la part du voisin* (the neighbour's share) of a good piece of meat.

Les battages au moulin (Grain Threshing): Finally, another autumn occurrence was the threshings. In earlier times the people beat the grain with the flail and winnowed it by hand. At the end of the last century, too, the smallest farmers, who had only a small amount of grain, beat it with the flail. It appears the first thresher used in Chéticamp was the property of Charlot Doucet. This thresher was passed from one farmer to another to beat the grain. As payment the owner kept for himself a percentage of the grain beaten. During this time there were no motors. This thresher was operated by eight horses who caused a horizontal wheel to turn; by using a method of multiple gearings the thresher functioned at the desired speed. This was quite a display. First there were eight horses and their drovers—even more sometimes, because the horses had to be replaced from time to time; then there were people who supplied the oats, men to operate the thresher, others to dispose of the beaten straw and, lastly, those who received the grain. With the exception of the owner of the thresher, no one was paid. This was the work party for the threshers. Here again an exhausting work became a day of pleasure, so much liveliness and gaiety did one put into it.

Later on Father Fiset brought in the threshers operated by two horses. Then came the motors. But the system of joyous work parties still exists.[41]

The *corvées* (work parties) did not lessen the work, for it is well understood that for a day received a day is expected in return. But they rendered the work easier to accomplish and much more agreeable. Often, however, there were corvées for purely charitable reasons, whether to help out a poor widow or to help someone suffering a hardship. Thus the *haleries*, *scieries*, etc., were often organized to furnish wood for a poor family when the father had passed away. If fire destroyed the home or the barn of a parishioner the pastor, from the pulpit, announced a corvée, sometimes even for a Sunday. Men arrived from all directions with their tools and, in one day, a house or a new barn rose up on the ruins of the old one. It was the same for someone who wished to move a house. This was a *halerie* of another type announced from the pulpit.

One can easily imagine what these corvées could do to create a spirit of charity and ties of gratitude and friendship among the people.

Nicknames

With the teasing spirit of the Chéticantins, their easy repartee, and their gracious witticisms, it isn't difficult to understand how nicknames multiplied by the hundreds. A mere list of these nicknames gives us a good idea of the imagination of the people:

A: Agneau jaune, Arbaque, l'As de carreau, sainte Anne.

B: Boingou, Bandet, Ballot, Benchire, Bichoure, Bigot, Braquette, Bill-Gaff, Bousquer, Baril à Dillon, Beurre-Net, la Bré, le Braillou, Binette, le Boeuf, Bouleau, Billotte, la Bosse de Pitche, Beurton, la Bouteille, la Blague, Gros Boute, la Belette, Brette, La Buche, la Broche, le Bac, Tanasse de Boeufs, le Balancier, Bebelle, Badlawine, Blanc-Bec, Brébaille.

C: Chieu-deboute, Caniche, Cacoune, Coyac, la Craque, Canivet, Chetisse, Carawiche, Conoque, Chomable, Chachulot, Curé, La Cuillère à pot, Cou fin, Cadet, Choupette, les Chiards, Cheière, Cap Sable, Cocourt, Cagnon, la Chatte, les Corbeaux, Chouragne, Césoeur, la Fausse Couette, Urbain Le Croche, Tom Crochet, Marie la Côte, Marie Cul Net, Chawèche, Cawain, la Charrue, Criche-Poque, Crosboy, Chie-en-Culotte, le petit Coquemar, la petite Chopine, le Coq, les Chats, le Chien, la Chienne, Chavèche, petit Coco, les Crêpes.

D: Damouk, Déboulé à Félix, Domingo, Damien la Côte, Dji-dji, De Vache.

F: Faillot, Fadico, Foutreau, la Furie, Fichère, Feutchonce, Fouaque, Fend le Vent, Félix des Vaches, la Fine.

G: Godouque, Gadou, Golo, Gamache, Godelle, Ganasse, la Petite Goélette, la Grolle, Grannoume, la Geude, la Grue, Grinchette, Gobeille, Godjin, Goliath, Gobèche.

H: Haddec.

J: Jactaire, Josais, Jèsouisse, Jobline, le Joker, petit Jaune, défunt John.

L: La Loutre, Luquine, la Luette.

M: Michons, Marteau, Marlouche, Mébisse, Marine, Maga, Machon, Menoque, Michouque, Médouche, Madeloche, Mangeurs de cendre, Mitouque, Margot, Mangeurs de mélasse, Mulot, Matagon, Mannawar, Madjusse, Mounette, Mailloche.

N: Nanoune, Nadouce, Nounon, Nouchon, le grand Nez, petit Noume, Nanouche, Nanon, Nanta.

O: L'Ours.

P: Pinquant, Pointu, Patouche, Pito, Petou, Pousse-nette, Piquet, Pet-de-

Loup, Panchette, Piquine, Pinandou, Portrait de pipe, Pot à Grof, Piseanne, Péch-
ien, la Prune, la Patte, la Plaise, la Pelle à Godouque, Gross Piche, Petit Piche,
Pentecôte, Poilu.

Q: La Queen.

R: Ruseau, Rigwèche.

S: Sept Soeurs, Skinner, Petit Singe, Sucriers, petit Sciau, la Squawl, Sambo, Souquie.

T: Traîneau, Talouche, Tiouette, Titie, Tazeau, Toussine, la Truite, Grand
Trou, Touquette, la Tèque, les Tanpa.

V: Venette.

W: Warrec.

Z: Zaillon.

For several the nickname was the only name used, even when one
spoke to them in person. Thus, in 1866 when the Chéticantins had to
practice military exercises on the occasion of the war against the Fenians,
Walter Lawrence served as interpreter between the English officer-
instructors and the improvised soldiers of Chéticamp. It was his duty to
call out the names. The actual name of "Petit Singe" was Hubert Poirier.
Three times Walter cried out, "Hubert Poirier!" No reply. He had to shout
"Petit Singe!" to be understood.

The Odd Ones

Even in a village with a small population, it is rare that there are not a
few mentally defective persons. Today these are placed in suitable institutions, but in the past, so long as they were not dangerously demented,
they were left at liberty.

Chéticamp has had only a few very rare cases of mental illness, more
or less pronounced, but they have remained famous. Two among them became almost legendary personnages, "Petit" Camille and "Petit" Constant.

"Petit" Camille was the son of André Poirier, brother of Pierre à André, and half brother of Charles, Alexandre, Dji-Dji and Élie. After the
death of his parents he went from house to house, eating at one, then another, and sleeping where he could.

"Petit" Camille had poor eyesight. One idea fixed in his mind was the
fear of having his eyelids stick together. He was afraid to go to sleep and
never accepted the offer of a bed in which to sleep. During the night he
would remain seated on a chair and, naturally, fell asleep there. Émilien à
Luc Chiasson, at whose home "Petit" Camille died, had all the trouble in
the world getting him to sleep in a bed. Once he had slept there, his fear
vanished.

"Petit" Camille always wore the same clothing and never washed himself. Naturally, until the time Émilien Chiasson took him home to live at his
place, he was full of lice. Deep down he loved his life of wandering and
his liberty. He stayed often at the home of Émilien Chiasson, but when he

learned that Émilien was going to take him in in order to look after him he ran away. He always had his pockets full of buttons and handkerchiefs.

With a perfect innocence "Petit" Camille loved girls very much. If one wanted him to rock the baby in the cradle it was enough to tell him the baby was a girl. He would rock her for hours. If told it was a baby boy he would stop immediately. He had developed a particular affection for Talouche. In talking to himself while walking, he ceaselessly repeated the name of Talouche, more and more loudly as he walked along.

If someone said, in his presence, "How pitiful!" Camille called them names and covered his head with his jacket. But if no one spoke to him, it would set him off, uttering incoherent phrases such as "Bears have no horns. They have ears like an ox. The church at le Moine is beautiful. They've played tricks on Camille."

"Petit" Constant was the son of Rémi Poirier from the Magdalen Islands. His life resembled that of "Petit" Camille, with whom, however, he did not agree at all. As soon as they met each other it was a fight. People had to keep them separated.

Like "P'tit" Camille, "P'tit" Constant went from house to house. Sometimes he arrived at daybreak. He occasionally found the doors still locked and, even if it was full in the month of August, he would say, "Cré djé! (Oh, for God's sake!). The doors are frozen shut!"

"P'tit" Constant had a mortal fear of a gun. It was enough to show him a gun for him to take flight. If a gun was fired, even one hundred paces from him, he collapsed, then disappeared.

He, too, never changed his clothing. If given a shirt, he accepted it and put it on, right over the other one.

"P'tit" Constant picked up and stored inside his bosom all the strange objects he could find, even dead and decomposing foxes. Loaded with these goods, he sometimes had a very prominent belly. One day he arrived at the home of Médouche Poirier, whose wife was several months pregnant, dressed in this way. On seeing "P'tit" Constant, she said, "Ah! Constant! You've stolen again!" Pointing his finger at her, he replied, "Cordjé! I believe you've stolen something, too!"

There were others less deranged, some of whom were even capable of very witty repartee. It is easy to imagine to what point these people could be, in a place like Chéticamp, the butt of teasing, jokes, and funny stories. Even Father Fiset didn't disdain to banter politely with them nor to laugh at the point-blank responses he sometimes received.

One day, when several members of the Fiset family were gathered at the glebe house, "La Furie" arrived. Father Fiset, to tease him, said, "I don't understand why you are permitted to wander around like this. In Québec it is forbidden for fools to circulate freely."

"I'm sure of it," replied La Furie, "their fools are sent to Chéticamp!" Father Fiset burst out laughing. (Father had come from Ancienne-Lorette, near Québec City.)

Common Sayings, Bad Omens, Good Omens, Etc.

Every working class group possesses a series of common sayings, as well as a catalogue of good omens or bad omens. Chéticamp is no exception. The people there believe in these—fortunately, less and less. However, through superstitious fear, there are still certain actions they avoid doing. Thus, the fishermen would never wear black mittens at sea because that attracts bad luck; a woodcutter would never leave his axe planted in a log overnight because the night would not bring him any rest.

Signs of Bad Luck: To dream of a bottle half-empty was a sign of illness. – To break a mirror brings seven years of bad luck. – For two persons to pass, each one on different sides of a pole, attracts bad luck. – The thirteenth of the month and Fridays are bad luck days. – If one says to a woodcutter, "Take care not to cut yourself," he is certain to cut himself. – To spill salt is a sign of a quarrel. – It is bad luck to make a chair spin on one leg; – to make a rocking chair rock while empty; – to open an umbrella in the house; – to wear black mittens on the fishing boats. – Whistling at sea brings on the wind. (This is why whistling is never heard at sea.) – To throw pennies at the sea brings on a storm. – If the right ear tingles, someone is speaking ill of you. – When the right eye blinks it is a sign of unhappiness. – Cutting one's nails on Saturday will bring shame on Sunday. – When one removes a hatch cover on a boat and leaves it upside-down on the deck it is a sign of bad luck.

Signs of Death: When the kettle whistles; – when a cock crows before midnight; – when a hen crows like a rooster; – when a cow sounds the knell (he turns his head around to the back and gives a special cry); – a crow on top of a house; – to dream of an empty bottle; – to find twigs of wood placed in the form of a cross. – If a person dies on Sunday, another person will die during the week.

Signs of Good Luck: To dream of a full bottle; – to find a horseshoe; – to carry a horseshoe; – having a horseshoe nailed onto one of one's buildings (in the past there was a horseshoe on the wall in several homes);– finding a four-leaf clover; – carrying a frog's leg in one's pocket; – carrying a fang of a snake in one's pocket. – Having a snakeskin in one's wallet would keep one from losing money. – If a small spider is found on one's person it is a sign of money. – When the left eye blinks it is a sign of happiness. – Carrying a rabbit's foot in one's pocket is a sign of luck at cards. – Finding a thread on one's person is a sign that one is going to undertake a voyage. – If your left ear tingles someone is speaking well of you.

Other Signs: Cutting one's nails on a Sunday: the devil makes combs of the pieces. – Tapping one's rakes or tools together: the two will still work together the following year. – If the children fast on Good Friday they will find birds' nests in the summer. – When the right hand is itchy you will shake hands with someone; – when the left hand itches you will receive a gift. – Always leave a house through the door by which you entered so as not to take away the good luck of this house. – When a dishcloth is dropped a stranger (someone who doesn't live in the house) is going to visit. – If the dishcloth falls in a bunch someone ugly will come; – if it spreads open someone handsome will come. – If scissors fall and stick in the floor strangers are going to come. – If the cat washes itself while pointing its tail to one side someone will come from that direction. – If a stranger is seen on Monday many more will be seen all week. – If one acquires a cat and doesn't want it to return to its former home, grease the undersides of its paws with butter; – for a dog, put on molasses. – White points under the nails are a sign that many gifts will be received. – If there is a person being waked, touching the body prevents fear of the dead later on. – One day, in the forenoon, we saw our father return from lobster fishing. He passed the gate and did not stop at the house but continued down towards the barn and disappeared. In reality our father did not return from fishing until the afternoon. This is a sign that he is going to live to a ripe old age. If we had seen him thus in the afternoon it would be a sign of a quickly approaching death.

Old Age and Death

If the parents owned enough land they gave a piece to their sons on which to build a house and have a garden and a potato patch. They kept with them on the old homestead the son with whom they got along best, and transferred the land to him. This custom persists today.

When parents grew old they continued to help the new household, the son and daughter-in-law. The elderly were always treated with great respect.

In olden times, there were no undertakers. When someone died, a neighbour—a woman for the women, a man for the men—washed the body, dressed it in the best clothes and laid it out on planks with a pillow under the head and a handkerchief over the face. Neighbouring carpenters offered, without any pay, to make the coffin, called the *coffre* (chest). This was made of hardwood and left completely bare. Unless the decomposition of the body was too rapid, the body was only put into the coffin at the moment of leaving for church.

Wakes

Wakes were held on two consecutive nights. Relatives and friends came in to say a prayer during the day and throughout the night; the house was packed until the wee hours of the morning. The night was spent in saying the Rosary and other prayers and in singing hymns. During the wake lunch would be served to everyone.

After midnight people would begin drifting home, little by little, and the group of visitors grew smaller. Prayers were recited at more widely-spaced intervals. Conversations began. Stories were told to help pass the time. With fatigue, laughing was easy, all the more so since no one wanted to laugh. And there were always comical people who told jokes. On the death of Lagode, Cécile à Gamache was singing for a long time. In one hymn, she sings, "I have chased God from my heart." Marcellin à Ben, who was present, said, "You're going to chase us all away, if you don't stop soon!" Another time Harriette à Nanta was reciting the prayer. It was interminable. She had been praying for well over an hour. William à Godouque said to his companion in a very low tone, "Will she ever finish! Will she ever finish!" Just at that moment in her prayer came the passage, "Good Virgin, at the hour of my death, when I will no longer be able to speak, you will speak for me." "Ah! The old...! She hires another!" said William. More proof that one jokes about anything and everything in Chéticamp.

Whether the deceased lived near to or far from the church, one or two choir members went to the house to sing for the funeral departure and accompanied the body to the church while singing the Miserere. Émilien à Luc Chiasson carried out this pious act all his life until a very advanced age.

Up to 1868 the pallbearers, who were never members of the family of the deceased, carried the coffin on their shoulders from the house to the church. Marie Larade, wife of Cyprien Deveau—the people called him Sépultien—was the first to be carried to the church in a vehicle on July 27, 1868, and this was in a cart. Afterwards, and until the beginning of the present century, it was a simple cart transporting the coffins from the house to the church, then from the church to the cemetery. Later it was a two-seater wagon with the seats removed, and was always drawn by a black horse. This last method of transport was quite restrained and very dignified. Unfortunately, after 1930 coffins began to be transported by simple trucks. This was a shameful and deplorable funeral procession. Fortunately, today Chéticamp enjoys the services of an undertaker, Louis Chiasson, who embalms the bodies and is the owner of a respectable hearse.

The grave was always dug by neighbours and friends. This job was never done by members of the family of the deceased. In the same way the deceased's family never aided in placing the body in its coffin nor in carrying the coffin. Everything was done willingly by friends or neighbours as a pious duty.

Today hymns are no longer sung at the wake. The Rosary is still recited from time to time.

Formerly the partner who was widowed stayed in mourning for a year and six months; the brother or sister for a year. Today the former stays in mourning for a year and the latter for six months.

SUPERSTITIONS

THE POPULATION OF CHÉTICAMP was too long without a resident priest, and later, the resident priests were too often absent in visiting their other missions; parishioners were spread over too vast an area for the influence of the priest and the teaching of religion to counteract the all-too-natural tendency towards superstition among the people. It is a popular belief in Chéticamp that there have been sorcerers who have cast spells, who have resorted to diabolical extortions, and that there are ghosts, imps and will-o'-the-wisps.

Sorcerers

In popular belief, and up to the present time, Chéticamp has always had its sorcerers whose evil spells are manifested by bewitching animals or people. Tradition tells us that from the beginning the Jerseys always had a few sorcerers among their number. Probably these Jerseys exploited the credulity of the people to play a hoax on them.

A belief still persists that the Jerseys practiced sorcery. On weekends a number of them would travel to their island of origin (Island of Jersey) astride a pig or in a canoe, going through the air, commanded and kept moving by cabalistic words and songs. They even offered to let a few Chéticantins accompany them. With the people's imagination helping things out, tradition reports numerous cases where some of them were bothered by Jersey sorcerers.

When returning from fishing by the portage route through the woods, old Timotheé à Thomas Chiasson, by no means prone to fear, saw himself pursued or accompanied by large barrels rolling around him. At other times it was pails full of fire. One evening he caught one and rubbed its ears with the fire that it contained. The next day, it seems, the Jersey suspected of doing this work had his ears burned and carefully bandaged.

One case, enlarged by imagination, became famous, that of "P'tit" Charlie Romeril. Romeril, a French Protestant (Huguenot) from the Isle of Jersey, worked for the Robin family and was reputed to be a Jersey sorcerer. An informant relates the story thusly:

At the home of Paddey à Bandaist Roche there was a servant girl named Marie. Paddey had an argument with Charlie Romeril. One day "P'tit" Charlie came to Paddey's barn to put some hay into the animals' manger. A short time later Marie had to go to the barn and she took out the hay remaining in the manger. She became bewitched while there.

Father Fiset had to come to remove the spell. But from that moment the spell settled on him. There was a disturbance in the glebe house. One night Jeffrey Crispou, who lived at the Rectory, woke up. His whole bedroom was on fire. Jeffrey ran to awaken Father Fiset. The whole glebe house seemed to be on fire. But nothing burned. Then Jeffrey said to Father Fiset, "If you don't want to get rid of this, I'm going to take charge of it." Father Fiset replied, "I'm not here to lose souls, but to save them."

This happened during the winter. Next day Jeffrey built a snowman. He took his gun and advanced towards the snowman. He advanced three steps and retreated two. At a certain distance he shot into the side of the snowman.

At the same time "P'tit" Charlie felt pain in his side. In the spring he began to waste away as the snowman began to melt. When there was nothing left of the snowman, "P'tit" Charlie died.

Imagination has kept alive many more cases of *sorcellage* (witchcraft). Some are mentioned here:

Lubin à Nectaire Maillet was bewitched by a sorcerer. Because of him, his father had to remain at home and so could not go fishing. One day he spoke of it to Walter Bertrand, a Jersey. "Go fishing," Walter told him. "I'm going to take care of it." He told Nectaire, "Go home, take your gun and shoot the first creature who enters your house!" Nectaire got his gun and placed it close beside him. But who should enter his house but a neighbour, Marcellin à Théophile Maillet. The sorcerer thus took on the form of a known person. Our man did not dare shoot. "You should have shot," the Jersey said. At the end of it all, Lubin received the order to go to the bridge of La Petite-Rivière to meet this Jersey so he could touch him in order to free him. That's what happened and Lubin was then free of the sorcery.

One day when Lubin seemed very ill, even dying, Sévérin à Félix Chiasson and Marcellin à Théophile Maillet went to get the priest at Le Moine. On the way the sorcerer or the devil went after them. The harness continually came undone. In the end the horse took fright. The men brought the priest just the same. But on their arrival, Lubin was on his feet and feeling well.[42]

•

Jérôme Aucoin and a companion were returning from hunting, carrying their guns. The Jerseys had told them, "You will be frightened!" Suddenly, on the road, what was that? A large barrel rolling all around them! Jérôme took his gun and bang! right into the rolling barrel. They heard ha! ha! And the barrel disappeared.

•

P.D. was married for a second time to a widow with a daughter from her first marriage. This girl was bewitched. There was a terrible racket in the house. Everything was flying around: lamps, chamber pots, etc. Buckets used to feed the pigs followed everyone. Overcoats came off the hooks and began to dance; axe-handles began to walk around and barrels of wool came down from the attic. All this confusion followed the daughter, even to school, as well as to the place where she was hired as a servant girl.

A Family of Sorcerers

In the middle of the last century Lazare Lizotte and his family came from the Magdalen Islands to settle in Cap-Rouge. Even today the Chéticantins believe this was a family of sorcerers. The number of their troublesome deeds is beyond reckoning. Everyone referred to them as the family of Le Canadien.

Marcellin à Eustache Bourgeois had had a quarrel with Le Canadien about a block of wood found on the shore. Le Canadien cast a spell on him: "Let him keep it! It will certainly turn into wood shavings! You will never cease *de chacoter* [whittling]." That's just what happened. From that moment on Marcellin began to whittle. He would take a stick and, with a knife, whittle away. He whittled everything in the house, bedposts, bed boards, chairs, etc. He saw large dogs coming into the house. Someone tried to make him drink some tea into which was placed a few drops of Holy Water. No way! If Holy Water was sprinkled on his bed he wouldn't go to bed that night.

Venette went to fetch a Gaudet from Margaree to remove the spell. During the trip they were accompanied by noises and howlings of all kinds. Having arrived at the house Gaudet said, "Do you want to see the sorcerers?" He made them appear. They saw arriving Le Canadien, his wife and his children. This Gaudet removed the spell from Marcellin.

•

One day Le Canadien said to Lubin à Jérôme Aucoin, "Lubin, I can bewitch an animal in its tracks." Lubin laughed at him. A few days later Lubin had a bewitched cow. Her eyes turned out, she rolled over, kicking with all fours, and made all kinds of gestures.

Lubin went to fetch those who took care of cows, but on their arrival the cow was well. As soon as these people were gone the cow again made these movements. Lubin wanted to kill her. But when he arrived at the barn with his axe the cow was well and normal.

Georges LeBrun said to him, "Take some of the cow's urine, put it into a bottle and insert new needles in it. Seal the bottle well and securely fasten it in a corner in such a way that it cannot open." That's what Lubin did. The same evening when he went outside Lubin was nearly knocked down by a large dog passing between his legs, the largest dog he'd ever seen. Lubin had scarcely returned when, on the stroke of midnight, he heard violent knocking on the door by someone who was uttering cries of desperation. He went to open the door. It was Le Canadien. At the time Lubin didn't think anything of it. It seems it is the custom of sorcerers to distract one's attention at times like this. Then Le Canadien told Lubin that he had slept at a neighbour's house and that he had felt ill during the night and needed some soda. The neighbours had none so he came to beg some from Lubin. The latter prepared some for him. Le Canadien drank the soda and went away. Next day Lubin learned that Le Canadien had not slept at the neighbours. It was only then that he understood the affair. Le Canadien had come, tormented as he was by the bottle. From that moment on the cow became normal.

•

One day Stephen à Michel à Angus Longuépée (a relative, I believe, of the wife of Le Canadien), watching a dog climbing a hill, said to his companions, "I can bring him down." He stuck a pin in the track of the dog and the dog immediately fell. "He will only get up when I wish it," said Stephen. He removed the pin and the dog dashed off.[43]

•

John à Onésime Poirier had a bewitched cow. Informed by someone, one day his wife decided to get rid of the sorcerer. She took a bottle, put into it some fire-clay, hawthorn prickle, and new needles, and set it all to boil. She locked her doors so no one could enter. After a certain time she began to feel she had forgotten something in her remedy. This feeling was so strong that she decided to get rid of it all and begin again later on. As soon as she had emptied the bottle she heard a great outburst of laughter in a corner of the house.

In earlier days several Chéticantins owned large schooners and transported animals, fish or wood to Halifax, the West Indies or Newfoundland and brought merchandise on the return trip. One of those was Venant Boudreau.

One day when Venant was in Halifax with a load of planks there happened to him this strange story:

A stranger came to buy some planks and appeared to look closely at the place where Venant put his moneybox. It was at the head of his bed.

In the evening everyone was ashore. Only Venant remained aboard the boat to keep watch. He had a lighted candle on the table with a large knife beside it.

Suddenly Venant heard steps on the deck coming towards the stairs. They were footsteps of a man. On the stairs it was no longer a man but an animal in the form of an ox. The candle went out and the intruder attacked Venant. He had become a man again. He only tried to push Venant aside to get at the moneybox. Venant, fighting all the while, passed his hand over the table to get the knife. But the knife was not there. Gifted with Herculean strength, Venant was knocking his adversary about when the latter dodged him and made for the stairs. Venant tried to recapture him and grabbed him by a leg, but it was as if he had passed his arm through wool. The sorcerer left.

Venant re-lit the candle. The knife was back in its place.

The following day the same man who had bought the planks came to the wharf. He said to Venant, "Were you afraid last night? How would you like to see the same animal again?" "Last night," said Venant, "it was able to get away. But if I see it again today, it will not escape!" "Let's not speak about it anymore," the stranger said to him.[44]

•

Simon à Damien Bourgeois had in his herd a young cow that was very wild. No one could approach her; to milk her it was necessay to lock her up. One day, on the dune, a person said to be a sorcerer came up, approached her easily and took her by the horns. From that moment on the cow was thought to be bewitched. Her milk gave a foul-smelling butter. Although every method imaginable was used to disinfect the milk cans, nothing worked. Milk from other cows in these same vessels remained normal, while that one had an unbearable taste and odour. That's when it was realized that there must have been some sorcery behind it all. Charles à Lagode was fetched to remove the evil spell of the sorcerer. He arrived and placed on the cow's manger a paper on which was written this magical prayer:

"Trotter head, I forbid thee my house and premises, I forbid thee my barn and cow stable. I forbid thee not to breathe on me nor upon any of my family until thou hast painted every fence-post, until thou hast crossed every ocean, and that thus dear dear day may come in the name of our Lord Jesus Christ. Amen."

Witnesses swear that the cow was immediately released from the evil spell.

Again, there was G. and his wife. The whole generation of those fifty years old and older knew them well. The fear of those two felt by the women and children is well remembered. The evil spells attributed to them are of the same nature as those we have described above. We give one example here:

G. went from house to house asking for charity. Ordinarily he asked for bread or something else to eat. Once, at the home of Jos à Fulgence Poirier, instead of asking for bread he wanted a blanket. "I have no blankets to give," Jos replied. "You will regret this," answered G. Jos was angry and went after G., who escaped with all speed.

The next day Jos' cow was bewitched. She was a real devil. It was impossible to catch her. She roamed everywhere and nothing could stop her from leaping into the air. She was crazy! Jos had to kill her.

Popular traditions tell us that a sorcerer who is going to accomplish his evil spells in a certain place sleeps with his mouth open and his soul flies away with his breath towards this place. If someone closed his mouth and his nose for too long a time, when his soul returned the sorcerer died.

Finally, according to the same tradition, on Fridays sorcerers hear everything bad that is said against them.

As can be seen, if there were any sorcerers, there were also people who could free us from the sorcerers. We have named a Gaudet, the Jerseys, Georges Le Brun and Charles à Lagode, whose services were required for this purpose. There were others. The alleged sorcerers and the sorcerer-fighters had recourse to a book of magical formulas. *Le Petit Albert* was the name of this book.

We have cited only a few cases of alleged sorcery. We could have compiled an almost endless list of similar cases. In what measure was there any basis to this popular belief in the homes of several Chéticantins? There are a few cases where supernatural intervention seems reasonable to believe. But ninety-nine percent of the cases are solely the evident fruit of an overactive imagination. Every strange illness, as often occurs to women during menopause, when a few of them even have hallucinations, every different type of behaviour or unexplainable event with the animals or objects, was easily attributed to sorcerers.

Besides, it is not impossible that the Jerseys named above had related frightening stories to the people to amuse themselves with their credulity. Finally, Le Canadien was a tinsmith, a repairer of pots and pans; G. was a beggar; both travelled from house to house in their work. It is likely that they exploited the superstition and fear of the people to their own advantage while plying their trade.

The Devil

It is said that, in earlier times, no one would have dared to go out alone at night to fetch the priest for a dying person. There was too much fear of being tormented by the devil on the way. Stories are told of huge black dogs suddenly appearing and following the vehicles for miles. They speak of horses being unhitched on the way or horses that didn't want to go on farther.

And that's about all that has been collected from tradition on this subject.

Elves

It is not such a long time since the people firmly believed in elves. These tiny beings in human form came at night to visit the horse stables. They chose the best horses, leading them outside and galloping off with them into the fields. The elves always sit on the neck of their charger and plait the mane so as to provide stirrups. The female elves plaited the mane on one side only. The horses thus teased, in spite of their night races, were always well treated and well nourished by the elves. But if the owner of the horse undid the tresses made by the elves these latter became furiously angry and treated the horses harshly.

Will-o'-the-Wisps

The people sincerely believed in will-o'-the-wisps. The story is told that Timothée à Thomas Chiasson ran through the meadows at night more than once trying to catch them.

It was midnight. Only the people at the home of Timotheé à Lubin Chiasson were still up. Paddey à Firmin Chiasson was crossing Timothée's field on returning home for a visit. Suddenly there was a will-o'-the-wisp! It was like a bird that was on fire under its wings, a bird making a tiny cry like a mocking laugh. It passed on each side of Paddey's head and blinded him. Paddey succeeded in reaching Timothée's house and pounded on the door with increasingly heavy blows while screaming, "Open up! Open up!" He was white as a sheet. He told his story. The others went to the door to try to see the will-o'-the-wisp. It could no longer be seen, but its mocking laugh could still be heard. Paddey didn't dare go any farther and slept at Timothée's that night.[45]

It is said that if one half-opens the blade of a pocket knife to make a right angle with the handle, and that if the knife is planted in a tree or on a fence in this manner, the will-o'-the-wisp is obliged to pass under the blade and cut its neck.

Today no one believes in will-o'-the-wisps.

Ghosts

Popular tradition is as abundant with ghost stories as it is with the evil spells of sorcerers.

Social Life

A visiting missionary had asked a few parishioners who were speaking of the dead, "How many damned souls, do you think, are in the cemetery?" Every parishioner present, even the broadminded, were in agreement in saying there were some, but how many…? "There is only one," the missionary told them in a mysterious but positive manner.

Shortly after the scene Father Vincent arrived in Chéticamp. That was in 1822. Father Vincent was a Trappist and a man of great virtue. He organized a ceremony for the dead in that very cemetery. This is more readily understandable since, most often, there was no resident priest and the people had to be buried without a priest to bless the grave. The story is told that the missionary, dressed in the sacred vestments, visited every grave, probably to bless them, then stopped at one of them. There he laid out the Pall (mortuary sheet).

Taking a large book, he began to read and recite prayers from it. Every parishioner assisted in the ceremony and made a circle around the missionary and the grave. At a certain moment the missionary pushed back the crowd to make a pathway on the side of the grave leading to the stream flowing nearby. Then he knelt down and redoubled the entreaties in his prayers. Afterwards he took the Holy Water sprinkler and sprinkled Holy Water on the grave. As soon as this was done an enormous snake left the grave, a snake of fire, completely red, which curled up in a ball, uncoiled itself and glided down the pathway now enlarged by the flight of the people, left the cemetery and was lost in the stream. This was the soul of the dead person which, no one could then doubt, was damned.

Since then people have discussed this event, but only in low tones, through charity or through superstitious fear.

This snake was, evidently, only a simple red-spotted snake, with no connection to the soul of the dead person. We have to realize the terrible fear the people of Chéticamp have for these small, inoffensive and beneficial creatures in order to understand this legendary transposition. Probably, through a biblical reminiscence, they see the devil in all snakes and sincerely believe them venomous and, unfortunately, kill them without mercy.

Baptiste à Granoume (Grand Homme) Aucoin was afraid of nothing. He was married twice.

His first wife, before dying, had promised a dress to someone. She died without keeping, or without being able to keep, her promise.

The second wife began to hear groans in the house. Baptiste didn't want to believe it. He was at the fishing cabins. But one evening when he was home the groans began again!

He still couldn't believe it. Just the same, he followed the groans sounding throughout the house. The groans led him right to the closet where the dress was. And there the noise sounded so loudly in his ears that he was afraid. Next day he gave the dress to the owner and the groans stopped.

•

Cyrille à Timothée à Thomas Chiasson, on his death, owed some flour. On one of the nights of his wake flour began to fall on the body.

•

Placide a Timothée Chiasson, when about four or five years of age, was playing near the threshing-floor doors. His mother, who had died a short time before, appeared to him. She said to him, "I'm coming for Mass." Masses were said for the response of her soul.[46]

On the occasion of the great storm of August 1873, many people drowned. Among them was David à Timotheé Chiasson who lived at the home of his brother, Jean, called "Petou."

A few days after this drowning, Judith, Jean's wife, had to enter David's bedroom. She was surprised to see, wide open, the chest in which she kept David's clothing, with all the clothing upside down, hanging from the chest and scattered on the floor. More serious yet, on the floor were three drops of blood. Judith bent down to wipe up these spots but they only appeared more clearly. Then she took a damp cloth to wash them away, but, far from going away, the blood seemed to spread. As her husband was fishing at the harbour and she was alone, she was afraid and ran to fetch her brother-in-law, Lubin, their neighbour. He felt she was being foolish, but followed her to see for himself. The spots were there, easy to see. He took his well-sharpened knife and began to chip away at the floor in order to lift the spots. Ah! The blood began to fill the holes made by the knife. Fear seized him. They went to tell this story to Father Girroir, who said to them, "Leave those spots alone and don't touch them. But pray for David." Those spots stayed there several years and disappeared all of a sudden.[47]

•

While she was a young girl, shortly after the death of her grandfather, Julite, wife of Damien Bourgeois, began to hear mutterings in her ears. She heard this muttering everywhere she went. One day, as she was weeding in the garden, an enormous weight seemed to fall near her and she saw her dead grandfather, Lagode, at her side. The murmuring continued. Masses were said for him, and the noise then ceased.

•

Timotheé à Lubin Chiasson was fishing one day with Joe à Firmin Chiasson and a few others. Speaking of Placide à Michel Romard, who had died in the spring, Timotheé said, "We played the fool together more than anything else. Now he is dead; I said a few Our Fathers for him, then I forgot him." In saying that, he heard a noise like the hum of a motor under their feet, which gave him a start. However, the motor was broken and didn't work. "Since that time," continued Timothée, "I have never forgotten Placide in my prayers."

•

During the famous storm of August 1926, Marie, wife of Jeffrey à Irénée Aucoin, had lost two brothers, Jos and Cyrille. On the evening of this unexpected drowning near Sable Island in the Atlantic, all was calm in Chéticamp and no one suspected the drama unfolding so far away. During the night Marie heard a noise in their attic, like the banging of a shutter on the window, blended as if with a noise of the ocean. At last, frightened to death, she woke her husband. Half-asleep, he heard nothing at first and laughed at her foolishness, but soon he heard it too. He got up and began to follow these mysterious groans. They led him to a chest belonging to one of the dead brothers. He heard something like a voice say to him, "A Mass." When Marie and her husband heard the news, they understood. They had Mass said for the men and heard no more noises.

How can we judge these ghost stories? The same as for sorcerers, we believe. In one case, as in the other, people's imagination plays a great role in the interpretation of facts and readily enlarges on them in transmitting them from one generation to the other.

Hidden Treasure

There is not a bay or a coastal village in Nova Scotia where belief in hidden treasure does not exist. Chéticamp is no exception. Here and there along the coast we've seen holes dug by people searching for these riches.

In Chéticamp legend related that these treasures have been buried by pirates. When they were pursued by empty boats or when their boat was overloaded with booty, these pirates ran ashore in isolated coves to hide their chests of gold and silver.

Every pirate for the boat went ashore. Then, seated around a fire, they drank mostly all evening. At the end of the visit the captain had a hole dug in which to bury the riches. He later asked, "Who wants to guard this treasure?" Hoping to seize some of the booty for himself, one was always found willing to be the guard. Bad luck for him! The captain had him beheaded and buried with the treasure. That's why, today, each of these treasures is guarded by the ghost of a man decapitated in this way.

According to legend, these ghosts cannot harm anyone. But their duty is to scare off any intruders. This is what they do, especially when the latter are on the verge of discovering the treasure. Seekers can then expect to see a headless man circulating around them or even to see it floating through the air; to see a sword, held by a thread, hanging over their heads, or an enormous rock ready to roll over them. There is no danger, but it is difficult not to run away.

Finally, the greatest silence is absolutely essential while the treasure is being located, dug up and carried away. Even when found, the riches disappear magically if one of the searchers has the misfortune of letting a single word pass his lips. And, according to the legend, many searchers have seen the object of their covetous eyes disappear the moment they expressed, by a shout, their joy at having found it.

TALES

CHÉTICAMP HAS KNOWN famous storytellers, such as "P'tit" Paul Leblanc, "Grande" Souquie (Mrs. Paul à Marine) Leblanc, John Marteau,

"P'tit" Paddé Roche, Charles à Lagode, Marcellin à Cyrille Haché, Jean à Sécime Deveau, William à Jules Deveau and others. In earlier times the storytellers were important figures in Chéticamp. During organized gatherings the services of a storyteller were just as necessary as the services of a violinist were for a wedding party. He was brought to the gathering by some vehicle and returned home at the end of the party, and was often given a small gratuity for his work.

Certain of the storytellers, such as "Grande" Souquie and "P'tit" Paddé, possessed a seemingly endless repertoire. Unfortunately, these stories haven't been collected and today the repertoire of the few storytellers we still have is very limited.

It would have been interesting to analyze these stories and conduct research on how they came to Chéticamp. Some of them were brought from the Motherland and passed down from one generation to another; others were learned from Canadian storytellers in the lumber camps; still others from Canadian or French sailors visiting Chéticamp, or heard in some other seaport. Lastly, a few among them, such as "La Belle et La Bête" (Beauty and the Beast), for example, perhaps were taken from collections of printed stories or from almanacs.

The storyteller, sometimes completely illiterate, was an artist. He knew how to describe his characters and make them come alive for his audience. He knew how to thrill his listeners by demonstrating the feelings of his heroes. "P'tit" Paddé is still remembered for beginning his stories while sitting on a chair, but soon, caught up in the excitement of his story, rising to his feet and completing the tale with all appropriate gestures.

We have collected about twenty stories from Chéticamp, a few relics among the hundreds originally held in the repertoire of earlier times. Mr. Gerald Aucoin of Sydney has also preserved about a dozen.[48]

Here below is related one of the famous tales from the collection of "P'tit" Paddé also told to us by Mr. Loubie Chiasson. This story, a much briefer version than the original, has never been collected in Canada, at least up to this time. We are including it here in its entirety because of its originality and its rarity. The French version, written in the archaic language of the storyteller, is a vibrant specimen of the language spoken by the people in Chéticamp. The English version follows here:

La reconnaissance du chien
(A Dog's Remembrance)

Once upon a time there was a man and his wife. They had a great handsome dog. The people were very poor. One terrible day the man said to his wife, "I believe we are going to have to kill the dog. We are so poor that I'm not sure if we are going to live." Now, it happened that the dog heard all this. He was near the table. When he finished eating he went to the door. They let him out. The dog took off as fast as he could go; they never saw him again. He never returned because he had heard them say they were going to kill him.

A few years later, about two or three years afterwards, things were going better for the old couple.

The man was a farmer.

One day he said to his son, "We have to go to town to sell some oxen." So saying, they left for town, he and his son. They went a certain distance to town and sold all the animals they had brought with them.

While the buyer was paying them for the animals he had bought, a man was watching them. He saw that they had some money. The others did not notice him.

After the sale the man and his son started off for home again. They were on horseback. They had led their animals to town in the same way. Night fell. When they arrived at a certain place, someone stopped them, the same man who had been watching them earlier with the buyer. They didn't recognize him. He said to them, "At a certain place ahead on this road, the bridge is out; you won't be able to pass. Take this other road; it will be a bit longer, but you will be sure to get through." They headed off in this direction. But, instead of the good road, he had convinced them to take the bad one. When they arrived at a certain place it was there that the bridge was out.

It was late at night. They found themselves blocked from going farther! There was a house not far off in the distance showing a pale light. The man said to his son, "By God! We cannot go home tonight. Now, before we can turn around and try to go back it's going to be too late. We're going to see if we can stay the night in that house."

So they went to see. They knocked on the door. A man and his wife came to open the door. The travellers told them that they had come to see if they could stay the night. "Well," said the man, "I think so."

Supper was prepared. While they were eating a great dog was watching them. He was near the table. The boy was afraid. But they didn't pay any attention to the dog.

When they were ready to go to bed, the man and his son went to the bedroom, accompanied by the dog. The man of the house locked the bedroom door, with the visitors and dog inside.

Then they understood the situation very well. These people were thieves, you know. They were in cahoots with the one who had sent the man and his son along the road.

It was dark in the bedroom. They tried to lie down on the bed, but the dog wouldn't let them go near it; he growled and tried to stop them from going to sleep. They were terrified and could understand quite well the trouble they were in! They didn't know what to do!

Suddenly the dog, near the young boy, was wagging his tail. The boy said to his father, "Do you remember the dog we had two or three years ago? Well," he continued, "this one resembles it!"

Instantly the dog understood him. He recognized them. He threw himself on them. He nearly ate them, he was so happy to see them again. "Well!" said the father, "I believe it is our dog! If it's ours, we're all right!"

A short time after the dog was near a small closet that was in the room. He scratched on the door. The boy said to this father, "I must open the door to see what is inside." There was a small iron bar there. The dog took it in its mouth and was trying to open a small door on the floor. The young boy said, "I have to open that door." On the door there was an iron ring for a handle. With the iron bar, the young boy opened the door. Underneath there were dead bodies....

You understand, it was the thieves had done this. They allowed people to stay overnight and had trained the dog to kill the visitors. The dog would accompany the visitors into the bedroom and there he would kill them. Afterwards the owners of the house would search the pockets of the dead and keep all the money they found there.

The boy's father said, "Close that! Close that door, for the love of God!"

They waited. The time passed so slowly! They spent the whole night in waiting.

Ah! The next morning the fellow who had told them to go by this road arrived. He asked if two men had come to the house the night before. The man of the house said, "Yes, they're in there. Chances are the dog has killed them. We'll go take a look later on!"

The two in the bedroom heard that. They thought: "We're certainly in great danger. The dog hasn't killed us, but it looks like those people are going to do the job!"

The man of the house said to the newcomer, "Smoke your pipe. We'll take a look later on. There's no hurry!"

After they had their smoke, they went to open the door. When the door opened, the dog leaped onto the owner, aiming for this throat! He strangled him! The others, the man and his wife, took to their heels!

Once the man and his son were in control of the house the dog went over to another closet and he scratched on the door. They went to have a look at it. It was filled with silver coins and bills!

They took all the money, then the man said to the dog, "You can come home with us. No matter how poor we become, you will always have a home with us!"

Then they all went off happily to their own home.

SONGS

FOLKLORE IS AN INHERITANCE. Even better, it is an atmosphere in which it is sufficient to bask a moment in order to feel abounding within oneself a vigour we believed exhausted. It is not an empty emotion that one experiences on listening to our old songs. It is the memory of a past poorly understood, often betrayed, but which, nevertheless, remains the very substance, the marrow of our life.[49]

Chéticamp is a patch of Acadian land particularly thick in folklore. Most of the legendary tales, unfortunately, are lost. The songs remain. The repertoire of these songs in Chéticamp seems inexhaustible. Mrs. Charles V. Boudreau alone, for example, knew the words and tunes of more than four hundred songs. With the help of Father Daniel, O.F.M. Cap., we have collected more than one hundred songs and laments.

As mentioned by music and folklore experts, the popular French songs of Chéticamp are "most precious and most interesting,"[50] "they give off a perfume which attracts, and a seductive enchantment"[51]; "songs like *Dessus la fougère*...and many others, are of great inspirational delicacy...true poetical and musical works of art."[52]

For the most part, they are pretty Cantilenas from Old France, completely fresh and innocent, which lull and charm us. They contain shyness, as well as the fragrance and freshness of snowdrops and other spring flowers.

These songs express, in their own way, the truly sympathetic soul of the Acadian people. Though they often sing of the sea, the really popular songs of Chéticamp do not speak of fishing—so familiar to the Acadians—nor do they speak of the Expulsion and the hardships following it. Songs haven't been composed on these themes, nor on the occasion of historical events that affected Acadia. It is not, then, in their words that we must search for the expression of all those things that make up the soul of a people; it is in their specific melodies that uncomplaining suffering, salty air, and vast horizons have been strongly characterized and rendered so humanely gentle and touching. It is through all this that these songs are truly Acadian.

There is a marine shellfish, a conch, which when held to the ear permits one to hear the faraway roar of the waves. The ocean registers its eternal song in it. It is the same for the Acadian refrains. Sung by sailors that the ocean has rocked from generation to generation, these refrains are blended and synchronized to the great voice of the ocean. They exude an atmosphere of the wide-open sea, the rhythm, the cadence, the rocking of the "flowing immensity" that is the ocean.

The gentle melancholy of some of these songs discreetly recalls the sad memories of the past. As is expressed in the Preface of the first published collection,

These songs are filled with memories of the past. They have rocked our infancy, as well as that of our ancestors. They have enlivened, for the most part, the beautiful days of the dawning Acadia. They have accompanied the Acadian people during the trials of the "Grand Dérangement" (Expulsion). And, during the dark days of our fathers, who were hidden here and there, hunted like animals, they have been like a ray of sunshine. The laments tell of their sufferings, while the hymns guard their faith during the tough years when the guidance of the priest was wanting. These songs are too attached to the soul of a people which has suffered and is reborn, not to be able to move every French heart that sings them or hears them being sung.

The joyous voices raised in song express the sentiments of a pure-hearted people kept young by their music, people who have no fear of an honest and wholesome love of their people, their culture, their whole way of life.

These songs gain a great deal in being heard. Terms, such as *amant* (lover) and *maîtresse* (mistress) can surprise one on first hearing them. But we must recall that in a folklorist style these expressions have preserved the original meanings and do not contain any derogatory connotation. It is *l'ami* (the boyfriend) who visits and *l'amie* (the girlfriend) who is honourably visited, with marriage in mind. And, on hearing them, one does not read more than what is in the verse: "I have lost my mistress without deserving to..." from our famous *À la claire fontaine*.

In 1942 two cousins, both Religious in the Congregation of the Capuchins, grandsons of Mrs. Charles V. Boudreau, timorously published a first collection of twenty-five songs from this repertoire. In 1945 and 1948, respectively, two other series of songs by the same Religious, carrying about one hundred and twenty-five tunes, were published.[53]

Their goal was to have these beautiful songs live again in the hearts of the people of their region who were turning more and more to the American songs of Hollywood. Their success was greater then they had hoped. This publication was the occasion of a dazzling reawakening of the popular song in Chéticamp. Not only are the people singing these songs, but a great number of other marvellous and beautiful tunes have been uncovered.

The encouragement of folklorists like Marius Barbeau, Luc Lacourcière, François Brassard, Thomas Leblanc; of musicians like Oscar O'Brien, whose accompaniment and harmonization are real works of art; of Hector Gratton, famous musician from Montréal; of artists of interpretation, such as Jacques Labrecque who has since sung them with huge success in Québec and Acadia where he made a great concert tour in 1945, continuing on to Europe; of frequent programmes on radio and even on television; an Acadian choir, *Le Coeur d'Acadie*, founded in Montréal for this occasion; of recordings made by Jacques Labrecque, Allan Mills, Hélène Baillargeon, by the chorale from the University of Bathurst; several of these songs are heard today on the lips of young girls, of fishermen, of travellers, of the learned, as well as the uneducated, of mothers who rock their babies, even of priests, for diversion; all this gives us an idea of the success of these songs and also, we believe, of their value.

LANGUAGE

PASCAL POIRIER WROTE:

It would be possible to discover, solely by an examination of the language spoken by the Acadians today, the province of France from which their ancestors came.

This language is not a dialect exclusively characteristic of them; it is still less a patois; it is the same French which was spoken in Touraine and the northwest of Berri, in the middle of the XVIIth century.[54]

And so

...of all the provinces of France, it is perhaps in Berri and Touraine that the ancient language of oui is the least altered....The language in Acadia, even more so...remained untouched by outside influence, having been, from 1710 onward, completely isolated from the rest of the world, and only having come in contact with that of the French-Canadians after the agreement in 1867, which united in Confederation all the provinces of Canada.[55]

But what is true of all of Acadia is particularly true for the community of Chéticamp. Here the means of communication were such that even the agreement of Confederation changed nothing of the isolation of the Chéticantins. It is only in the past few years that the highway, enlarged into a great national route encircling all of Cape Breton, leads a growing wave of American and French-Canadian tourists into Chéticamp each summer.

It isn't necessary to make a complete analysis of the language of the Chéticantins here. It would be too long and outside the sphere of our competence. Besides, the thorough study of Senator Pascal Poirier on French-Acadian speech and its origins applies, with few differences, to the speech of the Chéticantins. The following is drawn largely from Poirier's work.

Let us point out a few characteristics of the Acadian language, transmitted in its archaic form by the pioneers to the Chéticantins of today.

Conjugations

"Henry IV sang: 'J'aimons les filles et j'aimons le bon vin' (We love the ladies and we love good wine) and it is he, we are told, who composed the words of that song. An Acadian would not do otherwise, or better."[56]

Here, below, is the method invariably used by the Chéticantins in conjugating their verbs, in the style of the Île-de-France of the seventeenth century. In the present indicative: j'mange, tu manges, i'mange, j'mangeons, vous mangez, i'mangeont. The "je" in place of "nous" and the third person plural ending in "ont" are seen in all tenses in the indicative, conditional, and subjunctive moods: j'mangions, i'mangiont; j'manterons, i'mangeront; j'avons mangé, il'avont mangé; j'disons, i'disont, etc. Auxiliary verbs follow the same rules: j'sons, i'sont; j'avons, il'avont.[57]

The *ont* endings in the third person plural...closely resemble the Latin form, amant, dicunt, faciunt.... The advantage here of the final sound is that to the ear the plural of the verb is not confused with the singular. The peasant says: il parle, ils parlont; the life-long secretary of the Académie will say: il parle, ils parlent. The silent ent says nothing to the ear.

The passé simple, j'aimai, je fus, j'allai, is no longer used; it is replaced by the passé indéfini: j'ai aimé, j'ai été, j'ai passé, etc. When our people have to use it, they confuse, most often, by analogy, the verbs of the first conjugation with those of the third, and say: je parlis, il mangit, ils tombirent, just as they say je rendis, il vendit, ils finirent. This ending is preserved among the people in France. No other is heard in Poitou. The preterit tenses in i, for all conjugations, were commonly used in the old language. It is found elsewhere:

"Je lui demandis s'il avoit presché" (Favel)
"Dont me trouviz au large" (Marot, etc.)[58]

In Chéticamp, as nearly everywhere in Acadia in the olden days, the *o* becomes *ou* in front of every *n* or *m* and certain other double consonants: *poume* for pomme (apple), *boune* for bonne (good), *houme* for homme (man), *brousser* for brosser (to brush), etc. The same phenomenon is also seen, but more rarely, before other consonants: *arrouser* for arroser (to water), *routir* for rôtir (to roast), renfrogné will be *renfrougné* (frowning), while, like the modern Frenchmen, we say: cochons (pigs), bosse (hump), notre (our), votre (yours), porter (to wear or to carry), gorge (throat), etc.

Instead of *un*, we say, as in Touraine and Beri, *ien*, or rather, *yin* (in Chéticamp: *yon*) with the yod consonant, when the numerical adjective is not followed by another word, and *in*, when it qualifies the following word: *in* cheval (one horse); il n'en reste plus qu'*yien* (I've only one left); il n'y en a qu'*yien* (There is only one). In the feminine form, we say: *eune* femme (a woman); j'en veux *yeune* (I would like one).[59]

The *c* followed by the vowel *u* and diphthongs *ui* and *ai* give a sound alien to official French that the alphabet is completely inadequate to render. The ordinary spelling translates it by *tch*. "Thus, in cul-de-sac (blind alley), culbute (somersault), cultivé (cultivated), culotte (trousers), curé (parish priest), culture (cultivation), etc., the Acadian *c* softens and takes on a sound very similar to the English *ch* in chip, cheese, Charles, choice."[60]

The cacuminal sound of *tch* comes to us, perhaps, from the Latin. It was not without some probability that we believe it comes from both the Latin and the Celtic languages. This sound exists in nearly all human languages, with the exception of official French, revised, corrected, improved, polished, and considerably impoverished, by the grammarians who prevailed in Paris in the first half of the XVIIth century.[61]

The *d* is pronounced here in the same manner as elsewhere, with a sound more pure perhaps, "except before the syllabic diphthongs *ia*, *io*, iu, and before the diphthong *ieu*, where it is softened. It is, then, a very strongly hissing consonant."

"This softened sound, known to the academic language, seems to be a relic of the Celtic language.... Its present territorial distribution would indicate that it was universally used at a given time, perhaps during the Middle Ages, in France.... It is found in all writings of the old French authors...."[62] In Acadia Dieu (God), diable (devil), and diamant (diamond) are pronounced Djeu, djable, and djamant, the *d* having the sound of the English *j* as in jib, job, jaw, Joe. This Acadian *dj* gives a very soft sound.[63]

The *g* equally is softened before *e, ei, i* and *ui* and is pronounced *dj*, as in the English *j:* guetter (to wait for), guerre (war), guère (not much), guêpe (wasp), gueule (mouth), guéret (fallow land), anguille (eel) and aiguiser (to sharpen) are pronounced djetter, djère, djêpe, djeule, djéret, andjiulle, and aidjusier.

In the French language of France, before a vowel, before any vowel, *qu* always gives the hard sound of *k*, which is also that of the c before *a*, *o*, *ou*, and *u*.

In qualité (quality), quand (when), quasiment (almost), and quatre (four), that is, when *qu* is followed by *a*, and then by a consonant, the pronunciation is the same here as in France; but, if the *a* is followed by a vowel, it softens and is strongly hushed: quai (wharf)—I know no other example—is pronounced tchai....

Followed by a final mute *e*, *qu* is pronounced in Acadia, as it is in France: que (that), quoique (although). If the silent *e* is then followed by one or more vowels, the sound becomes hushed, as in queue (tail)—I can find no other example—which is pronounced *tcheue*. "*Qu* is equally hushed, if the silent *e* is followed by *l*, *m*, or *s*. Quelquefois (sometimes) is pronounced *tcheuq'fois* (by the loss of *l*), quémander (to beg), is pronounced *tchémander*, question is pronounced *tchestion*, and quête (quest) is *tchête*." Also, Québec is pronounced *Tchébec*.

As in France, we pronounce the words where *que* is followed by *r* or *n*: quenouille (bedpost), querelle (quarrel), etc.

Qui alone or followed by any consonant is pronounced like the Italian *ci* in cicerone: *tchi* (who?), *tchille* (keel), *tchinze* (fifteen), *tchitter* (to leave), etc. for qui, quille, quinze, and quitter.

Followed by an *o* or by the diphthong *oi*, the sound remains hard, as in France, whatever is the vowel or consonant that follows: quolibet (gibe), quoi (what).[64]

The *t* has two official sounds in the language: the hard sound, in modestie [medesti] (modesty), and the soft sound, as in prophétie [prefesi] (prophecy).

The Chéticantins, like Acadians in general, "give to the *t*, in combination with *ie*, a third sound, like that of the Italian *ci*, or more exactly, that of the English *ch*. Pitié (pity), amitié (friendship), tiède (lukewarm), tien (possessive pronoun, "yours"), tiens (verb in the imperative, "hold"), say *pitché*, *tchède*, *tchien*, the *ti* being pronounced like the English *ch* in peach, chin, and patch."[65]

In front of oi, *v* takes, in our region, or conserves, rather, the sound of the English *w* (double *v* or double *u*). We say une *ouelle* (or welle) for une voile (sail), *ouêture* or *wêture* for voiture (vehicle), *aouène* or *awène* for avoine (oats). The Picards seldom pronounce them otherwise. At the court of the Sun King (Louis XIV), where Bossuet and Racine shone, the courtiers on guard begged benefits for themselves and *avouène* (oats) for their horses, while giving to this word the pronunciation it has today in Acadia. We, too, say: Attends que je *waye* (Wait until I see). Voir is pronounced *ouair* and pouvoir *pouair* in the mouth of our people.[66]

There are few really French words beginning with z.

We possess one, however, universally used, that has not been collected in the Dictionnaire, one that, truthfully, I can find nowhere, the word *zire*, a synonym for a deep dislike. That meat fait *zire*—disgusts me, that is, inspires me with distaste, nauseates me; il fait *zire*—he dresses disgustingly: he is slovenly, distasteful about his person. From this root word, we have formed *zirable*, having the same sense: c'est *zirable* (It's disgusting, foul, nauseating).

From where does *zire* come? Would it be from the Latin ira, colère (anger), fureur (fury), dépit (spite), which have left in the language *ire* (anger), a word that the people, after a vowel, would have caused to be preceded by an euphonic *z*? It is quite probable.[67]

The speech of the Chéticantins has many other distinctions which would take too long to relate here. Many sailing terms are transposed in the current language. Thus, *on amarre* (ties up), a horse, a package, as one does a schooner. *On embarque* (embarks), *on vire de bord* (turns back) in a vehicle as well as a boat.

A few Indian words, though rare, are now part of the French language. We have come across these words in Chéticamp. Besides the ones universally accepted, like boucanier (pirate), ouragan (hurricane), tabac (tobacco), savane (swamp), canot (type of boat), etc., we also have: doré (dory), ouaouaron (bull-frog), pimbina (edible viburnum), tobagan (toboggan), caristeau (footwear), césain (piece of moccasin covering the toes), mashkoui (fine white bark of the birch tree), mataché (spotted), mocassine (moccasin), nigogue (harpoon with two flexible jaws with a dart in the middle), ouaouari (uproar, racket).

Even today the Chéticantin dialect has many similarities to the language of Marot, Ronsard, and Rabelais. It is close as well to the speech in usage at the court of Versailles. It has, then, a fine lineage.

I have named Rabelais [1494?-1553]. Pascal Poirier has shown that the Acadian speech is studded with a variety of archaic expressions, of old French terms lost elsewhere, but found in the writings of Rabelais. We must add that the speech of Chéticamp has retained a vigour, a forthrightness, that is quite Rabelaisian. Let us add, however, that these crudities in the current language have no obscenity in the expressed sense, even if the terms used may sometimes sound that way.

If the vocabulary of the Chéticantins is poor in modern terms, if it borrows ready-made technical terms too easily from the English language, it is due to the lack of contact with all French civilizations. Before the Machine Age the Chéticantins possessed an astonishingly rich vocabulary. Within the limits of their knowledge, within the domains of fishing, temperature, cultivation of the soil, hunting, building houses and barns, rudimentary anatomy, etc., they used the perfect and quite vivid word. One example among many others: The Chéticantins would not use carelessly the words "amarre," câble, cordage, corde, merlin, bitord, fil à "drague," ligneul, lacets, licou, fil d'arichal, ficelle, and fil, even if one or the other is in current usage and can serve for "amarrer" (to tie up).

The language of the Chéticantins is especially replete with old French words, formerly respected but hardly used today, as chalin (flashes without thunder) or éloize (lightning), or, unfortunately, lost, as rarir (to become rare), bazir (to destroy), embelzir (to beautify), ravigoter (to revive). A list, though very incomplete, of a few of these old words can give us an idea of the richness of this vocabulary.

A

Amoureux (botanical): burdock, a plant whose flower heads stick to clothing.

Attiraille: a pile of mixed-up things.

Avoindre (pronounced aouindre): to take an object out of a drawer. Il aouindit—He took it out of the drawer. Il a aouindu—He has taken it out of the drawer.

B

Baille: wash up.

Baluches: chaff of oats after the threshing.

Baranquer: to be delirious; to talk nonsense. That delirious man. (Probably the same origin as *baragouiner*—to talk gibberish.)

Battures: elevations from the bottom of the ocean, beaten by the waves. Boats often run aground on the battures—reefs.

Baume: ointment, salve. As in the song: "J'vends du baume pour les brûlures"[68]—I sell salve for burns.

Bazir: this verb is both transitive—meaning to destroy or to make disappear: bazir un objet; to destroy an object—and intransitive—meaning to disappear: je bazis, i.e. je disparais—I'm disappearing.

Bluette (pronounced beluette): small sparks.

Boudrier: seaweed.

Bouette: "For the catching of cod, it is the bait that one puts on the fish-hook." [Nicolas Denys]

Bouillée: talle in Québec; clump of trees, strawberry bush, etc.

Brangeler, ébrangeler: to shake (one's head, legs, etc.); to loosen, unsettle.

C

Chaffraille or *chafrail:* many objects jumbled together and cumbersome; confusion. Figuratively, a great deal of noise.

Chalin: flashes of lightning with no thunder.

Clapets: "culottes à clapets"—a pair of breeches or trousers buttoned on the side so that the front part and the back part could fold down. These parts that could be folded down are called clapets. Clapet was also the word used for a vizor, as in a helmet vizor or cap vizor.

Cloches: women's breasts.

Cobir: to make a scored mark on sheet metal.[69]

Collouetter: to blink one's eye.

Cordelle: to haul by tow-line

Couleurs: paints—"J'vends des couleurs" as the song says[70] (I sell paint).

Courge: a yoke for carrying buckets. The word "joug" is reserved here for the oxen.

D

Dalter: to passionately desire something. Il en dalte. He has an extravagant desire for something.

Déblâme: a pretext; a not very justifiable excuse for something.

Déconforté: discouraged.

Dégonder: to run away, fleeing with all speed.

Désamain, à: difficult to reach, not at hand.

E

Ébarouir: see Larousse.

Égaïl: dew.

Éloize: flash of lightning.

Emborver: to imbibe. From abreuver—to drink; to soak.

Émoyer, s'émoyer: to inquire about something.

Épivarder: to make one's toilette with exaggerated care; to "show off"—more refined than "escarer."

Essherber: to weed a garden.

Escârer, s': to show off, giving oneself pretentious airs.[71]

F

Flaguescent: soft, to look as if it's moving. Like soft Jello in a dish; floundering.

Flâtre: weak, limp, flaccid.

Fouailler: this is said of waves which, in a storm, lash the bridge of a ship, the wharf, or the coast; waves which buffet or tear everything away.

Fourbir: to polish, making shiny by rubbing: the stove, the floor, the knives.

Fourgailler: to pester, plague, or worry someone.

G

Gargoton: the throat of a man or animal. Pascal Poirier enumerates thirty-two derivatives of the word "gargoton" and one hundred sixty-seven of the word "got," of which "gargoton" is composed.

Gorziller: this is the reaction of shivering done by one who hears the writing on a slate.

Gourd: swollen; swollen fingers with no feeling; insensitive.

Gratte-cul: wild rosebush.

H

Haute heure: getting up late; late.

Hucher: to yell.

Horiotte: alder stick or a stem of any kind of forest species which serves as a whip.

J

Jongler: to reflect, to think: Je vais y jongler—I'm going to reflect on it. Jongler, être jongleur: to be pensive, to be flooded by and to be somewhat paralyzed by an idea of sadness, or remorse, or of disquiet.

L

Laîche: earthworm.

Longi: slow to work.

Social Life

M

Marionnettes: Aurora borealis.

Mâtrouiller: to nibble, to chew something which isn't swallowed, for example, rubber.

Mâter, se mâter: a horse rearing, i.e. kicks, bucks.

Mitan: middle.

Mouvée: shoal of fish.

N

Neuillace: a one-year-old calf.

Neuillère: barren cow; a cow that has not and will not have a calf during the current year; a non-calver.

Nippes: clothing, in a pejorative sense, somewhat in the sense of rags. Ramasse tes nippes—Pick up your old clothes.

O

Ouêtrer, se ouêtrer: to take a nap, a snooze.

P

Pouîne: uproar, racket, noise.

Pourgynée: numerous children; a large group of children.

Pruce or *prusse:* spruce; white spruce, black spruce, red spruce. This deals with the spruce tree (Picea).

R

Rabousiner: to put in a bundle.

Ramander: insistent and repeated request on the part of children.

Rarir: to become rare or more rare.

Raveston: a jungle.

Remeuille: udder of a cow, of a mammal.

Ribotte: churn.

Roue de neige: snowbank.

S

Sagant: negligent; neglected

Siler: to cause one to hear a sharp sound. Gémir: to whine. The dog whines at the door. Siler un chien—to send a dog chasing after animals or someone.

Sirouane: poultice; plaster.

Sourge: a light paste, well-raised, or a cake or bread made with such a paste.

Subler: to whistle.

T

Tamarin: made with molasses, this is Canadian taffy; with sugar it is fudge.[72]

V

Veauriou: lactic milk; first milk of a cow freshly calved.

Ventraîche: the hide from the abdomen of an animal.

Vezes: bagpipes.[73]

Volatif, volative: not attached; not nailed down: loose planks on a floor or on a bridge.

Vournousser: to occupy oneself in working at different things.

Z

Zire, zirable, faire zire: distasteful to the highest degree.

In Chéticamp many words have kept the meaning they had in early times, though they may not have exactly this meaning in the official language of today. We meet there very expressive old French phrases, the disappearance of which, in the scholarly world, is to be regretted. Putting aside the too-numerous anglicisms recently introduced into the language, we believe, without chauvinism or prejudice, that the speech of the Chéticantins is still very rich and savoury. We would even go so far as to say that of all corners of old Acadia, this is probably the region where one finds the purest old Acadian speech. Yes, even with respect to his language, this following assertion of Frère Bernard, C.S.V., fully applies, in our opinion, to the Chéticantins. "Where can you find, today, the most faithfully preserved type of the Acadian of long ago? Go to the shores of Chéticamp," he said.

In the semi-solitude of these rocky shores, in the salty atmosphere where the billowing ocean waves roll in, the Acadian soul [of the Chéticantins] preserves the qualities inherited from the pioneers of the old region of the Bay of Fundy. Added to this is the softness of the language and manners, a smile tingled with sadness which seems to be the distinguishing mark of the region. Go listen to the singing of a French hymn in the Chéticamp church, or some lament from olden times hummed by a fisherman…and you will feel your eyes fill up, and you will have the impression of "the soul of the ancestors watching over the sons." [Chateaubriand][74]

Unfortunately a serious danger threatens and will continue to threaten this beautiful speech of Old France in Chéticamp. I'm referring to the anglicisms and the anglicizations that have crept into our language. As a matter of fact, the school teaches more English than French to the young Chéticantins. The home, which up to this time remained a haven closed to any English influence, no longer exists as such today. Each day the mail pours a quantity of English magazines and newspapers into the region. The radio in New Carlisle allows French broadcasting, but too often the people listen to the English programmes from Antigonish and Charlottetown. And now English television, the only possible programming for a long time, has invaded the area. Tourism attracts a goodly number of English visitors. Business is conducted, necessarily, with English firms in the Maritimes and the United State. All of these constitute a danger for the mother tongue of these small groups, isolated from all other French centres in the country. Already numerous anglicisms on the lips of too great a number of our Chéticantins are despoiling this beautiful language.

The safeguard will come, if safeguard there is, through the clear-sightedness of the parish clergy, the teaching nuns and the teachers who will train energetic and proud secular leaders, who will well understand that French is a richness for Chéticamp, and who will face the danger and, as a result, organize themselves to conquer it.[75]

THE CHARACTER OF THE CHÉTICANTINS

THE CHARACTER OF THE CHÉTICANTINS is no different from that of the other Acadians of the Maritimes. The Acadian is the same, or nearly the same, wherever he is found. He has his own mentality, a special character which distinguishes him even from his French-Canadian compatriot. This is so true that one can recognize him simply by studying his facial features.

What is this particular Acadian characteristic? It is a gathering of subtleties difficult to describe. By studying its causes, perhaps we might succeed.

The Acadian carries in his soul the traces of past sufferings. He has lived a long time dispossessed, hunted, reviled. The initial pages of his history are written in blood. He still carries the scars of this. Brutally deprived of his lands, he turned to the sea, which he adopted as his own. The sea, in return, has molded his soul. The sea has rocked in its bosom the generations of Acadians, and imprinted its mark on them.

A tree which holds on under the force of the hurricane that is tearing it up by its roots leads a hard life, but if it endures it only becomes stronger. It does not have the spread nor the bloom of the tree growing in shelter, in the light. It is smaller, more humble, less arrogant, but nevertheless strong. If pulled out by the violence of the storm it settles elsewhere and these characteristics will reappear, only more prominently. The tree, thus transplanted in a slipshod manner by a violent storm, rarely finds proper nourishment.

Like that uprooted tree, the Acadians have grown for a long time without schools, without priests, without even the invigorating sap that can be supplied by the intellectual and moral contact of another brotherly or friendly people.

For a long period in their history the Acadians have lived in isolation. On the whole they are late, or at least they have been, and for that reason they feel inferior. Their subconscious is imbued with this feeling, and they suffer under the influence of this secular atavism. Just the same, they have survived. They have withstood the storms. They have been dispersed, hunted and massacred for decades; the debris caught hold again, here and there; they hold on; they have revived with a life that today, except for a few groups, blossoms out in the light of God's sun with magnificent accomplishments. But the Acadian, probably because of past sufferings, remains a shy person. Rather reserved, he doesn't open up easily to others. He doesn't confide in anyone on the first meeting, nor is he impressed with the beautiful words of a stranger. He confers his trust only with prudence. But, once given, his confidence is total and sincere. He rarely acts highbrow or superior. In him there is nothing of that proud and arrogant self-conceit which believes itself above others and shows itself unconsciously. In general, he is humble, and because he is humble he is frank. Having suffered, he is kind to others, understanding, sensitive, sympathetic, compassionate, hospitable. Any kindness, any attention makes him very responsive. Tactlessness causes him to suffer, but he will suffer alone in his heart.

With a rather modest opinion of himself, he easily believes himself, at least in the beginning, unsuited to carrying out important tasks. But if a field of endeavour presents itself and he recognizes the possibility of his being able to handle it, then he is capable of every effort in order to succeed, even to the point of obstinacy. He is said to be stubborn.

For every Chéticantin, fisherman or the son of a fisherman, the land holds no attraction. The sea is his true domain. He makes his living by it. But the ties binding him to the sea are stronger than the meagre pittance it provides. The sea, for him, has a language, a music, an irresistible appeal. It is through the sea and with the sea that he ceaselessly communes with the magnificent harmony of nature. It is, for him, the chorale, forever blending its voice to the canticle of creation, the orchestra continually accompanying it.

In the spring, before dawn, the sea is piously hushed as the fishermen leave for the open waters and it combines their prayers with the reflections of the stars whose light caresses the waves. The ocean is, at this hour, full of mysteries. At sunrise the light illuminating the heavens battles against the shadows of the waves, is lit and extinguished by the rise and fall of the sea. Like merry-go-rounds of small devils, its reflections hop, extend, contract, disappear, and begin again. Apparently subdued by the light of day, the sea allows itself to be caressed in order to make it dance, jump and gleam like a thousands fires; to be transformed completely on all sides in long trails of sparkling diamonds which is its daylight raiment; to reunite with it in the evening in the grand finale of the colours in the fire of blazing sunsets.

The ocean lends itself to the feelings of nature and man. It sleeps, calm and clear, under the beautiful summer skies. It is agitated by storms and hurls its frantic waves, like panic-stricken horses. When the heavens are unchained, the ocean becomes angry; with fearsome howlings it rushes to the assault of the cliffs, sweeping all in its path and tearing away at the headlands. The sea weeps with those who weep, sings with those who sing, and laughs with those who laugh. Sometimes, however, it makes one cry with the cruellest indifference: when it swallows someone up and changes nothing in its song in front of a desperately distraught mother, or a widow in mourning.

On land man leaves his traces, but the sea, even if it is ploughed in all directions, always remains virginal. Everything in it, waves, foam, bubbles, and reflections take form, ripple, and are erased. Here and there are clumps of seaweed, torn from God knows where, and surrendered to the whims of the waves. These lively waves that dance, rising up and crashing down again, murmur or moan, eternally; these sea gulls that skim the crest of the waves and, climbing, wheel and dive down, indifferent to the boats, to the poor humans passing by; these uprooted trees; a length of plank; a stick; wreckage of unknown origin—all that gives to the sea a character both eternal and human, indifferent and sensitive. The sea is there, always the same, everlasting and unlimited. However, everything in it, as in a meadow, "is movement, uncertainty, and secret."[76]

The sea has been rocking the Chéticantins for two centuries. It is, then, not surprising that the people carry within their hearts, as in a dream, a type of indefinable nostalgia that is expressed in their songs, their speech, and their customs. Like the sea, they are simple, yet great. There is depth in their vision, nobility in their hearts, dignity in their manners; all this interwoven with the yearning for the open sea, of white sails on the horizon, of sea gulls gliding in high winds. In other respects very jovial, they love to sing and laugh, like the sea which sings and plays with the pebbles on the shores.

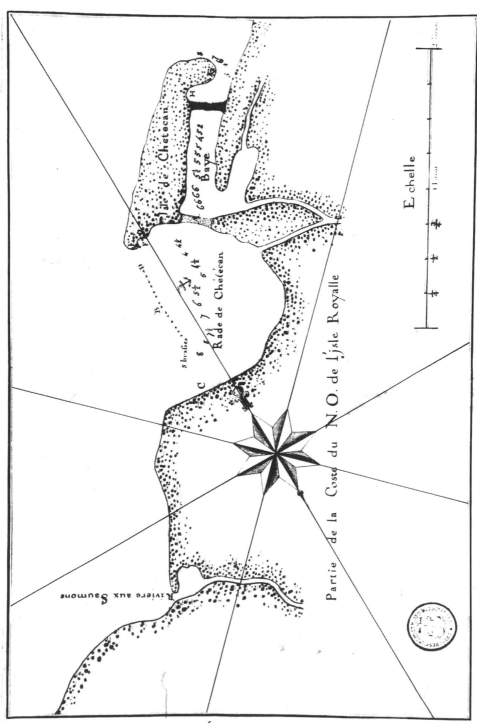

1752 MAP OF THE CHÉTICAMP WORLD BY FRANQUET

CHAPTER ELEVEN

Supplement: Chéticamp Since 1961

THE FRENCH VERSION OF THIS BOOK was published in 1961. The next two printings (1962, 1972) simply reproduced the first edition without mentioning additional noteworthy events which took place since 1961.

A complete book could be written on the evolution Chéticamp has known since that date in the religious, educational, economic, social and cultural fields. We wish to use this English edition, if not to give a lengthy discourse on this evolution, at least to give a summary outline.

Field of Religion

The Eudist Fathers had the pastoral care of the parish of Chéticamp from 1953 to 1988. There have been numerous changes among the pastors and curates during this period. Father Jules Comeau was succeeded in 1964 by Father Emmanuel Gallant, who was replaced in 1973 by Father Robert Desjardins. In 1981 Father Henri Tremblay, a former curate who had been loved by the people, returned to Chéticamp, this time as a pastor, to the great satisfaction of the parishioners; but in 1985 he was replaced by Father Hector Comeau, who left in 1988 and was the last Eudist pastor in Chéticamp.

If the people of Chéticamp were sorry to see the Eudist Fathers leave, they were happy to receive as their pastor a young diocesan priest who could speak their language well, Father Bill Burke. A still younger priest, Father Lester Marchand, took charge in 1992 and left in 1997, to be replaced by Father Jean-Baptiste DeCoste, a White Father, born in Arichat, who as a missionary has passed many years in Zaire, Africa.

From the time they assumed the care of the parish, the Congregation of the Eudist Fathers has always provided curates for Chéticamp who have accomplished admirable and highly appreciated work. After 1961, we had Fathers Henri Tremblay, Harland D'Eon, Roger Saint-Laurent, Louis Antoine Lachance and Jean-Paul Roy.

From 1961 to 1997 much work was done on the church building: new roofing, the main steeple and the small one rebuilt, the statues, one on each side of the main steeple, were replaced by new ones, and the parking area was paved. Inside, a ramp was installed on the left side of the sanctuary for the aged and the handicapped; two new furnaces were installed to replace the old one; an altar was set up in front of the sanctuary so that the priest can celebrate Mass facing the congregation. And the whole interior was painted anew in 1988.

A special event happened in 1993: the centenary of the church was highly celebrated. First, there was a great feast Friday evening, the 30th of July, at the Centre Acadien. His Excellency Colin Campbell, Bishop of Antigonish, attended, as well as eleven priests, forty-five nuns, two brothers, those who were born in Chéticamp and those who accomplished apostolic work there. The hall was full of parishioners, both for the celebration and to buy the fine brochure on the history of the church written by Charlie Dan Roach.

The next day, a High Mass was celebrated by the bishop, accompanied by many priests. And on Sunday night in the sanctuary of the church what they called "Symphony in the Heart of Acadia" was performed. It was produced by the Acadian Cultural Council of Nova Scotia, the Society of Radio-Canada and two renowned choirs of Chéticamp, L'Echo des Montagnes and Les Voix du large, under the direction of Michel Aucoin, and finally Symphony Nova Scotia under the direction of Scott MacMillan.

The Mass and this concert Sunday night were broadcast all over Canada by Radio Canada Television.

Field of Education

All the small schools of the district have been closed. The large school, Notre Dame d'Acadie, built in 1963, takes in all the students of Chéticamp, St-Joseph-du-Moine and Pleasant Bay. This school contains sixty-two classrooms, four science laboratories, an auditorium with a capacity for 500 persons, a gymnasium, a darkroom for developing photographs, an Industrial Arts Department, and another for Domestic Science.

The school has over forty-five teachers and an enrollment of around 700 students, of whom some 70 or more complete their twelfth grade each year.

Field of Economics

Chéticamp has experienced a remarkable economic development over the past forty years. New industries have sprung up and former ones have grown to the point that this locality has finally become a prosperous village.

New Industries

G. Boudreau soudure électrique (G. Boudreau Electrical Welding): In 1958 Gérard Boudreau, who had taken advantage of a stay in Toronto to take a course in electrical welding, returned to ply his trade in Chéticamp. He bought a building at the harbour, later enlarged in 1965. His business continued to prosper and employed a few men in the winter and four in the summer. In 1993 Gérard retired and sold his business to his nephew Claude Poirier.

La compagnie Industrial Welding (Industrial Welding Company): Founded in 1974 by Roger and Raymond Deveau, this company specialized in the work of high-pressure welding, as well as the planning and manufacturing of hydraulic pumps, winches, etc. This company already had twenty employees and worked all over Cape Breton and even beyond. The founders dreamed of even greater projects like building equipment for the drilling of oil wells at sea and obtaining a "share of the work created by the exploration and exploitation of offshore resources." Unfortunately these dreams did not materialize. A reversal of fortune forced them to sell their huge workshop. It was bought by Johnny MacEwen in 1992 who rents it to Riff's Company.

Le Gabriel, a magnificent restaurant that Raymond Deveau had built in 1986-87, was sold to René Lefort in 1991.

The Deveaus continue in the welding business.

A.B.C Welding Shop had also been opened, by Bernie Lapierre. Later on, the building and the business were turned into Chéticamp Coin Car Wash.

Boat Builders: Till nearly sixty years ago, Chéticamp always had carpenters who built boats. But the last ones to build them of any significantly large size were Fraser and Chiasson, Associates.

A company, *The Chéticamp Boat Builders*, was begun by Joseph, Jean Paul and Yvon Gaudet. In 1979 a building, one hundred and forty feet by eighty, was erected at the waterside at Redman and work began. They build and repair boats of all sizes, some over forty feet long.

La Co-opérative artisanale (The Crafts Co-operative): The industry of hooking rugs with wool has existed for a long time in Chéticamp. The shops where these can be bought have multiplied. One which deserves special mention because of its organisation and its volume of business is La Co-opérative artisanale.

It is more than a shop or store. It is a co-operative founded in 1964 by a group of twelve women. They bought the old fire station in order to turn it into a store for the sale of crafts, especially hooked rugs. In 1967 they set up a small museum; in 1970 they enlarged the building and opened a restaurant on the basement floor where, for a reasonable price, one could sample tasty Acadian dishes, made and cooked before the eyes of the customers.

Then the museum too was moved to the basement where, ever since, a lady explains to the tourists by actual demonstration the whole process through which the wool passes, from sheep, to carding, to the spinning wheel, right up to the craft of the hooked rugs. Later on, a garage nearby was bought and brought to be a part of the store as the restaurant.

The people bring their craft work to this store which then sells it to the tourists for a small profit. Sales grow year by year and the turnover amounts to hundreds of thousands of dollars.

We cannot mention all the shops selling rugs and crafts that have opened in Chéticamp during the last forty years. Two of them deserve a mention, *Flora's Gift Shop*, opened in 1964, for its success, and *Le Gabion (The Lobster Trap)* built in 1978, for the originality of its building in the form of a huge lobster trap. After Simon-Pierre Boudreau, the first owner, Le Gabion passed through different hands and closed in 1997.

New Stores

In Petit-Étang, Simon LeBlanc started a family business, *LeBlanc's General Store*, in December 1988. Elias Larade opened in 1977 a large garage, *Larade's Tire Shop Ltd.*, which employs five men full time. Mr. Larade also owns the *Chéticamp Auto Parts* store built in 1981.

At the harbour, a Frenchy's store, called *L'Entreprise Poirier du petit coin*, has been opened by Yolande and Anselme Poirier. Jean Chiasson operates a favourite convenience store called *Chez Luce*.

The Robin Jones ceased their fishing business several years ago. In 1965, they built a huge department store, now part of the IGA chain, where one can find everything one needs: groceries, hardware, furniture, etc. They also rent Pierre Bourgeois' store which permits an extension of their business.

A nice-looking store *Le Coin des Dames*, owned by Yvette Aucoin, sells women's clothing. Gloria Aucoin opened a small studio, *1 Hour Photo*, in 1989, where she sells and develops films.

In a store opened in 1996, Cyril Camus and his wife Lorette LeBlanc sell computers and the Internet.

Au Havre Ltee, La librairie: In October 1987 an important store opened its doors in Chéticamp, a library of French and English books. Its daring promoters were Maurice Poirier and his wife.

Chéticamp also has a liquor store.

Improvements and Transformations

The last forty years have seen several businesses transformed or expanded.

La Co-opérative Chéticamp ltée. (Chéticamp Co-operative Limited) opened its store in 1937. Yet it has experienced a development during the period 1961-1997 which deserves our wholehearted admiration. On November 21, 1978, a new building of 10,000 square feet, built at a cost of $585,000, was officially opened, replacing the old store which had become too small. This store was again enlarged in 1984, 1987 and 1992. This consumer's co-operative, after some difficulties in the past, now only experiences positive progress. Sales climbed constantly to attain $8,500,000 in 1996.

La Caisse Populaire (The Credit Union), with its humble beginnings in 1936, has known enormous progress since then and especially during the last forty years. The large building in which the Credit Union operates was newly-built in 1989 and its 1996 assets amounted to $14,500,000.

Fisheries: Chéticamp has always been known as one of the best fishing harbours on the Gulf of Saint Lawrence. A mass of 15,000 metric tons of fish were unloaded on its wharves each year, worth $8,000,000, with lobster and crab of equal worth. But the scarcity of the codfish that has happened lately has changed the picture and put stress on other kinds of fish.

Unfortunately the *Fishermen's Co-operative*, which held such great promise, continually encountered economic difficulties, and its fish plant finally closed in 1995.

New fish plants have been built in Chéticamp. Ned LeBlanc started in 1982 on his own land at Petit-Étang, a plant named *Ned LeBlanc Fish Supplier Ltd.* He bought cod, lobster, crab, and sole. A company, *Landry and Landry* from Cap-Pelé, New Brunswick, bought Ned LeBlanc's business in 1987, then sold it in 1992 to the company of Claude Moore: *Pleasant Bay Fish Ltd.* Ned LeBlanc continues as manager. During 1997 only, they have sold 100,000 pounds of lobster, 1,500,000 of ground fish.

Pierre LeBlanc from Cap-Pelé owns a plant, *Chéticamp Packers*, at L'Anse-du-Bois-Marié, and also the *Digue Fisheries Ltd.*, where he buys mostly lobster and crab.

Poirier Fish Haven, owned by Millot and Calixte Poirier, buy fish at the harbour and ship it outside.

While many people of Chéticamp are looking for work, it is sad to see most of their fish pass by their wharves, shipped out to be treated elsewhere.

New Restaurants: Ronnie Roach in 1995 opened a coffee shop restaurant called *Home Town Kitchen*. The restaurant *Lick-a-Chick* built in 1971 by Pierre Deveau changed its name to *Mr. Chicken* and with the *Harbour Restaurant* is now owned by Linus Deveau. A *Tim Hortons* was built in 1996 and is already very busy. The summer restaurant *La Chaloupe*, built in 1990 at the end of the promenade along the seashore, is very popular with musicians and singers. The owners are Sylvia Lelièvre, Judy Wakefield and Rita Kemp. Nearby a *Wabo's Pizza Restaurant* was started in 1993 by Jeannot Chiasson. The former Evangeline Theatre has been transformed into the *Restaurant Évangéline*. Finally, a new restaurant called the *Brigadoon Restaurant* was opened by Calvin and Caroline Martel in 1992.

Tourists' Accommodations: Many new cabins have been built. Patrice

Poirier owns nine cabins, family style, since 1988, called *Les Cabines du Portage*. Twelve cabins, *Cabot Trail Sea and Golf Chalets*, were built in 1997 near the golf course by Maurice Doucet. A beautiful inn named *L'Auberge Doucet Inn*, with twelve rooms and restaurant, was built in 1992 at a prime Redman elevation. Finally, six two-storied cabins, named *Pilot Whale Chalets*, were built in 1997 at L'Anse-du-Bois-Marié by Johnny Power. *Laurie's Motor Inn* has expanded to the capacity of fifty-three rooms, some very sumptuous.

The Royal Bank of Canada has been in Chéticamp since 1914. In 1969, a new building was constructed where the bank set up business. With eight employees, this bank does a great deal of business.

La Pharmacie Acadienne: This drugstore, well furnished, with registered pharmacists, was opened in 1977. Begun in a trailer, it was moved the following year to a new building worthy of a large town.

La Taverne Doryman (The Doryman Tavern) was constructed and opened its doors in 1965.

Salon funéraire (Funeral Parlour): The funeral parlour under the sacristy of the church consisted of only one room. It was not always sufficient for the needs of the parish. In 1976 Mr. Louis Chiasson and his son Bernie, the undertakers, built one with two rooms, and that of the sacristy ceased to be used. The Chéticamp Co-operative Limited acquired this funeral home and its business in 1996 and it is administered by the board of directors of its store. The Chiassons also operated an ambulance service of particular importance to the whole region. It was sold a few years ago to Amédée Muise and Marcel Larade.

Chiasson Brothers, Roger and Tommy, have a gravel pit at La-Cave-à-Loup. Equipped with heavy machinery, employing five or six men, they do great business.

La Boulangerie Aucoin (Aucoin's Bakery) was opened in 1959 at Petit-Étang by Alex Aucoin. Alex retired and his son Leonard took over in 1988.

Richardson Printing Ltd.: Joseph-Luc Chiasson started to operate a printing press, named *L'Imprimerie du Nord-est*. The property and business were sold first to Wilfred Boudreau (Dr. Gabriel's son), then to Louis-Paul Aucoin, then to La Société Saint-Pierre, and finally in September 1981 to Mr. Richardson, who has been running it successfully since.

Lawyers: Chéticamp is now served by three lawyers, Carmel Lavigne, Camïlle Deveau and Réjean Aucoin.

Other Improvements

Sidewalks: The road through the village along the harbour is very crowded in the summer, the peak season for tourists. With a considerable increase in vehicles, as well as the fact that pedestrians had no alternative to walking on the road, traffic became particularly dangerous. It was a great improvement when the municipality built sidewalks in 1972.

Sewers: Every house in Chéticamp has its well from which an electric pump draws water. Up to 1974, each house used its own septic tank as a sewer or, along the harbour, a pipe which discharged all waste into the bay.

The bay and the wells became dangerously polluted. In 1974 the municipality judged it necessary to begin the installation of a public sewage system all along the harbour, completing it in 1975 and extending it to Petit-Étang in 1977.

Telephone: In 1972, the Maritime Telegraph and Telephone Company Limited installed automatic dial phones throughout Chéticamp. Since then the people are able to make their calls, even long distance ones, without having recourse to a central operator based in Sydney, especially as the service there is unilingual English.

La Plage Sainte-Pierre (The Beach): A group of parishioners obtained government grants and in 1963 began to commercially develop the beach of Le Banc on the island. Because of financial difficulties this whole beach and its installations were ceded to La Société Saint-Pierre in 1977, which obtained subsidies to improve the hygienic and physical conditions of the place. This magnificent beach, without flies or mosquitoes, could experience great development if financial means permitted it. Already tourists with tents or trailers register there in large numbers.

Works at the Port: Important works were undertaken in the port of Chéticamp in 1981. The federal Minister of Public Works agreed to spend $160,000 to renew harbour installations. These works concerned what is called Le Petit Havre (The Small Harbour) and were carried out on three levels: repairs to the drydock (slip) at a cost of $25,000; construction of a breakwater along La Digue in order to protect Le Petit Havre, at a cost of $100,000; and lastly, a thirty-foot extension to Job's Wharf at the harbour entrance at a cost of $40,000.

Le Quai Mathieu (Mathieu's Wharf): A group of dynamic persons formed a committee for the economic development of Chéticamp. Among other plans they built a promenade wharf along a part of the harbour seashore. This promenade has become a rendezvous every summer night for artists, musicians and singers, who attract crowds of tourists as well as the people of Chéticamp.

The Social Point of View

We include in this field activities which are social in nature, for the well-being and development of the entire community or of a particular group in the community. In this field, also, Chéticamp has seen important developments.

Le Foyer Père Fiset: One of the most important projects, without any doubt, was the building of *Le Foyer Père Fiset*, a nursing home for the aged. Its construction began in 1969 and on December 8, 1971, the institution, with the capacity of forty-four residents, opened its doors. Highly qualified in administration, Sister Louise Boudreau of Les Filles de Jésus was its first administrator. She skillfully endowed the Home with a fine family spirit that still endures, continued by her successors.

In 1979 the building was enlarged and sixteen more beds were added. This Home presently lodges sixty residents and has a permanent waiting list. The residents found themselves very happy and never ceased praising it.

Le Foyer Pére Fiset is a member of The Association of Homes for Special Care that includes all the homes in Nova Scotia.

Residence Père Patrice LeBlanc: Le Foyer Père Fiset responded to a need: that of aged persons who cannot look after themselves for reasons of health, age or other handicap.

Another need was felt, too, that of persons also relatively advanced in age but still capable of taking care of themselves in an appropriate setting, capable of doing their own cooking, washing, and ordinary chores, but who would have difficulty taking care of a house. The Father Patrice LeBlanc Residence was then constructed in 1976, and later enlarged, where single persons or couples are lodged in their own apartments (consisting of kitchen, bedroom, and living room). These people only have to take care of their own apartment and are freed from the care and bother of the upkeep and repairs of the building, the heating, the shovelling of snow, etc.

Another building was constructed close by in 1991 adding fifteen more apartments to the thirty previously built.

Low-Cost Housing: Another valuable social initiative started in Chéticamp was the construction of modestly-priced houses. Several families with small incomes could not ever hope to own their own home. Aided by government agencies, the Kinsmen and the pastor of the parish, Father Robert Desjardins, set in motion the building of attractive homes for families with low incomes. These families paid for their homes in monthly installments in proportion to their incomes. Twenty of these homes were erected through the Kinsmen, and twenty-five more through La Société Saint-Pierre who had taken over.

Le Manoir Saint-Pierre (Housing Co-operative Ltd): A group of persons incorporated as a co-operative movement obtained loans from governments to erect a huge building of twelve apartments to lodge each couple of its members. A first building opened its doors in 1987; another one of twelve apartments was built close by in 1989. There has never been an empty apartment since the beginning. There exists a great family spirit that assures the happiness of the residents.

Arena: A further proof of the resourcefulness and spirit of initiative of the present generation of Chéticantins has been shown by the construction of a huge artificially-iced arena which opened in November 1978. This was a gigantic and very expensive undertaking launched, not by wealthy individuals, but by a group of relatively young people without very much financial backing. They completed this enormous project thanks to government subsidies, no doubt, but also to all types of organizations working to gather funds, and especially thanks to the great devotion and many sacrifices on the part of the promoters.

With the presence of the arena, numerous hockey teams and other games for the young have appeared. The arena also serves as a showplace for great exhibitions, major entertainments and large assemblies.

Le Portage Golf Course: The same group, or almost the same, who successfully carried off the arena project had further ideas in mind. For several years Chéticamp had been in need of a golf course. This dynamic group acted on this idea in 1980.

Understanding how to benefit from government subsidies for work creation, and having obtained ownership of huge plots of land in La Frênière behind the arena, they put people to work clearing away the forest and preparing the ground for a nine-hole golf course, already called *Le Portage Golf Course.* The size of the project did not frighten these people; they took their time in accomplishing it, only going ahead according to their financial means. They would open it in 1985, during the festivities of the bicentenary of the founding of Chéticamp. Pushing ahead their initiative, they enlarged this golf course to eighteen holes in 1997.

New Horizons Club: A small school building, no longer in use after the construction of the N.D.A. School, was retrieved by a group of persons "in their golden years" who placed it on parish property behind the church and use the building for their social activities. This building, called *La Salle des Retraités*, also served the handicapped as a workshop and classroom. But these handicapped now have their own building where they live and are trained to work and learn according to their capacities.

Skidoo Club: With prosperity, Chéticamp has developed numerous organized leisure-time activities—ball and hockey games, etc. Snowmobiles or skidoos became tremendously popular after 1970. Most homes possess one, sometimes two of them. In winter, fields were furrowed with their tracks and people were deafened by the noise of their motors. They widened the skidoo territory, their tracks invading the neighbouring mountains, sometimes crossing from one side of Cape Breton to the other.

In 1970 the Skidoo Club was founded, and a clubhouse for the members was built in Belle-Marche.

Today Japanese-made motorbikes, having three or four wheels and able to go nearly everywhere in both summer and winter, give serious competition to the skidoos.

Knights of Columbus: A Council of the Knights of Columbus was founded in Chéticamp in 1954. In 1966, they bought the abandoned school at Point Cross, which has served them ever since as a club and meeting room.

Kinsmen: The goal of the Kinsmen Club is to give assistance where it is most greatly needed in the community in which it is established. Since its founding in Chéticamp on January 11, 1977, this club has not ceased to extend its co-operation and assistance to the following important works: the construction and running of the arena, financial aid to the Home for the Handicapped, to Le Foyer Pere Fiset, to l'Hôpital Sacré-Coeur, to the firemen, to the minor hockey, to figure skating, to the golf course, etc.

Volunteer Firemen: Volunteer firemen have moved their vehicles and equipment to a new, more spacious building. These men are well-trained, perfectly equipped and wonderfully dedicated. Their organization constitutes an incomparable protection for the whole region.

The Cultural Point of View

The economic progress of a region produces a certain cultural advancement. This was the case in Chéticamp.

La Société Sainte-Pierre: An essential factor of this cultural development was, certainly, the revival of La Société Saint-Pierre. Founded in 1947, this society had been placed in abeyance following the founding of the FANE (Acadian Federation of Nova Scotia). But in 1974, when its definite dissolution was questioned at a meeting convened in Port Hawkesbury for this purpose, there was a veritable turnaround. Not only was its disappearance opposed, but it was decided to give it a new intensive life. New directors were elected.

The first order of business for the newly-elected directors was to find a place to serve as offices, as well as the head office of the society. After trying in vain to obtain a small abandoned school, the directors came up with a magnificent project, that of erecting their own building to become an important cultural centre for the entire region. The idea of the monument of Les Trois Pignons was born.

La Société Saint-Pierre, a member of La Fédération Acadienne de la Nouvelle-Écosse, in collaboration with it and other agencies, can claim all the merit or most of the merit for the following cultural activities:

Les Trois Pignons: With outstanding vision, the directors of La Société Saint-Pierre decided to erect one of the most beautiful buildings in Cape Breton which would not only serve as a head office for their society, but would also include, for the whole Acadian population of the region, a room for films and crafts exhibitions, a reception and tourist information centre, an Acadian library, as well as a centre for documents and information on history, folklore and genealogy.

Begun in 1976 with a subsidy from the Cape Breton Development Corporation, and built according to plans drawn up by the very same architect who reconstructed Louisbourg, Yvon LeBlanc, this magnificent centre opened its doors in 1978. Since then, La Société Saint-Pierre has set up in this centre the Marguerite Gallant musuem, and a showroom for hooked rugs, especially those of Elizabeth Lefort, a world-renowned artist in this domain. Les Trois Pignons is the driving force, the soul of all the cultural activities of the region, and its influence continually increases in this domain as well as in many others.

Department of History and Genealogy: A very important department at Les Trois Pignons is that of the history and genealogy of the Chéticantins. Under the able direction of Father Charles Aucoin, Charlie Dan Roach and Edmund Burns, there is accumulated here all possible documentation on these subjects: books, copies of parish registers, census lists, listing of names from all the headstones in the cemetery, old photographs, etc. And, as must be done, this material is organized to make it available to researchers.

This department is having a wide influence on the area and abroad. Students and adults are interested in doing research. Some descendants of people from Chéticamp gone for several generations write to obtain or to complete their ancestral line (family tree); others, also in large numbers, come themselves, sometimes from great distances, to gather this information firsthand.

La Société Sainte-Pierre founded an historical society which published from March 1984 to September 1994, at the rate of four issues a year, a Bulletin very rich with information on the history and genealogy of the people of Chéticamp.

Organized Courses: La Société Sainte-Pierre organized different interesting courses in painting for adults, for children, courses in folk dancing, singing and crafts. For some years, each winter Mr. and Mrs. Gérard Deveau have been giving lessons in rug-hooking to about forty people in a series of courses. The hooked rugs of Chéticamp still remain popular. They are more and more beautiful and are sold at better prices. We must not forget that as they make a substantial economic contribution to the locality, their creation has also become an art. When Elizabeth II visited Nova Scotia in 1976 the gift presented to her by the government in the name of the province was a rug hooked in Chéticamp by Mr. and Mrs. Joseph-Luc Muise.

Other Activities: The list of activities organized by or participated in by La Société Sainte-Pierre and Les Trois Pignons is endless: the sale of Acadian books; various study sessions; participation in provincial or national congresses; welcoming of groups from Saint-Pierre and Miquelon, from Québec, from Louisiana, even from France; as well as encouragement and aid to groups of musicians and singers.

One of these singers, Ronald Bourgeois, merits a special mention. Ronald composes his own songs and has rapidly become a Canadian celebrity. In 1982 alone he won a prize at the Gala of Granby (Québec), first prize at the fourteenth Song Festival of Caraquet, and first prize Aurèle Seguin in the national competition organized by the Cultural Federation of French Canadians and the Conseil de la Vie Française in America. There are other remarkable singers like Sylvia Lelièvre, the opera singer Bruno Cormier, and his sister Aurélie.

The Escaouette Festival: A demonstration of rejoicing and of Acadian pride, the Escaouette Festival has been organized for several years. The programme that lasts several days includes the official opening, a Solemn Mass sometimes outdoors, conferences, banquets, parades and entertainment for children, craft and arts exhibitions, diverse gatherings, and a long procession of allegorical floats for the closing.

Chéticamp and Saint-Joseph-du-Moine unite to organize this festival and the two parishes celebrate together. The Acadian flag waves in front of most of the houses and commercial buildings, and a feeling of Acadian pride cannot fail to move hearts.

In 1980, Nova Scotia celebrated its 375th anniversary of the founding of Port Royal and solemnly concluded this pageant at Chéticamp-Saint-Joseph-du-Moine on the occasion of the festival.

C.H.N.E. Community TV Channel: In 1989 a group of shareholders, a non-profit association, established and operates the Acadian Communications (TV Cable) in Chéticamp and a community TV channel. This was an important improvement for this locality.

Community Radio Station: Another important acquisition for Chéticamp was the opening on October 6, 1995, of the community French radio statio C.K.J.M., administered by a committee as a non-profit co-operative. It is open from 6 o'clock in the morning till 9 in the evening. In June 1997, this radio station was declared the Community Enterprise of the year by the Alliance of Community Radios in Canada.

Choirs: Chéticamp, during all of its existence, was renowned for its church choirs. It is remarkable now for its numerous groups of singers, and its fiddlers are among the very best in the Maritimes. Two famous mixed choirs were founded and directed by Michel Aucoin, one constituted of young persons called *L'Écho des Montagnes*; the other one of adults named *Les Voix de la Mer*. This latter was discontinued in 1996 because its director who is also a schoolteacher had too much work.

Books Published: Several books concerning Chéticamp have been published. One in 1985 was *L'Histoire des tapis "hookés" de Chéticamp et de leurs artisans*, written by Father Anselme Chiasson, with research done by Annie-Rose Deveau. It was translated by Marcel LeBlanc and published in English in 1988. *The Genealogy of the Poirier Family in Chéticamp* (the André line), written by Jean Doris LeBlanc, was published in 1985; another one by the same author *The Poirier Family of Chéticamp* (the Raymond line) in 1993. Charlie Dan Roach published his booklet *L'Église Saint-Pierre, Chéticamp, 1893-1993*. Gérald E. Aucoin's collection, *L'oiseau de la vérité et autres contes des pêcheurs acadiens de l'île du Cap-Breton*, was published in 1980. *Les Contes de Chéticamp (Fairy Tales of Chéticamp)*, published in 1994 by Father Anselme Chiasson, was translated by Rosie Aucoin Grace and published in English in 1996 as *The Seven-Headed Beast and Other Acadian Tales from Cape Breton Island*, by Breton Books of Wreck Cove. *À l'assaut des défis*, his memoirs written by Alexandre Boudreau, was published in 1994. The book *Chéticamp: Mémoires* by Anselme Boudreau was published in 1996. In 1986, Réjean Aucoin from Chéticamp and Jean-Claude Tremblay as co-author published a novel *Le Tapis de Grand-Pré*, which won the France-Acadie award.

Conclusion

This supplement, though short and necessarily incomplete, suffices just the same to demonstrate the progress accomplished in Chéticamp since 1961. This evolution on all levels has changed the appearance of the locality.

Homes are improved, business has progressed, social services have been developed, communications with the outside have been expanded: French television around 1970, *Le Courrier*, a weekly French newspaper, delegations to congresses, frequent travellings, etc. Cultural life is also making great strides. On the whole it can be stated that Chéticamp is the most dynamic Acadian centre in Nova Scotia.

Unfortunately its French aspect and Acadian culture are seriously threatened. The anglophone students coming from Pleasant Bay attending N.D.A. School, or the Chéticantins returning from Ontario or the United States, constitute the greatest threat of anglicization that Chéticamp has known in its history.

However, French is an asset for Chéticamp and for Cape Breton, even from an economic viewpoint. This was recognized and affirmed by the Cape Breton Development Corporation when, for this reason, they granted subsidies to La Société Sainte-Pierre. This pronounced French character of an Acadian village in Cape Breton is a richness by itself, but is also an element that attracts tourists and, with them, money.

DEVCO understood it, La Société Sainte-Pierre and several individuals understood it, but will the population in general and groups in particular understand it sufficiently to combine their efforts with a view to preserving this treasure which is their French culture? Let us hope so.

Appendices, Footnotes and Bibliography

APPENDIX A

MEMORANDUM ON THE PENINSULA OF CHÉTÉCAN
ISLE ROYALE, 1751, ADDED TO FR. FRANQUET'S LETTER
May 25, 1752

The peninsula of Chétécan is situated to the north of Isle Royale, twelve leagues from Cape North and seven from Les Îles de la Madeleine. It is connected to the mainland by a gravel bed, A, about one league in length by 30 to 40 fathoms in width, and is used to dry the cod, the main fish caught along this coast, lying bare at all times, even during the severest storms.

The reef, at B, is a collection of rocks covered by four feet of water at low tide. The breakers they form make one aware of the danger of approaching too closely. At each end of this reef is a passageway to enter the sheltered basin of Chétécan. The one at C, separating the reef from the mainland, is wide and good, and the other at D, although narrower, is used more often. There is good depth of water, and the edges at point E, on the peninsula, are so abrupt that one can touch them with the end of an oar, without running any risk. The establishments of the fishermen are built at the above mentioned point E, as are also their cabins and their sheds. The anchorage is good here in this area, and except for the areas marked on the plan, one is sure to find 10-12 feet of water and a sandy bottom all around the small cove, F.

Towards part G, to the east of the said peninsula, is a Harbour, H, situated in the bay formed by point G and the gravel bed, I, where all ships can take shelter during any bad weather. This bed, I, is always dry at both ends, but in the middle there is four feet of water at low tide. The extent under water is wide enough to allow ships to sail through at high tide, thus entering the bay.

This peninsula is covered with woods, the most common being the oak; we find there a large bed of building stone near the above-mentioned point, C.[1] It is of a greyish colour and from 3-15 inches in height.

243

Besides the fishing for cod, which is done in the Gulf and along the coasts of this peninsula, there can also be taken many sea-cows.

Franquet

Isle Royale at Louisbourg, May 28, 1752.

Mr. Franquet

Note that the plans and memos added to this letter have been sent to the office of maps and plans.

Your Excellency

The small amount of knowledge that we have about the coasts of the northern part of this island makes me understand certain remarks made by a practical fisherman from the peninsula of Chétécan on different voyages. They seemed interesting enough to me to collect, then write a memorandum and draw a plan that I have the honour of sending to you.

I wish that, convinced of my zeal in all respects for the service, you be not less convinced of the profound respect which I have the honour of being

Your Excellency,

Your very humble and obedient servant

Franquet

Naval Archives, Series 3 JJ:
Northeast Coasts of America, Vol. 198.

APPENDIX B

PLACES OF ORIGIN OF THE PIONEERS OF CHÉTICAMP AND MARGAREE AND OF THEIR PARENTS

PIONEERS OF CHÉTICAMP

Born in Nova Scotia (other than Cape Breton):
Pierre Aucoin, of parents born in Nova Scotia
Joseph Aucoin, of parents born in Nova Scotia
Augustin Deveau, of parents born in Nova Scotia
Raymond Poirier, of parents born in Nova Scotia
Lazare Leblanc, of parents born in Nova Scotia
Cyriac Roche, of parents born in Ireland
Régis Bois, of parents born in Port-Toulouse

In Cape Breton
Pierre Bois, born in Port-Toulouse, of parents born in France
Joseph Richard
Maximilien Gaudet, born in Louisbourg, of parents born in Nova Scotia
Louis Gaudet, born in Louisbourg, of parents born in Nova Scotia
Joseph Gaudet, born in Arichat, of parents born in Nova Scotia
Benjamin Poirier, born in Arichat, of parents born in Nova Scotia

André Poirier, born in Arichat, of parents born in Nova Scotia
Pierre Deveau, born in Arichat, of parents born in Nova Scotia

Those Who Came from Margaree
Joseph Galland, of parents born in the area of Bay of Chaleurs
Simon Doucet, of parents born in Prince Edward Island
Alexandre Broussard

Born on Prince Edward Island
Joseph Chiasson, of parents born in Nova Scotia
Joseph Leblanc, of parents born in Nova Scotia
Thomas Chiasson, of parents born in Prince Edward Island
Charles Chiasson, of parents born in Prince Edward Island
Louis Doucet, of parents born in Nova Scotia
Joseph Aucoin, of parents born in Nova Scotia
Simon Doucet, of parents born in Nova Scotia
Joseph Cormier, of parents born in Nova Scotia
David Chiasson, of parents born in Nova Scotia
Germain Chiasson, of parents born in Nova Scotia
Polycarpe Chiasson, of parents born in Nova Scotia
Charles Mius, of parents born in Nova Scotia
Pierre Deveau, of parents born in Prince Edward Island
Laurent Chiasson, of parents born in Nova Scotia
Pierre Mius, of parents born in Nova Scotia
Firmin Chiasson, of parents born in Nova Scotia
John Chiasson, of parents born in Nova Scotia
Basile Chiasson, of parents born in Nova Scotia
Joseph Chiasson, of parents born in Nova Scotia

Born in France
Pierre Aucoin, of parents born in Nova Scotia
Joseph Deveaux, of parents born in Prince Edward Island
Jean Bourgeois, of parents born in France
Louis Breuillat, of parents born in France
Joseph Boudreau, of parents born in Nova Scotia
Firmin Deveau, of parents born in Prince Edward Island
François Lefort, of parents born in Prince Edward Island
Anselme Aucoin, of parents born in Nova Scotia
Louis Luhédé, of parents born in France
Étienne Rambeau, of parents born in France
François Levert, of parents born in France

Born at Bay of Chaleurs
Jean Deveau, of parents born in Nova Scotia
Joseph Deveau, of parents born in Nova Scotia
Raymond Poirier, of parents born in Nova Scotia

From the Magdalen Islands
Cyprien Deveau, of parents born in Prince Edward Island

Born in Tracadie, Nova Scotia
Jean-Marc Romard, who came to Chéticamp before 1809

From Newfoundland
Jean Camus, who came from Bay St. George

From Québec
Jean Shumph

From the Isle of Jersey, Europe
Jacques Avy, of St. Élier
Probably Jean Lelièvre, a Jersey who converted to Catholicism

From Ireland
James Bulter
George Flinn
The Odle Family
The Harris Family

PLACES OF ORIGIN OF PIONEER ACADIANS OF MARGAREE AND OF THEIR PARENTS

Charles Galland, born in Cape Breton, of parents born in Prince Edward Island
Jean Cormier, born in Cape Breton, of parents born in Prince Edward Island
Firmin Etchevery, born in Cape Breton, of parents born in France
Judon (Judes?) Etchevery, born in Cape Breton, of parents born in France
Jean Blanchard, born in Cape Breton, of parents born in France
Simion Leblanc, born in Cape Breton, of parents born in Nova Scotia
Joseph Leblanc, born in Prince Edward Island, of parents born in Nova Scotia
Matthieu Galland, born in New Brunswick, of parents born in Nova Scotia
Lazare Leblanc, born in Cape Breton, of parents born in Nova Scotia
Charles Galland, born in Prince Edward Island, of parents born in Nova Scotia
Meuran Leblanc, born in Prince Edward Island, of parents born in Nova Scotia
Lazare Leblanc, son, born in Prince Edward Island, of parents born in Nova Scotia
Élie Leblanc, born in Cape Breton, of parents born in Nova Scotia
France (François?) Leblanc, born in Cape Breton, of parents born in Nova Scotia
Jacob Galland, born in Prince Edward Island, of parents born in Nova Scotia
Paul Doucet, born in Prince Edward Island, of parents born in Nova Scotia
Jean Chiasson, born in Prince Edward Island, of parents born in Nova Scotia
Prosper Leblanc, born in Prince Edward Island, of parents born in Nova Scotia
Raphaël Aucoin, born in Cape Breton, of parents born in England
Basile Mius, born in Prince Edward Island, of parents born in Nova Scotia
Joseph Broussard, born in France, of parents born in France
Simion Galland, born in Cape Breton, of parents born in Prince Edward Island

Appendices, Footnotes and Bibliography

Peter Bass (?), born in Cape Breton, of parents born in France
Jean Leblanc, born in Cape Breton, of parents born in France
Joseph Bass, born in Cape Breton, of parents born in France
Noré (Honoré) Leblanc, born in Prince Edward Island, of parents born in Nova Scotia
Charles Blanchard, born in Cape Breton, of parents born in France
Siméon Leblanc, born in Prince Edward Island, of parents born in Nova Scotia
Georges Leblanc, born in Prince Edward Island, of parents born in Nova Scotia
Georges Leblanc, Jr., born in Cape Breton, of parents born in Nova Scotia
Charles Leblanc, born in Cape Breton, of parents born in Nova Scotia
Germain Leblanc, born in Cape Breton, of parents born in Nova Scotia
Bertrand Deraspe, born in Cape Breton, of parents born in Nova Scotia
Jean Hubert (Hébert), born in Cape Breton, of parents born in Cape Breton
Bélonie Leblanc, born in Cape Breton, of parents born in Nova Scotia
Jacob Leblanc, born in Cape Breton, of parents born in Nova Scotia
William Leblanc, born in Cape Breton, of parents born in Nova Scotia

*(Source: **Holland's Description of Cape Breton**
pp. 156-58, and Parish Registers.)*

APPENDIX C

CENSUS OF CHÉTICAMP TAKEN AT END OF AUGUST 1809
BY FATHER LEJAMTEL, MISSIONARY

CATHOLIC INHABITANTS OF CHÉTÉCAN

In the village of Grand-Étang
François Cormier and Anne Hachet, his wife
      Cyprien,* Barbe,* François*
Joseph Cormier and Susanne Leblanc, his wife
Simon Doucet and Scholastique Cormier, his wife
      Simon, Henriette, Marie, François, Marguerite, Barbe,
      Félicité, Céleste, Sophie, Scolastique
Étienne Raimbeau and Louise Cormier, his wife
      François
David Chiasson and Celeste Cormier, his wife
      Maltide, Charles, Celeste

At Le Platin
Louis Doucet and Magdeleine Aucoin, his wife
      Joseph, Magdeleine, Marie Judith, Dominique
Jean Bourgeois and Angélique Poirier, his wife
      Laurent, Jean, Charlotte, Marie, Raimond, Thomas, Genevieve, Eustache
Firmin Devaux and Marie-Luce Godet, his wife
      Charles, Sophie, Gervaise, Anne, Céleste

Maximin Godet and Genevieve Bois, his wife
    Angélique,* Jean, Marie, Elisabeth, Ursule, Marguerite
Louis Godet and Marie Bourg, his wife
    Luce, Amand, Barbe
Anne Richard, widow of Joseph Godet
François Marie Lefort and Anne Godet, his wife
    Joseph
Louis Bruyard, widower of Marie Magdeleine Deveaux
    Charles, Marie, Marguerite, Rosalie
Joseph Boudrot and Anne Chiasson, his wife
    Charles,* Luce Aucoin* (domestic)
Anselme Aucoin and Rose Chiasson, his wife
    Marie,* Hubert,* Raphael,* Pierre,* Magdeleine,
    Agnès, Joseph, Thomas, Susanne
Simon Aucoin and Élisabeth Poirier, his wife
Joseph Aucoin and Marie Hébert, his wife
Cyriac Roche and Rosalie Harnois, his wife
    Modeste, Joseph, Hubert, Marie
Genevieve Godet
Pierre Aucoin, widower of Félicité Leblanc,
Joseph Aucoin and Ysabelle Leblanc, his wife
    Joseph Charles, Pierre, Luce
Augustin Devaux and Marie Poirier, his wife
    Joseph,* Frédéric, widower of Théotiste Leblanc, Jean Baptiste
Joseph Godet and Ysabelle Aucoin, his wife
    Osithe, Ysabelle, Marguerite, Henriette, Victoire, Françoise, Joseph
Jeanne Dugas, widow of Pierre Bois
Régis Bois and Apolline Arsenaux, his wife
    Marie-Magdeleine,* Genevieve, Hélene
Joseph Devaux, widower of Angélique Hébert
Bruno Poirier and Marie Devaux, his wife
    Renauld, Moyses, Félix, Meloine
Pierre Devaux and Marie Aucoin, his wife
    Marie, Luce
Jean Devaux and Eulalie Poirier, his wife
    Susanne
Raimond Poirier and Marie Bois, his wife
    Raimond, Henriette
Jean Lelièvre and Marie Angélique Devaux, his wife
    Marie, Susanne, Jean, Ester, Elisabeth
Ysaac Leblanc and Genevieve Aucoin, his wife
    Alexis, Julienne, Simon, Henriette, Catherine, Felicité, Genevieve
Anastasie Girouard, widow of Jean Romard
    Magdeleine Olive,* Jean François, * Marguerite Rose,* Anne Marie,
    Anastasie Angélique, Sophie, Julie Rosalie, Julien Alexandre

In the village of Petit-Étang
Elisabeth Boudrot, widow of Jean Chiasson
Lazare Leblanc and Modeste Chiasson, his wife
    Cyprien,* Jean,* Simon,* Lazare,* Euphrosine, Marie
Étienne Chiasson and Monique Godet, his wife
    Urbain,* Charles,* Anastasie, Michel, Joseph, Prosper
Joseph Leblanc and Marie Chiasson, his wife
    Jean,* Joseph, Lazare, Placide, Marie, Grégoire, Sophie
Jean Baptiste Maillet and Françoise Chiasson, his wife
    Marie, Michel
Anne Leblanc, widow of Grégoire Maillet
Joseph Chiasson and Marie Maillet, his wife
    Joseph, Charles, Magdeleine
Rosalie Maillet, widow of Simon Cormier
    Simon
Pierre Aucoin and Luce Babin, his wife
    Magdeleine,* Barbe,* Pierre, Marguerite,
    Simon, Charles, Félicité, Marie, Joseph
Joseph Devaux and Euphrosine Godet, his wife
    Magdeleine,* Anastasie,* Ysidore,* Ester, Marie,
    Ysabelle, Angélique, Joseph, Françoise, Susanne
Joseph Chiasson and Dorothé Poirier, his wife
    Hubert, Ursule, Céleste

On Chéticamp Island
Basile Chiasson and Anne Arsenaux, his wife
    Thomas,* Jean,* Marguerite,* Basile
Firmin Chiasson and Hélène Poirier, his wife
    Susanne, Jean, Hélène
Marie Pitre, widow of Germain Chiasson
    Maturin,* Charlemagne,* Laurent,* Polycarpe,*
    Marie Barbe,* Charlotte, Germain
Pierre Devaux and Marguerite Godet, his wife
    Agnés, Pierre, Rosalie, Charles, Marie, Joseph, Marguerite
André Poirier and Marie Blandine Benoit
    André,* Marie,* Casimir, Benjamin, Henriette
Joseph Poirier and Euphrosine Devaux, his wife
Thomas Doody and Marie Power, his wife
    Thomas, Brijitte
Joseph Mathe and Marie Zace, his wife
    Marie, Emilie
Alexandre Mcdonald and ..., his wife
    His children.

Those designated by baptismal names only are the children of those immediately preceding them. Asterisk (*) denotes those who have made their First Communion.

CENSUS OF MARGAREE IN CAPE BRETON IN 1809
BY FATHER LEJAMTEL, MISSIONARY

Joseph Cormier and Osithe LeBlanc, his wife
    Laurent, Henriette, Pélagie, Charlotte, Marguerite, Théotiste, Joseph, Pierre
Joseph Chiasson and Marguerite LeBlanc, his wife
    Henriette, Luc, Isabelle, Dominique, Jean-Baptiste, Jean, Placide
Isidore Chiasson and Marie Madeleine LeBlanc, his wife
    Marie-Modeste, Armand, Simon, Isidore, Isabelle, Charles, Marguerite
Prosper LeBlanc and Marguerite Poirier, his wife
Pierre Cormier and Félicité LeBlanc, his wife
    Firmin, Edesse, Marie
Joseph LeBlanc, and Martine Arsenaux, his wife
Paul LeBlanc and Marguerite Haché, his wife
Bénoni LeBlanc, and Joseph Bourg, his wife
    Euphrasine, widow of Lazare Doucet, Marie Jardin* (domestic)
Jacques LeBlanc and Angéline LeBlanc, his wife
    Catherine
Marguerite LeBlanc, widow of Joseph LeBlanc
    Rufine,* Anastasie,* Marie,* Suzanne* (married), Joseph
Hilaire LeBlanc and Scolastique LeBlanc, his wife
    Étienne,* Célestin, Simon, Maturin, Paul, Charlotte
Charles Haché and Félicité Gautreau, his wife
    Marthe,* Maturin,* Jacques,* Simon,*
    Euphrozine,* Charles, Marie, Joseph, Pierre
Honoré Michel, widower of…
Felix Haché and Luce LeBlanc, his wife
    Gilbert
Françoise Haché, widow of Jean Blanchard
    Charles, Judith, Jean
Paul Doucet, widower of Félicité Michel
    Anne-Marguerite*
Paul Doucet and Tarsilde LeBlanc, his wife
    Martin, Simon, Marie
Marie Doucet, widow of Martin Larade
    Marie,* Madeleine,* Félicité,* Henriette,*
    Pierre, Simon, Lazare, Barbe, Osithe, Joseph
Pierre Arsenaux and Marie LeBlanc, his wife
    Luc,* Barbe,* Simon, Madeleine, Thaddée,
    Anne, Mélanie, Angélique, Suzanne
Jean-Baptiste LeBlanc and Marguerite Bourg, his wife
    Honoré,* Jean,* Angélique
Paul Daigle and Osithe Arsenaux, his wife, widow of Simon LeBlanc
    Bibiane LeBlanc,* Ursule, Daigle (mentally defective), Nicolas Daigle*

François LeBlanc and Osothe LeBlanc, his wife
    Marie
Marguerite Daigle, widow of Jean-Baptiste Chavary
    Prosper,* Jean,* Ester,* Isidore, Firmin, Simon
Ange Muce and Ursule Chavary, his wife
    Pierre, Charles
Madeleine Bourg, widow of Barthélémy Muce
    Marie,* Françoise,* Pierre,* Sifroy,* Rosalie
Isabelle Boudrot, widow of Guillaume Cormier
    Urbain,* Guillaume, * Isidore, Jean, Anne-Marie, Marie-Modeste
Marin LeBlanc and Marie Cormier, his wife
    Marie, Céleste, Luce
Germain LeBlanc and Madeleine Cormier, his wife
Lazare LeBlanc and Théotiste Cormier, his wife
    Polycarpe, Dominique, Henriette
Jean Chiasson and Anastasie Cormier, his wife
    David, Germain, Basile
Bénoni LeBlanc and Marguerite Cormier, his wife
    Sophie, François, Julien, Suzanne, Placide
Basile Cormier and Marguerite Arsenaux, his wife
Georges LeBlanc and Marie Doucet, his wife
    Madeleine, Hélène, Georges, Lazare
Simon LeBlanc and Scolastique Doucet, his wife
    Charles
Charles LeBlanc and Apolline Cormier, his wife
    Germain, Charles
Bertrand Deraspe and Marie LeBlanc, his wife
    Françoise, Bertrand
Jacques Moore and Flore McNeill, his wife
    Catherine

Between Margaree and Chéticamp
Joseph Ryan and Elizabeth Darabie, his wife
    Basile, Joseph, Brigitte, Marie, Jean, Catherine, Thomas, Louise

Those designated by baptismal names only are the children of those immediately preceding them. Asterisk (*) denotes those who have made their First Communion.

(Source: Archives of Archbishop of Québec, Nova Scotia, VII-22.)

APPENDIX D

CHARTER OF 1790
Chetican, 29th Sept. 1791

Rec'd of the Proprietor of this grant all fees and surveying thereon to this date which fees I have paid heretofore at Sydney to all persons concerned in this grant.

Palk Ry. Nugent

Letters Patent for Lands at Chetican to Pierre Bois and Associates. 7,000 acres. Registered 27th sept. 1790. Book C. No. 41.

J. Crawley, Ry.

Island of Cape Breton

William Macormick.

George the Third by the Grace of God of Great Britain, France and Ireland, King, Defender of the Faith and so forth. To all to whom these Presents shall come, Greeting,

Know ye, that We, of our Special Grace, certain knowledge and mere motion have given and granted, and by these presents for us, our Heirs and Successors, do give and grant unto Pierre Bois, Peter O'Quin, Joseph Boudroit, Joseph Godet, Paul Chiasson, Bazile Chiasson, Joseph Desveaux, Gregoire Maliette, John Chiasson, Lazare White, Raymond Poirier, Anselm O'Quin, Joseph O'Quin, and Justin Desveaux and to their heirs and assigns forever all that Parcel Plantation or Tract of Land situated, lying and being in and contiguous to Chétican or Macclesfield Harbor in Caermarthen County and is butted or bounded as follows viz, beginning at a Stake and Stones on the sea shore on the south side of said harbor two Chains North of Lands assigned unto Philip Robin and others, thence running by the magnet due East twenty-two chains of four Rods each to a Blazed Fir Tree, thence South forty-five degrees East, one hundred and forty-two Chains, thence North forty-five degrees East four hundred and eighty Chains thence North forty-five degrees West one hundred and twenty-four Chains more or less to the seashore from thence to be bounded by the several Courses of the sea-shore and of the south side of Marclesfield Harbor to a stake and stones forming the North West corner boundary of ungranted or Crown Lands, thence South forty-five degrees East sixty nine Chains, thence South forty-five degrees West one hundred and sixty-five Chains more or less to the East side of Chetican or Macclesfield Harbor aforesaid and from thence to be bounded by the several courses of said Harbor to a Barreachoix at the South West end thereof, thence by the several courses of the South side of said Barreachoix to a stake and stones at the South West end thereof, thence South forty-five degrees West two chains more or less to the Seashore and from thence to be bounded by the several courses of the Seashore to the Boundary first mentioned and measuring by estimation five thousand acres of Arable Land and two thousand Acres of barren and mountainous Land forming in the whole a Tract of Land containing seven thousand acres more or less.

and hath such Shape, Form and Marks, as appears by a Plan thereof hereunto annexed; together with all Woods, Underwoods, Timber Trees, Lakes, Ponds, Fishings, Waters, Water courses, Profits, Commodities, Appurtenances, and Hereditaments whatsoever thereunto belonging or in any wise appertaining, together also with Privilege of Hunting, Hawking and Fowling in and upon the same, and Mines and minerals; Saving and reserving Nevertheless to us, our Heirs and Successors, all white Pine Trees if any shall be found growing thereon, and also Saving and reserving to us, our Heirs and Successors, all Mines of Gold, Silver,

Appendices, Footnotes and Bibliography

Copper, Lead and Coals, to have and to hold the said Parcel Lot or Tract containing in the whole by estimation seven thousand Acres of Land and all and singular other Premises hereby granted unto the said Pierre Bois, Peter O'Quin, Joseph Boudroit, Joseph Gaudet, Paul Chiasson, Bazil Chiasson, Joseph Desveaux, Gregoire Maliette, John Chiasson, Lazard White, Raymond Poirier, Ansem O'Quin, Joseph O'Quin, and Justin Desveaux their — Heirs or Assigns Yielding and Paying therefore unto us, our Heirs and Successors, or to our Receiver General for the Time being, or to his Deputy or Deputies for the Time being Yearly, that is to say, at the Feast of Saint Michael in every year at the rate of two shillings for every Hundred Acres, and so in Proportion according to the Quantities of Acres hereby granted; the same to commence and be payable from the said feast of Saint Michael which shall first happen after the Expiration of two years from the Date hereof; Provided always and this present Grant is upon Condition that the said Pierre Bois and His Associates above mentioned their Heirs or assigns shall and do within three years after the Date hereof for every Fifty Acres of Plantable Land hereby granted, clear and work three Acres at least in that part therefore as they shall judge most convenient and advantageous; or else to clear and drain three Acres of Swampy or Sunken Ground, or drain three Acres of Marsh if any such contained therein. And shall and do within the time afore said, put and keep upon every Fifty Acres thereof, accounted Barren, three Neat Cattle, and continue the same thereon, until three Acres for every Fifty Acres be fully cleared and improved, and if there shall be no Part of the said Tract fit for present Cultivation without Manuring and improving the same, they within the time aforesaid shall be obliged to erect on same Part of said Parcel or Tract of Land, one good Dwelling House, to be at least Twenty Feet in length and Sixteen Feet in Breadth, and to put on said Parcel or Tract of Land the like Number of three Neat Cattle for every Fifty Acres or otherwise if any Part of the said Tract shall be stony or Rocky Ground, and not fit for Planting or Pasture, shall and do within three Years as aforesaid, begin to employ thereon and continue to work for three Years then next ensuing, in digging any stony Quarry or Mine, one good and able Hand for every Fifty Acres, it shall be accounted a fulfilment, cultivation and Improvement; Provided also, that every three Acres that shall be cleared and worked, or cleaned and drained aforesaid shall be accounted a sufficient Seating Cultivation and Improvement to have forever from Forfeiture Fifty Acres of Land in any Part of the Tract hereby Granted; And the said Pierre Bois, Justin Desveaux and their associates aforesaid their Heirs and Assigns be at liberty to withdraw their Stock or forbear working in any Quarry or Mine, in proportion to such Cultivation and Improvements, as shall be made upon the Plantable Lands, Swamps, Sunken Grounds, or Marsh therein contained.

And if the said Rent hereby reserved shall be in arrear or unpaid for the Space of One Year from the Time it shall become due, and no Distress can be found on the said Lands, Tenements and Hereditaments hereby Granted or if this Grant shall not be duely Registered in the Register's Office of our said Province within Six Months from the Date hereof, and a Docket also entered in the Auditor's Office of the same, then this Grant shall be void, and the said Lands, Tenements and Hereditaments hereby granted; and every part and Parcel thereof shall revert to our Heirs and Successors; And Provided also, and upon this further Condition, that if the Land hereby Given and Granted to the said Pierre Bois and his associates above mentioned and their Heirs as aforesaid shall at any Time or Times hereafter come unto the Possession and Tenure of any Person or Persons, whatever inhabitants of our said Province of Cape Breton either by Virtue of any Deed of Sale, Conveyance Enfeoftment or Exchange or by Gift, Inheritance Descent, Devise, or Marriage, such person or Persons being inhabitants as aforesaid, shall within twelve months after his, her, or their Entry and Possession of the same, take the Oaths, prescribed by Law, and make and subscribe the following Declaration, that is to say, "I   do promise and declare, that I will maintain and defend to the utmost of my power, the Authority of the King in His Parliament as the Supreme Legislature of this Province" before some one of the Magistrates of the said Province, and such Declaration and Certificate on the Magistrate such Oaths have been taken, being recorded in the Secretary's Office, of the said Province, The Person or Persons so taking the Oath aforesaid, and making and subscribing the said Declaration, shall be deemed the lawful Possessor or Possessors of the Lands hereby granted : And in Case of Default the part of such Person or Persons in taking the Oaths, and making and subscribing the Declaration within Twelve Months aforesaid This present Grant, and every Part thereof, shall and We do hereby declare the same to be Null and Void to all Intents and Purposes, and the Lands hereby Granted and every Part and Parcel thereof, shall in like manner revert to and become vested to Us, our Heirs and Successors, any Thing contained to the Contrary Notwithstanding.

Given under the Great Seal of our Province of Cape Breton Witness our Trusty and Wellbeloved William Macormick Es'qre Our Lieutenant and Commander in Chief in and over our said Province, this twenty-seventh day of September in the Year of our Lord One Thousand Seven Hundred and ninety and in the third year of our Reign.

By His Excellency's Command
T. Crawley Secretary

Entered in the Auditor's Office
Book C No 24
Ach Cha Dolb
A.A.

APPENDIX E

RELIGIOUS SISTERS WHO ARE NATIVE TO CHÉTICAMP
Vocations to the Religious Order Les Filles de Jésus

Name in Religion	Year of Profession
Sister Marie Ste-Candide (Luce), daughter of Placide Leblanc	1909
Sister Marie Ste-Séraphie (Sophie), daughter of Édouard Aucoin	1909
Sister Marie Ste-Colette (Zabine), daughter of Pascal Haché	1912

Sister Marie Ste-Gaudence (Hélène), daughter of Charles Broussard   1914
Sister St-Étienne Marie (Marie-Hélène), daughter of Amédée Broussard   1916
Sister Marie Victorine du Sacré-Coeur (Marie),
   daughter of Charles (à Amédée) Aucoin   1917
Sister Marie St-Fiacre (Marie), daughter of Henri (à Fidèle) Poirier   1917
Sister St-Théophile-Marie (Marguerite), daughter of Marcellin Maillet   1921
Sister Marie Ste-Vénérande (Marie), daughter of Philippe Bourgeois   1923
Sister Marie St-Henri (Annie), daughter of Henri (à Fidèle) Poirier   1923
Sister Marie Théobaldine (Marie-Louise), daughter of Thomas E. Boudreau   1929
Sister Candide-Marie (Marie-Pétronille), daughter of Polycarpe Maillet   1929
Sister Marie Joséphine de Jésus (Marie-Louise),
   daughter of Denis (à Michel) Chiasson   1929
Sister Oliva-Marie (Marie-Madeleine), daughter of Luc Chiasson   1930
Sister Marie St-Paulin (Joséphine), daughter of Denis (à Michel) Chiasson   1931
Sister Marie-Géraldine (Deveau), of parents formerly from Chéticamp   1931
Sister Esther-Marie (Marie-Éthel), daughter of Placide Boudreau   1932
Sister Bertha-Marie (Louise-Béeatrice), daughter of Éphrem Chiasson   1932
Sister Marie Catherine-Aurélie (Sophie), daughter of William Cormier   1933
Sister Marie-Laurentia (Louise), daughter of Placide Boudreau   1933
Sister Marie-Marthe-Hélène (Lucie), daughter of Thomas Deveau   1933
Sister Arsène-Maria (Lucie-Anne), daughter of Willie Lefort   1937
Sister Marie-Yvonne des Anges (Edna), daughter of Samuel Cormier   1936
Sister Esther-Maria (Marie-Adèle), daughter of Lazare Boudreau   1942
Sister Marie Hélèna du Sacré-Coeur (Marguerite-Marie),
   daughter of Léo Bellefontaine   1943
Sister Léon-Marie du Sacré-Coeur (Stella), daughter of Léo Bellefontaine   1943
Sister Marcellin-Marie (Élisabeth), daughter of Marcellin Haché   1943
Sister Marie-Pierre-Vincent (Mathilda), daughter of Patrice Roach   1944
Sister Marie-Placide du Sacré-Coeur (Marie-Luce),
   daughter of Dan Chiasson   1945
Sister Louise-Marie du Sacré-Coeur (Marie-Mathilde),
   daughter of Willie Maillet   1945
Sister Marie-Gabriel des Anges (Marguerite-Alma),
   daughter of Lazare Boudreau   1946
Sister Marie de l'Emmanuel (Catherine-Rita), daughter of Pierre Poirier   1946
Sister Marie St-Gérald (Marguerite-Thérèse), daughter of Alex Leblanc   1947
Sister Hubert-Marie (Marguerite-Rita), daughter of Hubert Deveau   1947
Sister Marie-Rose-Yvonne (Évangéline), daughter of Henri Aucoin   1947
Sister Anne-Marie-Marguerite (Marie-Rita), daughter of Joseph J. Chiasson   1948
Sister Monica-Marie (Patricia), daughter of Joseph D.D. Aucoin   1949
Sister Luce-Emmanuel (Jeanne), daughter of Charles P. Deveau   1949
Sister Bertrand-Marie (Mercédès), daughter of Joseph (à Henri) Deveau   1949
Sister Marie-Dorothée (Marie-Dora), daughter of Sandy (à David) Bourgeois   1950
Sister Marie-Jean-André (Esther), daughter of Jean Poirier   1950
Sister St-Lucius-Marie (Marie-Hélène), daughter of Jean Poirier   1950

Sister Marie-Ste-Marguerite (Agnès), daughter of Léo Bellefontaine   1950
Sister Marie-Adéline (Marguerite-Martha),
     daughter of Joseph (à Henri) Deveau   1952
Sister Rosaire-Marie (Victorine), daughter of Jean Poirier   1954
Sister Marie-Saint-Georges (Joséphine), daughter of Georges Deveau   1954
Sister Luce-Marie (Pauline), daughter of Amédée Larade   1956
Sister Marie-Saint-Vallier (Olive), daughter of Charlo Poirier
Sister Jeanne Chiasson, daughter of Sévérin Chiasson (died as a postulant)
Sister Esther Aucoin, daughter of Charles Aucoin (died as a postulant)

Sisters of Charity of Providence of Montréal

Sister Sophie Aucoin—father: Victor Aucoin; mother: Anne Lefort
     Born: May 25, 1873; professed: February 11, 1897; died: March 6, 1925
Sister Marie Aucoin—father: Victor Aucoin; mother: Anne Lefort
     Born: August 4, 1879; professed: March 14, 1901; died: November 19, 1928
Sister Mathilde Chiasson—father: Léonard Chiasson; mother: Cordule Chiasson
     Born: October 9, 1856; professed: March 14, 1901; died: May 2, 1915
Sister Louise Romard—father: Charles Romard; mother: Sophie Gaudet
     Born: May 13, 1876; professed: March 14, 1901; died: January 7, 1912
Sister Mathilde Haché—father: Nectaire Haché; mother: Cécile Deveau
     Born: October 22, 1878; professed: March 14, 1901; died: January 18, 1956
Sister Cécile Lefort—father: Servant Lefort; mother: Judith Aucoin
     Born: November 15, 1875; professed: March 14, 1901;
     died: December 13, 1912
Sister Sophie Doucet—father: Romuald Doucet; mother: Brigitte Roger
     Born: June 21, 1874; professed: March 14, 1901; died: June 13, 1937
Sister Agnès Lefort—father: Stanislas Lefort; mother: Luce Roche
     Born: April 8, 1867; professed: March 14, 1901; died: June 28, 1944
Sister Luce Roche—father: P. Alexandre Roche; mother: Suzanne Cécile
     Bourgeois
     Born: July 25, 1872; professed: March 29, 1901; died: October 30, 1947
Sister Laurentin (Marie-Louise Leblanc)—father: Lazare Leblanc; mother: Résine
     Leblanc
Sister Henriette Doucet—father: Jean Doucet; mother: Sophie Galland
     Born: June 22, 1863; professed: February 11, 1895; died: April 13, 1949
Sister Justine Doucet—father: Calixte Doucet; mother: Félicité Roche
     Born: November 30, 1868; professed: March 14, 1901; died: July 4, 1956
Sister Olive Aucoin—father: William Aucoin; mother: Barbe Doucet
     Born: November 1, 1878; professed: March 14, 1901;
     died: November 2, 1918
Sister (Marie Roche)—father: Marcellin; mother: Luce Bourgeois

Sisters of St. Martha of Antigonish

Sister Marie-Philomène (Marie), daughter of Hippolyte Lelièvre
Sister Marie-Gabriel (Marie), daughter of Marcellin Doucet

Sister of Charity of Halifax
Sister Paul-Carmel (Marie), daughter of Paul Chiasson

APPENDIX F

"TRAVAILLER AUX GRAVES"

The expression "travailler aux graves" meant the laying out of cod on the *vignaux* (flakes) to be dried. But it was not enough to lay out the cod and leave it there; on the contrary, this drying of the fish encompassed a series of operations extending over a period of several weeks. Here is how an old fisherman, Tom (à Patrick) Leblanc, described this work to us:

The fishermen brought in the codfish and threw it on the wharf.

The employees of the Jerseys sliced the fish and cleaned it thoroughly, removing the head and the backbone, salting it, then leaving it in a pile for five or six days. On the sixth day, they washed the cod. Next day, in the afternoon, they spread the cod out on the flakes—the inside of the fish to the sun. About four or five o'clock in the afternoon, the workers turned the fish over and placed it with the outside skin facing the sun. On the following day, about nine or ten o'clock in the morning, the fish were again placed with the inside flesh to the sun. Towards evening, the fish were placed on top of each other four or five in a pile; they were left like that for two or three days. Afterwards, they were placed in large piles of 125 quintals each [one quintal = 100 pounds], and left for another three or four days. On the morning of the fifth day, the fish were once again placed with the outside skin to the sun, but were turned over before dinnertime. Then, in the evening, the fish were put into large piles again. Here the piles were covered with *machecoui* (birchbark) and left for five or six days.

All these operations took five or six weeks in all. Afterwards, the codfish were put into tubs and were ready for market.

Footnotes

Introduction
[1]Brother Antoine Bernard, *Histoire de la Survivance Acadienne* (Montréal: Les Clercs de Saint-Viateur, 1935), p. 302.

Chapter 1: Dawning of Acadia and the English Conquest
[1]Antoine Bernard, c.s.v., *L'Acadie Vivante* (Montréal: Le Devoir, 1945), p. 24.
[2]*Ibid.*, p. 25.
[3]Father François Lanoue, *St.-Jacques L'Achigan*, p. 5.
[4]Letter addressed to Nicholson, dated June 23, 1713. See Edmé Rameau de Saint-Père, *Une Colonie Féodale en Amérique*, "L'Acadie" (Paris and Montréal: 1889), Vol. 2, p. 357.
[5]*Pennsylvania Gazette*, September 4, 1755, Arch. Can. 1905, third part, p. XVI.
[6]"Petite Histoire de l'Île du Prince-Édouard," in *l'Évangéline*, June 13, 1958.
[7]Bernard, *L'Acadie Vivante*, p. 88.
[8]"Persecutions more inhuman than even those of Grand Pré." Pascal Poirier, in *Voyages aux Îles de la Madeleine: Le Parler franco-acadien et ses Origines* (Québec: 1928), p. 4.
[9]Report to Amherst, General-in-Chief.
[10]According to a report of 1763 preserved by the Naval Ministry in Paris, "there were only 3,000 to 3,500 Acadians who arrived in France, including all those who were able to make their way there by various routes from America and England, after the first deportation." Father H.R. Casgrain, *Une Seconde Acadie* (Québec: 1894), Ch. 13, p. 349.
[11]Henri Blanchard, *Histoire des Acadiens de l'Île du Prince-Édouard* (Moncton: 1927), pp.30-32.
[12]Émile Lauvrière, *La Tragédie d'un Peuple* (Paris: 1922), Ch. XVI, Vol. 2, p. 73.
[13]Father Casgrain, *Une Seconde Acadie*, pp. 362-63.
[14]Blanchard, *Histoire des Acadiens de l'Île du Prince-Édouard*, p. 35.

Chapter 2: Geographical and Political Position of Chéticamp
[1]Report of the voyage of the Intendant, Jacques de Meules, in Acadia, between October 11, 1685, and July 6, 1686, in *Revue d'Histoire de l'Amérique Française* Vol. II, No. 3 (December 1948), pp. 432-39.
[2]D.C. Harvey, editor, *Holland's Description of Cape Breton and Other Documents*, Publication No. 2 (Halifax: Public Archives of Nova Scotia, 1935), p. 7.
[3]J.L. MacDougall, *History of Inverness County* (1922), pp. 11-16. He gives the names of the governors and the councillors on page 12.
[4]*Ibid.*, p. 16.
[5]C.W. Vernon, *Cape Breton, Canada* (Toronto: 1903), p. 85.
[6]MacDougall, *Inverness County*, p. 17.
[7]Rameau de Saint-Père, *Une Colonie Féodale*, Vol. 2, p. 283.
[8]Letter of December 8, 1942, located in the Capuchin Archives.

Appendices, Footnotes and Bibliography

[9]Ganong, cited in Nicolas Denys, *Description and Natural History of Acadia* (Toronto: The Champlain Society, 1908), note, p. 185.

[10]Nicolas Denys, *Ibid.*

[11]On an undated anonymous map, a manuscript in the possession of Mr. Ganong. See *Ibid.*

[12]Map of 1758 according to the Chevalier de la Rigaudière, reproduced by Lauvrière, *La Tragédie d'un Peuple*, Ch. 8, p. 272.

[13]Census of Sieur de la Roque. See *Canadian Archives*, Vol. 1905, pp. 63, 65.

[14]Archives of the Archbishop of Québec, Nova Scotia, Notebook 5, p. 12. Located in Québec City, Québec. (Hereafter cited as AAQ.)

[15]First Parish Register of Chéticamp, p. 27.

[16]"It is ridiculous enough to suppose that this name is due to 14 Acadian families from Prince Edward Island, established there many years later, and who would find there a 'chétif camp.'" Father Pacifique, o.f.m., Cap., "The country of the Micmacs (continued)," in *Études Historiques et Géographiques* (Restigouche: 1935), p. 252.

[17]Bishop Plessis, "Journal of The Mission of 1812," *Le Foyer Canadien* (1865), p. 226, AAQ.

[18]Up to 1879 the present parish of Saint-Joseph-du-Moine was also part of Chéticamp.

[19]Bishop Plessis, "Journal," AAQ.

[20]*L'Evangéline*, August 19, 1949.

[21]First Parish Register of Chéticamp, p. 23.

[22]*Ibid.*

[23]June 13, 1813, N.-É. VI, 59, AAQ.

Chapter 3: Founding of Chéticamp

[1]James Phinney Baxter, *A Memoir of Jacques Cartier* (New York: Dodd, Mead & Co., 1906), notes: "There is much confusion in Cartier's account after leaving the Isle of Brion. Bourinot and other writers suppose his 'Cap de Lorraine' to have been Cape North on the Cape Breton shore; but this view cannot be reconciled with the account. Hakluyt gives the latitude as forty-seven and one half degrees, which is more nearly correct if Cartier's 'Cap de Lorraine' was Cape Ray; but it was more likely Chéticamp, and the latitude Cartier gives, namely forty-six and one half degrees, is evidence of this. It is probable that he was a few miles east-north-east of the northern extremity of Cape Breton Island when he took his latitude."

[2]*Bref récit et succincte narration de la navigation par le capitaine Jacques Cartier aux îles du Canada* (Paris: Librairie Tross, 1863), p.46. (Hereafter cited as *Voyage de Cartier.*)

[3]Lauvrière, *La Tragédie d'un Peuple*, Vol. 1, p. 289.

[4]Harvey, *Holland's Description of Cape Breton*, p. 62: "...there is scarce a Place, hereabouts without the remains of Wrecks."

[5]Nicolas Denys, *Description de l'Amérique Septentrionale*, Chap. VI. Note from Ganong: "This place, Chady, seems to be the same as our modern Cheticamp (or Chetican). It appears on an undated, anonymous MS map in my posses-

sion as Le Grand Chady, suggesting the possibility that Cheticamp is a corruption of Chady Grand, the Chady being Micmac Indian. It appears on the Coronelli map of 1689 as Ochatis, evidently taken from the Creuxius map of 1660." See Denys, *Description and Natural History of Acadia*, p. 185.

[6]Naval Archives, Series 3 JJ, *Côtes du Nord Est d'Amérique*, vol. 198. See Appendix A for this document and the map which accompanies it.

[7]"Chatican or Macclesfield Harbour affords Shelter for small fishing Craft; many of which the French built here, the Woods producing proper Materials." Harvey, *Holland's Description of Cape Breton*, p.62. And Sieur de la Roque said in his Census of 1752, p. 65: "The inhabitants who are in the large harbour of Scaterie Island (to the east of Cape Breton) wished to leave to found a settlement at Chéticamp harbour."

[8]There is, evidently, an error here. He means the American Revolution.

[9]Rameau de Saint-Père, *Une Colonie Féodale*, Vol. 2, p. 390.

[10]Monsignor Henri Têtu, Visites *Pastorales par Mgr. J. Octave Plessis, év. de Québec*, 1815 trip (Québec: 1903), notes, p. 176.

[11]Blanchard, *Histoire des Acadiens de l'Île du Prince Édouard*, pp. 39-40.

[12]Lauvriére, *La Tragédie d'un Peuple*, Vol. 2, p. 454.

[13]*Ibid.*

[14]Public Archives of Canada, Treasury Out-Letters, Various, America 1763-1778, T.28/1 F.175, p. 163. (Hereafter cited as PAC, America.) The Jerseys, coming to establish a fishing station at Chéticamp, asked for a customs house in 1770.

[15]Rameau de Saint-Père, "Notes de Voyages en Acadie," *Les Cahiers*, 31st Notebook of the Acadian Historical Society, Moncton, New Brunswick, Vol. IV, No. 1 (April-May-June, 1971), p. 35.

[16]Dates verified in the Acts of the Register of Carleton. Pierre Bois and Joseph Richard were of the group from the Bay of Chaleurs but seemed to be part of the first ones who went to Chéticamp.

[17]Harvey, *Holland's Description of Cape Breton*, p. 158.

[18]Henri Blanchard, *Rustico* (1938), p. 45.

[19]For more details on the places of origin of the pioneers of Chéticamp (comprising Saint-Joseph-du-Moine) and Margaree, see Appendix B.

[20]Rameau de Saint-Père, *Une Colonie Féodale*, Vol. 2, p. 261.

[21]The parents of these three Leforts came from Prince Edward Island. François, at least, was born in St. Malo, France. Luidée was born in Brittany of French parents. See *Registres Paroissiaux de Chéticamp*, Vol. 1; Harvey, *Holland's Description of Cape Breton*, p. 158.

[22]Augustin Haché, *L'Évangéline*, February 12, 1903, p. 1.

[23]*Registres de Chéticamp.*

[24]Radoub drowned in 1812. The Rambeau family emigrated to Cape North. These two names disappeared in Chéticamp.

[25]It isn't certain he was a Jersey. There were some Briards in 1767 in the passage from Bras d'Or Point (1 Reg. Car. 50), as well as some Miuses. The name of Breuillat, Breuillard, Briard, or Brillant become extinct in Chéticamp with the death of Anastasie Breuillard, wife of Timothée Chiasson, in 1925. Germain Chiasson

states that he came from the islands of Saint Pierre and Miquelon.

[26]Letter from Father Lejamtel to Bishop Plessis, July 30, 1799, N.-É. VI, 28, AAQ. Father Courtaud, a little later, would have to re-marry several couples that he had already married invalidly, for reasons of kinship.

[27]Letter from Father Jones, October 5, 1790, cited in A.A. Johnston, *A History of the Catholic Church in Eastern Nova Scotia*, Vol. 1 (Antigonish: 1960), p. 170.

[28]Letter from Father Lejamtel containing this Census, September 3, 1809, N.-É. VI, 53, AAQ. See Appendix C.

[29]Reg. of Québec, H.F. 322, AAQ.

[30]There was "le gros" 'Polite Chiasson and his son, William à Joachim Mius, Henri à Fidèle Poirier, Frédéric à "Petit" Philippe Lelièvre, the widow Cecile Haché, Fidèle and Joseph à Konock Chiasson, and their families. Only the sons of Konock Chiasson remained there. The others went to Shawinigan, Québec, then returned to Chéticamp.

[31]Bishop Plessis, "Journal," p. 226.

[32]Even at the beginning of our century, some old ladies of Chéticamp had an uncontrollable fear of the English, to the point of never leaving their homes by themselves, e.g. Anastasie Breuillat (widow of Timothée Chiasson).

[33]Since that time, we call them "les quatorze vieux" (the fourteen original settlers), and we honour them as the founders of Chéticamp. Their names are: Pierre Bois, Pierre Aucoin, Joseph Boudreau, Joseph Gaudet, Paul Chiasson, Basile Chiasson, Joseph Deveau, Grégoire Maillet, Jean Chiasson, Lazare Leblanc, Raymond Poirier, Anselme Aucoin, Joseph Aucoin and Justin Deveau.

[34]The land granted by the Charter comprised all of Point Cross, beginning about a mile to the southwest of Le Banc. Diagonally, towards the east, the line extends 1,442 feet then runs southeast for two short miles (9,372 feet), which reaches into the mountains. It then travels northeasterly about five miles, then northwest for a mile and a half to the shoreline; finally, it advances to the middle of the harbour, where it skirts the rest of the harbour, La Pointe-à-Cochons, and Redman, which remained Crown property. For the complete text of the Charter, see Appendix D.

[35]See Appendix C.

[36]Document in the possession of Amédée W. Aucoin à Calixte.

[37]*Ibid.*

[38]Letter from Arichat, where he had met Father Blanchet, October 10, 1823, AAQ.

Chapter 4: Economic Life

[1]Rameau de Saint-Père, *Une Colonie Féodale*, Vol. 2, p. 203.

[2]Account Book, Robin and Company, September 25, 1788.

[3]Letter from Father Lejamtel to Bishop of Québec, September 3, 1809, N.-É. VI, 53, 54, AAQ.

[4]Letter from Father Manseau to Bishop of Québec, January 7, 1814, N.-É. II, 148, AAQ.

[5]Letter from Father Lejamtel to Bishop of Québec, September 3, 1809, N.-É.

VI, 53, 54, AAQ.

[6]Letter from Father Manseau to Bishop of Québec, January 7, 1814, N.-É. II, 148, AAQ.

[7]This mill is indicated, as are its owners, on the sketch which accompanies the Charter of 1790.

[8]Stony ground where huge wire nets or lattices on posts were erected in order to spread out the cod to dry.

[9]Placide Labelle, "Faire du feu," in *La Revue Moderne* (October 1959), 19.

[10]In Chéticamp the people say *brocher* for *tricoter* (to knit).

[11]A ring of wool to protect the hand against the biting of the fishing lines.

[12]Bishop Plessis, "Journal," p. 29.

[13]This cereal was attacked by a disease, then unknown.

[14]Second Parish Register of Chéticamp.

[15]This was the sound of the bells ringing for them. They were believed dead.

[16]They were in Lowland, beyond Grand Anse.

[17]This tale, from the very lips of Hyacinthe Chiasson, written by Joséphine Aucoin, sixteen-year-old student of the Convent of Chéticamp, appeared in the Paris publication *Les Amitiés Catholiques Françaises* (July 16, 1939), 106-07, with a mark of seventeen out of twenty—about eighty-five or ninety-five percent.

[18]Fir tree, also called *chenave* in Chéticamp.

[19]Letter of June 12, 1813, N.-É. VI, 39, AAQ.

[20]Letter from Father Champion to Bishop de Canath, June 10, 1802, AAQ, VII, 6.

[21]Bishop Plessis, "Journal."

[22]Letter from Father Lejamtel to the Bishop of Québec, June 13, 1813, N.-É. VI, 39, AAQ.

[23]As told to the author by Arsène (à John) Bourgeois. There seems to be an error in the date given.

[24]Victor Hugo, *Océano Nox*.

[25]PAC, America, p. 163.

[26]Stony ground; cod-drying yards. *Travailler aux graves*. See Appendix F.

[27]Words of Captain Breuillard.

[28]This store was situated above the present establishment of The Fishing Co-operative, on the northwest side of the road.

[29]In Chéticamp the lobster companies took the name of factories. From that came the name given to the first two co-operative societies of Chéticamp, the Small Factory of La Pointe and, farther away, the Small Factory of the Harbour.

[30]This lobster factory and wharf were built on the lots of Pat Maillet, Luc (Hyacinthe) Chiasson and Johnny (à Eusèbe) Chiasson, where the buildings of the Fishing Co-operative can still be found.

[31]Listed here are the names of the first members of The Small Factory at the Harbour: Pat Maillet, Lazare Boudreau, Jeffrey Lefort, Jos Poirier (à Fulgence), who was president for a long time, Simon Bourgeois, Timothée Chiasson, Daniel (P'tit Den) Chiasson, Joseph (à Cacoune) Deveau, David (à Sambo) Chiasson, Joseph (à Édouard) Camus from Cap-Rouge, Joseph (à Amédée) Camus from

Appendices, Footnotes and Bibliography

Cap-Rouge, Joseph (à Hubert) Poirier, Charles (à Mesmin) Roach, Charles (à Caniche) Mius, Joseph (à Éloi à Victor) Roach, Élie (à Éloi à Victor) Roach, William (à Marcellin) Roach, Baptiste (à Jovite) Lefort, Luc (à Hyacinthe) Chiasson, John S. Mius, and Amédée (à Paddey) Aucoin.

[32]On February 1, 1959, Edmond (à Sandey à Lazare) Aucoin was named manager. In 1983 the position was taken over by Robert Maillet. The present manager is Denis Larade.

[33]The first manager was a Mr. Arthur Bourque of Louisdale, who stayed only a year. Then came Leo Cormier, Arthur Godet of Moncton, Berth Leboutellier, ex-manager of Robins, Louis-Philippe Chiasson, John (à Claude) Chiasson of Reserve, and, in 1948, Edmond Aucoin of Rogersville, whose parents were originally from Chéticamp.

[34]L'Évangeline, April 7, 1948.

[35]Ibid., May 22, 1957.

[36]The following was obtained from the Ministry of Fisheries, Ottawa:

Fish handled in Chéticamp in 1957	7,428,921 lbs.	$190,930
Lobster handled in Chéticamp in 1957	95,793 lbs.	25,717
	7,524,714 lbs.	$216,647

[37]Its first name was *Santiago de Cuba*, a boat, it is said, that the Americans had sunk in the harbour at Manila to prevent the Spaniards from leaving it during the Spanish-American War of 1898. Father Fiset had paid $5,000 for it. Before his death he sold it to his nephew, Dr. Louis Fiset, who lost it at sea shortly afterwards.

[38]The French version of this song is sung to the tune of "Casey Jones" or "The Parking Meter" song. The French words were obtained from Mrs. Padée Aucoin of Chéticamp.

[39]It appears that the evolution in this domain of craftsmanship was the same in Chéticamp as in the province of Québec. If one compares the hooked rugs formerly made there, one is astonished to find the same ideas and very similar designs. See Marius Barbeau, *The Hooked Rug: Its Origin*, Third Series, Section II, Vol. 36 (Ottawa: Royal Society of Canada, 1942).

[40]Miss Lefort worked in Margaree in the showroom of the Paul Pix Shop. Her works can be admired at the White House (the Eisenhower portrait), at Buckingham Palace (the Queen's portrait), and at the Vatican (the portrait of Pius XII).

[41]Original French version composed by Mr. Lubie Chiasson of Chéticamp.

[42]Property of J.F. Road of Halifax.

[43]Property of A.J. Burke Company of Halifax.

[44]Property of J.F. Road of Halifax.

[45]Property of Bras d'Or Steamship Company.

[46]This service was inaugurated in 1952 by Joseph (à Georges) Aucoin.

[47]PAC, America, p.163.

[48]Present Post Offices: Chéticamp (1868), Pointe (1868), Petit-Étang (1889), Point Cross (1891), Belle-Marche (1902), Plateau (1905), and Chéticamp Island.

[49]Following is a list of the garages in 1957, along with their opening date: Aucoin Imperial Esso Service, 1937; North End Garage (David P. Chiasson), 1939;

Chéticamp Motors (Alphonse D. Chiasson), 1946; Central Service (David Bourgeois), 1947; Trail Garage (another garage of the Robins), 1949; in 1955 another garage owned by Marcellin Lelièvre; and in 1959 a garage at Petit-Étang owned by Henri Maillet.

[50]Acquired by Mr. David Chiasson and Mr. Paul Cormier in 1955.

[51]There are some hen houses.

Chapter 5: Religious Life

[1]Letter from Father Maillard, Vicar-General of the Diocese of Québec, September 17, 1761, *Archives Canadiennes 1905*, appendix I, pp. 167-68. "Being Vicar-General of the whole parish of North America, I have the right to choose a trustworthy person to receive the same consents as I, and it is you whom I choose...."

[2]*Rapport de l'archiviste de la province de Québec*, Vol. 1931, Reg. D.f. 53 R, p. 189.

[3]Mandate of Bishop Plessis, June 26, 1798.

[4]According to the Parish Registers, it was he who baptized the newborn; he who made declarations to the travelling missionaries as witness to the death of such-and-such a parishioner.

[5]The Canticle of the Passion was composed of twenty-six couplets.

[6]Letter from Father Ledru to Bishop of Québec, June 1, 1787, N.-B. III, 5, AAQ.

[7]Formerly, in Chéticamp, the title of "Messieurs" was given to priests: Monsieur Lejamtel, Monsieur Fiset. Today, they are called "Père": Père Leblanc, Père Samson. But we speak of Monsieur Girroir, Monsieur Courteau, when we speak of the old ones. Rarely heard is the term "Abbé" as in Québec. In carrying out this work, we accordingly use one or the other of these titles.

[8]Letter from Father Jones to Bishop Hubert, October 8, 1792, AAQ.

[9]Têtu, *Visites Pastorales*, p. 33.

[10]Letter to Bishop Hubert, June 4, 1793, N.-É. VI, 23, AAQ. This Census is untraceable.

[11]Letter of August 21, 1795, Îles de la Madeleine [I.M.] 7, AAQ.

[12]Letter of July 27, 1800, I.M. II, AAQ.

[13]Letter from Father Allain to the Bishop, July 27, 1800, I.M. II, AAQ.

[14]N.-É. VII, 5, AAQ.

[15]I.M. 9, AAQ.

[16]Letter from Father MacEachern to Bishop of Québec, May 30, 1801, I.P.E. 22, AAQ.

[17]From Chéticamp, June 10, 1802, N.-É. VI, AAQ.

[18]Letter of May 30, 1801, I.P.E. 22, AAQ.

[19]June 1, 1801, N.-É., V, 7, AAQ.

[20]N.-É., VII, 7, AAQ.

[21]Letter of June 1, 1807, I.M. 22, AAQ.

[22]August 10, 1805, AAQ.

[23]Letter of June 1, 1807, I.M. 22, AAQ.

[24]Letter of May 5, 1808, N.-É. VI, 18, AAQ.

[25]Letter from Father Lejamtel to the Bishop, June 29, 1808, N.-É. VI, 50, AAQ.

[26]Letter from Father Lejamtel to the Bishop, September 3, 1809, N.-É. VI, 53, AAQ.

[27]*Ibid.*

[28]*Ibid.*

[29]Letter from Father Lejamtel to the Bishop, September 10, 1809, N.-É. VI, 54, AAQ.

[30]Letter of May 4, 1810, N.-É. VI, 55, AAQ.

[31]Bishop Plessis, "Journal," p. 230.

[32]Letter of April 17, 1801, N.-É. VI, 36, AAQ.

[33]Letter of June 10, 1802, N.-É. VII, 6, AAQ.

[34]Bishop Plessis, "Journal," p. 233. Seeing the importance of the narrative of Bishop Plessis, we publish *in extenso* the part which pertains to Chéticamp, pp. 87-89. The subtitles are ours.

[35]"At the church of Chétican there is missing a chalice, a ciborium, a monstrance, a Holy Water basin, a censer, a processional Cross, some red and purple vestments, a cincture for the lab, some labs, a surplice for the priest and for the altar server, amices, a washbasin, purificators, altar cloths, a mortuary sheet, and altar equipment." Bishop Plessis, *Cahiers des Visites Pastorales*, 1812, No. 7, pp. 23-24, AAQ.

[36]Letter from Father Lejamtel, August 27, 1813, Reg. H.F. 311, N.-É. VI, 60, AAQ.

[37]Têtu, *Visites Pastorales*, p. 64. Father Vézina, subdeacon, accompanied Father Dufresne to Chéticamp, probably to help him teach school, as well as religion.

[38]*Ibid.*, p, 62. A young man from the Magdalen Islands had escaped.

[39]Letter of June 13, 1813, N.-É. VI, 59, AAQ.

[40]Têtu, *Visites Pastorales*, p. 64.

[41]Letter from Father Lejamtel, October 4, 1814, N.-É. VI, 64, AAQ. It was Guillaume (à François) Leblanc who emigrated to the Magdalen Islands in 1839.

[42]He arrived on November 23. That is what he says in a letter to the Bishop, January 7, 1815. Besides, he recorded an act of baptism in the Registers on November 24.

[43]Joseph Bonin, *Biographies de l'honourable B. Joliette et de M. le grand vicaire A. Manseau* (Montréal: 1874), pp.177-215.

[44]Letter written from Margaree to the Bishop, January 7, 1814, N.-É. II, 148, AAQ.

[45]Bonin, *Biographies*, pp. 177-215.

[46]Letter from Manseau to the Bishop, January 7, 1814, N.-É. II, 148, AAQ.

[47]Notice given at Arichat on July 4, 1815, by Bishop Plessis. See, Têtu, *Visites Pastorales*, Appendix E, p. 203.

[48]Letter of June 4, 1818, I.M. 45, AAQ.

[49]Reg. H.F. 135, AAQ.

[50]Letter written from Arichat to the Bishop, August 4, 1817, I.M. 43, AAQ.

[51]Letter written from Chéticamp to the Bishop, March 4, 1818. In the autumn

of 1818 a Father Beaubien from Québec came to visit Chéticamp. He performed one baptism and two marriages.

[52]He died on May 8, 1857, and was buried in his cathedral in Kingston.

[53]Reg. I, f. 3-5, AAQ.

[54]Reg, I, f. 5, AAQ.

[55]Reg, K, f. 150 v., AAQ.

[56]"Father Joseph Moll, born in Montréal on February 28, 1794, of Michel Moll and Marie Vernier, was ordained priest on October 12, 1817. Curate at Deschambault (1817-19); pastor of Chéticamp (1819-22); of Saint-Anne-de-la-Pérade (1822-28); of Saint-Timothée-de-Beauharnois (1828-32); first pastor of Saint-Édouard-de-Napierville (1832-42); pastor of Saint-Charles-sur-Richelieu (1842-44); of Saint Sulpice (1844-55); died on April 8, 1857; buried at Berthierville." See Father J.B.A. Allaire, *Dictionnaire biographique du Clergé Canadien-Français*, Vol. I, *Les Anciens* (1910), p. 389.

[57]"You...remind me of my approaching term of aberration and offer me...employment in the interior of the diocese," said Father Gaulin. Letter, March 4, 1818, I.M. 43, AAQ.

[58]Letter from Father Moll to the Bishop, May 28, 1821, N.-É. VII, 18, AAQ.

[59]*Ibid.*

[60]*Ibid.*

[61]Record in the Reg. of November 25, 1822.

[62]Letter to Bishop Plessis, February 6, 1825, AAQ.

[63]Letter written from Arichat by Bishop MacEachern to Bishop Plessis, October 10, 1823.

[64]Letter of July 18, 1825. AAQ.

[65]Letter of March 3, 1826, Archbishop of Québec, Reg. of Letters, V. 12, p. 450, AAQ.

[66]Bishop Denaut had acted thusly during his visit to these missions in 1803.

[67]He died on February 25, 1887, at Vancouver, where he had been retired.

[68]Dated October 24, 1826, AAQ.

[69]Dated April 27, 1842, AAQ.

[70]Letter to Father Fortier, Secretary, April 5, 1827, AAQ.

[71]Letter to Bishop Panet, September 22, 1827, AAQ.

[72]Lettre to Bishop Panet, June 4, 1828, AAQ.

[73]Besides, from 1827 to 1832 he had to re-do at least four marriages he had previously celebrated because of the discovery of new relationships.

[74]Letter to Bishop Panet, September 22, 1827, AAQ.

[75]Letter to Bishop Panet, September 12, 1829, AAQ.

[76]Letter to Bishop Panet, February 15, 1830, AAQ.

[77]*Ibid.*

[78]Letter from Father Manseau to the Bishop, January 7, 1814, N.-É. II, 148, AAQ.

[79]Letter to Father Fortier.

[80]Letter to the Bishop, June 4, 1828, AAQ.

[81]Letter from Father Lejamtel to the Bishop, September 3, 1809.

Appendices, Footnotes and Bibliography

[82]Letter to the Bishop on behalf of Father Courtaud, September 12, 1829, AAQ.

[83]Letter from the Bishop to Father Courtaud, October 15, 1829, AAQ.

[84]*Ibid.*

[85]Written in the margin: Pastoral letter from the Bishop of Québec to the inhabitants of Chéticamp, Cape Breton, Québec, July 9, 1830, Reg. K. f. 150 v., AAQ.

[86]La Société Canadienne d'Histoire de l'Église Catholique [Ottawa], "Report, 1943-1944," p. 112.

[87]Letter to the Bishop, September 12, 1829. AAQ.

[88]Letter from the pastor of Arichat, Father Maranda, to Father Cazeau, April 27, 1842. Father Maranda is said to have eaten some prunes from trees planted in Chéticamp by Father Courtaud.

[89]*The Casket* (Antigonish), May, 1860. Was this in France? Or in Québec, where his brother Henry McKeagney was ordained on September 30, 1821? This latter, missionary to Sydney, had created or caused many quarrels and difficulties by his lack of tact.

[90]Letter from Arichat to Father Cazeau, April 27, 1842, AAQ.

[91]The parishioners pronounced it *Channelle*. It can be seen in the numerous wills he drew up for his parishioners that he had impeccable French and beautiful handwriting.

[92]This is the only case in which we find any sign of public penance in Chéticamp.

[93]Bishop Plessis, "Journal," p. 226.

[94]This LeClerc drowned in Margaree River.

[95]One can read the following inscription on its sides: "Cast by William Blake Co., Formerly H.N. Hooper & Co., Boston, Mass. A.D. 1871 Chéticamp, Rev. Hubert Girroir Pastor."

[96]A marginal note on her burial certificate written by Father Girroir.

[97]Allaire, *Dictionnaire*, Second Supplement (1911), p. 76.

[98]MacDougall, *Inverness County*, p. 43.

[99]Letter from Bishop Plessis to Magloire Blanchet, August 21, 1824, AAQ.

[100]"At the entrance to the village, still called Friar's Head, the first settlers had noticed on the seashore a blunt rock, cut by the winds and rain, closely resembling, in a way, the figure of a monk in prayer." See *Histoire commémorative, Saint-Joseph du-Moine, 1879-1954*, pamphlet, p. 3.

[101]Following is a list of the pastors and priests who have served this parish: Father Guillaume Leblanc, 1879-92; Father Théophile Richard, 1892-1911; Father Broussard, 1911-24; there were Fathers A. Boudreau and Théophile Maillet, successively, as curates; Father Joseph A. DeCoste, 1924-50; Father A. Briand; and, at present, Father Joseph Marinelli.

[102]It is still the Glebe House today, the fourth in Chéticamp.

[103]A fine "Casavant" pipe organ was installed in 1904; and a loud-speaking system in 1949.

[104]For the construction of the Convent, they used wood from the large store at La Pointe which Father Fiset had bought from the Robins.

[105]*L'Évangéline*, May 1909.

[106]This store was bought from Évariste Leblanc, left to Conrad Fiset, and finally, sold to the Co-operative in 1936.

[107]A debt of $5,000, it is said.

[108]December 14, 1908, AAQ.

[109]The author of this monograph.

[110]We must not forget to mention that the following priests served the area as curates.

Secular Priests:

John J. Chisholm	June 13, 1869 - September 6, 1869
Théo. Richard	October 26, 1869 – January 25, 1870
François Broussard	October 27, 1909 – August 13, 1911
Georges L. Landry	September 1921 – February 1922
(Native of Pomquet, September 3, 1895; named Bishop of Hearst, 1945.)	
Théo. P. Maillet	February 25, 1922 – March 27, 1924
Angus C. McNeil	November 1927 – September 5, 1929
Flavien Samson	September 1929 – 1939
Théo. Maillet	1938-
T.O.R. Boyle	November 2, 1939 – January 24, 1943
James A. MacLean	June 27, 1943 – October 24, 1950
Francis A Morley	November 12, 1950 – December 3, 1950
Sylvère Gallant	December 10, 1950 – March 30, 1952
John MacKinnon	April 20, 1952 – June 8, 1952
E.J. MacNeil	July 13, 1952 – August 24, 1952
Ronald D. Smith	September 2, 1952 – February 1, 1953
Father Bernard MacDonald	twice curate here

Eudist Fathers:

Louis-Philippe Gagné, C.J.M.	February 4, 1953 – July 28, 1953
Gerald Forest	August 12, 1953 – August 1, 1954
Joseph LeGresley	September 1, 1954 –August 1955
Liboire Amirault	September 1, 1955 – August 1, 1959
Jovite Doucet	August 26, 1959-

[111]See the names of these Sisters in Appendix E.

[112]Of the fourteen priests who left Chéticamp, counting two who are soon to be ordained, only three offered themselves or have been accepted in the diocese—Father Arsène Cormier, deceased; Father Théophile Maillet, deceased; and Father Ernest Chiasson—when the diocese had such an urgent need for Acadian priests!

[113]A term used in Chéticamp to designate those who no longer practice their religion.

Chapter 6: Field of Education

[1]Father Candide, O.F.M. Cap, *Pages Glorieuses de l'épopée canadienne* (Montréal: Le Devoir, 1927), pp. 140-42, 228.

[2]Father Groulx takes as his own this question of Father Omer LeGresley in *L'Enseignement du français en Acadie*, p. 81. See Father Groulx, *L'Enseignement du français au Canada* (1933), t. II, p.13.

[3]Nova Scotia Laws, 1766, chap. 7.

[4]As could Charles Boudrot, Hubert Aucoin, Joseph Aucoin, Charles Haché, etc.

[5]Letter from Father Manseau to the Bishop, January 7, 1814, AAQ.

[6]Letter from Father Lejamtel, October 4, 1814, AAQ.

[7]Father Cloutier, probably still a seminarian, also spent a winter in Chéticamp with Father Blanchet. Courtaud letter, March 25, 1830, AAQ.

[8]Nova Scotia Laws, 1786, chap. 1.

[9]LeGresley, *L'Enseignement du français en Acadie*, p. 101.

[10]Nova Scotia Laws, 1841, chap. 43, XIV.

[11]These pioneers were: Sister Marie-de-Sainte-Philomène, Sister Marie-Saint-Étienne, Sister Marie-Claire d'Assise, Sister Marguerite-Marie, Sister Marie-Dominique, Sister Marie-de-la-Circoncision, Sister Marie-Saint-Sébastien. Sister Marguerite-Marie never changed convents since 1903. She became part of the soul of Chéticamp.

[12]Bishop Beaupin, in *Les Amitiés Catholiques Françaises*, Vol. XX, No. 2 (February 15, 1939), p. 21.

[13]Nova Scotia School Laws, pp. 309-12.

[14]*Ibid.*, p. 308.

[15]Louis A. d'Entremont, *Le Devoir* (Montréal), July 29, 1939.

[16]Here are the schools, with the dates of construction or extension: Petit-Étang (1946)—three classes; École Lefort (1946)—two classes; La Prairie (1950); Belle-Marche (1950); École Évangéline (1950); Plateau (1950); École Leblanc at Le Lac (1950)—two classes; the new Convent School (1950) which, with the Convent (fifteen classes), became the Consolidated School. We must also mention a most modern Home Economics class, run by Miss Anne-Marie Fiset.

[17]*Le Petit Courrier*, May 25, 1950.

[18]"Constitution and Rules of La Société Saint-Pierre" (Pubnico, Nova Scotia: 1954), pp. 3-8.

[19]*Le Lien* (an Acadian newspaper in Montréal), July-August 1947.

[20]*Study of Bronchiestasy: considered from the bronchoscopical point of view* (Montréal: La Presse Médicale Canadienne); *Peroral Endoscopy: consecutive series of one hundred foreign bodies of digestive and respiratory tracts*, with Preface by Dr. Fernand Lemaître (Paris: Vigot Brothers); "Foreign Bodies in Respiratory Tracts: Emphysema and Atelectasy by Obstruction, Peroral Endoscopy and Physiotherapy" (paper presented to the meeting of French Language doctors from North America, Montréal, September 1930); "Remarks on the Foreign Bodies in the Bronchia" (paper presented to the meeting of the French Society of Otology-Rhinology-Laryngology, October 1930).

[21]Léo Bérubé, in *À pleines voiles* (Ste-Anne-de-la-Pocatière, Québec), June 15, 1948.

[22]*The Victoria-Inverness Bulletin* (Inverness, Nova Scotia), July 21, 1944.

[23]*Le Lien*, official organ of the Abbé Casgrain branch of La Société l'Assomption, Montréal, October 15, 1946, to January 1948, sixteen issues.

[24]It is worthy to note that of the number of Bachelor degrees earned by the youth of Chéticamp, at least a dozen were helped by bursaries from the college of

classical studies in Québec through the intervention of Father Mombourquette, pastor at Arichat, while other bursaries came from La Société l'Assomption.

Chapter 7: Health

[1]Carmen Roy, *Littérature Orale de la Gaspésie* (Ottawa: 1955), pp. 61-87.

[2]Coptis, probably, the savoyanne of the French-Canadians of Québec.

[3]Cherry trees from Pennsylvania; *prunus pennsylvanica*; wild cherries; wild cherry trees.

[4]A handful, a small amount. Here the quantity is precise: the quantity of roots that a person can hold between the thumb and the index finger, while permitting the ends of the roots to hang down in all their length.

[5]*Sonchus arvensis*. In place of milk-weed, it was more likely lynx plant: *Hieracium Pilosella*.

[6]Information provided by Marie Aucoin.

[7]Letter from Father Lejamtel, April 17, 1801, N.-É., VI, 36, AAQ.

[8]Letter from Father Manseau, May 26, 1817, AAQ.

[9]Dr. W. Grignon, *Le Livre d'or du cultivateur* (Montréal), p. 118.

[10]The children of Dr. Napoléon Fiset were: Berthe, died aged ten years; Léo, a mental patient; Zabine, wife of Daniel Chiasson; Pitre, deaf and dumb, unmarried; Lévis, husband of Marguerite Leblanc of Margaree; Conrad, husband of Sophie (à Men) Leblanc—the last two ran big businesses at La Pointe and the harbour; finally, Antoinette, wife of Wilbert Bellefontaine.

[11]*L'Évangéline*, June 11, 1958.

[12]The construction, in 1937, was entrusted to Mr. Rousseau, architect and businessman from Trois-Rivières, Québec; the expansion of 1956-57 to Downie Baker and Ahern Architects, Halifax, and the contract was given to M.F. Schurman Co., Ltd., of Summerside, Prince Edward Island.

The Sisters-Superior who succeeded to the position of hospital director up to this time are: Mother Aimée de Saint-Charles, 1931-36; Mother Marie Saint-Alexis, August to November 1936; Mother Élisa-Marie, 1936-43; Mother Marie-Hérina, 1943-46; Mother Marie-Colombe, 1946-51; Mother Marie-Éditrude, 1951-57; Mother Marie-Émerentienne, 1957 -   .

Chapter 8: Civil Life

[1]Anselme Boudreau has been councillor for twenty-six years and has presided over the County Council for six years.

Chapter 9: Different Events

[1]A harbour of Anticosti Island, say some old men. Henri (à Fidèle) Poirier believes it was at Île-aux-Oiseaux, to the north of the Magdalen Islands. An inquiry made by us among the Madelinots seems to confirm this latter opinion.

[2]In 1914, all received the sum of $100 as payment for this training session, half a century late.

[3]This is what tradition says concerning the departure of Briard.

Appendices, Footnotes and Bibliography

Chapter 10: Social Life

[1] Letter to the Bishop, September 3, 1809, N.-É., VI, 53, AAQ.

[2] Bishop Plessis, "Journal," p. 227.

[3] Letter to the Bishop, January 7, 1814, N.-É. II, 148.

[4] On his voyage of 1812 Bishop Plessis encountered the same tradition at Gédaïque (Shédiac).

[5] This story appears to be well known in Nova Scotia. See Helen Creighton, *Folklore of Lunenburg County, Nova Scotia*, Pt. X, Bulletin No. 17 (Ottawa: National Museum of Canada, 1950), p.18.

[6] From the Latin *puls, pultis*.

[7] *Année* is pronounced *Ânnée* in Chéticamp.

[8] Québec tourtières (meat pies) are unknown in Chéticamp.

[9] Related by Placide Boudreau, who played the part of the leader in his youth.

[10] Fathers Anselme Chiasson and Daniel Boudreau, Capuchins, *Chansons d'Acadie*, Vol. 1 (Moncton: Aboiteaux, 1943), p. 25. Mr. Roger Matton has entitled "Escaouette" an orchestral suite for a choir on the theme of Acadian folklore.

[11] Mrs. Charles L. Aucoin.

[12] Fathers Anselme and Daniel, *Chansons d'Acadie*, Vol. I, pp. 28-31.

[13] *Lycopod claviform, lycopodium clavatum*, commonly green currants.

[14] *Genevrier commun*, common juniper, juniper.

[15] *Lycopode foncé*, obscure lycopod.

[16] Simon Bourgeois, informant.

[17] Letter to the Bishop, September 3, 1809, N.-É., VI, 53, AAQ.

[18] Mrs. Marie Aucoin, informant.

[19] This happened and still must happen in the district schools. At the Convent the students are completely separated during recess.

[20] Sister Marie-Ursule, C.S.J., *Civilisation Traditionnelle des Lavalois* (Québec: 1951), p. 100.

[21] Fathers Anselme and Daniel, *Chansons d'Acadie*, Vol. I, p.11.

[22] This riddle is the residuum of the story-type 927, "Out-riddling the Judge," from the international classification Aarne-Thompson.

[23] Aouindre: avoindre, from aveindre, old French.

[24] Sister Marie-Ursule, *Civilisation Traditionnelle des Lavalois*, p. 121.

[25] *Ibid.*, p. 120.

[26] *Ibid.*

[27] *Ibid.*

[28] A practice known elsewhere in Nova Scotia. See Creighton, *Folklore of Lunenburg County*, p. 19.

[29] In several regions of Acadia *avoir honte* means *être gêné*, to be shy.

[30] Bishop Plessis, "Journal," p. 229.

[31] Fathers Anselme and David, *Chansons d'Acadie*, Vol. II, p. 26.

[32] Placide Boudreau, informant.

[33] Sister Marie-Ursule, *Civilisation Traditionnelle des Lavalois*, p. 118.

[34] *Ibid.*, pp. 118-19.

[35] The men working on the boat were Amédée a Sévérin Aucoin, Tom à Ra-

phaël Aucoin, Lubin à Suzanne Chiasson, Eusèbe à Thomas Aucoin.

[36]Lubin Chiasson.

[37]The road which goes up to the home of Alex à Magloire Poirier.

[38]Traps, cages; *sougner:* to take care of; sougner les attrapes: usual expression in Chéticamp to mean lobster fishing.

[39]A method of fishing squid using a stem, usually of lead to make it sink, with one end of the stem attached to a line while the other end holds a ball-shaped crown, to which are attached several hooks.

[40]This bait is called *effarts* or *éphards* by the fishermen.

[41]Threshing was done in half-hour sessions called a *chaude*, each one followed by a rest for a quarter of an hour.

[42]At this time Lubin lived in the house of Charles à Alexandre Broussard.

[43]Henri à Fidèle Poirier, informant.

[44]Mrs. Charles Boudreau.

[45]Related by witnesses still living.

[46]Heard related by Placide himself.

[47]Related to the author by the witnesses, now deceased.

[48]Gerald E. Aucoin, "Le Conte populaire au Cap-Breton" (M.A. Thesis, Laval University, 1960). [Editor's Note: This thesis has been published, as well as a book of tales collected by Anselme Chiasson. See page 241.]

[49]Victor Barbeau, *Initiation à l'Humain* (Montréal: Ed. De la Familiale, 1944), pp.156-157.

[50]Thomas Leblanc of the *Voix de l'Évangéline*, Letter, August 12, 1940.

[51]Marius Barbeau, Preface in Fathers Anselme and David, *Chansons d'Acadie*, Vol. I.

[52]Oscar O'Brien, Dom., Letter, 1948.

[53]Fathers Anselme and David, *Chansons d'Acadie*, Vol. III.

[54]Pacal Poirier, *Le parler franco-acadien et ses origines* (Québec: 1928), p. 2.

[55]*Ibid.*, p. 55.

[56]*Ibid.*, pp. 50-57.

[57]Here is what Chiffet, a contemporary grammarian of Molière and Bossuet, says about the pronunciation of this pronoun, and the rules which he gives: "The soft 'i' is not sounded before consonants: 'il dit' is pronounced 'i dit'; nor is it in questions: 'Que dit-il?' is pronounced 'que dit-i?' For 'Parle-t-il à vous?' say: 'Parle-t-i à vous?' But, outside of questions, 'il' sounds the 'l' before vowels: 'il a,' 'il aime.'" Cited in *Ibid.*, p. 138. "Plaist-i," writes Rabelais, Le Cinquième Livre, in Fragment de Prologue.

[58]Poirier, *Le parler franco-acadien*, pp.58, 59.

[59]*Ibid.*, p. 113.

[60]*Ibid.*, p. 120.

[61]*Ibid.*, p. 122.

[62]*Ibid.*, p. 120.

[63]*Ibid.*, p. 122.

[64]*Ibid.*, pp. 151, 152.

[65]*Ibid.*, p. 157.

[66] *Ibid.*, p. 162.

[67] *Ibid.*, p. 169.

[68] Nisard, *Chansons Populaires* (1867), Vol. 2, pp. 231-33.

[69] Rabelais, Le Quart Livre, Ch. XIII.

[70] Nisard, *Chansons Populaires*, pp. 231-233.

[71] La Société du Parler français au Canada, *Glossaire du Parler français au Canada* (Québec: 1930).

[72] Rabelais, Le Quart Livre, Ch. LII.

[73] Rabelais, Le Cinquième Livre, Ch. XXXIII Bis.

[74] Bernard, *La Survivance Acadienne*, pp. 302-303.

[75] Mr. Gaston Dulong, assistant professor of history, literature and the language of the Middle Ages, Faculty of Letters, Laval University, Québec, after a month of enquiry on the spot in 1957, said at a conference held in Québec: "The French situation is...very difficult in Chéticamp. This is an unequal battle existing between the French and the English. French is impoverished from one generation to another. It is more and more contaminated by the English. It is less and less read. Circumstances being what they are, we must foresee that, unless a miracle occurs, French is bound to disappear, with time, in Chéticamp." *Le Soleil* (Québec), December 14, 1957. This should act as a warning to those interested.

[76] Gaétan Bernoville, *Ste Thérèse de l'Enfant Jésus* (Grasset, 1926), p. 41.

Appendices

[1] It must be G.

Bibliography

Manuscripts

Archives of the Archbishop of Québec.

Archives of the Bishop of Antigonish.

Missionary Registers of Carleton and Caraquet.

Parish Registers of Chéticamp and Margaree.

Private Documents and Contracts found in the families of Chéticamp and Margaree.

Public Archives of Canada.

Newspapers

À Pleines Voiles. Ste. Anne-de-la-Pocatière, Québec.

The Casket. Antigonish, Nova Scotia.

Le Devoir. Montréal, Québec.

Le Droit. Ottawa, Ontario.

L'Évangéline. Moncton, New Brunswick.
Le Lien. Montréal, Québec.
Le Petit Courrier. Pubnico, Nova Scotia.
Le Soleil. Québec City, Québec.
The Victoria-Inverness Bulletin. Inverness, Nova Scotia.

Periodicals
Les Amitiés Catholiques Françaises.
Le Foyer Canadien.
Revue d'Histoire de l'Amérique Française.

Other Sources
Allaire, Father J.B.A. *Dictionnaire biographique du Clergé Canadien-Français*. Montréal: 1910.
Anselme Chiasson and Daniel Boudreau, Capuchin Fathers. *Chansons d'Acadie*. 5 vols. Moncton: Aboiteaux, 1943, 1945, 1946.
Archives Canadiennes, 1905.
Les Archives de Folklore. Laval University, Québec.
Aucoin, Clarence Richard. *History of Chéticamp*. Pamphlet.
Aucoin, Gerald E. "Le conte populaire au Cap-Breton." Typed manuscript.
Barbeau, Marius. *The Hooked Rugs: Its Origin*. Publication 36. Ottawa: Royal Society of Canada, 1942.
Barbeau, Victor. *Initiation à l'Humain*. Montréal: Ed. de la Familiale, 1944.
Baxter, James Phinney. *A Memoir of Jacques Cartier*. New York: Dodd, Mead & Co., 1906.
Bernard, Brother Antoine, C.S.V. *L'Acadie Vivante*. Montréal: 1945.
_____. *La Survivance Acadienne*. Montréal: 1935.
Blanchard, Henri. *Île du Prince Édouard: History of the Acadians of Prince Edward Island*. Moncton: 1927.
Bonin, Father Joseph. *Biographies de l'honorable B. Joliette et de M. le grand vicaire A. Manseau*. Montréal: 1874.
Bref récit et succincte narration de la navigation par le capitaine Jacques Cartier aux îles du Canada. Paris: Tross, 1863.
Candide, Father, Capuchin. *Pages Glorieuses de l'épopée canadienne*. Montréal: Le Devoir, 1927.
Casgrain, Father H.R. *Une Seconde Acadie*. Québec: 1894.
Constitution et Règlements de la Société Saint-Pierre. 1954.
Creighton, Helen. *Folklore of Lunenburg County, Nova Scotia*. Ottawa: 1950.
Denys, Nicolas. *Description and Natural History of Acadia*. Toronto: The Champlain Society, 1908.
_____. *Description de l'Amérique Septentrionale*.
Glossaire du Parler français au Canada. Québec: 1930.
Grignon, Dr. W. *Le Livre d'or du cultivateur*.
Groulx, Father Lionel. *L'Enseignement du français au Canada*. 1933.
Harvey, D.C., compiler. *Holland's Description of Cape Breton Island and Other*

Appendices, Footnotes and Bibliography

Harvey, D.C., compiler. *Holland's Description of Cape Breton Island and Other Documents*. Publication No. 2. Halifax: Public Archives of Nova Scotia. 1935.

Histoire commémorative, Saint-Joseph-du-Moine. Brochure. Cape Breton, Nova Scotia.

Johnston, Father A.A. *A History of the Catholic Church in Eastern Nova Scotia*. Antigonish: 1960.

Lanoue, Father François. *Saint Jacques de l'Achigan*.

Lauvrière, Émile. *La Tragédie d'un Peuple*. 2 vols. Paris: 1922.

LeGresley, Father Omer, Eudist. *L'Enseignement du français en Acadie*.

MacDougall, J.L. *History of Inverness County*. 1922.

Marie-Ursule, Sister, C.S.J. *Civilisation Traditionnelle des Lavalois*. Québec: 1951.

Nisard. *Chansons Populaires*. 1867.

Nova Scotia Laws and School Laws.

Pacifique, Father, O.F.M. Capuchin. *Études Historiques et Géographiques. Le Pays des Micmacs*. Restigouche: 1935.

Plessis, Bishop J-Octave. "Journal of The Mission of 1812," in *Le Foyer Canadien*. Québec: 1865.

Poirier, Pascal, Senator. *Voyages aux îles de la Madeleine*.

_____. *Le Parler franco-acadien et ses Origines*. Québec: 1928.

Rabelais. His works.

Rameau de Saint-Père, Edmé. *Une Colonie Féodale en Amérique: l'Acadie*. 2 vols. Paris and Montréal: 1889.

Rapports de l'Archiviste de la Province de Québec.

Rapports de la Société Canadienne d'Histoire de l'Église catholique.

Roy, Dr. Carmen. *Littérature Orale de la Gaspésie*. Ottawa: 1955.

Têtu, Monsignor Henri. *Visites Pastorales par Mgr. J. Octave Plessis*. Québec: 1903.

Vernon, C.W. *Cape Breton, Canada*. Toronto: 1903.